States, Nations and Nationalism

THE MAKING OF EUROPE

Series Editor: Jacques Le Goff

The Making of Europe series is the result of a unique collaboration between five European publishers – Beck in Germany, Blackwell in Great Britain and the United States, Critica in Spain, Laterza in Italy and le Seuil in France. Each book will be published in all five languages. The scope of the series is broad, encompassing the history of ideas as well as societies, nations and states, to produce informative, readable, and provocative treatments of central themes in the history of the European peoples and their cultures.

States, Nations and Nationalism

From the Middle Ages to the Present

Hagen Schulze

Translated from the German by
William E. Yuill

BLACKWELL
Publishers

First published in 1996 by Blackwell Publishers and by four other publishers:
© 1994 Beck, Munich (German); © 1996 Critica, Barcelona (Spanish);
© 1996 Editions du Seuil, Paris (French); © Laterza, Rome and Bari (Italian).

First published 1996
First published in paperback 1998

Blackwell Publishers Inc
350 Main Street
Malden, Massachusetts 02148, USA

Blackwell Publishers Ltd
108 Cowley Road
Oxford OX4 1JF, UK

Library of Congress Cataloging in Publication Data
Schulze, Hagen.
[Staat und Nation in der europäischen Geschichte. English]
Nations, States and nationalism: from the Middle Ages to the
present / Hagen Schultz; translated from the German by W. E. Yuill.
p.   cm. — (The making of Europe)
Includes bibliographical references and index.
ISBN 0–631–19633–1 (acid-free paper)
ISBN 0–631–20933–6 (acid-free paper/pbk)
1. State, The—History. I. Title. II. Series.
JC131.S3813   1996   95–36139
940.2—dc20   CIP

British Library Cataloguing in Publication Data
A CIP catalogue record for this book is available from the British Library

Typeset in 11.5 on 13pt Sabon
by Grahame & Grahame Editorial, Brighton
Printed and bound in Great Britain
by T. J. International Limited, Padstow, Cornwall

This book is printed on acid-free paper

Contents

Contents

PART III
Nation States

PART IV
Nations, States and Europe

Series Editor's Preface

Europe is in the making. It is founded on great hopes. But these hopes will not be realized if we neglect history. A Europe lacking history would have neither a past nor a future. For today stems from yesterday, and tomorrow comes from all that has gone before. What is past, however, ought not to paralyse the future, but enable it, whatever it may choose to preserve, to assume new and progressive shape. Our European continent, situated between the Atlantic, Asia and Africa, has long existed as shown on our maps and as it has been shaped by history ever since the Greeks gave it the name it still bears today. The future must be built on this heritage which has enabled Europe since classical – indeed since prehistoric – times, precisely because of its unity in diversity, to develop such a wealth of culture and such extraordinary creative power.

The series, *The Making of Europe*, which has been launched as a joint venture by five publishers of different nationalities and languages, is designed to throw light on the shaping of Europe and on its not inconsiderable potential for successful integration, without disguising the problems it has inherited. The series does not mean to conceal the fact that this continent, in its striving for unity, has had to overcome so many conflicts, so much that divides the nations, so much that is contradictory; for anyone who embarks on the European enterprise must be familiar with the continent's past and fully aware of its future prospects. This explains the 'active' title of our series. It does not seem to us, in fact, that the time is yet ripe for the compiling of a definitive universal history of Europe. We wish to encompass our subject in a series of essays by the most able contemporary historians, irrespective of whether they are Europeans or non-Europeans, whether they are established authorities or as yet scarcely known. They will deal with the essential themes of European history in the fields of economics, politics, sociology, religion and culture, drawing on the long tradition of historical writing founded by Herodotus, but also on the new ideas that have fundamentally changed the writing of history in the twentieth century, and especially during the last decades. They will endeavour to make the issues clear, so that they may be understood by all.

Our aim is to provide those involved in the building and development of Europe, as well as interested individuals throughout the world, with evidence and material to answer the fundamental questions: Who are we? Where did we come from? Where are we going?

Jacques Le Goff

Preface

In the course of the last few years, following the collapse of the Soviet Union and of socialism as an actual political system, optimism has spread throughout the western world, especially the Anglo-Saxon world. Ever since this radical transformation of the European political landscape, in works like Francis Fukuyama's much acclaimed study, we have read about 'the end of history'. We are, it seems, living in a utopia which is unique in so far as all rival utopias have vanished from the scene. Political liberalism, allied with the doctrine of the free market economy, has triumphed over the entire globe and put an end to socialist and communist dreams, while fascism went into liquidation a generation ago. A new world order of liberal democracy, with no serious challenger, will bring mankind peace, stability and tolerance. At the same time, it is true, interest in political argument will dwindle. Since all history is based on the clash of rival doctrines, history will forthwith 'come to an end'.[1]

But this new optimism is not shared by everyone. In Europe especially, we are faced with the revival of an irksome phenomenon that apparently resists all our efforts to establish a more or less uniform society throughout the world based on a radical foundation of liberal and democratic values. Fukuyama may be right in predicting the final collapse of totalitarian ideologies, which formed the main obstacle to a new world order, but he is apparently ignoring – among other things – the surviving doctrine of nationalism. In the Balkans, in Transylvania, in what was once Czechoslovakia and in the territory of the former Soviet empire, but also in many ways in Western Europe, the decline of communism has been accompanied by an upsurge of national sentiment which everyone had believed to be long since defunct. At the same time, enthusiasm for political integration seems to be on the wane; the nation states and their vested interests are once again bestriding the political stage of our continent. It looks as if Europe is on the point of reverting to the condition in which it was prior to the first world war. The metaphor that springs to mind is the situation in the Sleeping Beauty's castle following the Prince's kiss that wakened her: after slumbering for some eighty years, everyone springs into action and carries on with what he was doing at the moment he fell asleep – down to the cook, who now at last delivers the long overdue box on the ear to the delinquent scullion.

It seems only sensible to look more closely at the disruptive element of nationalism and its political manifestations. Why, in fact, were we Europeans organized into states in the first place? How and why did the European idea of the nation evolve? What purpose does it serve? How have state and nation combined to shape Europe, and ultimately the whole world into a precarious unity? Are nations and nation states an unavoidable evil casting a baleful shadow on the future, and blighting hopes of a united Europe within a liberal world order?

Historical study, aided by the findings of sociologists, political scientists, anthropologists and social psychologists, has produced a vast volume of research into the idea of the nation and of nationalism; the bibliography at the end of this volume can offer no more than a modest selection. If we look more closely at the ground covered, however, it turns out that researchers have concentrated their efforts mainly on two diametrically opposed aspects: on the one hand there are meticulously documented dissertations on individual phenomena, especially on the development of particular nations; on the other hand there are large numbers of highly abstract and generalized theories of a speculative kind. Compared with the flood of historical commentaries on the idea of the state that appeared after the first world war and the years between the wars, relatively little has been written recently on the subject from the point of view of historical research – with a single significant exception: the emergence of the modern state during the middle ages and the early modern era has increasingly attracted the attention of historians and has produced some fresh findings. It is generally true, however, that academic discussion of the nature and function of the state has tended to become the preserve of the political sciences, which are more concerned with actual political systems than with historical issues.

In what follows I have tried to sketch a provisional outline history of the state and the nation in Europe since the middle ages. The present work is not meant to be the kind of manual in which every issue is systematically dealt with, nor is it a totally comprehensive account of the subject – that would require a whole range of monographs and would be feasible only when we have achieved the necessary standard of pre-liminary research. Instead, the present work is meant to be an initial approach, providing a historical survey, highlighting connections and European continuities and pointing out certain discontinuities. Since there are often glaring gaps in the relevant research material, even this is a bold enterprise, con-sidering also that any attempt at a history of Europe largely lacks axiomatic data, logical premises and those definitions of historical eras that help to shape accounts of individual nations. Consequently, the account given here of certain topics may mean less to the reader than to the author, while, conversely, the reader may miss certain topics and arguments with which he is familiar from other sources.

In its mode of presentation the book tries to appeal to readers without a specialized academic knowledge of history: I have tried, as far as possible, to avoid abstract theoretical speculation, although this does not mean that what I write is not based on theoretical premises. I start from the assumption that the 'state' and the 'nation' are cultural concepts that have evolved in the course of European history and that have undergone continual changes. I begin with the period around 1000 AD, because it was at this point that the traditional concept of the state obtaining in the ancient world had been disrupted, or else survived only imperfectly here, while there could be no talk of a 'nation' in any meaningful context. State and nation change in the course of history, so that the classic constitutional definition, according to which statehood is marked by the exercise of effective authority, occupation of a given territory and identification with a 'nation', seems to me as inadequate as the common assumption that a nation may be defined as a sovereign people, or else as a linguistic or cultural community. My view of the state is largely indebted to Otto Hintze's historical typology of statehood. Like him, I draw distinctions between:

1   the sovereign authoritarian state in the context of a European system of states;
2   the virtually self-contained trading state with middle-class capitalist social and economic features;
3   the liberal constitutional state under the rule of law, with the emphasis on personal freedom of the individual; and
4   the nation state, which combines and reinforces all these trends.[2]

It need hardly be pointed out that we are dealing here with a series of models which never existed in concrete historical terms: what we have, in fact, are categories that help to classify and interpret our empirical findings. The same applies to the concepts I have used to reconstruct the history of the 'nation'. I draw a distinction – and, in so doing, owe much to my discussions with Karl-Ferdinand Werner – between the older idea of the nation as a system of 'estates' or an aristocratic hierarchy, and the more recent view of the nation as an ethnic community, which emerges more or less at the end of the eighteenth century. This frame of reference may be more narrowly defined by introducing a further distinction between the nation as a cultural phenomenon and as a political organism. These concepts, too, should be regarded as denoting theoretical types marking the terminal points in a system of co-ordinates by which an actual nation may be located within the system, described and compared with other nations.

Some readers may take exception to the fact that Eastern Europe does not play a more prominent part in our account. To me it seems plausible that, since the division of the continent into a Western and an Eastern Roman Empire about the year 330 AD, two European spheres of civilization have emerged and developed over the two thousand years down to the present day, not without influencing each other, but certainly without merging. The tale I have to tell unfolded unequivocally in the western cultural sphere and describes a civilization which, as opposed to the Byzantine and Russian Orthodox East, was marked by the early divorce of the secular from the spiritual authorities and by a process of intellectual secularization featuring concepts like the Renaissance and Enlightenment and, as result of such movements, sovereignty of the people and democracy. This is the history of the 'Westernization of the Occident', and for that reason I have concentrated mainly on France, England, Germany, Italy and Spain. I have, however, permitted myself, for purposes of comparison, occasional brief glances at Northern and Eastern Europe. Detailed treatment of Scandinavia or the regions of Eastern Europe, e.g. Poland or Hungary, would doubtless have broadened the picture, but would also have exceeded the limited scope of this volume.

In conclusion, I would like to point out that my concept of a 'pivotal period' in the history of the world and its significance for the history of European culture and politics is based on categories which the Committee on Comparative Politics of the American Social Research Council has worked out to describe the modernization of political systems.[3] The fact that 'modernization' in certain circumstances may have dubious normative undertones is quite another matter.

Part I

States

1

The Advent of the Modern State

The Roman Empire had passed away. But even then, a thousand years after the birth of Christ, the wide open spaces of Europe were still spanned by the network of dead straight, paved highways that had knitted the empire together over half a millennium earlier. Now, however, these roads had fallen into disrepair. Nature had reclaimed its rights over long stretches of them, the expertly designed bridges had collapsed, and a detour to reach the nearest ford might take several days. Wayfarers who nevertheless kept to the ancient highways – and there were no others – had to reckon with untoward incidents: attacks by robbers, encounters with contingents of foreign troops. The arable land of Western Europe, once cleared of virgin forest, had reverted to its former condition, the great cities of late antiquity had fallen into ruins, their aqueducts, and hence their water supply, had dried up, and the population had dwindled to the point where there could be no suggestion of normal urban life. Grass and weeds encroached on city streets, such buildings as had survived gradually fell into ruins, cattle grazed in the market places, while in the amphitheatres herms and statues still stood incongruously amidst the cornfields.

By the year 1000 AD the Roman Empire of the West had long ceased to exist, but traces of it were still visibly present. Were the inhabitants of Germany and Italy not still living in the *imperium romanum*? Had not the Roman emperor been crowned ruler of the Reich, invested with the titles of Augustus and Protector of the Faith, as the successor to Caesar and Constantine? And side by side with him was there not the church with a hierarchy modelled on the ancient Roman bureaucracy, and a supreme pontiff, successor to the prince of apostles, Peter, unrivalled in his authority over the universal Christian church? Like a vast triumphal arch the Latin language, the manifest vehicle of faith and philosophy, spanned the vernacular speech and dialects of the nations as it had done for the previous thousand years, while in their monasteries the monks still pored over the works of Boethius and Cicero.

Thus, in the early middle ages and at their height, people lived simultaneously in the Roman Empire and in a totally different, archaic world. The Germanic tribes at the time of the migration of the peoples had taken up their abode in the vacant dwellings of the ancient, dilapidated *imperium*, adapting the infinitely complex, sophisticated and hybrid civilization of Rome and the Near East during late classical times to match the simple cultural patterns they had inherited. The defeated empire that had once held sway over the Mediterranean and Western Europe had been succeeded by a host of conquering tribes – Franks, Bavarians, Langobards and Visigoths, Saxons and Swabians. But for the unifying influence of the church and the surviving memory of Rome, Europe would have disintegrated into a jumble of primitive clans.

The church and the idea of a Roman Empire proved to be so tenacious that, more than three centuries after the fall of Romulus Augustulus in 476 AD and the end of the Western Roman Empire, a new empire made its appearance in Rome. Charles, King of the Franks, known as Charlemagne, by dint of victories over the Langobards and the Saxons, had become the supreme ruler of Western Europe: he was crowned Emperor by Pope Leo III in the basilica of St Peter on Christmas Day in the year 800 AD. Henceforth, Charlemagne's seal bore the inscription 'Renovatio Imperii Romani', the renewal of the Roman Empire.

It may be seen as one of the major ironies of history that this reconstitution of the Roman Empire was in fact the cradle of that motley collection of states that makes up modern Europe.

For the Roman Empire that Charlemagne attempted to resurrect could not survive. It is true, for an uninterrupted period of a thousand years, Roman emperors continued to exist: the last of them, the Habsburg Emperor Francis II, did not renounce the title until 1806. But, although in the West, in Gaul and in Italy, remnants of the Roman administration survived, although the lands settled by Germanic tribes east of the Rhine, with their *Gaue* (counties), parishes, monasteries, cathedral chapters, secular and ecclesiastical estates represented a rudimentary administrative structure, this was not the same thing as an integrated and stable empire. A letter sent by the emperor from Aachen to Rome would take two months on the way, and a reply would take just as long. How could an empire possibly be held together in these circumstances? Even without the quarrels over the succession amongst Charlemagne's heirs, the empire was bound to fall apart. The haste with which Charlemagne had clapped the Roman crown on top of tribal traditions ruled out any true empire in Europe for the foreseeable future. It was precisely because an attempt had been made to assume an imperial style of government far beyond the economic, judicial and technical resources, actual or potential, of the early middle ages, that disintegratory forces took on enduring forms of their own. 'So now everything that had been stable for the Roman world', Hegel remarked astutely, 'was understood by the Germanic world as a point of departure, so that the shape taken by this world essentially represents reaction and resistance to all that is stable and straightforward, rather than conformity to the course of nature. The initial outcome of the process is the formal rule of law, arbitrary force, individuation as the norm.'[1]

There was another reason why the future multiplicity of states in Europe was destined to endure: Rome had become so firmly lodged in the European mind by reason of its Carolingian revival that all the successor states of the continent were designed against the imposing antique dome of the universal Roman state. This was equally true of the East Frankish empire, whose rulers had inherited the imperial crown and from which ultimately Germany emerged; it applied also to the West Frankish kingdom of France, to Anglo-Saxon and Norman England, the Christian kingdoms of the Iberian penininsula and Northern Europe. For all of them, the myth of a Roman Empire had become the obligatory model. That is why jurists were able, with a semblance of legitimacy, to invest their monarchs with the imperial emblems of the ancient world and the middle ages as well. And so Europe did not disintegrate as the Carolingian empire had disintegrated with the Treaty of Verdun in 843, but achieved an inner cohesion, precisely because of its plurality of states. 'The genius of Napoleon', claimed the Spanish historian Diez del Corral, 'had already been frustrated a thousand years in advance by the phenomenon of Charlemagne. Although Napoleon and others like him constantly harked back to this ancient emperor, claiming to rule under his auspices as his successors, what Charlemagne had founded was not in fact a single united empire.'[2] It was the motley conglomeration of European states, in which only a sense of their common identity had survived.

Certainly, in medieval Europe there could be no suggestion of 'states' in our modern sense of political entities embracing all the inhabitants of a major territory. It is only recently that we have come to realize that, in the history of Europe, 'states' are a relatively novel phenomenon. The image of the middle ages, as it existed in the minds of educated Europeans during the nineteenth century, did not differ essentially from their view of the political cosmos on the eve of the French Revolution. They believed in the existence of fairly stable feudal states ruled by kings who held sway over a population divided into classes or 'estates', with the nobility at the summit; below them was a middle class, and at the base the peasantry. This impression of a stable and peaceful system could be confirmed by a glance at any historical atlas, where the sovereign territories of the medieval states appeared as they still do to this day, as uniform patches of colour. The impression prevailed that all the inhabitants of each of these coloured areas were politically organized in the same way as the citizens of our modern states. It was reckoned that states represented an age-old, indeed eternal, principle of human organization – 'original creations of the human mind', Leopold von Ranke called them, 'one might almost say, God's thoughts'.[3]

Modern research has moved away from this view. We now know that the structure of medieval communities was far more complex and diverse. It is certain in fact that well into the middle ages there could be no question of royal authority governing an entire land and its people, i.e. nothing resembling a state. A medieval monarch had direct political relationships with relatively few individuals. His power was based on the land that was owned by him and his relatives, and on the fact that other landowners acknowledged him as the most powerful member of their class and were prepared to submit to him. It was on this basis that personal relationships developed and were subsequently formalized by contract: an oath of allegiance obliged a liege lord to protect his vassal, while the vassal undertook to do his lord's bidding. In the course of time it became customary for the lord to transfer certain powers or privileges to his vassal by virtue of this oath, i.e. the tenure of land or even specific offices. The vassal might also be a liege lord in his own right, investing others with subsidiary fiefs on the basis of the authority he had been granted. It was a highly ramified system of legal obligations, complex and not easy to understand, for a vassal was free to accept fiefs from a number of feudal overlords, which might compromise his loyalty to one of these lords in a particular case. Even kings might be vassals: the English king, John Lackland (1199–1216) was a vassal of the French crown until he forfeited most of his French fiefs for failure to meet his feudal obligations. The popes claimed that in fact all the European monarchs held power by virtue of fiefs granted by St Peter. In most of Europe political power was based on the feudal system: medieval Europe was unfamiliar with the idea of states on a purely territorial basis, it acknowledged only personal bonds based on an oath of allegiance. States, as we know them, are built to last, they are impersonal and linked to institutions: the medieval personal bond, however, was limited in duration, it came to an end with the demise of the overlord or his vassal, and had to be repeatedly renewed.

The modern European state developed from this medieval personal bond. Since the feudal system had evolved mainly in the Carolingian empire, European states began to be formed in those areas which constituted Charles the Great's legacy, or which had been conquered from bases in imperial territory, i.e. in France, Germany, Spain, England, Italy and the Norman states of Normandy and Sicily. It is not easy, however, to trace the transition from the feudal system of personal allegiance to the territorial state with its centralized bureaucratic authority. It was a process that extended over centuries and took place through innumerable minor stages. No coherent impression emerges from the thousands of documentary sources in the form of taxation records, military archives, judicial verdicts etc.: they do not reveal with any clarity how a multitude of administrative sectors and functions were formed, or how they evolved, how they came to be transferred from a municipality to the state, or from a vassal to his sovereign prince. The fief tended to lose its personal character and become an object, an asset which the feudal lords attempted to regain, embodying it in their own property and thus restoring their sovereign authority. The vassals, on the other hand, tried throughout the middle ages to convert their fiefs into permanent holdings that could be passed on by inheritance. In this way two types of property emerged as the basis of political power. The king owned crown properties which comprised a considerable proportion of the land. Besides this, however, there was property in the form of fiefs, over which the king indeed exercised sovereign rights, but which in the course of time had become the hereditary property of his vassals. Thus, from the feudal system of personal bonds, there developed a state based on 'estates', or social classes: the prince and his vassals shared rights over landed property. While the king, or some other sovereign monarch, sought to extend his power, those who shared power with him banded together to take common action. The secular and ecclesiastical aristocracy, ambitiously aspiring cities, and in some states even the yeomanry, formed estates in defiance of their territorial overlord, claiming their rights in local assemblies and seeking to curb his powers.

The 'reification' of the fief changed the nature of political authority in still another respect: the monarch no longer ruled over individuals, but over land, which included his own property as well as that of his vassals. This was a consequence, not only of the change in the nature of the fief, but also of the demographic revolution that had taken place throughout Europe at the height of the middle ages: a sudden population explosion led to the clearing of woodland, the draining of marshes and the cultivation of fallow land. The increased acreage of pasture and arable land supported a larger population, producing more food for the towns that were now springing up and expanding. From the eleventh century onwards men began to emerge from their isolated existence in villages, castles, monasteries and market towns, the exchange of goods increased, as did the efficacy of communications and the speed with which news could be transmitted. The infiltration of authority into freshly developed and newly organized regions was bound to bring about changes in the nature of authority itself.

But this transformation entailed further changes. The feudal relationship was originally a bond for life: if the overlord or the vassal died, then the fief lapsed. The newly emerging state, however, was intended to be permanent, its authority was to be on an enduring footing that was not confined to particular individuals. This idea was not entirely novel. The king was not simply the person at the apex of the feudal pyramid, and hence the first among equals, but also a kind of hallowed figure. His office combined features of the biblical royal priesthood and the pre-Christian Germanic idea of the wellbeing (*Heil*) of the tribe that was personified in its leader. On the occasion of the coronation the king was anointed with holy oil, thus acquiring something of the character of the Old Testament combination of monarch and high priest. He was ordained by god to secure the rights of the individual and the commonwealth, to keep the peace within and outside his realm and to defend the church. He was credited with mystic supernatural powers and was seen as a kind of hybrid personality (*mixta persona*), as 'human by nature, but divine through grace'. The king embodied a divine and eternal principle, and this applied also to his rule on earth. Thus, the person of the ruler became divorced from his office: 'The King is dead! Long live the King!' ran the proclamation of the death of the death of the French monarchs: the king was indeed mortal, like other men, but the royal office, and hence the state, lived on. That is the reason, too, why the chancellor at the court of the French kings did not wear mourning dress during the period of official mourning. The king's office, and hence the state which the king embodied, were immortal.

Immortal, too, was the law which the king solemnly undertook to observe and practise on his accession to the throne. The nature and function of the law in fact for long remained unclear. At the time of the migration of the peoples and during the Carolingian period the laws of individual tribes had been recorded in writing on the model of Roman law: the Franconian *lex galica*, the *leges langobardorum*, the *lex visigothorum*: for the most part lists of offences and the appropriate penalties. By the tenth century, however, these time-honoured codes had been forgotten north of the Alps, and case-law had taken the place of royal legislation: i.e. whenever a legal verdict had to be arrived at, similar, earlier cases were cited as precedents. Occasionally, if a judgement was considered specially important, it was formally recorded in writing for the benefit of future generations. That is why we have a mass of medieval forgeries designed to support specific legal claims: the Donation of Constantine, which allegedly gave the pope the right to nominate the Emperor of the Western Roman Empire, hundreds of pastoral letters and decretals produced by a ring of forgers operating within the church during the ninth century ('pseudo-Isidorian forgeries') which have left their mark still on today's canon law, and some 270 surviving documents relating to Charlemagne, of which only three out of five are authentic.

The old Roman law had not been entirely forgotten, however, and it went on evolving in an environment where elements of the classical Roman administration still survived: in the church. The ecclesiastical hierarchy, the only administrative apparatus that had endured from late classical times until the middle ages, was modelled on the civil service of the ancient Roman Empire. In the church the tradition of keeping judicial records had never entirely died out, and in Italy, from the middle of the twelfth century onwards, a collection of ecclesiastical legal principles had evolved which rapidly gained general acceptance as a code of church law: *corpus iuris canonici*, the canon law of the Roman church.

Roman law also aroused the interest of the lay authorities. *Corpus iuris*, the code of Roman law from late classical times, had remained in force in a number of Italian cities during the middle ages, and now became the starting point for the development of general principles of jurisprudence – for a strictly rational and incontestably logical basis for reforms calculated to eliminate the tangle of case-law and curb the privileges of certain social groups and the church. It was in the interest of the towns to arm their administrators with permanent judicial norms to help them keep order and ward off attempts by the landed aristocracy to encroach on their rights. Thus, the *codex Iustinianus* was rediscovered, a compendium of imperial laws from late antiquity, along with the collection of relevant commentaries by legal authorities known as the digests. The sons of the urban middle class crowded into the universities of Bologna, Montpellier, Paris and Orleans to pore over Roman law. It was hardly surprising that, during the thirteenth century, the administration of the upper Italian cities advanced more rapidly than in the agrarian areas of Europe where the feudal system still obtained.

Lawyers versed in Roman law also made their appearance at princely courts, offering a legal apparatus that justified the prince's sovereign power and helped him to exercise it. Until then the monarch had taken decisions in a council of magnates, the *curia regis*; if he intended to enact laws, he had to make sure that the major nobles accepted them. Now, however, the lawyers pointed to the principle of Roman law: '*princeps legibus solutus*' a prince is not bound by the law, for it is he who makes the law. The monarch's law, the commentators on Roman law explained, had a special status, and they referred to a principle: it may be assumed that anyone who has recourse openly to force, does not do so without just cause. Thus, in the late middle ages, lawyers trained in Roman law were able to offer monarchs and territorial rulers an entirely new concept of the ruler's office. The power to lay down the secular law, and to determine the rules by which the state was governed, lay exclusively in the hands of the ruler.

The principle that no one but the monarch had the power to lay down the law and to put it into practice was admittedly at odds with the facts of medieval society. In fact, anarchy prevailed pretty well everywhere: it was taken for granted or regarded as inevitable that a man had to claim his rights himself, even if he had to resort to force. Except for the clergy, who were forbidden to bear arms, any individual who failed to resort to violence was reckoned to have compromised his honour. Anyone at all was at liberty to wage war against anyone else – the medieval term was 'feud'. Feuds were waged for the most part by those who possessed power and the necessary armament, i.e. the nobility, princes, or even towns and cities – but that did not mean that the blameless population were not affected. A feud meant vengeance and plunder, and it was the peasant subjects of the hostile party who were plundered, cattle were stolen, harvests burned. Attempts were made to secure at least local armistices and to establish zones that were exempt from hostilities for specified periods – but without much success. Emperor Frederick Barbarossa, for example, tried in 1152 to ban self-help through the use of force throughout the Reich, except in clear cases of self-defence. Barbarossa was reckoned to be a powerful ruler, but his armistice proposal failed because it was opposed by the nobility, who were determined not to be deprived of their right to declare feuds. In the course of the middle ages such armistices (*'Landfrieden'*) were proclaimed time and time again. In certain parts of Europe, in England and the Italian cities, and in France since the thirteenth century, the right of feud was limited up to a point, but otherwise such attempts at pacification failed in the absence of a powerful state that could enforce them. At best, they led to stricter regulation: church property was to be spared, peasants working in the fields and travelling traders were not to be molested, and specific days, in Advent, for instance, were exempted. It was not until 1495 that Emperor Maximilian I was able to proclaim a 'Perpetual Truce' (*'Ewiger Landfrieden'*) which gradually came into effect throughout the Reich.

These attempts by sovereign rulers to pacify their domains nevertheless suggest that legislation by the state was at least theoretically possible: the real problem was enforcement. That is why Sicily under the rule of the Hohenstaufen Emperor

Frederick II (1194–1250) appeared to be such a prodigy in the eyes of his contemporaries and of later generations. This was a realm governed by a closely knit civil service, with a legally qualified elite responsible only to the emperor himself, with ministries and administrative departments and a hierarchical organization. The civil servants were paid fixed salaries and were regularly transferred from one appointment to another. The higher officials and their subordinates kept a check on each other and their performance was recorded. Senior civil servants were not permitted to hold office in their home province, and were not even allowed to marry local residents, so as not to compromise their objectivity and impartiality in the discharge of their duties.

This bureaucracy did not simply run the country, it also handled the finances of the state through an ingenious system of taxes on property, income and commerce, through customs duties and other taxes for the maintenance of the imperial civil service, for the waging of wars, the construction of highways and the upkeep of the imperial court. But the state did not draw its revenue exclusively from taxes and customs duties; it played an active part in the economic life of the country, producing grain, wine and cotton for export and setting up monopolies in raw materials, such as salt and iron ore, as well as luxury goods: bales of silk and other valuable textiles had to bear the monarch's stamp.

Frederick II's state tried to be omnipresent: physicians, surgeons, apothecaries and lawyers were licensed by the state and their fees were laid down by the civil service. The manufacture and sale of medicines were subject to bureaucratic control and prices were prescribed. Every trade or craft was regulated down to the last detail, and the daily lives of the emperor's subjects were supervised to the point where instructions to ensure clean air and water were issued. The state even took a keen interest in their private lives: marriage to foreigners was banned, and even knights and barons needed their ruler's permission before contracting marriage.

The authority of the state was absolute. Self-help, private justice and blood feuds were strictly forbidden, for the fight against crime was exclusively a matter for the monarch and his officials, who took action automatically as soon as an offence became known. The responsible magistrate laid charges in accordance with a standard code of practice, and the ancient principle of 'no plaintiff, no judge' was abolished. The administration of justice and the legal system as a whole were regulated on strictly rational and hierarchical lines. The royal courts of law in the provinces were subject to a supreme court, and for their part supervised the local magistrates and police officers. The courts conducted trials and handed down verdicts without regard to the status of those involved. The trial procedure was precisely regulated, irrational evidence like trial by ordeal was not admissible, and if a review of the evidence in a particular case revealed errors of procedure, then the case was retried before another magistrate.

A bureaucratic state under the rule of law, then, but on absolutist lines and with unmistakably utopian features. This was in fact the state that the Calabrian Dominican Tommaso Campanella had in mind when he wrote his *Sun State*, a utopian account of a tyrannical state lurching into communism, an apparatus for the enforcement of the common good. Campanella lived at the turn of the sixteenth and seventeenth century: the memory of the state created by the Hohenstaufen monarch, the Emperor Frederick II, had survived in the minds of the people of Southern Italy for no less then 350 years.

The utopian features of this political design are explained up to a point by the ruthless and brilliant personality of Frederick II, a man determined to have his own way at all costs and described by Jakob Burckhardt as 'the first ruler of the modern type who sat upon a throne'.[4] When Frederick came to power in 1215, he found the bureaucracy of his Norman predecessors already in operation: it was highly efficient, but also so novel that he was able to ignore tradition and the ancient law and plan a state on entirely new lines. His 'Constitutions of Melfi' of 1231, a basic set of laws with Roman, Byzantine and Arabic elements, represented nothing less than a bold attempt to organize a state on totally rational principles as the expression of one man's will: the state as an artefact. Frederick died nineteen years later, too soon for his plan to be put into practice in all its details. Nor did it in fact function as smoothly as the admiring – mainly German – historians of the first half of the twentieth century liked to claim. No one can now say how Frederick's political system might have evolved: the decline of Hohenstaufen power put an end to the Sicilian experiment.

The state planned by Frederick II, 'the prodigy who changed the face of the world', as his awe-struck contemporaries called a ruler so much in advance of his time, remained a unique phenomenon in its own age, although many of its features were to be found in the Italian cities as well as in England and Flanders. Following the proclamation of the 'Constitutions of Melfi' Pope Gregory IX wrote in dismay to Frederick: 'It has come to our ears that at your instigation, or on the wicked advice of depraved councillors, laws are to be promulgated from which it will inevitably follow that you will be decried as a persecutor of the Church who is bent on subverting our liberties.'[5] It was not so much the particular constitution of the royal Sicilian state that astonished and dismayed people, but the emergence of a 'state' at all. The Sicilian state was too novel, too much the creation of a single ruler in advance of his time.

The first modern state to come into permanent existence in Europe was France. Until the twelfth century the crown lands of the French monarchs, located in the Île-de-France had been of little account compared with the great duchies of the monarchy. But their situation in the centre of France had its advantages: the king was resident in Paris and had no need to travel round his realm in order to assert his authority, as other rulers were obliged to do. Thus, this little kingdom could be governed from a fixed centre, which was not just its capital city, but also the seat of the most celebrated of Europe's universities. Moreover, from the beginning of the twelfth century the territory over which the crown exercised direct control began to expand: the French kings began systematically reclaiming fiefs previously granted by the crown, and the death of numerous barons during the Crusades of 1190–1 and 1202–4 facilitated the reversion of large estates to the crown, so that the crown property was consolidated and enlarged. By the time of King Philip II Augustus (1180–1220), the overlord of the Île-de-France had become a monarch whose pre-eminence in France was clearly evident, although it still had to be formally confirmed: the territory of the emergent state had to be effectively governed, taxes had to be levied and delivered to the crown, the law had to be proclaimed and enforced according to the same principles everywhere. The developing state needed an administration.

It was obviously the church that had fostered the development over the centuries of an official bureaucracy, the most distinctive feature of the state in modern times: the church was itself a bureaucratic institution that had issued from the ancient Roman civil service, and the *officium*, i.e. devotion to the service of the state, characterized the clerical office holder, as did the fact that his office, given the rule of celibacy, could not pass from father to son. A priest might well advance within the hierarchy: the church guaranteed him a 'living' in return for loyal service. In the church there were defined areas of jurisdiction and competence, and hence a clear and rational division of authority; the proper discharge of an official's duties was open to inspection, and lapses might incur disciplinary action. The modern bureaucracy was already in place, it merely had to be duplicated by the secular authorities.

In France, the *curia regis*, the king's council, had fundamentally changed its character: the group of magnates who had advised the king on major issues had been superseded by a royal administrative and judicial body of minor nobles, clergy and commoners, all of them versed in Roman law and nominated and paid by the sovereign. In this way a central bureaucracy emerged which was independent of the country's major landowners. The royal civil servants handled the law and the country's finances expertly, they were responsible to the king alone, they might be dismissed at any time and their offices could not be inherited. The appointment in 1310 by King Philip IV, the Fair (1268–1314), of a commoner, Guillaume de Nogaret, to the office of Lord Privy Seal, and hence head of the civil service, was a sign of the times. It was no longer birth or property but competence and absolute loyalty to the crown that would open the way to the supreme offices of state.

The same was true of the lower ranks of the state bureaucracy. Local government had hitherto been the concern of local landowners, who were responsible for keeping the peace in their own area. But the more the vassals were inclined to regard their fiefs as hereditary, the less they tended to brook interference by their overlord. The French kings had long since handed over the management of the crown estates to royal officials called provosts (*prévôts*). King Louis VII (1137–1180) proceeded to appoint *prévôts* to govern other areas of his kingdom. Apart from the *prévôts*, a new office of *bailli* was instituted. The *bailli* was a senior civil servant who represented the king in a given region. He supervised a number of *prévôts*, and was magistrate, administrator and tax inspector in one person. When King Philipp II Augustus was preparing to take part in a Crusade in 1190, he could be sure that he had reliable officials throughout the kingdom who would keep order, should the king fail to return. The administrative apparatus was sufficiently well established to secure the succession of his heir. That is why the king addressed himself in his political testament primarily to his *baillis*, speaking not of his person, but of the 'royal office' (*officium regis*): 'the object of the king's office is to care for the welfare of his subjects in every way, and to place the common good above personal gain.'[6]

By the beginning of the fourteenth century at the latest, the main features of the modern, centrally governed state had begun to emerge, in a form that we subsequently find well-nigh perfected in the France of Louis XIV. The character of the kingdom's legislation underwent a corresponding change. Hitherto, the concluding sentence of a law had read: 'in the presence and with the consent of the prelates and the barons.' From the beginning of the fourteenth century the formula ran: '*Le roi a ordonné et établi par délibération de son conseil*', the king has resolved and proclaimed in his council.

Nevertheless, the states which made their appearance on the European stage from the end of the middle ages should not be seen as political structures governed by an anonymous centralized bureaucracy with a king at its head who had appropriated overall authority and exercised it as he thought fit. Even the kingdom of France, which was in many respects politically advanced, was able to impose the king's authority only indirectly in many regions: in those areas controlled by major landowners, the church or the cities, the royal administration was strictly limited. The legal situation was still complicated, because the owners of large estates, the barons and counts still retained autonomous jurisdiction on their own territory. Besides, the law of the land was divided into a Germanic circuit in the north and a Roman circuit in the south. It is true that the king possessed in the *parlement* of Paris a judicial instrument to which even the aristocracy were answerable in the last instance, but not even St Louis the Holy (1205–70), a monarch of great charisma and determination, succeeded in preventing private wars and suppressing the right of feud in his realm. Down to the time of the French Revolution the kingdom of France was regarded throughout Europe as a model in its concentration of political power; but this was rarely more than an intermediate or indirect power which functioned primarily as an arbitrator, judging, mediating and reconciling differences between largely autonomous regions of the country and between social groups, in the interests of the state as a whole.

There was no other way: the evolution of the European states did not tend towards a concentration or monopoly of power, but rather towards the division and control of power. The doctrine of the division of powers propounded by Montesquieu in the eighteenth century as a defence against state absolutism described precisely, albeit in a systematic and schematic form, the situation in the states of Western and Central Europe as they had evolved in the period since the middle ages – a motley variety in the relationships of the various authorities to each other. As communications and the instruments of power were continually improved, the system of power sharing within individual states was constantly threatened by attempts on the part of the monarch to achieve absolute powers, but the internal balance was continually restored: this was what mainly distinguished the European state from its Asian or African counterpart.

There were a number of reasons why, from the outset, the European state did not sanction a concentration of power in a single hand. There was, for instance, the separation of church and state as it had evolved following the medieval investiture dispute. The major states on the outskirts of Europe, Byzantium and its successors, the Russia of Ivan the Terrible, drew a great part of their despotic power from the circumstance that their temporal authority was not separated from their spiritual status. State and church were here one and the same; in the Byzantine Empire the emperor was a holy figure, standing like St Peter over the heads of the patriarchs as God's vicar, the head of the state church, who was able at any time to mobilize the forces of religion in the service of the state.

The monarch of the Holy Roman Empire had made the same claim, at least until the decline of the Hohenstaufens, for, after all, his office, no less than that of the Byzantine emperor could be traced back to the Roman emperors of classical times who had enjoyed divine status: ever since the conversion of Rome to Christianity the emperor had claimed the title and function of *pontifex maximus*, high priest and defender of the faith. In the course of the twelfth and thirteenth century, however, the papacy had contrived to gain a large measure of authority within the Roman church and to confine the emperor and king to his temporal function – only to be subsequently humiliated by the crowns of France and England, which were no longer prepared to accept a papal right of intervention in secular matters.

Certainly, secular rulers held their sovereign powers 'by the grace of god', they were crowned and anointed, and the French kings were even credited with miraculous powers. But the separation of spiritual and secular powers led in the long run, in those areas dominated by the Roman church, i.e. in Western and Central Europe, to a secularization of the power of the state. Up to that point every form of social order had been justified by reference to divine revelation, and every exercise of authority justified by reference to god. There was no escape from a social order ordained by divine sanction. An autonomous political sphere and the idea of the common good were unthinkable. At the height of the middle ages, following the protracted dispute between the emperor and the papacy, from which both emerged as losers, the situation changed. Had not Aristotle, who had been rediscovered in the thirteenth century as the fountainhead of political wisdom, defined the state as an autonomous institution? Had not the Greek philosopher defined political man as a natural creature who needed no justification on the part of the church? The Franciscan monk, William of Ockham, had declared as early as 1330: 'The secular is older than the spiritual power, and hence independent of the papacy. The pope has no right to confirm the election of princes: not from reasons of state, for no state would grant him any such right; not on the basis of canon law, because that law exists only in as far as the monarch approves of it; not by reason of precedent, for case-law based on precedent does not apply if it runs counter to the common good.'[7] At that stage such a doctrine was tantamount to heresy, but under the patronage of the Emperor Ludwig of Bavaria, William of Ockham was at liberty to teach it without fear of papal intervention. It was at this juncture that church and state began to go their separate ways, and two concepts of freedom began to evolve which were of fundamental significance for the subsequent history of the European states: freedom of belief without coercion by the state, on the one hand, and political freedom from the tutelage of church, on the other.

There was another reason, apart from the divorce of church and state, which militated against the concentration of political authority in a single hand – the dualistic constitution of the state, the rival powers of the monarch and the estates that had emerged from the feudal system. In this respect the constitution of European states differed significantly from the pattern of states elsewhere. There is evidence of this in the report of a visit by a delegation from the Emperor Otto I to the court of the caliph of Cordoba in 956. The caliph was not in the least impressed when the ambassadors of the Roman emperor extolled their master in somewhat undiplomatic terms as the mightiest ruler on earth. The Christian rulers, he replied, were obviously feeble and powerless, for even the Emperor permitted his princes and nobles to rule in their own right. In the vain hope that they would serve him loyally the emperor had divided his land among them and should therefore not be surprised if this gave rise to arrogance and rebellion.[8]

What the well-informed caliph (and local critics of imperial rule) found to criticize in the record of this conversation applied in various ways to all the Christian states of Europe. Everywhere power was shared by the monarch and the aristocracy, and this remained the case even into the late middle ages, when the monarchs consolidated and extended their territories, governing them with the aid of a hierarchy of officials, acquiring supreme judicial authority and thus laying the foundations of present-day statehood. But the sovereign's direct rule of the country and its people clashed everywhere with the power of aristocratic landowners and the judicial and administrative competence which the latter claimed. Nowhere in Western and Central Europe did any sovereign prince succeed in overcoming the obstacles to his absolute power which stemmed from the feudal system and which ultimately took the form of the more or less stable corporate bodies known as the 'estates'. These brought together all the influential representatives of a particular region, with the exception of the monarch himself, i.e. the secular and clerical nobility and the municipalities, which could thus form a united front in the form of regional assemblies (known in Germany as *Landtage* or 'Diets').

These assemblies were the forerunners of our present-day parliaments, although they were originally something entirely different. For the most part they had evolved from the *curia regis*, the circle of the great and influential who were responsible for advising the monarch. The allegiance of the vassals to their monarch had indeed changed, just as the fief had changed from a religiously based personal bond of loyalty and had been reduced to a title to property, but it was for this very reason that the monarch needed the support of the landowners all the more: the revenue from the crown lands alone was no longer adequate to meet the growing expense of the administration and the army. Taxes had to be levied, and the major landowners, as the most affluent social class, had to approve these taxes. That was the reason why the monarch convened the estates in local assemblies. The slogan, 'No taxation without representation' was not coined until the eve of the American Revolution, but it epitomizes the basic principle on which the division of power in the European states had rested since the end of the middle ages.

The classic example of the evolution of a balance of power

within the state was to be found in England. In the course
of the twelfth century, especially during the reign of Henry II
(1133–89), the English crown had established its authority to
an even greater degree than was the case in France. The royal
power extended to the point where no fortifications might be
built without the prior consent of the king. The counties were
governed by royal officials, the sheriffs, and since the king
spent a good deal of his time on his continental estates in
Aquitaine, a central bureaucracy had developed which no
longer accompanied a peripatetic court, but was permanently
settled in Westminster and Winchester, incorporating the royal
will and executing it. Judgements in the royal courts tended
more and more to replace feudal modes of jurisdiction, while
the head of the royal exchequer, the chancellor, was constantly
on the lookout for fresh sources of revenue for the crown.
It was the king's vassals especially, the barons and knights,
who were fleeced by the chancellor: if a vassal's son wished
to inherit the estate on the death of his father, their land was
taxed and subject to a substantial levy. There was also a levy
which a vassal might choose – or even be obliged – to pay for
exemption from military service.

At the beginning of the thirteenth century then, the English
monarchy seemed to have secured its power more firmly than
any of the continental monarchies; it turned out in the end,
however, that not even an English king was in a position to
rule against the united opposition of the nobility. The barons
felt that they were being exploited for the sake of the king's
continental interests. When King John (1167–1216) planned
a major campaign in France in 1213, the barons refused to
join his army. John went ahead nevertheless, mounted an
offensive in Poitou and suffered a heavy defeat at Bouvines
in 1214. Although his position had thus been weakened, the
king committed a grave error of judgement in demanding an
exorbitant indemnity from those of his vassals who had refused
to join in his campaign. He had thus overstepped the limits of
his royal prerogative: faced by the united opposition of the
higher nobility, the clergy and the city of London, he was
forced to back down, and on 15 June 1215, on the meadow
of Runnymede near Windsor, he was obliged to grant a whole

series of guarantees to the estates of the English kingdom: restoration of the traditional rights of those vassals who were directly subject to the crown, renunciation by the crown of arbitrary measures, improvements in the administration of justice to the benefit of all the king's free subjects, liberty for the church. From 1217 this document was known as '*Magna Charta Libertatum*' – 'Great' because of its format rather than its historical significance. A contract of this kind concluded between the crown and the estates of the realm was by no means unusual in the late middle ages. But such a contract did not constitute an attack on the monarchy or an attempt to safeguard liberties in the modern, liberal sense; it was more of a reversion to 'the good old laws'.

A revolutionary feature of the Magna Charta in fact was the inclusion of a clause providing for a committee of twenty-five barons who would ensure that the king observed the terms of the agreement. In this way the English estates had created a political organ of their own; although it did not exist in this form for very long, it was permanently established as a parliament in the reign of Edward I (1239–1307). Even before then it had been customary to convene a great diet almost every year attended by the higher nobility, and this had been known as *parlamentum* since about 1250. Under the terms of the Magna Charta this parliament had to approve the taxes payable to the crown by the barons. Being constantly in dire financial straits, Edward I conceived the idea of summoning representatives of the minor rural nobility or squirearchy and the cities to join Parliament as the so-called 'Commons'. From 1297 on the king acknowledged the right of Parliament to determine grants of money which went beyond the normal revenue of the crown. About the same time complaints and petitions to the crown began to play a part in the business of Parliament. There gradually grew up a dual system of rule by the monarch and the estates which governed not only the history of the English constitution, but also that of the European states down to the eighteenth and nineteenth century, and which ultimately led to the typical modern state with its parliamentary constitution.

In each country this dual system of government took a

different form. In France the crown needed the consent of the estates if exceptional expense required an increase in crown revenues. But, as distinct from England, the French crown usually contrived not to convene the *états généraux* of the whole kingdom, which would inevitably have limited the king's freedom of action. Instead, the monarch did his best to convene only certain regional assemblies in a consultative role – that of Languedoc in Toulouse, or of Langue d'Oeil in Paris or Poitiers. The smaller such assemblies were, the easier they were to handle. Since the *états généraux* were never furnished with a sound legal basis, they lacked the continuity needed to develop like the English Parliament into a permanent political institution. They were constantly dependent on the favour of the king who was prepared to summon them only in extraordinary circumstances.

The situation was different, again, in the Holy Roman Empire, where the Roman emperors and kings had failed to set up the kind of comprehensive administrative network that had begun to emerge in France or England. This was because the attempt of the Hohenstaufen rulers to secure the lasting supremacy of the emperor ultimately failed. The sheer expanse of the empire was an obstacle to the establishment of any kind of uniform government, while the premature death of Henry VI in 1198, and the preoccupation of his son Frederick II with his Italian possessions, tended further to weaken the imperial authority. The protracted dispute between the emperor and the papacy, the attrition of resources, the host of adversaries and a cultural advance that lagged behind the rest of Europe – all this meant that the empire retained its traditional archaic structure. While the neighbouring states governed more or less well defined territories and had capital cities that served as centres of culture and trade, the empire's frontiers remained uncertain and, down to the time it finally expired in 1806, it never possessed a capital city to rival London or Paris. It was generally regional overlords, or else the imperial free cities, and not the imperial authorities as such, that played the leading political role. In Italy there were autonomous municipalities which tended increasingly to move away from the empire.

Two levels of political authority thus came into being: on

the one hand the Reich, with its head, the emperor, wielding symbolic rather than real power, while, on the other hand, the imperial estates confronted him from positions which they had established at an early stage. The estates comprised the civil and clerical princes of the empire, among whom the electors had occupied a special position ever since the thirteenth century as the only individuals entitled to elect the emperor, those cities which were directly beholden to the monarch, and the counts and knights with similar status. They met in imperial diets – ever since the twelfth century it had been laid down in principle that the emperor required the agreement of the imperial estates in all issues affecting the empire. It was from these diets that the Reichstag evolved, which ultimately became a regular political institution playing a significant part in the affairs of the Reich. We may wonder how such a fragile structure, the head of which was constantly dependent on election by, and support from the electors and the estates, was able to endure as an integral whole in the very centre of Europe until the beginning of the nineteenth century. The answer is complex, the reasons range from the evolution of a European community of states that needed a weak and inherently divided centre as a field for settling conflicting interests, and as a theatre of war, to the fact that an imperial ruler of this kind, precisely because he was relatively powerless, represented a potential source of diplomatic initiatives. Another reason for the surprising longevity of the Reich was the uninterrupted practice of royal election; in the long run, the higher aristocracy were intent on mutual collaboration and on the preservation of the empire and the monarchical principle. Every election of an emperor was a fresh vote in favour of the Reich, so that it was in fact the electors who guaranteed its integrity and continued survival.

On the other hand there was the political arena represented by the territorial states that made up the Reich and on which an increasing degree of power and independence devolved. They included a bizarre conglomeration of electorates, duchies, principalities, bishoprics, counties, imperial cities, abbeys and bailiwicks. In these territories, too, the principle of dual authority obtained; here, too a local ruler was liable to be confronted by regional assemblies or *Landtage* in which the estates were represented and which were often the only factor guaranteeing the stability and identity of a given territory, given the ceaseless changes in the political map of Central Europe, the partition or consolidation of states through wars or dynastic accident. In certain critical situations the *Landtag* might act as a stabilizing factor, i.e. during the minority of the monarch. It was not only the princes of Europe, but also the *forces intermédiaires*, the estates, the parliaments, the *Landtage* that played a part in the formation and stabilization of our modern states.

2

Christianity and Reasons of State

To constitute the modern state in its full range of sovereign power more was needed than just the gradual dissemination of civil servants and magistrates over the realm, and an agreed definition of the monarch's powers and those of the estates. The forms of late medieval government as they had developed in Christian Europe were less than efficient; they largely depended on the personality of the individual ruler, on the authority enjoyed by his house, his relations with other rulers, the estates, the church – and on the fact that the monarch's territory tended to be regarded as his private property. The main function of Europe's rulers was to offer their subjects the protection of the law and a defence against foes at home and abroad, but they exercised this function less and less as the middle ages came to an end.

In the course of the fourteenth and fifteenth centuries events on the continent took a catastrophic turn.

A whole series of disasters began in 1309 with the exile of the popes in Avignon and assumed even more drastic features with the beginning of the Hundred Years War between France and England in 1339. Increasing famines and plagues reached a climax with the Black Death of 1348–9. There followed the Jacquerie, the French peasant insurrection of 1358, the great ecclesiastical schism from 1378 to 1417, risings in England and France in 1381–2, and the victory of the Swiss confederation over the chivalrous might of the Habsburgs at Sempach in 1386. Nine years later came the destruction by the Turks of a Hungarian army under King Sigismund at Nikopolis – and so the tale of woe continued until the fall of Constantinople in 1453: an endless succession of misfortunes and evil tidings, each of which shook Christendom to its foundations.

In this autumnal season of the middle ages Europe was over-populated. Since the dark ages of the ninth century, when some 30 million inhabitants were scattered over the wide open spaces of the continent, the population had grown at an alarming rate to reach an unprecedented 80 million at the beginning of the fourteenth century. The traditional methods of agriculture no longer sufficed to fill men's bellies, the population was chronically undernourished and hence all the more susceptible to the plagues that regularly swept like sombre tidal waves across Europe. In the course of the fourteenth century something like a third of the population was struck down by the plague, the terrible Black Death. There could be no improvement in food supplies, for vast areas of fertile land lay fallow: men were doomed, it seemed, to a vicious circle of disease and famine.

Widespread destitution and distress led to the most drastic upheaval in society that Europe had ever known. Riots in the towns, peasant risings in the countryside, gangs of impoverished noblemen prowling the country in search of booty, looting by brutal and destitute soldiery – all these were everyday occurrences. 'The people', writes Johan Huizinga,

> were incapable of seeing their fate and the events of the day other than as an endless alternation of misgovernment and exploitation, war and robbery, rising prices and pestilence. The chronic state of war, the constant harrying of town and countryside by all manner of dangerous riff-raff, the unremitting threat of harsh and unpredictable law-enforcement and, moreover, the oppressive fear of hell, devils and witches: all this combined to engender a universal sense of insecurity . . . '[1]

It was not only the lives of the common people that were arduous and uncertain: even the great lived under constant threat. We need only recall the September of 1399, when the English King Richard II, defeated and taken prisoner by his cousin Lancaster, was forced to renounce the crown, while the German electors of Germany were assembled in Mainz to depose King Wenceslas. The king of the third great kingdom, Charles VI of France, was of unsound mind, and his land was shortly to be violently shaken by ferocious rivalry between the houses of Burgundy and Orleans. Louis of Orleans, the king's brother, fell victim to an assassin in 1407, while twelve years later the instigator of this murder, John the Fearless, Duke of Burgundy, was himself treacherously slain on the bridge of Montereau. Thus, law and order everywhere seemed to be on the point of collapse, while the church was in little better plight: the year 1409 saw three popes, and the following year three German kings, each of them denouncing the others as impostors and usurpers.

Law and order on earth were disintegrating: that was the fundamental impression in men's minds during the century, and it was matched by the sense that the medieval concept of a single cosmos was also falling apart. Thomas Aquinas (1225–74), basing himself on Aristotle and St Augustine, had still been in a position to acknowledge a secular authority as an element in the eternal rule of god. God, according to Thomas Aquinas, had ordained the forms in which men should live together, so that any change in authority and the social system was unthinkable, a sin against god's commandments. Two hundred years after the death of the great Aquinas, who had summed up medieval man's knowledge of god and the world, the foundations of his philosophy had been undermined. What did the divine order amount to, anyway? Even thought processes themselves had become confused: the Aristotelian concepts of medieval scholasticism had been corroded by nominalistic doubts. Philosophers like William of Ockham and Johannes Buridan taught that the universals, general ideas, were an illusion: only phenomena were real. God, on the other hand, and his order were inscrutable, not accessible to logical and conceptual investigation. And did not everyday experience suggest that the world was not governed by any recognizable divine plan, but by the fickle goddess Fortuna, whose emblem was the wheel and whose characteristic was perpetual, unpredictable change? Niccolò Machiavelli (1469–1527), erstwhile chancellor of the Florentine 'Council of Ten' and but recently released from unjustified imprisonment following an insurrection against the city government, was sufficiently familiar with Dame Fortune from his own experience: 'I would liken the power of Fortune to a raging torrent, which, having burst its banks, floods our fields, tears down our dams and dwellings, washes the soil away at one point, only to deposit it at another: everyone flees from it, yielding to its assault without offering the least resistance . . . '[2]

But that did not necessarily mean that men were hapless victims of Fortune's whim; in peaceful times precautions might be taken, dams and dykes constructed to stem the flood:

> So it is, too, with the power of Fortune: it, too, shows its strength where there is no force to resist it, and the waves of destiny surge on to the point where they find no dams or dykes. Italy, which is the seat of these changes, and that which hath given them their motions, you shall see it to be a plaine field, without any trench or bank; which had it been fenc'd with convenient vertue as was Germany, Spain or France; this inundation would never have causd these great alterations it hath, or else would it not have reach'd to us . . . '[3]

God's intervention in the world had become unclear and dubious, men were subject to blind fate, and what was more, experience suggested that they were not really concerned to save their souls: on the contrary, 'all men are evil and constantly give way to their evil inclinations the moment they have the chance.'[4] The only defence capable of coping with the vagaries of Fortune is the state – *lo stato*. This is a term which in its application to the organization of political power occurs for the first time in Machiavelli, and which in fact was long limited to the Italian language. Hitherto the terminology had been vague, as befitted the subject. There had been talk of 'rule' (*dominium*) or 'government' (*regimen*), of 'kingdoms' (*regia*) or of the 'principality' (*principatus*), of 'land' (*terra, territorium*), all of which implied both an association of persons and a legally incorporated territory. The term *res publica* had been borrowed from Aristotle and Cicero: it did not necessarily mean a 'republic' in the modern sense, but any political community, however constituted. But when Machiavelli and his Italian contemporaries, from Villani to Guicciardini, spoke of *stato* they had in mind a form of government that had not been thought of before: basically a situation in which a concentrated form of public political authority was exercised uniformly throughout a given territory, irrespective of the person who exercised it, or in whose name it was exercised; a self-justifying system without transcendental dimension or reference.

Since the extinction of the Hohenstaufen dynasty about the middle of the thirteenth century, Italy had been racked by an interminable succession of wars between her city states. By about 1500 it was mainly the *cinque principati* that had survived – Florence, Milan, Venice, Rome and Naples – largely thanks to the financial resources that enabled them to put powerful mercenary forces into the field. In any case, Italy had become the plaything of alien powers: the emperor, France and Aragon treated the Italian states as pawns in a game for which the prize was supremacy in Europe. It was not only rulers who had become insecure, but also the constitutional forms of the states: Machiavelli knew Florence as a republic, a monarchy and a dictatorship, so that the loyal performance of a man's duty in high office might overnight lead to indictment for high treason, banishment or worse.

The *stato* as conceived and described by Machiavelli, appeared in the mind's eye of an observer when the secular power was stripped of all illusory pretentions and reduced to essentials: it then became obvious that the essence of the state was indeed power, the power to master the vagaries of Fortuna through *virtù*, political energy, with the aim *mantenere lo stato*, the upholding of the state at all costs and by every possible means. The maintenance of the state and its power both inside and outside its frontiers required no justification: the end justified the means. 'A prince need only be victorious and maintain his rule, and whatever means he employs will be looked upon as honourable and will please everyone; for the vulgar is overtaken with the appearance and event of a thing: and for the most part, people are but vulgar . . . '5 Hitherto all life and behaviour on earth had been embraced by a divine scheme of salvation; now, however, theology and politics parted company; indeed, Machiavelli exhorted his readers to care more for their fatherland than for their immortal souls. His fellow countryman Francesco Guicciardini (1483–1540) admitted that the medieval idea of the subordination of politics to theology was unrealistic, and that 'no one can live truly according to God's will unless he withdraws totally from the world; on the other hand, it is hard for a man to live on tolerable terms with the world without offering offence to God.'6

The rise and fall of states was governed by laws that differed from the laws of religion or of personal morality: Machiavelli demonstrated this by reference to the example of Cesare Borgia, who employed his *virtù*, his political potential, unscrupulously to gain a principality by force and deceit. But when he trusted the promises of Pope Julius II, his father's successor, then he was deserted by Fortune and fell from power. The state has its own rules, its own code of behaviour, and it is reasons of state that must govern the actions of statesmen, if they wish to succeed. Machiavelli was not the only one who thought on these lines. As early as the fourteenth century Philipp van Leyden, a clergyman in the service of the Count of Holland, had declared that a sovereign ruler was at liberty to break his given word, if the *publica utilitas*, the public interest, required him to do so, while in 1408 a doctor of theology, Jean Petit, in a highly sophisticated address, defended his master, the Duke of Burgundy, against the charge of complicity in the murder of Louis of Orleans: promises and alliances between members of the chivalrous class need not be honoured if they were to the disadvantage of the monarch or against the public interest. The concept of 'reasons of state', incidentally, made its first appearance in Guicciardini, who considered the execution of Pisan prisoners to be justified: it was indeed an un-Christian act, but it was in keeping with the *ragione e uso degli stati*, the national interest and usage of the state.7

It is true that views differed as to how the state might best be constituted so that such reasons of state might be effectively implemented. In spite of his admiration of the strong-willed tyrant who forced Fortune to do his bidding, Machiavelli favoured the republican form of government, ' . . . for the end which the people propound to themselves is more honest than that of the great men, these desiring to oppress, they only not to be oppressed.'[8] But in the course of the sixteenth century the Italian city republics fell one by one into the grasp of their most influential families, who turned them into principalities. In 1462 even Venice, which contemporaries liked to compare with the ancient Roman republic, had deleted from the Doge's oath of office the reference to the 'commonwealth of the Venetians', and the city was ruled by a small clique of noble families. Filippo de' Nerli, a contemporary of Machiavelli, described republican Florence as a welter of conflicting parties, factions and vested interests, in which arbitrary rule carried the day. He saw absolute rule by the Medicis as the only way to solve the state's political problems and guarantee its existence in the long term.

It was in fact the political instability of Italy in the fifteenth and sixteenth centuries that made the country a kind of proving-ground where various political models might be tested: it is hardly surprising that the leading political theorists of the age were Italian. At this stage Italy was the centre of European prosperity and culture, and it was perhaps its political fragmentation, with a consequent multitude of cultural centres, that offered such a wide range of opportunity for the cultivation of music, painting, literature and architecture, even in the smallest of states – as was the case in ancient Greece, or as was to be observed in the politically divided Germany of the eighteenth century. But the mighty state imposing its will and policies on others and thus ensuring its permanent survival was not to be found in Italy. It came into being only gradually, and elsewhere, and was for long to remain no more than a utopian vision. It was no mere chance that Machiavelli's *Principe* and the *Utopia* of the English statesman and diplomat Thomas More (1478–1535) appeared at almost the same time. Like Machiavelli's treatise, More's *Utopia*, as a non-land, was a response to the trials and tribulations of the age – not just a

States

manual for the aspiring statesman, but an ideal model for the state. It envisaged a rational, mathematically designed state, in which human reason was manifested and which embodied a society that had abolished all outward distinctions between one man and another and that lived in accordance with a totalitarian communist plan. The contemporary reader may shudder when confronted with this totalitarian vision, but such a reaction does little justice to its author, the future Lord Chancellor of England. In this dawn of a new age he was describing with boundless optimism a state based on the reasoning faculty of its citizens, a mirror for the statesmen of his day, to whose voracious appetite for power Machiavelli was simultaneously appealing. The idealist Thomas More was ultimately sanctified by the Roman Catholic church, while the realist Machiavelli lives on in the memory of the English people as 'Old Nick', a cant term for the devil.

There were still many obstacles to the establishment of centralized political authority in the European states. A major problem was the slowness of travel and communication: a letter despatched from Venice took 12 days to reach Paris, 20 days to reach Nuremberg and 27 days to arrive in London. Wagons and coaches could cover at most 30 kilometres a day, travellers on horseback 40, and express messengers 100 kilometres – all of these are rough averages.[9] Crossing mountain ranges greatly reduced the rate of progress, attacks by highwaymen or bandits were a serious risk, and in extremely cold weather, or heavy rain, travel was well-nigh out of the question. The larger the state, the more cumbersome were the modes of communication between a ruler and his provincial administrations, the tardier his instructions and their implementation. The great diversity of languages and dialects was also an obstacle to integration, as were local customs and traditions. The multitude of intermediate authorities also tended to obstruct the implementation of the monarch's will. The church fought hard to retain its independence from the secular authorities, and its servants were often torn by conflicting loyalties, to their sovereign on the one hand and the pope on the other. Fortified towns posed a special problem: they guarded their rights jealously and were sufficiently wealthy to maintain their own armed forces. Access to the wealth of the cities was vitally important for territorial rulers: a ruler who was not in a position to collect direct or indirect taxes form the towns was bereft of a major source of government revenue. And finally, there were the powers exercised by the estates, represented as they were by bodies from which a monarch had to seek approval for the levying of taxes. Some of these bodies were powerful assemblies, like the English parliament or the Cortes of Aragon; others, like the French *états généraux* or the German *Reichstag*, were relatively powerless.

On the other hand, however, the factors making for centralization grew stronger as the power of the nobility declined. With great areas of arable land reverting to wilderness following a sharp decline in the population during the fourteenth century, many aristocratic landowners lost the basis of their economic independence, while serfdom virtually vanished throughout Western Europe. With the economic and demographic recovery of Europe after the end of the fifteenth century, agricultural improvement was stimulated by the investment of fresh capital: many prosperous city dwellers acquired land and cultivated new crops in the expectation of a good return on their capital as grain prices steadily rose. At the same time there was a general boom in trade and commerce, largely due here as well to urban entrepreneurs, with whom the monarchs allied themselves in opposition to a politically and economically debilitated nobility.

Revolutionary changes had taken place, too, in the organization of armies and in methods of warfare. In the middle ages wars had been waged under the feudal system with vassals on whose readiness to go to war the rulers of Europe were dependent. During the twelfth century the English King Henry II had recruited mercenaries, so as to be free of this dependence on his vassals, and the king of France soon followed suit. These soldiers, called 'Brabanzonen' in Germany after the province of Brabant, from which many of them came, were usually recruited from the lower classes of the population; they offered their services for money rather than from patriotic motives, so that it was only the most eminent and affluent monarchs who could afford mercenary armies. And such armies were indeed victorious: in the Hundred Years War, English infantry armed with longbows routed the cohorts of French knights on their chargers at Crécy (1346), Poitiers (1356) and Agincourt (1415). With the introduction of firearms, the military indispensability of the aristocracy came to an end. Cannon, in use since the middle of the thirteenth century, were capable of breaching the walls of any castle, while handheld firearms, which made their appearance on European battle-fields about the beginning of the fourteenth century, could pierce the knight's armour. The cavalry formations, which were hard to handle in action, tended to be replaced as the main body of an army by infantry, whose firearms were capable of killing at long range, and whose square formations of pikemen successfully resisted the enemy's cavalry. What was more, infantry were better disciplined and easy to command in action – provided they were adequately paid.

The *bandes d'ordonnance* which the French crown established in 1445 constituted the first standing army in Europe, apart from royal bodyguards, which had existed since the eighth century. To meet the increased expense of the military establishment the royal exchequer had to become more efficient. Revenue from the monarch's own property, the crown lands, was now less important, and revenue was now drawn more from crown privileges, i.e. from state monopolies like the minting of coinage, mining, the production of and trade in salt, as well as from customs duties – there were reaches of the Rhine where customs posts were no further than 10 kilometres apart. But all other forms of state revenue were ultimately overshadowed by taxes, which had originally been levied only in emergencies or on other special occasions and which began to be collected on a regular basis only in the sixteenth century. In this respect, too, France was particularly progressive, for there indirect taxes in the form of dues on goods and transport, the so-called *aides* and *traites*, as well as a tax on salt (*gabelle*) had been imposed ever since the fourteenth century, as had a direct tax, the *taille* – the last-named being assessed per head of population in the north, and by the landownership of commoners in the south. A complex financial bureaucracy and a rationally organized civil service were needed to collect revenue on this scale. Consequently, in the fifteenth century, following the Hundred Years War and the expulsion of the English from France, four revenue districts were set up: Languedoc, Langue d'Oeil, Normandy and Paris. The efficient running of the financial civil service, the very heart of the government's bureaucracy, was ensured by a corps of specially trained officials who were controlled in the provinces by financial committees, the *Cours des Aides*. Henceforth, the king was able to dispense with the co-operation of the estates, and his growing revenue ensured him more freedom of movement in his policies.

The church, too, was obliged to yield more and more to the power of the state. As late as 1302 Pope Boniface VIII, 'with sublime indifference to the actual state of affairs' (Ilja Mieck), had restated a claim to universal authority. But by 1309, under pressure brought to bear by France, his successor was forced into 'Babylonian captivity' in Avignon, hence under the shadow of the French crown. The papacy never really recovered from this loss of authority and prestige: monarchs hostile to France proceeded to cut off the flow of papal revenues to Avignon and to usurp the rights of the papacy. By the middle of the fifteenth century the English crown had seized control of almost all the church's property in the country, as well as the conferment of benefices and control of ecclesiastical revenues. In France, too, the papacy was largely stripped of its power following the return of the popes to Rome in 1377. In 1438 a council of French bishops passed the Pragmatic Sanction of Bourges and thus opened the way for the development of a Gallican church, which was further confirmed in 1516 by the Concordat of Bologna. Henceforward the French clergy enjoyed – until 1789 – a large measure of autonomy and rights of appointment under the overriding authority of the king, who was free to make appointments as he wished to all the archdioceses, dioceses and abbeys in his realm: applicants for high ecclesiastical office were ultimately dependent on royal favour.

It was the challenge of an almost permanent state of war, inner divisions, as well as the rivalry of crown, aristocracy and church in a power struggle that led ultimately to the emergence

of the modern state. This was most clearly demonstrated in
a politically and geographically extreme case – that of Spain.
It was here, if anywhere, that Machiavelli's dream came true
– a great kingdom was united and achieved the necessary
concentration of power, thanks to the sheer determination
and ruthlessly efficient rule of its monarch. Before the last
third of the fifteenth century there had been scarcely any basis
for the emergence of a coherent political entity anywhere on
the Iberian peninsula. In the Andalusian south there was the
Moorish kingdom of Granada, in the west the stable kingdom of Portugal. Then there were Léon, Asturia, Catalonia,
Aragon and Navarra, where there was a strong tradition of
rule by the estates, as incorporated in the *cortes* of Castile
and Aragon. Apart from Aragon, which played a major part
in the power struggles of the Mediterranean region and had
claims to sovereignty in Sicily and southern Italy, the forces
making for political concentration were relatively weak: the
reconquista, the recovery of the territory governed by the
Moors, which extended over centuries, was largely a matter
of private enterprise – grandees, colonies of settlers, municipal
corporations. Of Castile a contemporary chronicler wrote:
'In this realm such corrupt and depraved manners prevailed
that everyone lived just as he pleased, and no one felt the
need to reproach or to punish vice . . . Where no law was
respected, whole settlements were ruined and crown property
misappropriated, while the royal revenues declined to such a
low level that I am ashamed to quote the figure . . . '[10]

All this changed with the marriage contracted in 1469
between the heirs to the thrones of Aragon and Castile,
Ferdinand (1452–1516) and Isabella (1451–1504), whose
kingdoms were joined in a personal union in 1479. The
two *Reyes católicos* – the honorary title conferred on them
by the pope – were especially eager to bring to a successful
conclusion the *reconquista*, the last Crusade against the Moors
in Andalusia. They were both very much aware that it was the
enduring crusading spirit of the Spanish people – a blend of
religious zeal, thirst for adventure and lust for booty – that
would best bind the two kingdoms together. The homogeneity
of the Spain of the future suffered indeed from the fact that the

two kingdoms were not constitutionally merged until 1516. Castile, with Léon, Andalusia and Granada, was more than three times as large as Aragon with its associated territories of Catalonia and Valencia, and this predominance of Castile made itself felt in an economic as well as a political sense, all the more so as King Ferdinand had his residence in Castile and was represented elsewhere in his realm by viceroys. Thus, it was in fact Castile that tended to turn more and more into the unified Spanish state. It was not only the *reconquista* that helped the cause of integration, but also the growing dominance of the Castilian language. In the year when America was discovered the humanist Antonio de Nebrija dedicated his Castilian grammar to Queen Isabella, pointing out expressly that 'language had at all times been an instrument of government'.[11] The Castilian administration developed rapidly to the benefit of royal prerogatives: the crown claimed the overall right to legislate, whereas the Castilian *cortes* merely had the power to approve the repeal of existing legislation. Taxation was monopolized by the crown, and the king soon stopped inviting the nobility and the clergy to the *cortes*, so that only delegates from the cities remained. With their help the king was able to take even more effective measures against the privileges the higher aristocracy had previously enjoyed. It was the cities, too, which provided the Catholic monarchs with their most effective instrument in domestic policy: the *hermandades*, the municipal fraternities who were appointed to keep public order and watch over the interests of the municipality. They were merged by Isabella into a single Sacred Fraternity (*Santa Hermandad*) which, from 1488, had the right of jurisdiction and the execution of judgement and which took its instructions direct from the crown. The nobility were explicitly debarred from magisterial office in the Sacred Fraternity, and the feudal jurisdiction of the aristocracy was severely limited. In a very short time the Sacred Fraternity succeeded in regulating the administration of the law with barbaric stringency, and it was ultimately to develop into a staunch pillar of the monarchy.

The decisive step towards the unification of the Spanish kingdom, however, was the continuation of the *reconquista* by other means and to other ends. After the fall of Granada in 1491 the Catholic monarchs exploited the crusading mood of the country in order to bring about a religious unification of Spain. In 1492 an edict was issued which forced Jews to choose between compulsory baptism or banishment from the country within a matter of months. Ten years later the Moslem population was faced with a similar ultimatum. Even Richelieu, whose persecution of the Huguenots had a similar purpose, later called the edict expelling the Spanish Moors one of the most barbaric documents in the history of the world. Of the million or so Moslems, more than 300,000 left the country, along with about 150,000 of Spain's 200,000 Jews. Spain's cities never really recovered from this economic bloodletting, but the intended aim was achieved: the religious unification of the state and the disciplining of the population in the name of the faith and of Spain. The church served in this respect simply as an instrument of state policy. As was the case with the French crown, the Spanish monarchy had contrived to acquire the exclusive right to nominate incumbents of all the major offices in the church, and had even made good a claim on a share of the church tithes for the royal exchequer. Above all, however, there was the Inquisition, the supreme ecclesiastical court of Spain, which was utterly committed to the battle for the unity and purity of the Catholic faith. Unlike the Roman Inquisition, the Spanish Inquisition was from the very beginning under the direct control of the crown and run by a special royal counsellor, so that it constituted a mighty instrument of the inner homogenization of the Spanish kingdom. The unity of faith and statehood as the means to an indissoluble bond between the ruler and his subjects: this turned out to be a vital strategy for consolidating the inner integrity of the modern states of Europe.

Thus, Reformation and Counter-Reformation were not simply secular revolutions in faith, church and society, but also essential elements in the formation of the European states. This became perfectly evident in the case of Spain, where the assimilation of church and state was accompanied by clerical reforms in the sense of a tightening of discipline and a purge of the monastic orders as well as the diocesan and parish clergy – the only clerical reform before the Reformation that took place in the very bosom of the papal church. There had been an analogous development half a century earlier: an attempt by King Georg von Podiebrad (1420–71) to make the Bohemian crown independent of both pope and emperor by seeking an alliance with the moderate Hussites. The attempt failed in the face of opposition by the powerful Bohemian nobility, who feared an alliance between the Hussite population of the towns and the crown. With the pope and the emperor behind them, the nobles offered implacable resistance to King Georg.

In England the situation was entirely different: there was no resistance here on the part of the estates to the crown's efforts to gain supremacy over the church, because the political confidence shared by the crown, parliament, aristocracy, clergy and the towns had grown stronger since the Hundred Years War, while the power of the nobility had been weakened by the civil wars of the fifteenth century. King Henry VIII followed a policy similar to that of the French King François I, using the divorce he sought from his consort Catherine of Aragon as a pretext to deprive the pope of the authority he had once enjoyed in the internal affairs of Henry's kingdom. In setting up the Gallican Church, François had stopped short of a complete break with the Vatican in so far as he still formally acknowledged the pope as supreme head of the church. Henry VIII went a step further: in 1549 Parliament passed the Act of Supremacy, which declared that the king 'justly and rightfully is and ought to be the Supreme Head of the Church of England'. Henceforth, as far as the English state was concerned, there was no longer a pope, but simply a Bishop of Rome. The Anglican episcopal church continued in existence, but it was ruled by the king, who had usurped the pope's authority in matters of canon law, liturgy and dogma. The fact that, apart from this, there was initially little or no change in ecclesiastical organization or liturgy made the establishment of the Anglican Church a relatively painless process, and even gave rise to hopes that there would henceforth be one rather than two financially demanding masters.

In the heart of Europe, too, in the Holy Roman Empire, it transpired that the struggle for power in the state largely coincided with the battle for control of the church. In contrast to the development in the states of Western Europe, two rival political structures evolved here. On the one hand there were the emperor and the Reich, the latter represented by the estates assembled in an imperial diet, the Reichstag; on the other hand there was a multitude of territories and towns owing direct allegiance to the Reich. These were often far in advance of the Reich on the path to autonomous statehood, albeit in a variety of very different ways. Alongside tiny domains, which could often by surveyed with ease from the battlements of the lord's castle, there were the vast territories of imperial princes with elaborate governments and their own parliamentary assemblies (*Landtage*), like the duchies of Bavaria, Württemberg, Lorraine, Luxemburg or Savoy, the electorates of Saxony and Brandenburg, the Palatinate, the Landgravate of Hesse, the ecclesiastical electorates of Cologne, Mainz and Trier, to mention only a few of the more extensive territories. Maximilian I's efforts to reform the Reich had shown that it had not become a purely metaphysical entity: the setting up of an imperial supreme court (*Reichskammergericht*) in 1495, combined with the declaration of a 'perpetual armistice' (*ewiger Landfrieden*) throughout the Reich, the division of the empire into ten regions – all this had been only a beginning. The introduction of a central imperial government (*Reichsregiment*) and the levying of imperial taxes were intended as the next step towards a viable sovereign imperial authority. With the emperor's death in 1519, plans for a reform of the Reich came to a halt, although his successor, Charles V, took them up again and attempted to stabilize and bring up to date the *monarchia universalis* – now, however, in the form of a truly universal empire, including, apart from Germany, Bohemia, Burgundy and Milan, also Spain and the newly discovered Spanish possessions beyond the Atlantic. It was obvious to Charles that the Reich could be turned into a true state only if he limited the power of the pope and founded a state church, as had been done in France and Spain. He failed to achieve this, however, partly on account of the radical nature of Luther's Reformation, but also because of the opposition of the imperial princes who feared an effective central authority and regarded the *Reichsregiment* simply as a committee of the Reichstag, and hence as an instrument for safeguarding the rights of the estates.

When the Imperial Diet of Worms assembled in 1521, the dice had not yet been cast. Summoned to appear before it was the rebellious monk from Wittenberg, who had defied the pope and sought to renew the true church of Christ from the congregation of the faithful, for whom the sole religious authority was holy scripture, *sola scriptura*. This was the first time that a lay body had presumed to pass judgement on an issue of church dogma. The atmosphere in the Diet was distinctly hostile to current abuses in the papacy and the church in general, nd the imperial counsellors were inclined to use Luther in order to bring pressure to bear on the pope. But Luther was unwilling to make diplomatic concessions, and his refusal to retract even part of his doctrine was more than the emperor would stomach. Luther would have shared the fate of the Bohemian reformer Jan Hus, had he not been protected by a group of imperial princes. No doubt this protection was offered partly – and possibly even wholly – from sincere religious motives: 'Nine Germans out of ten have taken up Luther's battle-cry, while the others have at least adopted the slogan, "Down with the Roman curia"', the papal legate reported back to Rome. Above all, however, Luther's Reformation had the effect of frustrating the emperor's attempts to assert his authority over the estates, so that it ultimately strengthened the power of the territorial princes.

At the Reichstag held in Speyer in 1526 a compromise was arrived at, by which Lutheran rulers and town councils were permitted to specify the official denomination of their territory. Without further ado the reformed authorities assumed the function of 'emergency bishops' heading the ecclesiastical organization of their territories. Luther had actually thought of this measure only as an interim solution, but the princes had not the slightest intention of relinquishing control of the church once they had gained it, particularly as almost all church property had been sequestered by the state. Part of this property was sold off, but most of it was simply added to the estates of the local ruler. Government of the church by local rulers was made easier in the light of Luther's doctrine, which quoted the apostle

Paul: 'For there is no power but of God: the powers that be
are ordained of God.'[12] Thus, the apostle had assigned to the
secular power the duty of protecting Christians from evil. The
reformed monarch, then, was like the English king, *summus
episcopus* and head of a strictly hierarchical organization of the
church, so that the entire confessional complex was absorbed
into the bureaucratic apparatus of the state.

Even in those areas which had remained loyal to the old
faith, local rulers tried to bring the church into the grasp of
the state. To this end the Bavarian dukes allied themselves
with the University of Ingolstadt, aiming to establish the right
of the secular authority to supervise church dogma in defiance
of the official powers of the bishops. In this case, in fact,
the step was taken in the spirit of the Counter-Reformation,
for there were still too many clerics whose view of their
official function did not conform to the new moral stringency
of the Catholic church, or who had looked with too much
favour on Luther's teachings. In any case, both Reformation
and Counter-Reformation were exploited in the interests of
the states and their governments: territories that were just
emerging painfully from a tangled web of property rights and
claims needed, for purely political reasons, a kind of spiritual
bond to hold them together. And given the significance of
religion, which pervaded every sphere of life, such a spiritual
bond existed only in the form of a religious denomination. Hence
the Religious Peace of Augsburg of 1555, through which the
Lutheran estates of the Reich at least achieved equal rights with
their Catholic counterparts, proclaimed the *ius reformandi*.
This meant that the population of a given territory was obliged
to adopt whatever religious denomination their ruler had chosen.
Anyone who was not prepared to do so was offered the
provisions of the *ius emigrandi*, i.e. the right to move to a
state where his own denomination was officially recognized. The
homogenization of the German lands and cities had thus taken
a mighty step forward and fulfilled an essential precondition
for their growing autonomy and independence as states. At the
same time, however, the Holy Roman Empire was significantly
weakened, for its territorial fragmentation was now further
complicated by confessional differences. As the empire lost

more and more of its political actuality in the following years, the Habsburg emperors tended to withdraw more and more into their hereditary lands in Austria. The slow but certain exit of Austria from the history of Germany had begun even before the Reformation.

About the middle of the sixteenth century it might have seemed that the idea of the autonomous state as proclaimed by Machiavelli had evaporated in the stress of the religious quarrel. On the one hand, states gained in power and in internal coherence, if their rulers managed to introduce their own confession into the most remote hamlet of their realm. On the other hand, the explosive power of religious conviction was revealed wherever one denomination conflicted with another. The conviction that the truth must prevail still held good, and the unity of God's kingdom on earth was an essential part of that truth. In the conflict of faiths by which Europe was afflicted following the Reformation and Counter-Reformation, states were liable to be plunged into bloody anarchy, or simply to fall apart.

In fact, the real stumbling-block was not so much Luther's doctrine as the more radical movement led by John Calvin (1509–64), whose followers refused to accept Luther's authority, demanding that their version of the true faith be recognized at all costs. If a ruler persecuted his subjects on account of their religious faith, then, according to Calvin's teaching, active resistance became the duty of all those thus affected. This implied in fact readiness to embark on a civil war, and civil war actually broke out in France in 1562, after François de Guise, one of the leaders of the Catholic faction had perpetrated a bloodbath in Vassy among Calvinists assembled for a prayer meeting. Throughout France the Calvinists, who were there known as Huguenots, took up arms, and from that moment until 1598 one bloody religious war after another ravaged the country, with fanatical religious zealots committing fearful atrocities on both sides. The crown's loss of control led to an extremely grave situation: following the massacre of St Bartholomew's Night, 23 August 1572, when almost all the Huguenots in Paris, together with another ten thousand in other parts of France, were butchered, the Calvinists formed the Calvinist Union, a state within a state, with its own army, its own jurisdiction and financial administration.

Although the total collapse of the French state was ultimately prevented by the conversion of the Huguenot leader, Henry of Navarre, to Catholicism and his coronation as King of France, the civil war in France was no more than one episode in the protracted bloodbath in which most European states came close to foundering. In the seven northern provinces of the Spanish Netherlands the Reformed nobility rose in rebellion against Madrid's Counter-Reformation policy. The war raged from 1567, combining the features of a liberation struggle and a civil war, continuing far beyond the close of the century and coming to an end really only with the recognition of the independence of the Netherlands in the Treaty of Westphalia in 1648.

In Germany, however, the Treaty of Augsburg was followed by the longest period of peace in the country's history. It lasted from 1555 until 1618 and came to an end because, during that period, confessional alliances had been concluded between ambitious leaders who were awaiting their chance to strike. The chance came when the latent tension between the predominantly Protestant estates of Bohemia and the Catholic, Counter-Reformation Habsburg administration came to a head. On 23 May 1618 the Bohemian estates rose in rebellion, threw a couple of imperial officials out of a window in the castle of Prague, formed a provisional Bohemian government, expelled the Jesuits and raised an army. Emperor Ferdinand II, in alliance with the states of the Catholic league headed by Bavaria, intervened, while the states of the Protestant union took up the cause of their co-religionists. Thus began the Thirty Years War, in which almost all the European states became involved, one after the other, and which ended with the Treaties of Münster and Osnabrück in 1648. At the same time a civil war was also raging in England; it had begun in 1642, basically as a rebellion of the minor nobility, allied with the prosperous commercial middle class, against the fiscal demands of the crown. Here, too, the political power struggle was overlaid with conflicting confessional allegiances, for parliament inclined towards

Scottish Presbyterianism, while the Anglican episcopal church supported Charles. The parliamentary army, on the other hand, included Puritan and other, even more radical sects. In the end something outrageous and unprecedented happened: the defeated king was condemned to death by the House of Commons and publicly executed as a tyrant and enemy of the people.

All these events were connected and went to make up the same European civil and religious war. What was happening in the background was a historical struggle for supremacy in Europe between France and the house of Habsburg, with France, in spite of the religious unrest within her borders, siding with the Protestants. At a different level, in most European states there was resistance to the claims of their territorial rulers by the estates, which found in Protestantism a useful ally in their attempts to consolidate their position within the state. And, last but not least, the civil and religious war in Europe was fought for the Christian unity of the continent, and hence for the supremacy of universal political ideas which transcended the interests of individual states.

3

Leviathan

With the signing of the peace treaties of Münster and Osnabrück in 1648 an era of profound uncertainty was drawing to an end. A new continent had arisen from the shambles of the religious wars: the age of the absolutist state was about to dawn, the power struggle between the monarchs and their estates had been settled, religious confession and the state combined to form an indivisible union, and even in the most remote hamlet people knew what law and order and the true faith were. Someone who had been on the losing side, Paul de Gondi, Cardinal de Retz, who had taken up arms more than once against the King of France on behalf of the great noble families and the assembly of the estates, remarked plaintively towards the end of his life:

> France has had kings for more than twelve hundred years, but these kings never had the absolute power they enjoy nowadays. Their authority was never prescribed by written laws, as with the kings of England and Aragon, It was simply acknowledged by precedent and, as it were, given into safe custody, first in the hands of the *états généraux*, and then with the *parlements* . . . [1]

Now, in the year 1665, under the rule of the youthful King Louis XIV, the *états généraux* had not been convened for half a century, the *parlements* had been reduced to the status of mere lawcourts, and the entire power of the state was embodied in the person of the king – 'the most outrageous and dangerous tyranny to which any state has ever been subjected', declared Cardinal de Retz.[2] Louis XIV in fact never said, '*L'état c'est moi*', but he might well have done, as might most of the ruling princes of Europe.

We gain only an imperfect understanding of this statement, if we approach it in terms of current usage, i.e. taking the term 'state' to mean the epitome of comprehensive sovereignty and independence. In Louis XIV's day the word *état* – in the singular – was novel and striking: *les états* were the 'estates' in the sense of social and vocational groups, the nobility, the clergy and the commoners who ruled jointly with the monarch (who was also an estate himself). In English the relationship is not as obvious as it is in French: we have to recall the time-honoured term, 'States General', for the assembly of the provincial estates of the Netherlands, a term which has survived to the present day as the title of the Netherlands parliament. On the ancient continent of Europe 'estates' and 'state' coincided until well into the seventeenth century, so that the claim 'I am the state' was not just presumptuous, but revolutionary. Henceforth, all the powers of the estates were to be vested in the crown.

The novel idea that the royal authority should be the sole power in the state had been generated in the harsh and brutal civil war that had torn France apart during the last third of the sixteenth century and that had flared up again and again until the autocratic regime of Louis XIV began in 1661. Had not the slaughter in the name of the Christian faith proved that the quarrel over a just order did nothing but destroy that order? Faced by universal demoralization and the erosion of all civilized standards, faced by mass religious mania on all sides, a small elite of lawyers, civil servants, members of parliament and men of letters trained in the humanities rose up and declared: any regime that put an end to the civil war was preferable to that war. This group of individuals that included the chancellor, Michel de l'Hôpital, as well as the author and member of parliament, Michel de Montaigne, was dubbed *les politiques*, that is, men who were concerned with sound political action rather than with confessional gains, and were seeking peace, peace at almost any price. This meant ruling out any sort of judgement on religious truths. Religious issues were a matter for the church; they could not be settled by force of arms, nor should they be permitted to govern the policies of the state. *Les politiques* favoured a strong monarchy, because only a strong monarchy could guarantee peace, and because the monarch seemed to be the natural source of all laws. These ideas were summed up by the lawyer and philosopher Jean Bodin (1529–96), who, in his *Six Livres de la République*, argued consistently in favour of a confessionally neutral, rationally justified political community: '*République est un droit gouvernement de plusieurs mesnages et de ce qui leurs est commun, avec puissance souveraine*,' the state (this is how we should render *république* in its older sense) is the power of government under the rule of law and exercised over a host of households and whatever they have in common.[3] The essential, if not the sole feature of the state is its sovereignty. And sovereignty means 'an absolute authority assigned to the state without limitation of time'.[4] Sovereignty applies therefore to the supreme level of political decision, and since it implies a power which is by definition absolute and unlimited, it may be exercised only by a single individual, that is, by the monarch, the sole legislator. Just as god has laid down the laws of the universe, so the sovereign must lay down the laws governing the state. All further political authority, hence all other rights the monarch possessed, as well as the rights exercised by the lawcourts, the municipal authorities and the king's subjects individually, according to Bodin, were sanctioned exclusively by the monarch's legislative monopoly. That is why no transcendental, religious justification of the ruler's acts was needed – the sovereign was confessionally neutral. That did not mean, however, that the sovereign might do whatever he pleased: the object of sovereignty was fair government, which was manifested as the observance of divine and natural law – but also in the traditional principles of monarchy, the *leges imperii*. In setting up this psychological curb on the abuse of power Bodin differs from Machiavelli.

Bodin's theory of single and indivisible sovereignty served

to explain and justify the overthrow of the feudal aristocracy and the estates in the European civil wars of the seventeenth century and the consequent concentration of power in the hands of kings and princes. But Bodin's theory of government was still less than satisfactory in one respect: what gives a mortal ruler the right to wield such god-like powers, to impose laws on his fellow men? Here, Bodin has recourse to a historical argument: the sovereign's office is founded on the time-honoured concept of the kingdom. In an age so obsessed with logic, this argument was not convincing: men wanted some evidence of a law on which the emergence and continued existence of sovereign power was founded. An explanation of this kind did exist, but it tended to be quoted by the opponents of absolute monarchical power. This was the doctrine of a contract concluded between the people – generally in the form of a representative assembly of the estates – and the monarch, as a rule with a third party, the church, acting as guarantor. In later writing on constitutional theory it was mainly the so-called monarchomachs who advanced the contract theory in order to justify a right of active resistance to tyrannical rulers who had infringed the contract. The idea of a social contract arrived at by the ruler and his subjects was therefore a major argument in the arsenal of those who opposed absolutism. It was the English philosopher, Thomas Hobbes (1588–1679), who demonstrated that this weapon could also serve as a buttress to shore up absolutism.

Hobbes's line of argument also issued from the phenomenon of civil war, for he regarded civil war as man's natural condition. Originally, all men were free and equal, but also the victims of their instincts and selfish motives, and consequently embroiled in a war of all against all: 'Man is a wolf to his fellow-man.' Because men feared death, however, and aspired to a life of ease, they yearned for peace. To achieve this peace, Hobbes thought, men must have made a contract amongst themselves, by which they renounced their natural right to slay each other. They had handed this right over to the state, which combined in itself the total power of all the contracting parties: the state was actually the biblical monster Leviathan, which alone retained the wolf-like potential of man's primeval condition and was the sole arbiter over peace and war, friend and foe, life and death.

Faced with the question as to which form of state should be preferred, Hobbes decided in favour of monarchy, for it was only in monarchy that the state's sovereignty could be preserved intact. Any hybrid form of government in which power was shared between the monarch and a parliament was rejected by Hobbes in no uncertain terms. The purpose of the contract was achieved only when state, monarchy and sovereignty were merged: only then would there be security, peace and protection for the state's subjects, one against the other.

Was Hobbes's Leviathan actually achieved under absolutism? Were absolute rulers the kind of sovereign described by Bodin? Anyone who asked this question at this point in history was bound to have France in mind. A hundred years earlier he might have been thinking of Spain, and a century before that, of Italy's city states and principalities. Since the end of the Thirty Years War, however, i.e. since the middle of the seventeenth century, France had risen to a position of unchallenged supremacy in Europe, in a political as well as a cultural sense. Its population numbered some 20 million, about twice that of the Holy Roman Empire, three times more than the combined population of England and Scotland, more than four times that of Spain. Spain, once the leading power in Europe, had been defeated and was bound by a marriage contract to the French crown. It was France that had guaranteed the Treaty of Westphalia, and hence the constitution of the Holy Roman Empire. The Habsburg threat, France's nightmare for the past two hundred years, had faded into insignificance. In the second half of the seventeenth century at least, it was France that guided European politics, and Louis XIV, king since 1643, had, since coming of age in 1661, governed the policies of France without advisers or regents. 'The King', writes Paul Hazard, 'is eager for action, eager to create an aura; he creates a solar system, in which Versailles was the centre, and in which he meant to make the other European nations no more than satellites . . . '[5] In the age of Louis XIV Paris aspired to be what Rome had been in the ancient world, and it actually was a meeting place for the social and intellectual aristocracy of all Europe: their books, their language, their manners, their entire lifestyle became French.

At the summit of the state stood the king: he was supreme as judge, feudal overlord and warlord, the sole arbiter in foreign affairs, finance, administration and, to a large extent, the church. He was the law personified, *lex rex*. The basic principles of the French monarchy had been laid down by lawyers ever since the late middle ages on the model of the Roman legal tradition; this was one of the sources from which royal absolutism derived its justification. Another source was the bible, and it was on the bible that Jacques-Bénigne Bossuet, Louis XIV's court preacher and later Bishop of Meaux, based the case for absolutism. In his treatise, *Politique tirée de l'écriture sainte*, he wrote that god exercised his rule on earth through the monarch. This meant that the king's person was sacred, but it also meant that the king should show restraint in the exercise of a power entrusted to him by god – for god would call him to account. The exercise of restraint was a matter to be judged by the monarch alone: the most his subjects could do was to entreat god in their prayers to change the monarch's mind – something which no mortal might dare to do: the monarch's power was indeed absolute.

It was the court that provided the setting for the glorification of the monarch, it was a temple for the worship of the ruler, with a liturgy of strict and complicated rituals, in which every one of some ten thousand acolytes was expected to perform his function with total devotion. This was where the members of the royal household and the loyal subjects and servants of the dynasty met and often lived together. Anyone who was admitted to the court was a member of the royal household, and no greater honour could be imagined. In this way it had proved possible to domesticate the feudal aristocracy, to the great benefit of the state. The most eminent families had deserted their châteaux in order to spend their lives at Versailles under the eyes of a monarch who was in a position to dispense all manner of favours. The direst fate that might befall a courtier was to be banished to his provincial estate.

The Council of State (*Conseil d'état du Roi*), the cabinet
that advised the king and took major decisions was strictly
separated from the court. Princes of the blood royal and
members of the higher aristocracy who had traditionally been
members of the Council of State by virtue of their birth, had
been ousted from the cabinet. At best they might be summoned
on occasion by the king, in which case they owed their position
solely to the fact that they enjoyed the king's confidence.
Otherwise, their places had been taken by professional civil
servants, the 'nobility of the pen' (*noblesse de la plume*), most
of them of middle-class origin, who owed their titles to the
appointments they held, and hence to the king, and who, as
a rule were unable to pass their noble status on to their
heirs. The Council of State comprised a number of bodies or
committees which dealt with different branches of government
business: trade, finance, the judiciary, but their resolutions
were invariably framed as if they were personal decisions
by the monarch himself. The implementation of policy was
the responsibility of central authorities – government offices
for foreign affairs, for the royal household, for war, for the
navy. The chancellery was the supreme judicial authority, and
the department with overall control of finance was concerned
not just with state revenue, but also with the promotion of the
economy, the building of roads, canals and docks, and with the
maintenance of law and order in general.

Below the central authorities, which even at this stage were
tantamount to a rudimentary form of ministerial departments,
a network of civil servants was disposed throughout the country, which was divided into about one hundred judicial circuits;
these were usually known as *baillages* in the north of the
country and as *sénéchaussées* in the south. As a rule the administration of the law was no longer in the hands of aristocratic
magistrates, the *baillis* and *sénéchaux*, but was conducted by
their middle-class deputies, the *lieutenants généraux*, who were
responsible in their own districts not just for the courts at the
highest local level, but also for administration in general. The
next highest level was represented by the *cours présidiales* as
appeal courts, above which were the supreme courts (*cours
souverains*) and the *parlements*, which had lost their political

function as assemblies of the estates and now served merely as the highest appeal courts in all civil and criminal cases. There were thirteen *parlements* in the various regions of France, but only the *parlement* in Paris had retained a significant political function, for its members included the royal princes and representatives of the higher nobility: it had the right and duty to advise the king on current legislation, and, if it thought it expedient, to raise objections. The king was able to overcome the opposition of this parliament, if he appeared in person, but Louis XIV no longer observed this practice. It is significant that, after 1665, the *parlaments* were permitted to call themselves only 'high courts' (*conseils supérieurs*) and not 'sovereign courts': only the king was 'sovereign'.

The most important instrument of power in French absolutism, however, was represented by the *intendants*, whose powers were even greater than those of the prefects, who are in a sense their successors. The prototypes of these officials were the *missi dominici* of Charlemagne, who were despatched from time to time to outlying regions of the Reich to settle lawsuits or contentious revenue issues. Louis XIV went much further in this direct, spanning the whole of his realm with a network of 35 districts, each under the jurisdiction of an *intendant* as the representative of the central government. As head of the local judiciary he was responsible for supervising the operation of the law, for bringing criminal cases before the courts, and, where necessary, for presiding over judicial bodies. As police commissioner, the *intendant* was head of the highway police force (*maréchaussée*) and responsible for keeping law and order. Together with the local governors, the *intendants* inspected the armed forces in their area and checked the budgets and financial policies of towns and villages. As revenue authorities the *intendants* supervised the assessment and collection of taxes. The novel, indeed revolutionary, feature of government by the *intendants* lay not only in their overall competence, through which they and their deputies, the *subdélégués*, constituted the entire machinery of government at the intermediate level, but also in their immunity from intervention by other authorities in the civil service and from formal objections on the part of the estates: they were purely and simply instruments of the government, prototypes of bureaucratic authority dedicated to an ideal of efficiency.

The unity of the state was safeguarded by the standing army – about 100,000 men under Louis XIV – and it was the army that constituted the real preserve of the monarch. The regular regiments embodied not only the king's fame and glory, but also his personal sovereignty, abroad and – above all – at home. The standing army was the *ultima ratio regis*, the ultimate instrument for the enforcement of the royal authority in a case of emergency. The army consisted of enlisted mercenaries, but there were also regional militias, which were combined into a single royal militia in 1688. Apart from its strictly military duties, the army also acted as a police force, dealing with public disorder. Following the revocation of the Edict of Nantes in 1685 it was the army that helped to restore Catholicism throughout the country by means of billeting as a form of harassment in Huguenot areas and by so-called *dragonnades*. Command of the army in the provinces was exercised by royal governors, members of the higher aristocracy who had hitherto been regarded as notoriously unreliable as regards their loyalty to the crown. In the decades just past, insurrection and insubordination against the crown could always count for support on provincial governors and their troops. Louis XIV adopted the procedure of limiting such appointments to a tenure of three years and giving preference to officers from his own lifeguards.

> I have always adhered to this arrangement [he wrote in his memoirs] and observed that it had two beneficial effects. For one thing, the governor's subordinates were then not so dependent on him, and hence not so devoted to him as formerly; moreover, governors were able to maintain themselves in office only as long as they retained my favour, and consequently were a good deal more amenable then they had been previously.[6]

In effect, command of the army in the provinces tended more and more to devolve on the *lieutenants généraux*, while the office of governor became little more than an honorary appointment. Until the outbreak of the French Revolution the army remained a reliable instrument in the hands of the monarch.

The state now set about making its presence felt everywhere. It even intervened in that most exclusive preserve of the middle class – trade and business. The form of state trading that the finance minister Jean Baptiste Colbert, son of a cloth merchant from Reims, turned into a flourishing enterprise in Louis XIV's heyday was known as mercantilism and was based on the view that the status and reputation of the sovereign were dependent on the economic prosperity of his state, and that the state should therefore intervene in commerce and regulate it down to the smallest detail. The theory behind this view was that the amount of money circulating in Europe was more or less constant, so that a particular country could become wealthier only if it drew money away from other countries. Consequently, it was necessary to sell as much as possible abroad, and to import as little as possible. It was therefore the state's duty to encourage, and even to engage in, industries in which raw materials could be processed and the finished products sold abroad at the highest possible prices. If the state wished to gain a reasonable share of the profits from industry, it had to act itself as a producer, setting up factories and creating monopolies, as well as introducing an effective taxation system so as to skim off some of the profits of private enterprise. The results of this policy were spectacular: the standards of training in the arts and crafts in France far excelled those of any other European country. French textiles, porcelain and perfumes brought vast revenues to the state; the improvement of communications in the country was designed to encourage domestic trade, and the construction of canals and highways was unmatched anywhere in Europe.

This was the model of a successful state as revealed to the gaze of all Europe about 1700. The French model, it is true, had certain shortcomings: the discrepancy between Bodin's or Hobbes's vision of the state and the France of Louis XIV was considerable. The world of the seventeenth and the beginning of the eighteenth centuries was still static and hidebound. European civilization was founded on a deeply rooted sense of continuity. The delivery of a message, the speed of a journey, the carriage of goods – all this took place at the same leisurely pace as in ancient Rome. Concepts of time and space by which human experience is shaped had not changed in living memory. However much styles and modes of thought changed from one epoch to the next they were still based on fundamental patterns which had been evolved in the ancient world and which constantly recurred in renewed versions. If an educated Roman from the Augustan age had ben brought back to life in Paris after a lapse of seventeen hundred years, he would have found himself in a society to which he could adapt without too much difficulty. The revolutionary forces of absolutism collided violently with the forces of inertia, the problem of sluggish communications, traditions that represented a fossilized independence, deeply rooted habits and outmoded privileges – and all this set limits to absolutism.

After all, the French kings, right down to 1789, never succeeded in establishing their indisputable claim to sovereignty uniformly throughout the country. Round the ancient crown lands clustered the provinces, as it were on the outskirts of the realm, most of them incorporated in the monarchical state at a relatively late stage. In the provinces autonomous traditions of jurisdiction and government still persisted. A number of them – Brittany, Burgundy, Languedoc, Walloon Flanders, Artois, Cambrésis, as well as certain regions in the Pyrenees – had their own provincial assemblies, in which the nobility, the clergy and the towns were represented. These local parliaments had to give their consent, on behalf of the province, to the fiscal demands of the crown, but they also levied taxes of their own and were responsible for the economic life of the region, for the maintenance of law and order, for the building and upkeep of roads and a good many other things. There were also provincial governments set up by the estates and these tended to curb the power of the *intendants*. In all these provinces, too, there was an autonomous judiciary with provincial supreme courts which reinforced the autonomy of the provinces *vis-à-vis* the central government.

That is the reason why the government of France was not in a position to secure its undisputed rule in two vital areas of the state's authority – the law and finance. As far as the law was concerned, certain major proposals were implemented in connection with trial procedures and the constitution of the courts, but the crown never succeeded in overcoming the barrier that separated the area of codified Roman law in the south of the kingdom from the area of common law in the north, so that two major legal systems persisted more or less independently until the end of the *ancien régime*.

> Every little province insists on practising its own common law, recorded and codified in the sixteenth century and subsequently amplified by commentaries; the law ordained by the crown is only one code among many; it has to be registered with the supreme courts, and these courts are adept at delaying cases and discovering all manner of pretexts, as otherwise they are not in a position to reject the crown's law. In any case, the crown's writ does not run throughout the realm, and did not apply even to the revocation of the Edict of Nantes . . . [7]

And as far as taxes were concerned, the imposing façade of the royal revenue administration could not disguise the fact that a real tax system did not exist. The various provinces were taxed at different rates, while the large number of privileged individuals who paid less than their fair share obviously embittered the common people. Moreover, the collection of revenue from direct taxes was farmed out; tax farmers had more or less a free hand in the methods they used and they waged a brutal war, with the aid of countless inspectors, on smugglers and tax evaders, so that they were universally detested among the population. Colbert set out to simplify this inefficient system of taxes and to remedy its manifest defects, but he failed: there were too many powerful private interests involved, too many bad habits, too many formal privileges. His failure was to have fateful consequences for the monarchy.

French absolutism under the *ancien régime* fell markedly short of its theoretical model, and it was not until the advent of the French Revolution with its mass terror and its wars that a truly revolutionary unified state was imposed on the country and the idea of the absolutist state realized. In Europe during the seventeenth and eighteenth centuries the example of France nevertheless had a powerful influence. In this period almost all the European states were subjected to absolutist regimes. However, the outward similarities, the general fondness for theatrical court ceremonial glorifying the monarch, the prevalence throughout Europe of the French language and French taste should not blind us to the profound differences between European states, in spite of the general tendency to copy fashions set by Louis XIV. Each country had framed its own constitution, incorporating features of its historical evolution, so that the absolutist pattern was adapted in a variety of ways to fit circumstances that had grown up over the centuries. The absolutist state did not exist except as an ideal: there were as many different approximations to the model as there were political entities.

This may be illustrated by reference to an essential problem of the modern state in its early stages of development, a problem to which, in theory, absolutism was the answer: the relationship between the crown and the estates. In France the domestication of the nobility and the emasculation of the *parlements* had gone to considerable lengths, but the powers of the estates and their privileges had nevertheless survived unscathed in a number of provinces on the borders of the country, while on the estates of the nobles, judicial powers had remained in the hands of the *seigneurs*, the major landlords, who went on representing the authorities in the everyday lives of country folk. Besides, the aristocracy enjoyed substantial fiscal privileges, and they alone were eligible for appointment to many of the more lucrative posts.

Different again was the case of Württemberg, a state, after all, on the borders of France and, from 1658 to 1668, a member of the first Rhenish League (*Rheinbund*), an alliance of West German states sponsored by France and aimed against the Habsburgs. The absolutist model had its effect here, too. The new fiscal legislation of 1713, the modernization of the civil service and measures to stimulate the economy were all evidence of this trend, as were also such features as the habitual influence of court favourites on policy and finance, the building of extravagant castles and residences and the maintenance of a miniature standing army. Nevertheless, in Württemberg power was still shared between the monarch and the estates: ever since the Treaty of Tübingen in 1514 the Duke had been obliged to come to terms with a parliament, the so-called *Landschaft* which consisted exclusively of commoners – though in the course of the eighteenth century even yeoman farmers became eligible to sit in the *Landschaft*. This body had the right to debate and oversee all important matters of state, including the impositions of taxes, the command of the army and the conduct of foreign affairs. The nobility, on the other hand, not being represented in parliament, felt that they owed allegiance to the *Reich* rather than to the duchy, although members of the nobility occupied the most important offices of state. Duke Eberhard Ludwig (1676–1733) attempted to outflank the parliament in 1715 by replacing the executive committee, the Privy Council, which was answerable to parliament, by a body responsible to himself as Duke – a move which led to violent conflicts. When his successor demanded that his subjects should support a standing army equivalent to three per cent of the population and proposed to handle the state's debts without reference to the estates, the country found itself on the brink of open rebellion. The Duke did not feel strong enough, however, to strip the *Landschaft* of its powers – especially as the Treaty of Tübingen of 1514, to which parliament looked for support, was still the law of the land. The parliament of 1737 to 1739 was able to reaffirm the rights of the estates, and so the situation remained until the Napoleonic era – a triumph for the estates which gained a European reputation for the *Landschaft* of Württemberg.

In Denmark, events developed in the opposite direction. The country had narrowly escaped extinction in a war against Sweden in 1660 and now had to find its way out of defeat and put its ruined finances in order. The taxes levied for this purpose had to be approved by the estates, and the Danish parliament was duly convened in September 1660.

Denmark was an elective monarchy, so that the crown was heavily dependent on the estates, and particularly on the nobility: the Council of the Realm, the governing body delegated by the estates, which had a status equal to that of the crown, was to all intents and purposes in the hands of the nobility. The parliamentary session of 1660, however, took an unusual turn. While the estates representing the clergy and the commons set about planning financial reforms, the nobility refused to take any part in solving the financial crisis and threatened to walk out of the assembly. The citizen militia of Copenhagen then came out in force and barricaded the gates of the capital, so that noble members of the Council of the Realm were unable to depart. They and the Council of the Realm finally gave way under pressure from the other estates and the irate population. What ensued was a capitulation on the part of the estates that was unprecedented in Europe. Since the crisis could not be resolved by agreement among the estates, on 10 January 1661, in a motion endorsed unanimously, the 'Hereditary Monarchical Act' transferred all the powers of the state to the crown. Thus, absolutism was introduced into Denmark by a formal state treaty, the estates having abdicated in due legal form.

Absolutism took a totally different form in Prussia. The traditional image of a hierarchically organized state with a powerful monarch at its head is misleading. The Elector of Brandenburg, who had crowned himself in Königsberg in 1701, far beyond the borders of the Holy Roman Empire, much to the indignation and amusement of the Viennese court, as 'King in Prussia', was actually a relatively weak ruler. The power of the Brandenburg margraves and electors was of very recent date compared with that of the crowned heads of Western Europe. It was only in the sixteenth century that they had succeeded in asserting their authority, by force of arms in many cases. It proved impossible, however, to deprive recalcitrant landowners of all their power, and the danger of a renewed collapse of the monarch's territorial autonomy was never far off. It was also the case that the Prussian crown lands were widely scattered and had no internal cohesion: in the March of Brandenburg the population lived, prayed and even spoke quite differently from the inhabitants of Cleves on the lower Rhine, and certainly very differently from the people of Neufchâtel in Switzerland.

Under the Great Elector Frederick William, the first Prussian

King Frederick I, and the so-called 'Soldier-king', Frederick William I, i.e. during the last third of the eighteenth century, a kind of compromise between the monarch and the *Junker*, the major aristocratic landowners, was arrived at. Sovereignty was divided, as it were, horizontally between the crown and the nobility. The royal administration had its seat in Berlin and was responsible for all the Prussian states – until 1806 the concept of a single Prussian state was unusual; the provinces, with their various judiciaries and independent local assemblies, were regarded as states in themselves, whose sole bond was embodied in allegiance to the person of the monarch. The central government, known since 1723 as the General Directory (*Generaldirektorium*), consisted of four provincial adminis-trations, each of which was allocated a particular area of responsibility – the army, the minting of money, supervision of frontiers, finance. In the provinces the 'War and Estates Chambers' (*Kriegs- und Domänenkammern*) were responsible for ensuring that the decrees of the king's government were enforced.

The comprehensive powers of the king extended so far, but no further. At the next administrative level, in the counties (*Kreise*), the estates ruled; they elected one of their number as prefect (*Landrat*), i.e. as head of the local administration – the king was obliged to accept the nominee of the local council. And at county level, within the boundaries of his own estate, the noble landlord was his own master, with virtually unlimited authority. The Prussian monarchs had conferred on the nobility, along with their landed estates, sovereign powers over the peasantry on their land – in economic, judicial and political terms. In his own area the landowner was invested with police powers and magisterial authority as a summary court. As their patron, he supervised the school and the local church. As the lord of the manor was subject to his king, so the peasant was subject to his squire, and the royal authority stopped short at the boundaries of the landowner's property. This is the reason for the political significance of the virtually unlimited power of the aristocratic landowner at home – on the farm, in the village, in church and school. State policy as it affected the flat countryside east of the River Elbe was normally transmitted through the agency of the local lord of the manor.

The king did in fact have one expedient by which the Prussian nobility could be forced to submit to the authority of the state. Frederick William I had been unable to achieve fully the aim which he communicated to the Prussian estates in a celebrated letter of 13 January 1717. The estates had made representations to the king against the imposition of a new tax which they claimed would ruin the whole country. Frederick William I replied in his typically Prussian style – a jumble of barbarically broken German, French and Polish: 'Tout le pays sera ruiné? Nihil Kredo, aber das Kredo, dass die Junkers ihre Autoritaet Nie pos volam wird ruinirt werden. Ich stabilire die Souveraineté wie einen Rocher von Bronce.'[8] The whole country will be ruined? I don't think so, but I do think that the Junkers' power of veto will be ruined. I shall establish sovereignty like a rock of bronze.

And so the recalcitrant Prussian nobility was taken firmly in hand in a manner in which they had not been treated in any other European country; they were scarcely less firmly tied to the land than their peasant tenants, because their estates could not be sold, and because their status debarred them from any pursuit other than farming. Strict decrees banned the Junkers from leaving the country, from studying abroad or from entering the service of a foreign power. A young gentleman of quality had to reckon with enlistment in the royal cadet corps in Berlin, so that he had no possibility of earning an honest living other than through the only alternative career the King of Prussia offered his noble subjects – a commission in the army. In the words of Frederick William I, the Prussian nobility were 'to acknowledge no lord and master other than God and the King in Prussia.'[9] It was not service at court, as in France and other absolutist states, that bound the Prussian aristocracy to their monarch, but service in the army: to wear the 'king's coat' was reckoned to be the highest of honours – and the king's coat was in fact a uniform.

However alike the European states might seem to be at this stage, they turn out on closer inspection to be singularly varied. Moreover, absolutism was by no means characteristic of all the states of Europe. On the outskirts of the continent there were states that differed significantly from the normal European pattern. There was, for instance, Poland. Here, the course had been set as early as the fifteenth century, when the kings of the Jagelloni dynasty attempted to curb the power of the aristocracy by showing favour to the squirearchy, the *szlachta*. In doing so, however, they had underestimated the solidarity of the nobility as a whole: the crown became increasingly dependent on the nobles, who were able to enhance their constitutional and social status to the point where royal decrees could not be passed without the consent of the nobility in their regional assemblies. In the local parliaments, apart from the city of Cracow, only the nobility and the squirearchy were represented. Their constitutional privileges included the right to elect the king, the right to object to alleged infringements of the constitution by the king – in practice, a licence for rebellion – as well as freedom of religion. It was in fact rule by the nobility disguised as monarchy. In the end the Polish state was totally subordinated to the interests of the nobility, as when, in 1652, a delegate of the aristocratic assembly vetoed the regular dissolution of the national parliament. The *liberum veto*, the frustration of parliamentary legislation in this way, came to be regarded as a customary right and opened up the way to anarchy. By 1700 Poland was in effect no more than a confederation of some 60,000 magnates, who took their lead in foreign policy from Russia, Prussia or Austria. Long before the partitions of 1772, 1793 and, finally, 1795, Poland had become a mere parade ground for her neighbours, a fascinating negative proof of the blessings of absolutism.

That events might take a very different course was demonstrated by the Republic of the United Netherlands – in the seventeenth century a great colonial power, although there was no single ruler who combined all the powers of the state in his own person. Sovereignty was vested in the estates of the autonomous provinces and exercised by the assembly of the States General (*Statengeneraal*) in The Hague. In the emergency situation of the war with France in 1672 the hereditary Governor General from the house of Orange had been invested by the Dutch estates with almost dictatorial powers, although he could not alter the constitution. In the ensuing period, the party of the estates, who esteemed the liberties of the provinces and the States General above all else, stood in opposition to the party of the house of Orange, who advocated an increase in the powers of the Governor General. Nevertheless, the enduring balance of power embodied in the constitution was not disturbed: 'Thus, in the first half of the eighteenth century the Republic became a small, old-fashioned, aristocratic trading nation ruled by an oligarchy of wealthy citizens, aristocrats and prosperous farmers, who formed a distinct caste . . . '[10] Poland and the Netherlands were not the only exceptions to absolutist rule in Europe – there was also Venice, where an archaic constitution ensured the rule of a handful of noble families. And there was the salient exception of England, which had left its absolutist era behind with the end of the Stuart dynasty and had established the sovereignty of Parliament through the Glorious Revolution of 1688.

But these were exceptions which simply highlighted the motley impression of the overall picture without changing its basic character. By and large, as far as Europe was concerned, a predominantly secular state, freed from the tutelage of the church and wielding sovereign power, had emerged from the feudal system of the middle ages and the Renaissance. In the civil and religious wars of the sixteenth and seventeenth centuries the struggle for supremacy in the state, and hence the issue of sovereignty had been decided. State and ruler – at least in theory – had become one and the same. To quote a celebrated definition of the state by Max Weber, the sovereign commanded 'the monopoly of legitimate physical force'.[11] In other words, under the absolutist system the state had put an end to civil war by assuming control over the lives of its subjects. Only the state had the right to demand of its subjects that they should, in the event of war, be prepared to die, or to kill other individuals from another state. This power included the right to take life-or-death decisions in the form of penal sentences or pardon. All other features of the absolutist state derive from these facts: the sovereign's public display of his own person, the celebration of his god-like power over life and death and his power to pardon, his patronage in matters of religion and in the church, the subjugation of rival power groups, particularly the church and the – generally aristocratic – estates, the creation of a hierarchically organized bureaucracy performing its function impartially and dealing institutionally rather than personally with the population, and the establishment of a standing army. This would be in theory the perfect absolutist state, but the European states were never more than an approximation to this ideal. In reality the area beyond the direct control of the state during the era of absolutism was as a rule considerably greater than in our own time.

In the seventeenth and eighteenth century the state was defined in the last analysis by its monopoly of the use of force both within and beyond its frontiers. War was the *ultima ratio regis*, as might be read on the Prussian cannon, i.e. the final, but still legitimate instrument of royal foreign policy. The threshold of this *ultima ratio* was in fact relatively low; the main reasons for going to war included the claim of one state on the territory of another, but another reason might simply be the weakness of a particular state that tempted neighbouring states to adjust frontiers – and there was also a monarch's ambitious desire for military triumph. The community of European states found itself precisely in the condition to which absolutism had put an end internally – in a state of almost perpetual warfare, a negative consequence of its manifold diversity. In the period down to 1815 there was scarcely a decade in which there was not at least one battle fought on European soil; in the course of the seventeenth century, Europe experienced no more than a total of four years of perfect peace, in the eighteenth century the figure had actually risen to sixteen years. This readiness to wage war has been linked by a number of historians with the 'military revolution' that took place between 1560 and 1660 – the widespread use of firearms on the battlefield, an approximately tenfold increase in the size of armies, new ideas in strategy and tactics, with a consequent dramatic effect of warfare on society as a whole.[12] The increasing scale of military campaigns inevitably led to a strengthening of the state's authority. Only the state was in a position to put mass armies into the field, the partisan bands and private armies that had played a part in previous wars tended to disappear.

Problems of financing, provisioning and administering larger armies called for more rational and efficient bureaucracies and fiscal systems. The new tactics, the need to manoeuvre large bodies of troops with precision, called for stricter discipline. Since an increasing proportion of the population came into contact with the army, something of this discipline rubbed off on wider circles of society – Prussia is a case in point. All this led to a greater concentration of the power of the absolutist state at home, and since no state on the continent of Europe could afford to neglect precautions against the possibility of war, absolutism was bound to prevail – which explains up to a point why England, in its secure position as an island, never succumbed to absolutism.

On the other hand, we may well ask why, given the almost permanent state of war in Europe, a European Leviathan was not born – in the form, for instance, of a major power seeking a hegemony that would put an end to warfare on the continent and culminate in an absolutist super-state, a resurrected Rome, or a return to the Carolingian Empire. Major empires destined to endure come about as a rule when tribal communities that have not taken the final step towards statehood are consolidated. That was true of the Roman Empire and of Russia, of the Mogul Empire of the sixteenth and seventeenth centuries, of Japan and China, the Turkish Empire and the Empire of the Abbasids. In Europe, on the other hand, the Carolingian Empire, based on similar premises had foundered on problems connected with the succession, as well as problems of administration and communication. It had, however, passed on the basis of its legitimation to successor states; the idea of the worldwide supremacy of Rome, of the *Imperium*, of a *monarchia universalis* did in fact crop up in Spain, in France and in England, as well as in the Holy Roman Empire.

Any claim to supremacy by these states was opposed by the European community of states, 'a secularized version of the medieval community of faith and church'.[13] Above and beyond the power struggles, however, the states of Europe – and this was a unique feature in the history of the world – together constituted a cultural community by virtue of the family relationships between their monarchs and aristocracies, by their media of communication – the Latin and French languages, by a common climate of civilization – the Enlightenment, by their common roots in the ancient world and in Christianity. It was in fact reasons of state, the plain self-interest of their sovereign rulers, that prompted the European states to recognize each other as equals – at the same time as they acknowledged a kind of ceremonial hierarchy with the Roman Emperor at its head. Wars were subject to certain rules and were waged, as it were, in reserved areas under a system that has been described as 'cabinet warfare'. It was precisely because a sovereign ruler had the right to go to war that wars of annihilation were considered totally unjustified. The *ius publicum europeum*, the international law of Europe was not just a product of modern reason: it had also been influenced by medieval ideas of divine and natural law that may be traced via the philosophy of the church all the way back to the Stoa of classical times. On the basis of a batch of constantly changing conventions and agreements certain binding legal norms evolved which went beyond day-to-day politics and which were valid even in wartime: they defined diplomatic status, the form in which wars might be declared and terminated, the justification of war, the inviolability of state sovereignty, the maintenance of peace. This unstable, but nevertheless enduring community of states was regulated by a set of judicial procedures and crowned by the concept of a balance of power in Europe. The sovereignty, indeed the actual survival of certain states was based on the balance between the leading powers on the continent. In this context most people thought of Austria and France, both of which had been seeking for centuries to extend their power over the entire continent and had invariably failed in the face of more powerful coalitions of other nations. On closer inspection, this system of checks and balances turns out to be a highly complex phenomenon, with sub-systems and components of which the function is not always clear. There was, for instance, a balance of religious denominations superimposed on the balance of the great powers. There were purely regional balance systems, such as the Nordic system, which kept a balance in the Baltic region involving Sweden, Russia and Poland, or a Mediterranean system holding in check the rival influences of Spain, France, Turkey – and, more recently, England.

The Holy Roman Empire, that political patchwork in the middle of the map of Europe, might also be seen as a system of checks and balances, now between Protestant and Catholic countries, now between the Empire and its states, now between Austria and coalitions of medium-sized states like Saxony and Bavaria. That the impoverished state of Prussia, the 'sand-pit' of the Empire, would rise to be a European power to rival the Habsburgs was still written only in the stars. Whether, and how far Russia fitted into the overall system was a matter as much in dispute at the beginning of the eighteenth century, as was the part played by the Ottoman empire. Even the most enlightened political theorists of the day still had at the back of their minds the *res publica christiana* of earlier centuries, the commonwealth of Latin Christianity, an ideal that excluded the Islamic Turks and the Orthodox Russians.

This splendidly rational machine was kept going by statesmen and diplomats who all spoke the same language – French – and who, as members of an aristocracy with family ties spanning the whole of Europe, shared the same modes of thought and patterns of behaviour, and who, in the form of the *ius publicm europeum*, had at their disposal a set of implements with which to repair eventual damage, if the machinery ever came to a standstill.

Outside the system there was also an engineer who took good care to see that the machine constituting the European balance of power was always well supplied with fuel in the form of subsidies, and who never hesitated to intervene if the balance of power seemed to be in jeopardy, i.e. England. England did not see herself as part of the European system of checks and balances; indeed, one might even say, as the Austrian financial councillor, Gottlob von Justi did, that the whole affair was simply an illusion created to advance England's commercial interests. Certainly it was quite obvious that, as a rule, England was militarily engaged on the continent only when the ports on the estuaries of the Rhine, the Scheldt and the Maas were in danger of being occupied by a major power, since it was through these ports that the English wool trade was carried on, and the island's prosperity had long depended on that trade. But as far as British commercial interests were concerned, the continent of Europe was only one market – and not even the most important. England's political economic horizon was far wider: while the continental powers were trying to settle their differences within the narrow confines of Europe, or engaging in trials of strength with their neighbours, the perspective of England as a great maritime power ranged far and wide over the entire globe. The English author and merchant Daniel Defoe made the point: 'To have command of the sea is to wield power and carry on trade in Europe, Africa and America.'[14] England's command of the seas and her supremacy in trade ranged from the mouth of the Ganges to Jamaica in the West Indies. It was not the minor continent of Europe that represented the yardstick of British policy and British trade, but the vast area between the two Indies. Thus, following the Peace of Utrecht in 1713, it was England that aspired to replace France as the pre-eminent power in Europe, and hence to supersede the political model that had hitherto been represented by France.

4

The Constitutional State and the Rule of Law

It was in the Treaty of Utrecht which put an end to the protracted War of the Spanish Succession, that there was embodied for the first time (in Article 6 of the Anglo-French agreement) in a treaty valid under international law, the concept of a balance of power. The idea was thus acknowledged as a contractually enforceable principle of European politics. The British foreign minister, Henry St John, Viscount Bolingbroke, played a leading part in drafting the treaty. Only two years later, this favourite of Queen Anne had fallen from power: the Whig majority in the Commons accused him of having concluded a peace with the French on much too lenient terms, and Bolingbroke fled to Paris in order to escape the Tower, or an even direr fate. Henceforth, he devoted himself to political intrigue and philosophy, and although he never again held office, he remained until his death in 1751, one of the most brilliant minds in the Tory party.

Bolingbroke's political views, published in 1749 in *The Idea of a Patriot King*, suggested that monarchy was based on a notion of common law; that followed from the natural and universal law of reason as well as from the particular law to which every state submitted voluntarily. Whoever exercised power in the state was worthy of it only as long as he earned the respect, the trust and the affection of his subjects; power remained 'a voluntary gift of freedom, which finds its own security therein'. In future there should be none but 'patriot kings' who cared only for the well-being of their country and who accepted the law which that country imposed on them.

The fact that the atheist Bolingbroke made no mention of god, but referred only to the law was to be expected in a country so fascinated by natural law. In any case, Bolingbroke did not have eternal truths in mind, but rather the condition of the British monarchy, which in his view had degenerated under Whig rule into a corrupt one-party affair: Parliament had been reduced to a willing tool in the hands of ministers of the crown. England's constitution therefore needed checks and balances to set limits to the abuse of power by the establishment. Bolingbroke was thinking in the first place of the English squirearchy as an instrument for achieving this end. In describing such balancing elements in the constitution, Bolingbroke, with his experience in foreign affairs, recalled the greatest triumph of his career, the Peace of Utrecht. What could be more obvious than to apply the principle of the balance of power to the constitutional situation of England? A return, in fact, to the principles of the Glorious Revolution, to the independence of Parliament from the executive, a decentralization of power, lower taxes for the rural gentry, whose liberties would provide a balance between the monarch's ministers and the mass of the population.

This was a party programme designed for implementation in day-to-day politics. But the dazzling circle round Bolingbroke, who cut just as fine a figure in Parisian *salons* as he had done in London clubs, also fascinated personalities who were not politicians, among them Voltaire and Montesquieu, both of whom were deeply impressed by Bolingbroke's ideas. In particular, Charles-Louis de Secondat, Baron de La Brède et de Montesquieu (1689–1755) learned a great deal from Bolingbroke; the celebrated eleventh book of his major work, *De l'Esprit des Lois*, which appeared in 1748, deals with 'laws governing political freedom in relation to the constitution'. This chapter is entirely based on the partisan view of the English constitution that Montesquieu had assimilated through his association with Bolingbroke and the latter's friends during the years Montesquieu spent in England between 1729 and 1732. Montesquieu's idea of the division of power was an ideal never realized in England, but it was destined to have consequences outside England.

Like Bolingbroke, Montesquieu believed in laws and their power to regulate, pacify and liberate. Had not the brilliant new sciences, astrology, cosmology and physics begun their triumphant advance because human reason had succeeded in reducing natural processes to the laws which lay behind all phenomena? Was not man himself a creature of nature and hence subject to these laws? On this point Montesquieu remains vague: for him 'laws' meant both the laws of nature, to which man as a natural creature was subject, and the laws by which a human community was governed. It was only necessary to let man's innate reason have its way, and we should become aware of the laws applying to man's nature! Certainly, Montesquieu did not believe that one law would apply to all nations: on the contrary, he took the view that every state needed its own particular legislation, adapted to its physical configuration, climate, mode of life, manner of production – in short, to its individual character. A community is rational, hence in keeping with nature, when it devises laws to regulate the anarchic urge for individual liberty. 'Political freedom does not consist in doing whatever one pleases. In a state, i.e. in a community of individuals in which there are laws, freedom can consist only in doing whatever is permitted and not being constrained to do something that one may not legitimately wish to do.' The freedom of the individual must be limited by the freedom of others; it is the responsibility of the state to frame those laws that are needed to strike a balance between the liberties of individuals in their relations to each other: 'Freedom is the right to do anything that the law allows. If one citizen were able to do something that the law prohibited, then he would no longer be free, for others would have the same right . . . '[1]

This beneficial effect of the law applied in fact to no more than two forms of government: the *gouvernements modérés* of republics and of monarchies. Republics in which the people as a whole exercised sovereign authority were feasible only on a small scale, where the situation could be viewed as a whole, in a few Alpine valleys, or in classical antiquity. Monarchy was the form of government best suited to modern states. It was true that monarchy constantly ran the risk of degenerating into despotism, an anti-state in which the monarch had arbitrarily abrogated the laws and ruled by brute force alone. In order to avoid this kind of abuse of power, authority would have to be shared by a number of institutions which had to be carefully separated from each other: the executive, i.e. the monarch, the government and administration; the legislature, i.e. the representatives of the people, augmented by representation of the nobility, which, as an independent body, would hold the balance vis-à-vis the monarch; and the judiciary, which should be thought of as a system of independent jury courts. These three authorities would maintain a balance, each constituting a check on the others, just as, in social terms, monarch, nobility and commons would maintain a balance. These were the preconditions for the kind of moderate, rational legislation that would promote and secure freedom.

France did not offer Montesquieu anything like his ideal model of a liberal monarchy bound by law and a system of mediating authorities. The French system of government, once so admired throughout Europe, no longer enjoyed the good reputation it had had in the middle of the eighteenth century. Montesquieu was only one of many mordant critics who deplored the decline of the monarchy and were inclined to draw comparisons with oriental despotism: with the monarch as the most eminent prisoner of his own court, given up to vice and indifferent to matters of state, an aristocracy long devoid of its original function as the guarantor of the liberties of the estates, and long reduced to the dull and dreary existence of sycophants and lackeys, rule by viziers, i.e. irresponsible ministers and councillors as the henchmen of a despotic power, with religious superstition taking the place of sound laws. This is the image of French monarchy as described by Montesquieu and many other authors and journalists of his day, recorded in a host of versions, printed in Geneva or Amsterdam and circulated throughout the continent. The France of Louis XV and Louis XVI had been exposed and denounced by its own men of letters long before the Revolution.

In England, on the other hand, these new ideas seemed to have been put into practice. Had not the separation of the executive, the legislature and the judiciary been achieved here? Enlightened individuals from all over Europe duly made their pilgrimage to this blessed island and on their return told of the merits of the English constitution. One of the most influential publicists of the eighteenth century, Johann Wilhelm von Archenholtz of Danzig, wrote in 1785: 'Apart from a large number of privileges and concessions of all kinds that the English gained from their *Magna Charta*, partly through their various revolutions and other favourable circumstances of the times, the main privileges of the nation may be summed up under five headings: 1. freedom of the press, 2. The *Habeas Corpus* Act, 3. Public tribunals, 4. Jury trials, 5. Parliamentary representation.'[2]

These liberties and the independence of the judiciary – this was what most fascinated visitors from abroad. The *Habeas Corpus* Act of 1679, which prevented arbitrary arrest, had contributed significantly to an increase in public confidence in the judiciary, but what mainly guaranteed every citizen effective protection under the law was the institution of jury courts. With the *Bill of Rights* of 1689 the Westminster Parliament had established its sovereignty by a legislative act, whereas the monarchy had relinquished its divine right and became henceforth a normal office of state, sanctioned by Parliament, albeit furnished with certain extraordinary powers. It was in fact a parliament that had little resemblance to the parliaments of the nineteenth and twentieth centuries: it was still an assembly of the estates, dominated by a relatively broad cross-section of the higher aristocracy, the squirearchy and wealthy commoners. It was not the king, but Parliament and the courts that defined the monarch's privileges and what was in the common interest; the king was still responsible, however, for the appointment of ministers, the allocation of higher administrative posts and national policy. In his *Two Treatises of Government* (1690), John Locke (1632–1704) had described the new situation as based on *trust*, with the crown and Parliament acting as joint trustees of the commonwealth: that was what was meant by 'the King in Parliament', the formal rendering of the British monarch's status. The king was bound by his oath to the religion and the constitutional statutes of his kingdom, obliged to confirm 'ancient rights and privileges', renouncing the ancient right of the monarch to suspend the law. The law, after all, stood above the crown.

With the triumphant advance of the Enlightenment, these political ideas of the day came into their own in other European courts as well. Monarchs surrounded themselves with enlightened advisers and their sons with tutors charged with instilling the new ideas into the younger generation. And, after all, were ideas concerning the supremacy of natural law so much at odds with absolute rule? Was not the absolute ruler also concerned to standardize the laws of his state, to ensure equal rights before the law for all his subjects, to eliminate the privileges of the nobility, to prevent abuses by the clergy, to involve the citizenry in the service of the state, to centralize the civil service, to increase the prosperity of his people through sound economic policy – in short, to apply the principles of reason to the government of his state?

Let us take the case of Prussia. The Crown Prince Frederick, who succeeded to the throne in 1740 as Frederick II, was the idol of the philosophers; his correspondence with Voltaire, in which the Crown Prince was hailed as a new Solomon, circulated throughout the learned world and even impressed Rousseau, who otherwise detested monarchs. Admittedly, every trace of philosophy was erased once Frederick had mounted the throne – the invasion of Silesia by Prussian troops that took place that same year was a blatant affront to any sense of law and order that prevailed in that age. Nevertheless, in the eyes of an enlightened public attuned to the idea of progress, Frederick remained the philosopher king: he not only corresponded with philosophers and accepted them into his academy when they were persecuted by other monarchs, he ruled his kingdom according to enlightened principles of government.

Frederick's view of the state had been shaped by Montesquieu and Christian Wolff. In 1721 the latter had declared, in his *Rational Thoughts on the Life of Society*, that the government and the governed 'were obliged to honour the contract between them'. An enlightened monarch was therefore bound by laws calculated to promote the prosperity of his people. Frederick took a similar view:

> The great truth, that we should do unto others as we would have them do unto us, forms the basis of all law and of the social contract . . . But since laws can neither endure nor be applied without unremitting supervision, authorities were established, elected by the people, to whom the people submitted of their own free will. We should take careful note of this: the upholding of the law was the sole reason that prompted men to appoint governments over them, for this is what the true origin of the ruler's power signifies. He who occupied this office was but the first servant of the state . . . [3]

Here we may find the crucial difference that distinguishes Louis XIV's absolutism from the enlightened absolutism that began to gain the upper hand in Europe during the second half of the eighteenth century – not even stopping short of the throne of the Empress of Russia. It was not god who sanctioned the monarch's right to rule, but the law that issued from man's reason and from the social contract. The monarch was no longer the state, but merely the first servant of the state and hence justified only if he served it well, i.e. for the benefit of its people. State and ruler were thus separated: the state forfeited its brilliant appearance as embodied in the monarch and became an abstraction formed by laws and institutions, tangible only in the actions of its officers, becoming a social entity governed by law and bureaucracy.

Among the characteristic features of the state – especially the Prussian state – during the course of the eighteenth century was the process by which the civil service acquired, as it were, a specific gravity of its own as the authority of the state was increasingly centralized and subjected to legislation. This was one result of increased administrative activity in the more remote regions of the monarchy, but also of an improvement in the qualification of civil servants and their increasing awareness of their status. In the newly acquired provinces of Silesia, West Prussia and Friesland, effective government from a centre in Berlin was hardly feasible, even for a 'first servant of the state' who ceaselessly patrolled his realm, summoning mayors and magistrates to the door of his carriage and interrogating them, questioning the peasantry about the prospects for the harvest, the condition of their livestock or the supply of salt. The growing ponderous burden of the Prussian civil service led to a functional *étatism*, to government by a 'formalistic un-personality', as Max Weber describes the ideal of bureaucratic rule embodied in the Prussian official state: 'Without animosity, dispassionately, under the compulsion of a simple concept of duty, without regard to persons, formally equal for all'.[4]

That the juxtaposition, cheek by jowl, of abstract legality and the personality of an absolute monarch involved inherent contradictions often became apparent, as in the case of the miller, Arnold. A miller, Christian Arnold, had rented a water-mill near Pommerzig in the Neumark on hereditary lease from Baron Schmettau. The working of the mill had been impaired by carp ponds which had been constructed upstream by the local prefect (*Landrat*) von Gersdorff. In 1778, when Arnold then failed to pay the rent due under the lease, he was evicted. His appeal, addressed in the first instance to the local authority, and then to the court in Berlin, was dismissed. In the end the miller appealed to the king who, convinced that the local magistrates had not been impartial but had shown favour to their aristocratic colleague, decided to make an example of them. He summoned the justices of the Berlin *Kammergericht*, cross-examined them and, ignoring their objections, had them imprisoned in one of his fortresses. The Justice Minister, von Zedlitz, however, refused to overturn the verdict of the *Kammergericht*, and Frederick did not dare to dismiss his refractory minister.

In this case the contradiction inherent in enlightened absolutism is obvious: if the king was an element in the rule of law, then he had no right to interfere with the course of justice as dispensed by the courts. But what if, in fact, the principle of 'equal rights for all before the law' had been infringed by the justices? Frederick had evidently decided to resume his former role and ensure that justice was done through a purely arbitrary pronouncement – although, as it happened, he was in the wrong. The judges of the *Kammergericht* were duly rehabilitated after Frederick's death. The case of miller Arnold, however, which was debated all over Europe, was taken as a popular pretext for embarking on a codification of the law which would simplify or sweep away the jumble of antiquated regional or parochial laws and legal usages, and which would lay down once and for all the principles of a monarchical state under the rule of law. A privy councillor and high court judge, Carl Gottlieb Svarez, was appointed principal author and editor of the revised code and, like his royal master, took as his starting point the social contract into which the monarch had entered with his subjects. Svarez deduced from the terms of the contract the right of the citizen to make certain demands on his sovereign. Legislation in general ought to 'define sure, certain and enduring principles of right and wrong which, especially in a state lacking a formal constitution must, in a sense serve in place of the same, and which must include rules binding on the legislator, which he may not infringe'.[5] This *General Code of Law for the Prussian States*, which took effect in 1794, had lost in the course of its gestation a good deal of its original enlightened enthusiasm. Under the impact of the Revolution in France, the proposed prohibition of arbitrary royal decrees had been deleted, as had any reference to 'the natural rights and liberties of the citizen'. What remained was, in its ambiguity, a symbol of Frederick's state: in 19,000 paragraphs the General Code regulated the relationship between the state and its citizens. On the one hand, the social structure based on the division of classes or estates was specifically endorsed: peasantry, commons and aristocracy were dealt with under separate headings, with the aristocracy in a privileged position, 'as far as the defence of the realm' and the 'support of the outer dignity and the inner constitution of the same' were concerned. On the other hand, the monarch and the state were now legally separated. The state was defined as a 'civic association' which had entrusted its authority as a state to the monarch. But the monarch was bound by the law, once it has been enacted: he was the highest officer of state, no less and no more. This was how Friedrich Schiller had conceived the monarch in his tragedy, *Plot and Passion* (*Kabale und Liebe*). In it Lady Milford remarks to Major Ferdinand von Walter, 'This sword was given to you by the Prince.' The Major replies, 'The state gave it to me by the hand of the Prince.' The reason for the existence of the state in the world, in the light of the General Code of Law, is explained by Svarez in the following terms: 'The establishment and maintenance of public order and security, the facilitation and promotion of those means by which every individual is provided with the opportunity to pursue his private happiness, without injury or detriment to that of other . . .'[6]

That the state existed in order to promote the 'private happiness of individuals' was a commonplace of the age. Jeremy Bentham (1748–1823), an expert in constitutional law, went so far as to declare that the ultimate aim of the state was to promote the greatest happiness of the greatest number of people; to this end constitutions and codification of the law were necessary. 'The whole world was on the point of giving birth to plans for codification of the law' (H. Hattenhauer), from Florence to St Petersburg. Scarcely one of these plans was ever realized, but the direction in which they tended was everywhere the same. The absolutist state was well on the way to being turned into an enlightened welfare state – everything for the people, but nothing by the people. Professor Georg Friedrich Lamprecht of the University of Halle, in his *Outline of a Complete System of Political Theory* (*Versuch eines vollständigen Systems der Staatslehre*, 1784), emphasized that 'the first principle in all the business of government is the promotion of the citizens' happiness.' He then proceeded to design a model police state which would compel the citizen to enjoy to the full his good fortune and wellbeing. Each and every impulse on the part of the citizen would be subject to police supervision – from the consumption of tea, chocolate or coffee, on the grounds that they were liable to harm the digestive system, to a ban on the colouring of Easter eggs, since this practice might also be detrimental to the citizen's health.

The innovations which well-meaning philosophers, philanthropic citizens and enlightened rulers meant to prescribe for their people's benefit were greeted everywhere with suspicion and vigorously resisted. Society was governed by force of habit and time-honoured precedent, there was a profound aversion to any departure from what had been the custom for as long as anyone could remember. Anyone who carried innovation too far was liable to come to grief. A prime example was the Emperor Joseph II: in the ten years (1780–90) when he ruled by himself following the death of his mother, Maria Theresa, he tried hard to introduce Enlightenment ideas of liberty and equality into the Austrian states. Peasants were freed from servitude to their landlords and the unpaid labour known as 'robot' was abolished. A patent of toleration decreed freedom of worship; a modern judicial system was inaugurated, with a clear separation of the judiciary from the civil service; the special status of the nobility before the law was abolished, as were the fiscal privileges of the nobility and the clergy. The initial stages of a programme of social legislation were begun with the control of child labour in factories; the civil service was slimmed down and centralized and its procedures simplified so as to accommodate reforms. This was a vast and revolutionary undertaking, which largely failed to achieve its purpose in Joseph's lifetime because it was resisted by the estates in Belgium, Hungary and Lombardy. The monarch's uncompromisingly rational will was effectively obstructed by the old laws, traditional privileges and practices to which the estates still tenaciously clung. Joseph's brother and successor, Leopold II, was obliged to retract the greater part of Joseph's planned reforms.

Something similar happened in America in 1774, when the British government annulled the Massachusetts Charter of 1691 in an attempt to rationalize the constitutional position, thus weakening the powers of the municipalities and strengthening those of the governor general. It was the infringement of the existing old law that provoked the resistance of the colonists as well as that of the Whig opposition in the House of Commons – an ominous prelude to the American Revolution of 1776. The same situation arose in France in 1788: the leading minister, Loménie de Brienne, attempted to deprive the *parlement* of Paris of its powers. This body had the right to raise objections to royal decrees, and since it consisted of members of the *noblesse de robe*, i.e. of civil servants who had been granted full aristocratic status only in 1715, it blocked any attempt at reform by the king that might have impaired the privileges of the nobility. In this case the point at issue was a decree proposing improvements in the condition of the peasantry, abolishing judicial torture, guaranteeing freedom of worship to Protestants and liberalizing the grain trade – a relatively moderate programme of reform, then, but it met with fierce opposition in the Parisian *parlement* – ostensibly in the name of liberty and on behalf of a nation that allegedly had to be protected from the crown's mania for legislation and innovation. Lawyers and civil servants went on strike, gangs of youths roamed the streets of the capital, looting and fighting pitched battles with the police that often ended with fatal casualties. There were risings in Béarn, the Dauphiné and Brittany. The king gave in: it was obvious that henceforth reforms might only be achieved through an appeal to the *états généraux*, which had not been convened since 1614.

The remarkable thing about all these events is not so much that the privileged classes clung to their privileges, but that they were able to do so, because they had contrived to form an alliance with the underprivileged under the auspices of the time-honoured traditional order. And wherever, as in America in 1776, or in France in 1789, the old state perished in the inferno of revolution, the same thing held true: down to the end of the eighteenth century, revolution did not mean the removal of what was old and the rise of something totally new, but the restoration of 'the good old order', which had been thrown into disorder by the enlightened tyranny of some monarch or other.

Back to Nature: that was the slogan that, in the general view, during the closing years of the eighteenth century, would lead into the future. The prophet of this new faith was a citizen of

Geneva, Jean-Jacques Rousseau (1712–78) who had conceived the brilliant idea of simply turning the current theory of a social contract upside down. Hobbes had claimed that, in his primitive condition, man behaved like a wolf towards his fellow men, hence the need for a universal agreement leading to his present state, which ensured peace and granted everyone his due. In reality, Rousseau declared, the opposite was true: once men had lived in extended families as nomadic herdsmen; they had owned no property and were consequently as happy as they were virtuous: it had been a golden age. Nowadays, however, society was governed by wealth and self-interest: 'This is where we find the poisonous source of violence, deceit, malice and any number of other horrors, which inevitably bring about a state of affairs in which each individual, while pretending to promote the happiness, welfare and prestige of others, in fact does his best to place his own interests first at their expense.'[7] The social contract on which the states of the day were based was simply a confidence trick on the part of the 'haves', who had persuaded the 'have-nots' by specious reasoning to found the state. The present-day state rested on foundations that were unjust, the principles of its laws were null and void: what mattered now was to form a new state, a true *association*, a community, a political body in which every individual would surrender his rights voluntarily to the community.

If everyone thus virtuously renounced his selfish private interests for the benefit of the community, then, in some mystic manner, a *volonté générale* was generated, a common purpose: the welfare and maintenance of a community, to which all virtuous citizens of the state submitted, so that true sovereignty in the state, the sovereignty of the people was established. In theory the state was a democratic republic in which all decisions were taken by the citizens in common, but it was obvious to Rousseau that this would be possible only in small communities which could easily be overseen – as, for instance, in the Swiss cantons. For purely practical reasons, larger states would have to be governed by delegates elected by the people, hence by a kind of republican aristocracy, while exceptionally large states would have no alternative to accepting a monarch with democratic credentials. It would certainly not be possible for even the most virtuous state to revert to the golden age of a simple pastoral people living under some kind of communistic dispensation: what really mattered was to prevent any further advance leading to the division of labour and a unilateral accumulation of wealth. That was why labour-saving machinery should be banned: Rousseau's sound state would consist of autonomous and austere crofters and craftsmen.

The model state proposed by Rousseau was by its very nature revolutionary, and it was no coincidence that the American Declaration of Independence of 1776 repeated Rousseau's argument almost word for word when it declared that the contract between the British crown and the English colonies in America was null and void:

> We hold these truths to be self-evident, that all men are created equal, that they are endowed by their Creator with certain unalienable Rights, that among these are Life, Liberty and the pursuit of Happiness. – That to secure these rights, Governments are instituted among Men, deriving their just powers from the consent of the governed. – That whenever any Form of Government becomes destructive of these ends, it is the Right of the People to alter or to abolish it, and to institute new Government, laying its foundation on such principles and organizing its powers in such form, as to them shall seem most likely to effect their Safety and Happiness.[8]

Natural innocence and the moral superiority of the transatlantic wilderness might almost have been created expressly to provide room for a new state on Rousseau's principles. The thirteen states of New England which had risen in rebellion against the British crown were looked upon as a model for Europe, as

> The better half of the world,
> Where sweet equality does dwell and the noble brood,
>
> That pestilence of Europe, no longer
> Stains the moral code of innocence.

as an anonymous contributor exultantly wrote in the *Berlinische Monatsschrift (Berlin Monthly)* in 1783. The old world must follow the example of the new, and itself become a new world. And when that happened – when in July 1789 news came from Paris that the Third Estate of the *états généraux* had declared itself the sole legitimate representative of the French people and was about to promulgate a constitution based on the sovereignty of the people and the Rights of Man, then it did seem certain that the old world was indeed an *ancien régime* – finished and done away with.

But it was not to be: Rousseau had indeed provided the ideas without which no revolutionary people's state could claim to be legitimate, but the attempt to base the new state on a social contract drafted by virtuous men, a paradise for craftsmen and smallholders, was to end in a bloodbath, dictatorship by the Committee of Public Safety under Robespierre from 1792 to 1794, and a reign of terror directed against all those who were lacking in true republican virtue. The ideal was wrecked by the inhuman philanthropy of a handful of ideologically inflamed Jacobins. The subsequent influence of Rousseau may properly be relegated to the history of ideas: he had introduced into the world the demand for popular sovereignty and the rights of man, but also the two opposing faces of popular rule – democracy, cheek by jowl with brutal oppression in the name of the people and the *volonté générale*: 'The individual must be forced to align his will with the interest of the state, the people have to be told what it is they want.'[9]

It took a long time for the shock of the French Revolution to abate to the point where people who had witnessed those events could see them in their wider European context. It was then apparent that, in spite of all the innovations that had been introduced since 1789, the real character of the European states had not basically changed – except in one respect: revolution and the Napeolonic dictatorship had actually given birth to the kind of state to which absolutism had aspired without ever achieving it. The first writer to point out this apparent paradox was Alexis de Tocqueville (1805–59) in his book, *L'Ancien Régime et la Révolution*, which appeared in 1856. It had been the old absolutist state that first set about curbing

the power of the nobility, restricting the competence of parliaments and courts, interfering with the traditional rights of
the provinces and spreading an increasingly dense bureaucratic
network throughout the country. Absolute monarchy, declared
Tocqueville, had forestalled more than three-quarters of the
revolution. The reason why a revolutionary mood developed
in France was that the last vestiges of the feudal rights and privileges enjoyed by the estates, which the king had been unable
to eliminate, subsequently seemed to have no justification and
thus constituted a perpetual thorn in the nation's flesh. The
actual revolution represented no more than a process of acceleration. The civil servants and lawyers, who already occupied
vital administrative posts under the monarchy, simply stepped
into the foreground and took the place of their erstwhile
aristocratic superiors. Once they had at last succeeded in
centralizing the administration of the country, often at the cost
of bloodshed, they proceeded to put an end to the rights and
liberties of the provinces, simplifying not merely the system of
weights and measures, but also the entire judicial system. What
nineteenth-century Europe witnessed as the direct and legitimate successor to the absolutist state was in fact the modern
centralized bureaucratic state, which – just like the enlightened
despots of the *ancien régime* – took as its ultimate aim the
happiness of the bureaucratically administered citizen.

The original model of this state was the Napoleonic Empire,
with its departmental ministers heading the civil service, and
under them the prefects and sub-prefects in the *départments*,
the successors to the *intendants* and *subdélégués* of the *ancien
régime*. The ministers, prefects and sub-prefects passed orders
and instructions down from the summit to the smallest municipality, and relayed information in the opposite direction to the
central bureaucracy. The system was constructed on entirely
rational principles of superior and subordinate authorities –
a geometrically exact power pyramid designed in the rational
and mathematical spirit of the Enlightenment. In every office
or appointment, the principle of expert competence prevailed
with a consequent professionalization of the civil service. The
bureaucracy consisted of career officials who could neither purchase their appointments nor pass them on to their heirs, and

who were promoted on grounds of competence and political reliability. Of the officials in the municipalities, the government nominated the mayors, who were formally agents of the government, but actually subordinate to the local prefect. There were representative bodies in the *départements*, the districts and the towns, but they had no more than a consultative function. What was in fact the military principle of command and obedience also governed the civil service. The state aspired to be a perfect political machine, from the most humble village mayor up to its pinnacle, the emperor.

As with the example set by Louis XIV, this model state broadcast its influence over the whole of Europe – no wonder, in view of the hegemony that revolutionary France and, even more, imperial France had achieved on the continent up to 1812. Wherever French satellite governments had been installed – and this applied to the Italian monarchies, Holland, the Swiss Republic, the Kingdom of Westphalia and the Grand Duchy of Berg – the administrative and judicial systems of France were imposed. France's allies, especially the states of the Rhenish League (*Rheinbund*) adopted French institutions and judicial standards in a variety of ways, and it was a fact that reforms on the French pattern – codification of laws, independence of the judiciary and centralization of the bureaucracy – were most successful where absolutism had already prepared the way. But even those states outside the Rhenish League, notably Austria and Prussia, reformed their structures essentially on the French pattern.

For the rulers of Austria and Prussia what most mattered was rapid recovery from the defeats of Austerlitz and Jena, and the restoration and extension of their political and military potential. France was the model here, too, in so far as it implanted in the minds of the reformers two ideas: we must never again suffer defeats like those of 1805 and 1806, and: we might wish some day to do what Napoleon did to us. In Prussia especially, which proved to be more radical and also more flexible in its reforms than the unwieldy Danube monarchy, the new state was considered unprecedented in the range and concentration of its powers. In Prussia, as elsewhere, it was the social class of civil servants and lawyers that mainly supported the reforms, tending to regard themselves as representative of the state as a whole. With almost revolutionary zeal they set about reshaping the state by decree. The reformer, declared Minister Altenstein, ought not to take the inner essence of the state as it is, 'but as it might be, and shape it to his purpose so that it conforms to the supreme aim of the state as a whole . . . Something entirely new must be created'.[10] The Prussian civil service, then, was a demiurge, 'an instrument chosen by the world order to educate the human race', as Chancellor Hardenberg put it at the end of the reform era.[11] There was, here again, something of the same trust in the rule of reason that had inspired men like Robespierre and Napoleon.

The refashioning of the Prussian state had some success in spite of resistance and its ultimate failure to achieve a radical reorganization of the government, civil service and army but it was essentially no more than one more triumph of the Prussian absolutist tradition. Centralization and rationalization of the state's authority, a reduction in the powers of the estates, to the benefit of a monarchical head of state, extension of the state's monopoly of power to every regional, social and cultural area and, last but not least, a bureaucracy independent of the estates and answerable only to the state and the monarchy – all this had long existed in embryo and was illustrated in the history of Brandenburg and Prussia. Even following reform there was an unmistakably patriarchal element in the new dispensation: Prussia as a state never quite lost the features it shared with large agrarian estates east of the River Elbe, with the king, as it were, the principal landowner or manager, whose Christian duties included the paternal care of his tenants.

Thus the European states, as they emerged from the abyss of the revolution and twenty-two years of a world war, varied in their internal structure. In essentials, however, they owed much to the French model; this was no doubt partly a consequence of Napoleonic hegemony, but it probably also owed something to the wide distribution of earlier absolutist regimes which, as had once been the case in the eighteenth century, embraced all but the states on the outskirts of the continent: Russia and England – Russia, because its autocratic tradition proved strong enough to resist the temptations of modernization *à la française*; England, because the sovereignty of Parliament and the privileges of the squirearchy had survived the Napoleonic wars unimpaired.

With the increasing encroachment of the state on the domain of public life, one major aspect had indeed changed: following the French example: revolution by force of arms might now be considered legitimate. Rousseau's dictum: 'Man is born free, but is everywhere in chains'[12] was firmly lodged in men's minds. The prospects of happiness on earth offered by all parties in the battle for the legacy of the revolution, the increasingly prominent part played by ideology in politics, the retreat from pragmatism and compromise – all this fostered the readiness to sacrifice human life and glorify violence and terrorism. As distinct from pre-revolutionary times, the masses were now prepared to man the barricades for political and social causes. This was true, not just of the motherland of the revolution, but of all Western and Central Europe. Even in Prussia, which was outwardly so formidably disciplined and well organized, ominous social stresses and fissures had become apparent. It was not possible to introduce universal military service, improve educational standards and perform on the instrument of public opinion, arousing the nation's emotions to fever pitch in the wars of liberation between 1813 and 1815 – and then expect the people to submit tamely to wise educational policies prescribed by a bureaucratic elite. Besides the growing social tensions in the period preceding the revolution of 1848, there was widespread indignation over broken promises of new constitutions, and over the policy of governments who, fearing the radical trend of public opinion and perhaps even a recurrence of the events of 1789, had tightened the screws of censorship, and used police chicanery to quell the clamour for economic freedom and political representation.

In this way the state and society were driven apart, and European statesmen had to pay the price of this divorce – in the revolutions of 1830 and 1848. The key concepts of European diplomacy, renaissance, regeneration and restoration, were as bloodless as the 'Holy Alliance' into which the Russian tsar wished the European powers to enter. In a sentimental access of sincerity Alexander I was convinced that the monarchs of Europe and their subjects could be bound together in this way. The British Foreign Minister, Castlereagh, however, called this return to the principle of divine right a mixture of sublime mysticism and nonsense. A powerful state needed powerful justification if it was not to be engulfed by revolution and civil war. What was called for was a fresh rationale of the national community, a renewed mandate to govern, an idea that would seize the minds of the masses, rising above all individual interests and ideologies and binding the nation to its state. What prevented Europe from once more disintegrating into religious strife and civil war, as it had done following the Reformation, was an idea that fostered a sense of community, the idea of the nation.

Part II

Nations

5

What is the 'Nation'?

The Hermann Monument near Detmold, in the murmuring depths of the forest, surrounded by swarms of tourists, shows the prince of the Cheruscans in heroic pose and towers up to a height of nearly a hundred feet. His sword bears in golden letters the inscription: 'German's Unity is my Strength, my Strength is Germany's Power.' At the unveiling of the monument in 1875 Emperor William I had hailed the Cheruskan chief as Hermann the German. When, on the occasion of the centenary of this ceremony in 1975, the historian Thomas Nipperdey ventured to pass a few critical remarks on this bold appropriation of the Cheruscan tribal chief and Roman knight Arminius, the consequent storm of indignation went far beyond the local patriots of Lippe: the million and a half visitors who annually made their pilgrimage to the monument were unmoved by the niggling doubts of a mere historian: the link between the bronze colossus and their own past was certified by the dozens of commemorative plaques that surrounded them, and at least the more elderly could still recall Viktor von Scheffels's verses, 'When those Romans grew too bold', which ended with the lines:

> And in honour of this tale
> They put a statue in the vale
> Proclaiming German unity,

Her strength is there for all to see:
'So let them come, just let them dare!'

'Them' – that had originally been the Romans, whose legions
led by the governor P. Quinctilius Varus had been annihilated
by the Germanic tribes led by Arminius in the year AD 9. Later
on, it had been the French against whom the bronze Hermann
had raised his sword. And so the thread of history reaches from
the past into the present. The author of a recent, astonishingly
popular account of Arminius speaks of 'the first great figure
of Germanic and German history', erecting a grand arch that
spans the whole of German history and reaches forward into
the future. We must bear Hermann in mind, we read, whenever
we speak of overcoming the division of Germany, for was not
his battle, too, fought in the cause of German unification?[1]
From Hermann the Cheruscan to Helmut Kohl: two thousand
years of German history?

The popular view is not all that different in France: what
Hermann the Cheruscan is for German history, Vercingetorix
is for the history of France. In fact, most European nations have
their quasi-mystical heroes who once led the fight for freedom
against the Romans: for instance, Viriathus, the hero of Spanish
nationalism, Civilis, the leader of the Batavian rising, whom
Rembrandt painted for the city hall in Amsterdam, Boadicea,
who fought against Nero's legions and who now stands in her
chariot in front of the Houses of Parliament in London. The
monument to Vercingetorix towers over the ruined ramparts of
Alesia, the town that Caesar besieged and finally conquered in
52 BC. On the pedestal of the monument is an inscription taken
from Caesar's commentary: '*La Gaule unie, formant une seule
nation, animée d'un même esprit, peut défier l'univers.*' That was
just the nineteenth century? Not far from this spot on Mount
Beuvray near Autun, stands a commemorative monolith dated
1958 and recalling that François Mitterand, President of the
Republic, had declared this site a national memorial, for it was
here that the chieftains of the Gallic tribes had once formed
an alliance under the leadership of Vercingetorix.[2] Has France,
then, been one nation since the days of Vercingetorix?

Following the Franco-Prussian War of 1870–1, the theologian, Ernest Renan (1823–92), prompted by the situation of Alsace, torn between France and Germany, addressed himself to the question: What is a nation? In his address,'*Qu'es-ce qu'une nation?*' delivered on 11 March 1882 in the Sorbonne, he took up, dispassionately and methodically, one familiar definition after another. A nation was not the same thing as a race, for obviously all modern nations were ethnically mixed: France is Celtic, Iberian, Germanic; Germany is Germanic, Celtic and Slavonic; it is scarcely possible to disentangle the races of Italy. Any policy which employs the argument of race to define the unity of a nation is clearly chimerical and would destroy European civilization. Nor is a nation the same thing as its language – otherwise, how could the separation of the United States from Great Britain, or South America from Spain be accounted for? Or, conversely, the unity of Switzerland? Nor can religious faith be considered the basis of the contemporary nation, as is clear from the disparity of political frontiers and the distribution of the various confessions. Common interests? A customs union (*Zollverein*) is not a fatherland. And geography? There is no more arbitrary and perilous theory that that which seeks to fix a nation within 'natural frontiers': the past shows that the 'living space' of nations has always been subject to change.

A nation, Renan concludes, cannot be adequately defined and established simply on the basis of material circumstances: he comes to the conclusion that

> a nation is a soul, a mental principle. Two things that are in fact one and the same constitute this principle. One of them is a store of memories, the other is the currently valid agreement, the wish to live together . . . A nation, then, is an extended community with a peculiar sense of kinship sustained by an awareness of the sacrifices that have been made in the past, and the sacrifices the nation is prepared to make in the future. A nation presumes a past, but the past is summed up in one tangible fact: the agreement, the desire to continue a life in common.[3]

Ernest Renan's definition is still valid today: a nation is a state of mind, a community that exists as long as it is willed and lives in the hearts and minds of its members and which perishes when it no longer exists in their thoughts and aspirations. Nations are founded on national awareness. Nations come to know themselves through their common history, their common reputation and the sacrifices they have made in common. It ought to be added, that their common history as a rule has no more than limited reality, it is more the product of dreams and visions than the product of facts.

What Renan terms 'communal solidarity' has been the subject of research by group sociologists. Following the lead of the American psychologist, William G. Sumner (1840–1910), a distinction has been drawn between so-called 'in-groups' and 'out-groups' as a basic feature of all identifiable groups. The 'in-group' is held together by an 'us-feeling' – which is no doubt what Renan meant by his 'mental principle' – while the 'out-group' are 'the others'; there is a strong tendency to look on the fellow members of one's group as equals, and members of other groups as inferior. Within the group there is agreement, peace and order; outside it, tension, if not actual conflict prevails. The 'us-group' conveys to its individual members a sense of belonging, security, and a feeling that whatever they do within the group or for the sake of the group gives meaning to their lives. The significance of the 'us-group' is affirmed, not only by the criteria for membership and the members' patterns of behaviour – by virtue of which the members form their association in the first place – but also by identification symbols, such as signs, heraldic devices and other emblems. A group needs continuity in order to establish its standards and select its symbols, thus acquiring a sense of permanence and legitimacy extending beyond the lifetime of its members – hence the inclination to trace the existence of the group back to its origins, or even to invent its history as a means of strengthening the integration of the group. But no one belongs to one group only. Beginning with a group of only two members, i.e. a friendship or marriage, through the family, the clan, the local parish and society in general to larger discrete groups like a nation or a church, there are any number of groups to which an individual may belong simultaneously, and each of them may claim his loyalty, offer him security in certain circumstances, but each of them may also provoke a conflict of loyalties, and membership of different groups may call for a number of different modes of behaviour.[4]

Among all these groups, the power of the nation to bind individuals together has proved to be especially effective in political terms. This was by no means always the case; like every other form of political or cultural association, the nation has long been a feature of European civilization and has consequently evolved historically, undergoing change and development: and, like everything else that has grown up in the course of history, it, too, may in time pass away, losing something of its political and cultural significance to make way for some other form of human association. It is true that the term 'nation' has existed for a long time, much longer than the 'state', but in its contemporary sense, embracing an entire population, a nation can hardly be defined without reference to the state – in this sense nations may still by very young.

Natio is a traditional term derived from ancient Rome and it originally meant 'birth' or 'descent' as a distinctive feature of groups of all kinds. Cicero used it to mean a section of the population, namely the aristocracy; for Pliny, a school of philosophers was a *natio*. In a remarkable number of cases, however, we find *natio* as the opposite of *civitas*, i.e. in the sense of an uncivilized tribe without a regular constitution, more or less in the same sense as the English might use the term 'natives', the French 'natifs' or the Germans 'Eingeborene'. The heathens of the Vulgate, Isidor von Seville's barbarians, the heathen Mohammedan hordes of Bernard of Clairvaux – these were *nationes*, and the main Germanic tribes of the early middle ages, the Franks, the Langobards or Burgundians, were also described as *nationes* because, although they were of common descent, they seemed to have no internal political or social structure, those features that were characteristic of a civilized people. Together with kindred terms like *gens* or *populus*, the use of the word led to the late medieval meaning of *nationes*, which referred to the major European peoples, each of which in turn might include several *gentes* or *nationes*.

The limits of a *natio* were ill-defined and long remained so, but the word in its original Latin sense ultimately came to denote a community under the law to which an individual belonged by reason of his birth. The aristocrat subjects of a particular regime might differ in birth, manners, law and language: e.g. in the East Frankish kingdom that was ultimately to become Germany, a member of the imperial aristocracy might belong to the Saxon, Frankish, Alemannic or Bavarian *natio* and assert his right to conduct himself according to the laws of that *natio*. The judicial circuits to which each individual was subject by birth was generally known as his *patria*: his subjective, personal loyalty was to the community in which he had been born, and to the law of which he was subject. 'Birth and the homeland, as in the perpetual classical theme of death for one's fatherland', the historian Karl-Ferdinand Werner sums up, 'were to endure over the centuries in close association with the 'nation' as the most potent expression of the ultimate solidarity of a group and its difference from other groups.'[5]

Even the current names of nations took a long time to emerge. The Germans in particular took a long time to realize that they *were* Germans. This was because there had been no German tribe: what had existed since the collapse of the Carolingian Empire during the ninth century was a number of tribal duchies which could not be traced back to the tribes that had existed at the time of the migration of the peoples, but which had evolved from the administrative districts of Charles the Great's Empire. The regions settled by the Thuringians, Bavarians, Alemans and later, the Saxons, were *ducati*, hence subject to a *dux*, not a tribal chieftain, but a senior Frankish official, whose title reached as far back as the administrative reforms of Constantine the Great. This Frankish imperial nobility disintegrated in the course of the ninth century into families and factions. It was not 'German' tribes, but an aristocracy of a Frankish complexion that formed the political bond holding together the region east of the Rhine that had been known since Roman times as '*Germania*'. Ever since 833 this aristocratic section of the population had acknowledged the rule of the emperor's son, Ludwig, in the East Frankish kingdom, so that Ludwig became *rex Germaniae*, king of the territories situated east of the Rhine, rather than 'Ludwig the

German', as nationally minded historians have been prone to call him since the nineteenth century.

Far into the eleventh century the kingdom that had emerged east of the Rhine was to be regarded as a Frankish realm founded on Frankish traditions that reached back via the Carolingians and Merovingians all the way to Rome and Troy, and this was equally the case with the west Frankish part of the empire. The monarchs of the east Frankish kingdom avoided any precise ethnic designation of their realm, calling themselves simply *rex*, not, for instance, *rex Francorum*, and certainly not *rex Teutonicorum*, i.e. king of the Germans. Only one totally isolated reference to any such title crops up in sources from the tenth century. After 919, when the Saxon dynasty succeeded to the crown through Henry I, Saxony took over the lead from the Franks and retained that position for more than a century. For Widukind of Corvey the Ottoman Empire consisted of the *regnum saxonum* in the north, and the *regnum latinorum* in the south: Germany was not mentioned. It was unlikely that it would be, since, with the coronation of the Emperor Otto I by Pope John XII in 962, the Ottoman royal house had been elevated to inherit the tradition of Charles the Great and the Roman Empire. It had hence acquired supreme authority in all those secular issues that mattered in the middle ages. Ever since the time of St Augustine it had been reckoned that the empire occupied a firm place in the history of the world, which was also the history of mankind's salvation: it was the last great worldwide monarchy. These were pretensions that far outstripped the mere royal title of the east Frankish monarchs, so that the empire looked towards Rome rather than Germany.

The word 'deutsch' is derived from 'thiutisk', a concept, starting with Bavaria, which spread through Central Europe in the eighth and ninth centuries and which meant simply 'the tongue of the people' – by no means a uniform language, but a medley of German tribal dialects which were obviously distinct from the learned Latin of the Church and the Romance or Slavonic languages of the country's neighbours. The later translation *teutonicus* is misleading: there was in fact no link with those Germanic Teutons who suffered a crushing defeat by the Romans under Marius at Aquae Sextiae in 102 BC, and thus made their exit from history. The terror inspired by the first Germanic incursions into Northern Italy lived on, however, and it was natural for the Italians to describe as Teutons people who came from *Germania* and who claimed to have succeeded to the title of Roman Emperor. There was no doubt a hint of condescension here, given the invaders' uncouth and barbaric demeanour. In this way *thiutisk* and *teutonicus* merged and began to acquire a political significance when Gregory VII, at the height of the investiture quarrel in the year 1076, called the Roman-German King Henry IV '*rex teutonicus*', meaning in this way to deprive the claimant to the title of emperor of his presumptuous messianic status and relegate him to that of an ordinary Christian monarch.

The empire continued nevertheless to be called 'Roman' and, after 1157, the Holy Roman Empire, while *thiutisk/teutonicus* gradually came into use, because feudal personal allegiance to the Roman Emperor in his capacity as (east) Frankish king denoted more than just a conglomeration of tribes and hence required a name. The term 'Frankish' had already been appropriated by their western neighbours, from whom they wished to distinguish themselves, as they had distinguished themselves from Italy and the Roman curia. Thus, in the course of the eleventh and twelfth centuries *regnum* and *teutonicum* gradually coalesced. The German nation, however, was and remained a somewhat nebulous concept, because for centuries following the fall of the Hohenstaufen dynasty no single dynasty succeeded in holding on to the crown of Germany for any length of time. As distinct from England or France, where the royal houses came, in the course of the thirteenth century, to represent nuclei round which national forces crystallized, the German crown remained weak. The German nation stood in the shadow of the overwhelming idea of the Roman Empire with all its mythical potency, while its political emblems were associated with the empire rather than the kingdom – the Holy Lance, the imperial crown, the imperial throne of Charlemagne in the Cathedral of Aachen.

Besides, tribal groups and their territorial successors from Saxony to Bavaria, tended to come to the fore and it was these territories which were regarded as *patriae* (fatherlands). As far as the individual subject was concerned, the country he belonged to was actually his fatherland: he called himself a Saxon or a Bavarian and regarded his local ruler as *pater patriae*, the father of his country. The empire was not his fatherland; affiliation to the empire was essentially a matter for the territorial ruler or for town and city councils. As late as the beginning of the nineteenth century, Ernst Moritz Arndt could still put the rhetorical question: "Where is the German's fatherland, Bavaria or Swabia?" In Germany, 'fatherland' and 'nation' had parted company. The German nation as a political entity did not consist of the population that lived in Germany or spoke German, but of a social class of imperial princes who, together with the emperor, constituted the empire, elected the emperor from amongst their number, or were at least involved in discussions about the succession, and had their seats in the Imperial Diet face to face with the emperor.

The birth of a nation proceeded more smoothly and more rapidly west of the Rhine. The west Frankish kings had always regarded themselves as Charlemagne's legitimate heirs. Even after partition into a west Frankish and an east Frankish kingdom had become irreversible about the year 888, it was the kings of the western kingdom who claimed exclusive rights to the traditions of the Carolingian and Merovingian dynasties and called themselves *reges francorum*, kings of the Franks. Not all the inhabitants of what had once been Gaul were Franks, but only those who owed allegiance and military service to the king: *franci* were the loyal subjects of the king, and a man from Brittany or Aquitaine might become a Frank through service to the king. The emergence of the French nation was thus an on-going process that kept pace with the growing power of the crown as it extended its rule across the Loire towards southern and western France: the nation was constituted in the main through its link with the crown, the sacred status of which shed lustre on the person of the monarch and his entourage, reinforcing national consciousness in a France that was just beginning to emerge. In that sense it might well be said that, in France, it was the state that gave birth to the nation.[6]

This was not a nation such as we know it today, however:

more or less until the time of the French Revolution in 1789, the French nation, like the other European nations, consisted in effect of those individuals who enjoyed *status politicus*, i.e. those who were in a position to initiate political action through direct relationship with the crown, or who were at least represented through the estates. The German nation consisted of the imperial aristocracy (*Reichsadel*), the imperial Church (*Reichskirche*) and the imperial cities (*Reichsstädte*), who were assembled in the imperial Diet (*Reichstag*). The English nation was embodied in the Westminster Parliament, the French nation in the States General (*états généraux*), and Montesquieu did not hesitate to declare in the middle of the eighteenth century, '*la nation, c'est-à-dire les seigneurs et les évêques*' – i.e. the nation, that is, the nobility and the clergy. When the Reich concluded the peace treaty of Szátmar in 1711 with the 'Hungarian nation', this term did not refer to the Hungarian people as a whole, but, as expressly stated in the treaty, to 'the barons, prelates and nobility of Hungary'. In the case of Hungary or Poland the term 'nation' applied to the aristocracy alone, whereas in Western, Central or Northern Europe, in certain cases the middle class, and occasionally even the peasantry might be included in the 'nation'. We ought to bear in mind, too, that, although our account deals with the major nations, the term was also used until the beginning of the nineteenth century in a narrower local or regional sense. For instance, around 1800 the East Prussians might still be referred to as a nation, because they had a regional parliament (*Landtag*) in which the 'country' was represented as a political entity, although it was under the suzerainty of the Hohenzollerns. From the height of the middle ages almost until the close of the eighteenth century it was not the population as a whole that constituted the nation, but only that sector of it that ruled or was in some way politically represented. We are not dealing here with 'people's nations' but with nations of the aristocracy.

Just as the idea of *natio* was used to mark distinctions in the political area, so it was a convenient term by which linguistic distinctions might be drawn. Although Latin prevailed throughout Europe as the universal mode of communication in the Church, in politics and in learning, the continent had nevertheless become multilingual during the middle ages, and so it seemed natural, wherever foreigners from many parts of Europe came together, to refer to their languages as distinguishing features. At the Council of Constance (1414–17) it was stipulated that votes would be registered by nation. The delegates of the ecclesiastical estates of the Holy Roman Empire were designated *natio germanica* in so far as they used the German language, but the clergy of England, Hungary, Poland and the Scandinavian countries also belonged to the German nation, whereas prelates from Savoy, Provence and Lorraine were assigned on the basis of their language to the French nation, although these regions were part of the Reich. The – politically non-existent – Italian nation included, in addition to Italian speakers, participants from Greece, Slavonia and Cyprus. Obviously, clear criteria for membership of a given nation were lacking, and the numbers of delegates and their 'nationality' remained a matter of dispute until the end of the Council.

The ill-defined nature of the link between language and nationality is apparent, too, in the case of students, who had been flooding into the universities from all parts of Europe ever since the twelfth century. Here they were divided in 'nations', although what mattered was not an individual's birthplace but his language or linguistic group, because this was a feature that could be more or less clearly identified. The University of Paris – with the University of Bologna the oldest in Europe – had since 1269 distinguished between a Gallic nation, to which Italians, Spaniards and Greeks also belonged, an English nation – including also Germans, Poles and Scandinavians – a Norman nation, and a Picard nation, whose members spoke a language which in the thirteenth century was reckoned to be as clearly distinct from French as were the idioms of Burgundy, Normandy or the Walloons. A century later the University of Orleans was divided into ten nations: France, Normandy, Picardy, Aquitaine, Champagne, Lorraine, Touraine and Scotland – and a *'nation germanique'* to which belonged students from the Holy Roman Empire, but also those from Poland, England, Denmark, Italy and Dalmatia. The principles on which these groups were formed seem confusing only at first sight: the system was actually purely pragmatic – students who came from adjacent linguistic areas were naturally more numerous and had therefore to be broken down into smaller groups, whereas those who came from further afield were fewer in number, so that more comprehensive categories sufficed. The fact that the division into nations was not entirely arbitrary or artificial was shown by the inner cohesion of these forerunners of later patriotic societies, as well as by the friction between the 'nations'. In 1328 a brawl between the nations of Picardy and Normandy, in which there were fatal casualties, culminated in something like a civil war in Paris. By this time the University of Oxford had already abolished the system of 'nations' so as to put an end to such disorders.

From such relatively trivial examples we may see how the principles of the 'us-group' and the alien group functioned among the 'nations' at the universities: members of the same linguistic family became aware of their common identity, not at home but abroad. The same applied to the political nations of the middle ages: their 'us-feeling' tended to emerge mainly in contact with foreigners. Following the growth of the population of Europe after the 1000, the number of travellers grew correspondingly: pilgrimages, trade, itinerant scholars making their way from one university to another had led to increasing contact with foreigners. Although reports of such encounters are too rare to furnish reliable evidence of national awareness at this stage, it may be assumed that pilgrimages especially, involving as they did relatively large groups of people, gave rise to prejudices and mutual resentment between different nations.

That is obviously even truer of the Crusades, and here we are on much firmer ground as far as evidence is concerned. In particular, the distinction drawn by both parties between the French and the Germans, the incipient growth of national awareness and the connection between 'us-feelings' and the negative image of foreigners began to be apparent: about 1165 Johann von Würzburg, in his *Descriptio terrae sanctae*, a kind of guidebook for pilgrims to the Holy Land, constantly emphasized the doughty deeds of the German knights during the first Crusade (1096–9). It was not the *Franci*, i.e. the

French, but the mighty *Francones*, Germans from Franconia on the Main, who had freed Jerusalem from the infidels' yoke. True, the German knights, a prey to homesickness, had returned to their native land, and their place in Palestine had been taken by other nations – the French, men from Lorraine or Provence, Normans, Italians, Spaniards and Burgundians. Although Gottfried von Bouillon, the conqueror of Jerusalem, and his brother Balduin, who was crowned King of Jerusalem, both came from Germany ('from our lands of Germania'), the feats of arms performed by the Germans had simply been suppressed, indeed, 'those who slandered our nation' had maliciously tried to erase 'our memory from men's minds' by removing German tombstones. If only the Germans had stayed, claims the outraged author, whose national pride had clearly been deeply wounded, then the borders of the Crusaders' state would have been advanced far beyond the Nile and Damascus. But, following the departure of the Germans, the other nations had achieved virtually nothing. A particularly sore point was the fact that the Imperial Duke Gottfried von Bouillon featured as the leader of the Germans, while the warriors from Lorraine who were in fact under his command, were numbered among those who had lorded it in the Holy Land after the Germans had gone. This situation arose, because our author refers to the Germans, not as *Teutonici*, but as *Germani* and is hence thinking only of the inhabitants of *Germania*, i.e. the territory east of the Rhine. The French speakers from Lorraine were thus excluded, although their province was part of the Reich.

Complaints of this kind grew ever more common during the course of the Crusade, which eventually generated a good deal of international hostility. Counter-charges came from the French side: Odo de Deuil, who took part in the second Crusade (1147–9) as Chaplain to Louis VII admits that his fellow countrymen were arrogant, but states that the Germans ('*Alemanni*') were simply insufferable. Germans and Frenchmen, he claims, could not even share the same camp without the Germans picking a quarrel – for one thing, neither nation understood the other's language. Thus, the Germans had done nothing but spread confusion, and that was why the joint assault on Damascus, and hence the entire Crusade, had come to grief. What is interesting about this account is not so much the fact that the blame for the failure of the Crusade is attributed to others, but the reason given: that no one could understand what the Germans were saying and that this had caused muddle and confusion.

Already at the time of the Crusades, apparently, the peoples east and west of the Rhine had a sense of their own identity, as well as a view of their neighbours which was often linked to specific stereotypes. French successes in the Holy Land were the occasion of deep-seated envy in their German neighbours. When the bishops and magnates of East Saxony appealed in 1108 for recruits to join a crusade against the heathen Wends, they referred to the heroic deeds of the French in the Orient: it was a matter of vying with and excelling those warriors from the neighbouring kingdom who were generally regarded as vainglorious. It was often the negative features of others that helped to establish a nation's own identity. Two hundred and fifty years later, national stereotypes were already fully formed. Philippe de Commynes, a French diplomat and historian (1447–1511) described a meeting between Charles the Bold, Duke of Burgundy and Frederick the Victorious of the Palatinate that took place in Brussels in 1467:

> The Duke's people said the Germans were dirty, that they took off their boots and flung them on the freshly made beds and had no such manners as we have; and so they had a lower opinion of the Germans than they had had before they met them. The Germans, on the other hand, as though consumed with envy, disapproved of all the luxury. In truth, they have had no liking for each other since then, and neither has been willing to do the other the smallest service.

This experienced diplomat came to the conclusion that the rulers of the two nations would do well never to meet, if they wished to stay on friendly terms.[7]

Even more dramatic than the hostility between the French and the Germans was that between the latter and their Slav neighbours, which also played a major part in establishing the identity of the peoples in question. That was particularly true of Bohemia, which had been linguistically divided as a result of German colonization of the eastern territories in the course of the twelfth and thirteenth centuries; the urban population for the most part spoke German, the rural population and the nobility mostly spoke Czech. As was the case with France in relation to Germany, there was a 'modernity gradient' from Germany to Bohemia and Poland, and consequently a tendency with the peoples on the Slav side, to set themselves apart in a national sense from their western neighbours. The Germans, so it was claimed in sources from the thirteenth century, despised Wenceslas, the patron saint of Bohemia: their arrogance was, for the Slavs, every bit as insufferable as the arrogance of the French was for the Germans. Crucial evidence of this tendency on the part of the Czechs to establish their own national character by way of contrast with their adversary is the anonymous rhymed chronicle of the fourteenth century known under the title *Dalimil*. While out hunting Duke Oldrich (Ulrich) comes across a peasant maiden called Božena who is of such surpassing beauty that the Duke at once marries her. His peers mock him because he has married a commoner, but he explains to them:

> I would rather laugh with a Czech peasant wench than take a German queen to wife. For a man's heart yearns for his native tongue, and a German wife would care little for my people. A German wife would have German retainers and would teach my children German, And so there would be a divorce of our tongues, and certain ruin for our land. My lords, you know not what is good for you, if you taunt me about my marriage. Where would you find interpreters, if you were to stand before a German princess?[8]

The Germans are depicted by the anonymous author as the enemies of the Czechs: for him the essential distinguishing feature is language, which overrides even the discrepancy in social status – sooner a Bohemian peasant girl than a German princess. In the background there is a further implicit conflict: that between the countryside, where the Czech nobility and peasantry were equally at home, and the towns, which were still mainly inhabited by German citizens at the time when *Dalimil* was written.

The degree to which language was the vehicle of national consciousness may be observed in many late medieval sources. Thus, one of the earliest signs of the merging of the Norman–French class of conquerors and the older Anglo-Saxon population which generated a new English sense of identity is Edward I's summons convoking Parliament in 1295: a common danger threatened, arising from the King of France, who had not only cheated the Plantagenet King of his land of Gascony, but was now threatening to invade Edward's kingdom. With his vast fleet and a host of warriors the king of France meant to destroy the English tongue altogether, which God forfend.[9] The equation of *lingua*, i.e. tongue or language, with 'nation' is also evident in the way in which the English looked on the western part of their country, where there was a language barrier between English and Welsh speakers. In 1283, two representatives from each borough were summoned to a parliament convened to try and condemn the Welsh prince David ap Gruffudd, who had led resistance to the invading English army of Edward I. The summons opened with the words: 'With what manner of deceit and treachery the Welsh tongue, like the foxes of old in the time of our fathers, has beset us and our realm . . . can scarcely be told by human tongue in all its detail.'[10] 'Tongue', then, may mean the Welsh people as well as their language – the affinity of nation and language is clear enough. 'Woe unto thee, German tongue, how sad thy disarray,' cried Walther von der Vogelweide in 1198, apostrophizing the German nation and its princes, who could not agree on the election of a king.

It was the the small nations, especially, that often discovered their national identity in the struggle for their independence, an emblematic situation that had proved effective since classical times and which was frequently taken up and assimilated into indigenous traditions. This was so, for instance, in an epistle from the Irish kings to Pope John XXII in 1317, in which they complained bitterly of the atrocities committed by the English, and in which they justified their claim to independence in the following terms: 3500 years previously the ancestors of the Irish kings had come from Spain, and since then 136 kings had ruled the land without a drop of alien blood flowing in their veins until St Patrick had converted Ireland to Christianity; since then kings of 'purest race' had always reigned and defended Ireland's native liberties until the country was finally conquered by the English in the year 1170. The right to independence, then, consisted in the antiquity of the nation, the ages that had passed since its conversion to Christianity, and the purity of the Irish blood.[11]

The common language, which differs from that of the – generally wicked – neighbouring nations, and the liberty of the fatherland, rooted in time-honoured laws and traditions, were bound up with the glorification of the 'us-group'. Victorious battles were readily raised to mythical status and used to reinforce 'us-feelings'. We need only think of the Battle of Bouvines in 1214, when a French army under the command of the Capet King Philip II defeated the combined forces of John Lackland and the German King Otto. As a result the territory north of the Loire was lost by the English crown and the power and prestige of the French king were brilliantly enhanced – Philip I called himself henceforth Philip Augustus. The historical significance of the battle was thus considerable, but its reflection in the chronicles and epics of the time magnified it into a struggle between Christ and Antichrist, between the French and the German king, the 'children of France', who steadfastly stood by their king, and the Teutons, who fought like wild beasts and were nevertheless no match for the chivalrous French. In Brito's *Philippide*, a brilliant interpretation of which we owe to Georges Duby, all those features were combined which in the view of the middle ages defined a nation – except that the word 'nation' does not occur. We may find tradition – for Philip Augustus wears the garments of Aeneas in the battle and recalls that the French are descendants of the Trojans and destined, like the Romans, to lead the world. There are also the symbols – the oriflamme, the royal banner that was said to have flown before Charlemagne and that was dedicated to Saint Denis, the patron saint of the Franks. We find, too, the typical distinction drawn between the French and their foes in simple black and white terms. And finally we have the 'children of France', those knights who had sworn loyalty to the king and who surrounded him in battle. They were a community of the elect and their intimate personal bond with the monarch laid the foundations of the French nation.

There were any number of battles equally evocative of patriotic emotion and capable of being exploited for propaganda purposes by the victors – and even by the vanquished: the Battle of the Marchfeld in 1278, in which King Ottokar of Bohemia was defeated by a German army under Rudolph of Habsburg; the battle of Bannockburn in 1314, a victory of the Scots over the English; the Battle of Morgarten, 1315, when the Swiss Confederation triumphed over the Austrians; the Battle of Kosovo Polje (the Field of Blackbirds) in 1389, when a Serbian army, and with it the Serbian kingdom, were destroyed by a superior Turkish force; or the Battle of Tannenberg-Grunwald, 1410, a joint Polish and Lithuanian triumph over the Teutonic Order. Alongside these epic battles stands the memory of great wars: the Hundred Years War between France and England, the campaigns of Charles the Bold in the Reich, the so-called Swabian War in Switzerland, 1499, which led to the ultimate independence of the Swiss Confederation; or the War of the Sicilian Vespers in Southern Italy, fought in the years from 1282 to 1302 against the house of Anjou, which gave rise to the most memorable of liberation myths.

Nations do not invariably have their origins in wars, but war often acts as a catalyst. From the very beginning, it was through the erection of frontiers against their neighbours, through hostility and strife that Europeans tended to discover their own identity – a process, it is true, that might extend over centuries and for long be the sole concern of the nobility, and a handful of patricians and intellectuals. There were periods of stagnation in times of relative political calm, but the process flared up again and again in times of political instability. It was not until the end of the eighteenth century, however, that the trend began to involve the mass of the population in actual force and violence. From the start, nations were vague, protean entities, except where they were explicitly and legally defined – for instance, as we have seen, in the case of the universities, or in the political assemblies of the estates.

It is true that nations existed before they were so called, as a sense of community rooted in collective emotions, as language, shared traditions and simple comradeship in arms – features that aspired to permanence, and in fact offered permanence, thus setting up fertile and dynamic tensions in relation to states – those political forms of organization that had begun to evolve simultaneously with the nations following the end of the European middle ages.

6

Nation States and National Cultures

Following the end of the middle ages, the history of the European nations was a tale of idiosyncratic approaches, even before the curtain rose on the era of nation states, i.e. before the end of the eighteenth century. The motley collection of national communities that peopled the continent, even before such expressions as 'nationalism' or 'national consciousness' were thought of, did not come about by mere chance. The image of each of these national communities, at first only dimly glimpsed, was governed by certain assumptions: their geographical or historical proximity to the ancient civilization of Rome, their share of the Carolingian heritage, the part played by trade and the towns, the relative ease of communication, the number of those who used the facilities for communication and transport, the degree to which a state had imposed its judicial and administrative system on its territory – and, last but not least, their actual geographical location.

The range of possibilities becomes apparent if we look at two states in contrasting geographical locations: first, that patchwork in the centre of Europe that went by the name of the 'Holy Roman Empire'. In 1512 the title was changed to the 'Holy Roman Empire of the German Nation' – a change which did nothing to clarify its nature: 'Empire' and 'Nation' were just as incongruous as were 'German' and 'Roman'. The Empire was singularly fluid, it had no geographically defined frontiers, although it had more neighbours than any other state in Europe. Nor was it clear where its central authority was located. What the Seine basin was for France, and the south-eastern region between the Thames and the coast was for England, the Rhineland might have become for Germany, had the centre of political power not shifted eastwards during the middle ages, while the major commercial centres grew up on the outskirts of the Reich, in places adjacent to transalpine trade routes like Nürnberg or Augsburg, or else on the North Sea or the Baltic, like Hamburg or Lübeck. No other state in Europe has ever had in the course of its history so many royal residences, places of coronation and royal burial, or as many capital cities: Aachen, Speyer, Goslar, Bamberg, Magdeburg, Frankfurt, Nürnberg, Prague, to mention but a few of them.

Even as late as the eighteenth century, when all the major European states had long been consolidated, no one could say with any certainty where the capital of the Holy Roman Empire of the German Nation was: Vienna was the capital of the super-power Austria, rather than the capital of the Empire, which offered a much higher profile in other cities: Regensburg, where the Imperial Diet sat; Frankfurt, the time-honoured coronation site; or even Wetzlar, the seat of the Imperial court of appeal (*Reichskammergericht*), which Goethe describes so vividly in his autobiography. In 1782 the Russian ambassador to the Reich, Count Rumjantzeff, reported that the Emperor Joseph II had asked him why he had chosen Frankfurt to set up his embassy. In reply the ambassador had asked the emperor which city he regarded as the capital of his empire. The emperor's reply was, 'Actually, of course, the capital and true centre of the empire is Rome.' The ambassador took this to be a royal jest, but he never received any more satisfying reply.

The empire, then, was a distinctly nebulous entity and tended to melt away into contradictions – in 1667, after all, Samuel Pufendorf, the great authority on international law, had referred to the empire in his book on its constitution as 'an amorphous monster of a political body'.[1] And even at the end of the eighteenth century Friedrich Schiller had put the rhetorical question: 'Germany? But where is it? I cannot find any such country . . . '[2]

Another land, another poet:

> This royal throne of kings, this sceptre'd isle,
> This earth of majesty, this seat of Mars,
> This other Eden, demi-paradise,
> This fortress built by Nature for herself
> Against infection and the hand of war,
> This happy breed of men, this little world,
> This precious stone set in the silver sea,
>   which serves it in the office of a wall . . .
> This blessed plot, this earth, this realm, this
>   England.[3]

Unlike Schiller, Shakespeare had known 200 years earlier
exactly where his country was: England was an island, and
her frontiers were clearly defined, even if she shared the island
with Wales to the west and Scotland to the north. Wales had
been joined to the English crown by an act of union in 1536,
and Scotland's king was to mount the English throne in 1603 as
King James I. Scotland was linked with England in a personal
union, and in 1708 a single state was founded – the United
Kingdom of Great Britain, although there was little change in
England's political and cultural domination of the Union.

The insular location clearly facilitated the emergence and
consolidation of a compact kingdom. Following the Norman
conquest of 1066, royal authority had been rapidly imposed
on the whole of England. A single jurisdiction incorporating
local bye-laws prevailed throughout the country, and since the
thirteenth century a system of government had been set up
which combined Norman–French and Anglo-Saxon elements
and which was felt by the subjects of the crown to be appropriate to a specifically English community. A further factor
that made for the cohesion of England was the pressure of the
Celtic belt – Ireland, Wales and Scotland – as well as the battle
for the continental heritage of the English crown that was to
make England and France arch-enemies for centuries to come.
A precocious sense of an English national identity is clearly
expressed, for instance, in the middle of the fourteenth century
through the panegyric verse of Laurence Minot, in which 'our
gracious King' Richard III figures as the glorious victor over

Scotland and France: he had behind him, Minot claimed, the whole English people, against whom the country's foes battled in vain. They were mere braggarts and poltroons, whereas there had never been warriors to match the English since long before the birth of Christ. Richard III had taught the Scottish king a fine lesson, and it was under Edward's leadership that England had trampled the French lilies underfoot, humiliating that country that had always been so arrogant and vainglorious.[4]

This access of nationalistic enthusiasm derives its significance from the fact that it was written during the Hundred Years War and couched in a northern English dialect that was obviously not primarily addressed to a courtly audience. The war against France in fact hastened the advance of the English language: in 1363 an English Parliament was for the first time opened by the Lord Chancellor in English, in 1368 a royal decree was published for the first time in Middle English alone, and in 1399 King Henry IV used English to deliver his claim to the throne before a kind of parliamentary assembly. The triumphant advance of English had purely practical aspects: in the Hundred Years War the English archers with their longbows had proved their superiority over the mounted French knights, so that the archers had become the backbone of the English army, and their commanders were thus obliged to use the language of the people. At the same time the English towns, especially London, were rapidly gaining in commercial importance; the merchants naturally spoke English, and their boroughs were represented in Parliament. Such factors encouraged ambitions to affirm the linguistic identity of the English in opposition to the French, so that a relatively compact and homogeneous English-speaking community emerged which embraced not only the common folk but also the nobility, Parliament and the court.

The process was protracted, extending over centuries. The multitude of English dialects was for long an obstacle to the development of a standard language: as late as 1589 the poet George Puttenham was warning his readers to steer clear of northern English, the speech of the villages, as well as the speech of the universities. 'The customary language of the Court is to be preferred, and such as is spoken in London and in

parishes situated in a radius of up to ten miles round London.'⁵
Nevertheless, the language of the Crown Chancellery, the
decrees of which found their way into the administration at
every level, ensured a measure of linguistic uniformity. The
standardization of the language was also fostered from the
end of the fourteenth century by the first translation of the
Bible into English. It was read for the most part by laymen
of the middle class, but also presumably by some members
of the nobility and clergy. About 1480 the introduction of
the printing press not only popularized the glories of English Renaissance literature, but also made possible the mass
production of tracts and pamphlets disseminating a popular
brand of Protestantism and placing Henry VIII's ecclesiastical
reforms on a solid national foundation.

Here, once again, it became apparent that the unity of
religious belief and standardization of the vernacular went
hand in hand. As far as England was concerned, the use of
the national language in the liturgy of the Anglican Church
was made mandatory by two Acts of Conformity in 1549
and 1552. The canon of Anglican devotional literature then
comprised the great Bible translation of 1539, the Book of
Common Prayer of 1549 and a popular history of the martyrs
by John Foxe (1563). Every Sunday there were readings from
these books in every Anglican church, even where English was
not the language of the common people, as in Wales or Ireland.
Pride in the English language as a bond holding the nation
together was a notable feature of Elizabethan authors: we
frequently come across statements like the triple credo of a
teacher, Richard Mulcaster, from the year 1582: 'I love Rome,
but London I love even more; I prefer England, even to Italy;
I respect Latin, but I honour English.'⁶

Attention was focused on religion, one of the most profound
and enduring elements in English national sentiment. The force
of religious conviction, as we have said, had already played its
part in the success of John Wycliffe's Bible translation, which
circulated until the end of the sixteenth century. Wycliffe's followers, the Lollards, who repudiated the Roman Church and
the doctrine of transubstantiation, propagated his teachings
until the Reformation, which assumed a distinctly nationalistic

aspect in England in two respects at least: the establishment of the High Anglican Church and the use of English as the liturgical language.

How closely religion and national consciousness were bound up was illustrated following the death of Edward VII: his successor, Mary Tudor (1515–58), known as 'Mary the Catholic' or 'Bloody Mary', attempted to convert England back to Roman Catholicism by the most brutal methods. In the subsequent flood of Protestant political pamphlets, mostly printed abroad, that poured into the country during Mary's reign between 1553 and 1558, national and theological arguments were closely combined. Fear of a revival of Roman Catholicism, and hence of renewed subservience of the Anglican Church to Rome, went along with a clearly defined image of the enemy – Spain now replaced France as England's archenemy (Philip II had married Mary in 1554). The reign of terror in countries subject to Spain – Naples, Milan, the Netherlands – was contrasted in graphic terms with the liberties of England, now threatened with extinction. The English nobility were solemnly exhorted to turn a deaf ear to the blandishments of the Spaniards. In many pamphlets the Spaniards were branded as secret infidels, half Jewish under a mantle of Popish piety. But that was not all: by her marriage to Philip, it was claimed, Mary had betrayed not only the country's religion, but England itself, and there were many voices clamouring for resistance to this un-English queen and reminding the nobility and Parliament of their prime duty to rid their oppressed fatherland of a tyrannical ruler.

The ambiguity of the religious argument in generating a common mentality throughout the nation is manifested here: wherever crown, nation and religious faith were one a powerful surge of national sentiment was generated, fostering and accelerating the integration of the state. If such unity was not guaranteed, then there was always a threat of civil war. The host of Protestant sects in England that were discriminated against or politically victimized by the Anglican Church and the crown was a major factor in precipitating the revolution of 1642–9. For that reason it might well be called a Puritan revolution, with Parliament taking up the cause of Protestant

Puritanism against the Crown and the episcopalian Anglican Church. In the course of the revolution it was mainly the Parliamentary party which relied on the argument of national unity and even had recourse to the Old Testament as additional evidence for their view: the English nation was God's chosen people, as the Jews had been until the death of Christ on the cross, England was the new Israel, its people were hallowed, their history was evidence of God's saving grace.

Henceforth the English nation was ' . . . a People that have had a stamp upon them from God',[7] as Oliver Cromwell declared in a speech in Parliament. The influence of Puritanism on the development of the English sense of nationality can scarcely be overrated. Although, following the collapse of the Puritan Commonwealth and the restoration of the Stuarts in 1660, Puritans, or so-called Dissenters, were largely barred from public office, their ideas have made a deep impression on English culture down to the present day and far beyond the country's borders. It was the Old Testament element in the English sense of national identity that subsequently endowed British imperialism with its providential features. Even as recently as 1940 it transformed the defeat at Dunkirk into a divine assurance of ultimate victory. The most famous photograph from the time of the Luftwaffe's raids on London during the Second World War shows the dome of St Paul's ('the parish church of the nation') rising unscathed from the smoke and surrounding devastation, symbol of a Protestant bastion that would triumph in the final battle between good and evil.

Apart from a common language and religion, it was an awareness of their common descent and of valiant deeds performed together – to paraphrase Ernest Renan once again – that forged the English nation. Works like Bede's ecclesiastical history of the English people from the year 731 had been handed down and had become the basis of historical study, along with Bishop Geoffrey of Monmouth's *History of the Kings of Britain* (c. 1136), in which the myth of the Britons' descent was first elaborated: the historical arch spanned the ages from Aeneas via his grandson Brutus, the founder of the British realm, and Arthur, the epitome of the perfect king and the perfect knight in one person, down to William the

Conqueror. As everywhere in Europe, the writing of history gained fresh impetus with the advent of the Renaissance. It is worth noting that there was never any doubt about the principal subject of historical writing. History was exclusively the national history of England, whether in Edward Hall's posthumous work, *The Union of the Two Noble and Illustre Families of Lancashire and York* (1548), in which the end of the Wars of the Roses and unification under Tudor rule was celebrated, or in John Ireland's antiquarian anthologies aimed at 'discovering the truth to the benefit of thy country', or in William Camden's opus of 1586 entitled simply *Britannia*, a work that was reprinted and enlarged time and time again and that appeared after 1610 with the express aim of defending 'patriae caritas, Britannici nominis gloria', i.e. love of the fatherland and the fame of the British name.

We would no doubt be overestimating the influence of academic historians on the spirit of the age if we suggested a direct link between their arguments, interpretations and explanations on the one hand and actual political events on the other. Nevertheless, the fact that over the centuries the history of England remained the main preoccupation of British historians has doubtless influenced the outlook of those select circles who actually took note of what historians were writing. These circles may well have been affected by the historians' tendency to see English history as normative, a yardstick by which to measure developments in the world at large. This tendency began at an early stage with William Harrison's *Description of England* (1577), in which the liberties and the noble character of the English nation were contrasted with the dissolute and depraved manners of the French. The trend persisted down to the Whig historians of the nineteenth and the early twentieth century, in the works of Thomas Macaulay and George Trevelyan, in which the evolution of the British constitution figures as the standard of a world history aspiring to the universal establishment of liberal parliamentary institutions.

Of more immediate consequence for the shaping of a popular image of national history was the treatment of historical themes in literary or dramatic form. The *Faerie Queene*, Edmund

Spenser's ambitious national epic, which appeared between 1590 and 1596, was based on the histories of Geoffrey of Monmouth and Edward Hall, spanning the period from the legendary King Arthur to Spenser's own day. Gloriana, the fairy queen, was Queen Elizabeth and also a female pendant to King Arthur – in Tudor mythology Elizabeth's ancestor. The source of all goodness, so the reader learns from the mouth of King Arthur himself, is the fatherland, England.[8] Arthur's speech is addressed to any English reader, not just to the political elite of the nation. The same applies to the English dramatized histories that began to appear when the Tudor dynasty came to power. They were blatant instruments of official propaganda, but became enormously popular on account of their mixture of history, spectacular crime, sex and crude comedy. The genre had been popular, even long before Shakespeare began staging his chronicles about 1580. Shakespeare's message: England as an island of peace, a 'second Eden, demi-paradise,' constantly threatened by foes abroad, by subversive agitators at home, and hence in need of a strong crown, already reflected a popular sense of national identity that may still be sensed in the atmosphere a visitor might experience on the last night of the 'Proms' in London's Albert Hall when the audience begins to sing William Blake's 'Jerusalem':

> I will not cease from mental fight,
> Nor shall my sword sleep in my hand,
> Till we have built Jerusalem
> In England's green and pleasant land.[9]

And so, relatively early, in the Elizabethan age, a cultural 'us-awareness' had developed in England, based on a common language, common historical prototypes, a common religion – common at any rate, as far as hostility to Roman Catholicism went – as well as a common notion of what England was, and what it was meant to be. One factor that helped to integrate the nation was a greater degree of social mobility than was common elsewhere in Europe. Social mobility between the higher aristocracy, the gentry and the commoners of the towns was also a factor in the cultural unification of the country. As far as the sixteenth century is concerned, it is true, and for some time beyond it, this statement would be subject to major qualifications. The horizon of the rural population, especially in the North of England, seldom extended even as far as the borders of the kingdom. Nearly all the business of their rural lives was conducted in the village or on the local squire's estate, and certainly within their own county. Nowadays it is hard for us to tell how far, if at all, a farmer from Lancashire or Kent considered himself an Englishman. In 1497 troops from Cornwall mutinied because they were expected to serve against the Scots in the far North: they obviously felt that a campaign so far from home was no concern of theirs. But the nobility, the clergy, the court and the burgesses of the larger towns – at least the political classes – were already united within a common culture. In that sense an English cultural nation has existed ever since the sixteenth century.

This relatively early – and what is more important – enduring formation of a common English identity was not rooted in the country's culture alone: cultural integration proceeded hand in hand with political integration of the state. Indeed, political integration often preceded cultural advances. Ever since the Norman Conquest, England's rulers had been wary of granting extensive or co-ordinated fiefs to the great noble families, so that it was much easier for the English crown than for continental rulers to extend its claim to supremacy and juris-diction over the entire kingdom. Nevertheless, the unification of England as a single state was a painful and laborious process. The kingdom had virtually fallen apart during the Wars of the Roses, the rivalry between the houses of York and Lancaster, the darkest and most bloody chapter in the history of the English middle ages. That episode had come to an end with the crowning of the Tudor monarch Henry VII on Bosworth Field in 1455. Henry reigned for twenty-four years and was succeeded by his son, Henry VIII. It was the Tudor dynasty which succeeded in establishing a stable political order in England. The king was in fact the largest landowner in the country, able to back his rule with all the resources of his personal property (*allodium*) and the considerable crown revenues. A civil service systematically organized by Thomas

Cromwell, a close associate of Henry VIII, was in a position
to co-ordinate the king's apparatus of power. The monopoly
exercised by the monarch in revenue matters and in the employment of armed force was unchallenged, and the king's judges
and 'justices of the peace' kept law and order in the name of
the crown.

Such a concentration of the authority of the state far
exceeded anything on the continent at this stage. The population throughout the length and breadth of England became
aware that the country had only a single ruler in the person of
the king. Ever since the time of Henry VIII, it had been obvious
that the king was the ruler of the entire English nation, and not
just the head of an aristocratic faction. The crown was not
only visibly present as a mighty organ of the state, it acquired
symbolic potency. Learned historians and strolling players alike
acclaimed the dynasty and its legendary forbears in Troy and
Camelot. The concord of crown and nation had been even
further underlined, for the king was now also supreme head
of the church.

And then there was Parliament, in which the unity of the
kingdom and the nation was also manifested. As the eulogists
of the Tudors never tired of saying, every single subject of the
crown was present in Parliament, either in person, or through
his delegate – not in fact through direct election, but by virtue
of his domicile. It was agreed that everything Parliament did
enjoyed the approval of the whole country. Parliament, for a
long time to come, was acting purely in the interest of the
crown, passing laws for the whole kingdom and endorsing
taxation by the monarch, but it was reckoned to be a political
body in which the country's vested interests came together and
– at least in theory – were resolved in compromises for the
common good. Parliament was the concrete proof that the
English nation really existed.

Crown and Parliament were the political institutions that
together created the nation state of England, the setting and
the prime condition for a culture that, for its part, sanctioned
and secured the institutions of the state. It was through these
institutions that the idea of the nation became a palpable
reality. The Englishman's patriotic sentiments had no need to

clutch at myths and a mere vision of his country's unity: these sentiments could be bodied forth in a self-confident account of his country's political institutions: 'Behold now this great state, a state of refuge, a house in which our freedom dwells, girded about with mighty ramparts.'[10]

The same was true, *mutatis mutandis*, of the other great states of Western Europe. France had made great strides towards discovering her own national identity during the Hundred Years War: the legend of the Maid of Orleans had arisen immediately after she had died a martyr's death as the victim of English and Burgundian treachery. From then on it was considered certain that God had intervened in the course of history to aid the cause of France. The national legend of St Joan and the voice that inspired her to liberate her country did in fact have a grain of historical truth. Besides, France possessed in the crown a long-standing state institution, round which the nation was gradually shaped. This was a relative lengthy process, delayed by much greater disparities and anomalies of a bureaucratic and judicial kind than had ever been the case in England. It was retarded, too, by a much smaller degree of social mobility. This meant that the French language and the literature of France were, until the Revolution, the preserve of the court, the nobility and the cities of Northern France – in spite of the efforts of the *Académie française*, founded by Richelieu in 1635, to give the language 'firm rules, and to make it pure, elegant and fit to deal with the arts and sciences', as stated in its royal charter.[11]

In Spain, too, the nation state evolved slowly, keeping in step with the country's cultural integration. In Spain, it was Castile that played a part comparable to that played by England in Great Britain. We read in Quevedo that the Spanish national character differed from that of the Germans, who were phlegmatic on account of their cold climate, and from that of the negroes and Indians, who had a more violent temperament because of the excessive heat of their clime: thanks to the temperate climate of Spain, sound morals and manners prevailed there. Consequently, the Crown was respected and the laws complied with by the whole nation.[12] This did not apply, however, to the constitutional situation in Aragon, where the estates, in the shape of the Cortes, played a distinctly more significant part than was the case in the politically dominant state of Castile, the language of which had spread throughout Spain at a relatively early stage. The ultimate outcome was a population with a common language, a common faith and a common culture, a people that, with certain exceptions, submitted readily to a ruling house with a modern civil service at its disposal. Spain's geographical isolation and its people's willingness to accept military discipline during the *reconquista* resulted during the sixteenth century in a measure of political and culture integration equal to that of Spain's arch-enemy, England – albeit in entirely different forms.

In Central Europe there was no suggestion of state institutions that might lend support to a national culture. The Cologne imperial decree of 1512 referring to the 'Holy Roman Empire of the German Nation' was evidence that the Reich was increasingly losing its authority and its universal character. As the Renaissance and humanism gained ground, the imperial crown tended to forfeit its medieval messianic status, and the more its alleged descent from the Roman caesars degenerated into an outmoded tradition, the more sensible it seemed to be to adopt the concept of the 'German Nation' as a kind of 'fall-back' position: after all, was it not in fact the Germans who had inherited the empire? Ever since the end of the fifteenth century there had been a clamour on all sides for a reform of the Reich, and in men's minds at that time a reform of the Reich was inextricably bound up with a reform of the church: were not church and Reich dependent on each other under the terms of god's plan of salvation? A tract by a canon of Cologne cathedral, Alexander von Roes, 'Memorandum on the Privilege of the Roman Empire', written as early as the thirteenth century, was now unearthed and circulated in numerous editions. Here it was boldly stated: 'It should thus be known that Charlemagne, the Holy Emperor, with the consent and on behalf of the Pope of Rome . . . determined and decreed that the imperial dignity shall rest for all time on legitimate election by the Princes of Germany . . . '[13] The German nation, then, was the enfranchised assembly of the German princes, who confronted the emperor collectively as the 'Empire'. The quest for a reform of the Reich which began in the middle of the thirteenth century had as its object the founding of some institution that would turn the medieval empire into a modern state. If the quest had been successful, then the 'German Nation' might have been established on an interim basis through the assembly of princes as a kind of aristocratic nation state.

In fact, the welfare of the 'German nation' was a powerful argument in the debate about a reform of the Reich. At the so-called 'Turkish Diet' in Regensburg in 1454 the leader of the imperial delegation, Enea Silvio Piccolomini, had called for a crusade against the Turks and the reconquest of Constantinople. The German electors replied sourly that the emperor should first look to the empire himself, since 'the same was a noble and worthy country of the German tongue . . . and the Holy Empire, so justly inherited by the German tongue, is in woeful disarray.'[14] In other words, without a reform of the Reich, there would be no crusade against the Turks. The emperor's German shirt should be nearer his skin than the imperial mantle. The 'German tongue' quite specifically identifies the German speakers among the estates. How closely a reform of the Reich was bound up with a reform of the church is evident from the 'grievances' of the German nation that were repeatedly submitted to the papal throne. The Roman throne, it is claimed in a summary of these 'grievances', had contrived a thousand devices to pick the Germans' pockets, so that this 'once illustrious nation', which had won the empire through her valour and her blood' and had 'been mistress and queen of the world' was now cast into penury and slavery.[15] At the beginning of the modern era, then, the 'German nation' was an idea linked with opposition to the universal powers of emperor and pope. In the long run, however, the idea was not politically robust enough to sustain the authority of a state.

On the other hand, the 'German nation' had made significant headway as a term denoting a cultural identity ever since the Italian scholar Pioggio Bracciolini had unearthed the text of Tacitus's *Germania* in the monastery library of Hersfeld and published it in Italy in 1455. In the age of the Renaissance and humanism, one aim of the search for classical Greek and Latin texts had been to find evidence for the age-old idea of the descent of tribes and modern nations from their legendary forebears. The historical studies of humanists in the sixteenth and seventeenth centuries were intended to confirm and reinforce the identity of their own nations by reference to the ancient world, the thought and experience of which were regarded as models and which provided, as it were, a cosmopolitan, pan-European seedbed for the cultivation of a distinctive national character. The discovery of the *Germania* consequently caused a great stir. It was now possible to learn from one of the great authors of antiquity, a respected and impeccable authority, that the Germans had been a nation – and, indeed, a very eminent nation – from time immemorial. Hitherto German scholars had lagged behind in the international race for national renown, for there had been no single German tribe from which the German nation had descended, as the French nation had descended from the Franks. 'German' was merely a collective term denoting a number of German dialects, otherwise it was a purely artificial term. Now the term could be simply translated: the Germans of the Tacitus were the ancestors of the contemporary Germans, Germany corresponded to the 'Germania' of the Romans. It was only now, about 1500, that the word *'Deutschland'* as a translation of Tacitus' 'Germania' crops up: hitherto authors had made do with the expression, *'die deutschen Länder'* ('the German lands').

Backed by the authority of Tacitus, German humanists were in a position to refute the disparaging remarks about the Germans that were current abroad. The widespread image of the uncouth, uncivilized, hard-drinking German was now set against the ideal figure from Tacitus – the unspoiled, loyal, valiant German with his unsophisticated view of life. It never occurred to anyone, apparently, that Tacitus might have invented these dazzling Germanic heroes as a literary device with which to satirize the corruption and decadence of Rome in his own day. Instead, the German humanists had a different, positive aim in mind: they saw the Germans as epitomizing a naive and uncorrupted nation destined to oust the old, effete civilization of the Italians and the French. The unblemished morality of the German race was not uncommonly contrasted with the depraved manners of the Roman Curia.

German scholars did not hesitate to parade their new-found self-confidence for the benefit of their French colleagues. That Charlemagne had been a forerunner of the Capets and the main basis for that dynasty's claim to the throne was branded as an absurd invention by Jakob Wimpfeling in his *Epitome Germanorum* of 1505: Charlemagne had actually been a German ruling over the French, whereas no Frenchman or Gaul had ever been Roman Emperor – in itself plain proof of the superiority of the Germans over the French. Wimpfeling came from Alsace, like a considerable number of German humanists, and for him it was an incontrovertible fact that the population of Alsace had been German ever since the days of Augustus, and Strasbourg and the rest of Alsace should never have fallen under French suzerainty.

It was about 1500 that the makings of a German national myth emerged within a single generation, a process that was taking place about the same time all over Europe. Erasmus of Rotterdam, although he himself firmly refused to be involved in the fabrication of national myths, conceded glumly that nature had not only implanted in every individual a personal conceit, but had also encouraged in each nation a kind of general *amour propre*.[16] It is true that in Germany the national myth lacked not only the political context of a unified state, but even the linguistic infrastructure that would have given it permanence: with rare exceptions, German humanists wrote in Latin. They were, after all, cosmopolitans and their mission to rehabilitate Germany led them on a roundabout path via the classical culture of the Latin world.

It was neither the academic labours of the humanists, nor the abortive attempt at a reform of the Reich that elevated German to the status of a national language, but Martin Luther's Reformation. Luther's theology was based on the Word; it originated with the opening phrase of the Gospel according to John 'In the beginning was the Word, and the Word was with God, and the Word was God.' The Bible, then, was the sole authority in the Christian faith, and since Luther's

Church was a congregation of all the faithful, the word of god had to be proclaimed in a language they understood. The translation of the Bible into Luther's robust Saxon dialect, along with his tracts and epistles, became the nation's primer. Luther's *Sermon on Indulgences and Grace*, for instance, first appeared in 1515 and had gone through 25 reprints and pirated editions by 1520, while 4,000 copies of his *Address to the Christian Nobility of the German Nation* were sold within 18 days, with a second printing appearing only a week after the first. The great reformer was joined by an army of other Protestant publicists, theologians, friars, educated burgesses and artisan-poets. This flood of literature in German, mainly on theological topics, was lapped up by a rapidly growing reading public. In those areas where the Reformation had found a foothold the educational standard of the laity, and literacy in general, improved enormously. But when Luther launched his appeal to the *Christian Nobility of the German Nation* in 1520, what he meant by the phrase 'German Nation' was indeed the aristocracy, i.e. the temporal and spiritual authorities, and what he was appealing for was not some political initiative on the part of a state that did not really exist, but 'the improvement of the Christian condition' and a reform of the Roman Church.

It is an extraordinary example of historical irony that it was the Reformation started by Martin Luther, 'the German Hercules' and the 'German nightingale', that constituted a major obstacle to the emergence of a common German culture, and possibly even to the establishment of a German nation state on the same footing as the other countries of Western Europe. The failure of the Reformation to prevail throughout the Reich, and the fact that Protestantism became the preserve of the reformed churches and the Protestant estates, meant that the battle between the confessions hung in a precarious balance, petrified by the territorial criterion of statehood: *cuius regio, eius religio*', by which each local ruler dictated the religious denomination of his own territory. Irrational territorial divisions within the Reich were confirmed, and the gulf between one state and another was rendered even deeper by confessional differences.

It was the Thirty Years War, finally brought to an end by the Treaties of Münster and Osnabrück in 1648, that did the rest: there could be no question then of the Reich becoming a single centralized state. The imperial estates were granted sovereignty within their territorial borders and had the right to conclude alliances among themselves or with foreign powers. Samuel Pufendorf, who summed up the Westphalian peace treaties in terms of international law, declared that the title 'Roman Empire of the German Nation' was anomalous, because the new German body politic (*modernam Germanorum rempublicam*) had no connection whatsoever with the Roman Empire – a remarkable admission, not only because it cut the ground from under the feet of those who argued for the uninterrupted existence of the empire, but also because the idea of the nation was thus casually deleted from the definition of the state. Pufendorf's colleague, Ludwig von Seckendorff, who was writing his *German Princely State* at about the same time (1656) did retain the idea of a German nation in a political sense, but observed that, within and below the level of this 'nation', there were other nations – including the numerous German principalities that were based on nations, from Württemberg to Anhalt, from Brandenburg to Braunschweig-Calenberg. Following the Thirty Years War the idea of the empire had, as it were, been watered down, becoming little more than a judicial institution for mediating in disputes and quarrels. Its potential statehood had devolved on the territorial states – more than three hundred of them – not counting the imperial knights' estates.

In the course of the next century and a half, 'German' denoted nothing but a language, and the prospects of it becoming anything more than that were at times distinctly dim. Here and there language societies were founded, like the 'Fruitful Society' in Weimar, or the 'Pegnitz Shepherds' in Nürnberg, learned bodies which, in rather pathetic attempts to emulate the *Académie française*, devoted their energies to purifying the German language, but which were often derided by their contemporaries on account of their rigorous purism. It is noticeable that efforts of this kind to purge the German language of foreign influences were largely confined to Protestant parts of the country – this is hardly surprising, considering that the canon of Protestant literature was the Saxon dialect of Luther's Bible translation. Even in the nineteenth century, the great German grammarian, Jakob Grimm, explained in the preface to his *German Grammar* that 'New High German might indeed by called the Protestant dialect.'[17]

During the eighteenth century a tendency became apparent that is of great significance for our theme: a new social class began to be formed in the Reich, comprising civil servants, professors, teachers, Protestant clergy, authors, booksellers and publishers, doctors and lawyers – members of the liberal professions who had one thing in common: they did not hold office or practise a vocation primarily by virtue of their social status, but by reason of their expertise. The guarantee of their competence was, as a rule, some kind of academic training. In the numerous Germany states a growing need for trained minds as a reservoir of talent for recruitment to the higher grades of the civil service had played a major part in the emergence of this new class. The German states did in fact provide facilities for academic training that were superior to those in most other European countries. Between Kiel in the north and Graz in the south, Königsberg in the east and Freiburg in the west there were no fewer than forty universities. As this new educated class grew larger, the German dialects began to coalesce and form the medium of a sophisticated German culture. A German national literature, a national tradition in music and on the stage created, far beyond the frontiers of the country's territorial states, a uniform standard of taste and judgement. Those authors who wrote in German during the second half of the eighteenth century did so, not simply because this was what the literary market demanded, but also because they were deliberately committing themselves to the standards and preferences of an enlightened middle class that crossed the borders of individual states. They deliberately eschewed the French language and culture that prevailed at court. In thus dissociating themselves from the cultural hegemony of France on the continent, the German educated class naturally became more keenly aware of their own national identity. As early as 1785 Justus Möser was exhorting his compatriots not to 'ape foreign manners'.[18] At about the same time Klopstock declared in one of his patriotic odes:

> Never was nation so just
> To foreigners as thou art –
> But be not *too* just. They think not so nobly
> That they might discover how fair is thy error.[19]

The public Klopstock was addressing was obviously the 'German nation', but such a nation existed only in the minds of an educated elite. It was a nation in fact where four out of five Germans were still firmly rooted in a bucolic environment in which high politics was epitomized at best by the prayers offered up in the parish church on behalf of the local ruler, or, at worst, by the trials and tribulations of war – billeting and looting by foreign soldiery; urban youth, like the young Goethe, had no political allegiance other than to 'Fritz', the Prussian King, Frederick the Great, who was respected as a national hero on account of his victories over French and Russian armies. There was little enough soil here for the cultivation of grassroots national sentiment. According to an estimate by the Berlin bookseller, Friedrich Nicolai, some 20,000 individuals in Germany had taken part in the public debate on the national issue around the year 1770: the concrete political consequences had been precisely nil. The unity of the German nation was initially purely linguistic and cultural. It is true that an increasingly dense network of communications linked cultured individuals in all the German-speaking areas; the vast increase in the number of new publications and reprints, a considerable expansion in the number of newspapers and periodicals, the establishment of flourishing reading societies, even in the small towns generated a reading public on a new scale and of a new kind. But, as Madame de Staël observed at the beginning of the nineteenth century, 'educated people in Germany do indeed conduct a most lively debate on theoretical topics and acknowledge no restraints as far as that goes but, on the other hand, they are somewhat inclined to leave the province of real life to their secular rulers.'[20]

A cultured nation, then, but a nation lacking the political

cohesion of the other cultured nations of Western Europe –
manifestly because no true nation state had as yet emerged in
Central Europe. Politics and culture did interact, each stimulat-
ing and advancing the other, to give birth ultimately to nations,
in which, it is true, only certain privileged groups played an
active political part before the end of the eighteenth century.
This development may be observed in the case of England
no less than in that of France. Again, the example of the
Académie française comes to mind – founded by Richelieu
in 1635 to cultivate and standardize the French language.
The consequent intellectual homogeneity of the French elites
inevitably strengthened the inner cohesion of the French state.

The case of Germany was by no means unique, the country was not pursuing its own special line of development.
Even a superficial glance reveals striking affinities with other
countries, especially with Italy. Here, too, the country was
politically divided and there were consequently a great many
different cultural centres. There had also been a revival of the
idea of an Italian nation state, encouraged by the Renaissance
and the development of the *volgare illustre*, the refined idiom of
Northern Italy. What Luther's Bible had done for German,
the poetry of Dante, Boccaccio and Petrarch did for Italian.
Nevertheless, Machiavelli's dream of a united Italy in his
Principe had remained only a utopia. During the sixteenth
and seventeenth centuries there were protracted civil wars in
Italy and a relapse into the provincialism endemic to such an
agglomeration of miniature states. For most Italians *la patria*
was their native town and the country round about. Certainly,
intellectual particularism had been broken down in the course
of the eighteenth century, but *Italia erudita*, the Italy of the
humanists, like Germany, was a nation in a cultural sense
only, literally a republic of letters, still far short of any kind
of political statehood.

In spite of such similarities, we should not overlook the
fundamental differences between the two countries. Rome
had always been present as the centre of Italy, in spiritual
and intellectual terms at least. The country had clearly defined
geographical contours, and the Latin foundations of its culture
inspired an enduring sense of its status as a civilized nation.

Moreover, Italy had remained solidly Catholic, knowing little of the major confessional differences that divided Germany. In Italy the counter-reformation had contrived to preserve a humanist tradition within the church, which had not been the case in Germany. Most of the Italian principalities, large and small, had alien rulers, which was not so in Germany: from Milan to Naples, Germans, Frenchmen and Spaniards ruled the land – a perpetual affront to *italianitá*, Italian national sentiment. On the other hand, French cultural hegemony during the seventeenth and eighteenth century did not arouse the kind of animosity in Italy that it did in Germany – on the contrary, French civilization was widely regarded by Italians as exemplary, and even in the eighteenth century there were Italian intellectuals who thought seriously of modernizing their native tongue by assimilating it to French.

But it is the structural affinities between Germany and Italy that bulk largest in any comparison between them, especially if we compare the strip of territory running from Jutland down to Sicily with Western Europe, where the consolidation of national states and national cultures had come about at an early stage. At the close of the eighteenth century, Eastern Europe also manifested certain typical structures in common. Here it was the great cosmopolitan empires that were dominant – the Habsburg monarchy, the empire of the Russian Tsars, the Ottoman Empire – to which might be added Prussia, following the partition of Poland. Here, under the stifling pressure of master races, Germans, Russians and Turks, there slumbered a multitude of latent national cultures which as a rule lacked the elites that might have led them, but which, in Central and Western Europe, included proponents of a national cultural identity. In Eastern Europe such cultures had been submerged and survived mainly in the countryside, but they included, for instance, the cultural traditions of the Poles, Bohemians and Serbs, which had already in the past advanced a long way on the path to a national cultural identity – in defiance of the ignorant, but momentous Marxist dictum referring to 'the people of Eastern Europe who had no history'. In their manner of government the European empires allowed for individual rights, but they also denied in principle the rights of national communities subject to their rule. They adhered to Montesquieu's principle that extensive empires called for despotic rule, in which instant and arbitrary decisions had to compensate for long chains of command over great distances. In Western Europe, on the other hand, the great diversity of relatively small states would not suffer such authoritarian methods.

Thus, as far as the emergence of its nation states was concerned, Europe consisted of three distinctly structured regions which moved from different starting points into that era of radical change which we might term the 'pivotal period' that lay between the old Europe, organized on agrarian lines and epitomized by its 'estates', and the Europe of industrial mass civilization with which we are familiar today, and in which the idea of the nation was to acquire a new actual and potential revolutionary significance.

7

The Pivotal Period

As the world passed over the historical threshold separating the French Revolution from the First World War, the idea of the nation underwent a fundamental change – not so much as far as its essential meaning was concerned, but more as regards its political significance and function. At the close of the eighteenth century this was an issue that had affected relatively few individuals. Up to that point the 'nation' had served as little more than a political slogan in the eyes of the political leadership while, as a term defining a cultural bond, it had appealed only to the educated members of all social classes. By the beginning of the twentieth century, however, the idea of the nation had, in the words of Karl Marx, seized hold of the masses and had become a force to be reckoned with, the most compelling proof of political legitimacy in Europe, and subsequently throughout the world. The background to this radical change was a break in historical continuity comparable only to that radical transformation that had once turned bands of neolithic hunters and food-gatherers into organized communities of arable farmers, stock-breeders and town-dwellers. Since the close of the eighteenth century, the Atlantic revolution had been turning an agrarian society, with its divisions into distinct social strata, into an industrialized mass civilization, the constitution of which swung between two polar extremes – the totalitarian repressive state on the one hand, and parliamentary democracy on the other. Whereas, however, the neolithic revolution had extended over a long period allowing people time to adjust to change, the headlong plunge into the industrial age had taken no more than a few generations. Never had mankind had so little time to adjust to so much in the way of change.

The initial problem was demographic: after many centuries of stability, with a balance cruelly trimmed by epidemic disease, war and famine, the population of Europe began to increase by leaps and bounds about the middle of the eighteenth century. In 1750 the continent had 130 million inhabitants, fifty years later the figure was 266 million, in 1900 it had reached 401 million. Even the departure of millions of emigrants during the second and final third of the nineteenth century made little impact on the figures. Catastrophes that had brought about major reductions in population – like the bitterly cold winter of 1783–4 when people froze to death as far south as Southern Italy – now had scarcely any effect. After Silesia had lost some 50,000 inhabitants in the famine of 1771–2, a further 70,000 souls had been added to the country's population during the succeeding three years. The population did not simply increase at a uniform rate: it was the *rate* of increase that actually grew, even though Europe by 1800 was already the most densely populated part of the world.

This unprecedented population explosion had a number of causes, some of which have still not been adequately explained. There was, for one thing, a steep rise in agricultural productivity. The old three-field system of cultivation, in which a third of the land lay fallow at any given time, was superseded by the modern method of crop rotation, so that crop yields increased everywhere. With the invention of the Brabant plough the soil could be tilled more effectively, the scythe replaced the sickle, new methods were used to improve sowing, fertilizing and harvesting. Governments and farmers alike were seized by a *fanatisme de l'agriculture*, as one contemporary put it. The fluctuation in yields from one harvest to the next grew smaller. Disastrous famines grew fewer, and finally vanished altogether.

People who are better fed are more resistant to disease.

New remedies in the fight against disease played their part in controlling epidemics, improved hygiene brought about a reduction in the infant mortality rate and deaths in childbirth. What was involved here was not just improvements in medical science, but also changing attitudes to children and the family. Regulations governing the guilds and social status in general, and the legal standing of the rural population in Central and Eastern Europe in particular, had hitherto barred many marriages. Now marriages became more frequent, and married couples tended to live together longer. It is true that the birthrate did not rise very significantly, and it even tended to decline from the second half of the nineteenth century onwards, but the mortality rate declined spectacularly, while average life expectancy rose correspondingly.

In this way a number of factors combined and interacted, culminating in a great surge in population density, such as the world had never experienced before – a kind of human inflation. Paradoxically, thanks to the improvement in the food supply, more and more people survived, only to suffer hunger for most of their lives. More and more individuals were competing for a dwindling number of jobs. And as the number of mouths to be fed increased after the middle of the eighteenth century so food prices also rose, especially the price of grain: in France, for instance, prices had risen by more than 60 per cent before the turn of the century, while during the same period incomes had increased by no more than 25 per cent.

People began to migrate. Surplus population from the countryside flowed mainly into the towns, swelling the army of beggars and casual workers, filling the almshouses and overloading what social services there were. London was flooded with Irish peasants, Paris with *pauvres montagnards* from the Massif Central and the Alps, Madrid swarmed with mountain dwellers from the Pyrenees and Galicia, while Naples attracted the impoverished rural proletariat from all over Southern Italy. Alternatively, people made for those areas where land was still available, often at the invitation of governments eager to populate their territory and open up new areas of cultivation. Frederick the Great settled more than 300,000 immigrants in the Oderbruch and elsewhere in his kingdom. The Hungarian plains and the Banat drew 11,000 families from south-west Germany, the Empress Catherine II set out to populate the steppes of the Volga region with Germans, while by the end of the century more than half a million Russians had settled in Siberia. There was mass emigration from the barren Scottish Highlands into northern England, but also into Ireland. Several thousand Germans were invited by the Spanish crown to settle in the Sierra Morena and cultivate land that had lain fallow ever since the expulsion of the Moors.

But habit and the law of the land were still more powerful than the pressure of population, and it took the upheaval of the Napoleonic era to change the situation radically. That was when, for the first time in history, armies numbering hundreds of thousands of men trudged backwards and forwards across Europe. When French, Italian or Württemberg soldiers became familiar with the Ebro as well as the Moscow River, when Cossacks from the Urals and militiamen (*Landwehr*) from East Prussia marched into Paris, then even recruits from the humblest circumstances became aware of totally new horizons: it suddenly seemed possible to overcome the obstacle of great distances. There was, too, the emancipation of the peasantry in the eastern parts of Central Europe. Restrictions on the marriage of peasants and labourers were abolished, as were the laws that tied the peasantry to the land. The average age of those entering into wedlock declined rapidly: the pressure of the population grew even more rapidly within a single generation, and even the landless farm labourer from the great estates east of the Elbe was at liberty to leave home and travel abroad. He tended to make for the nearest town in the first place, and from there he might make his way to the nearest large city. If living standards there proved to be little better, then it was a utopian vision of the New World that was likely to attract the masses of emigrants. Up until the outbreak of the First World War, some 15 per cent of Europeans had turned their backs on the continent that gave them birth. Most of them came from Great Britain, Ireland and Germany, and – from the end of the nineteenth century – from the industrially underdeveloped countries of Southern and Eastern Europe: Russians, Poles, Italians and Spaniards.

Some 45 million of them settled in America, Australia, New Zealand and South Africa. A further 6 million left Europe for the thinly populated region of Asiatic Russia, a migration which was in many respects no less important and dramatic than the settlement of North America.

But this was only the smaller part of a migratory movement that took place in Europe during the nineteenth century, affecting altogether some 85 per cent of the population, 70 per cent of whom remained in Europe, but moved from the countryside into the towns. The agrarian society of Western and Central Europe turned into an urban, and ultimately, a metropolitan, society. In 1801 there were no more than 21 cities in Europe with populations of over 100,000, but by 1901 the number had risen to 147, in which at least 10 per cent of the continent's population lived.

Behind these statistics lay squalor and poverty on a massive scale, of which social criticism in the literature of the day – the novels of Charles Dickens or Eugène Sue, for example, gives us only the faintest idea. In the countryside more than three-quarters of the rural population were either destitute or unemployed, 'without even a scrap of land', wrote a doctor tending the poor in Mantua, 'without hearth or home, with nothing save a superabundance of children, doomed to wander like Tartar nomads, changing their domicile from one year to the next . . . They are endlessly on the move, accompanied by a couple of sheep and a handful of chattels, comprising a tattered mattress, a mouldy wine-cask, a few crude utensils and a little basin.'[1] In some districts of Westphalia, the Palatinate and lower Austria the authorities marshalled the poor into regular troops of beggars who were then escorted round the neighbourhood to collect alms according to a pre-arranged schedule.

Those who sought relief in the towns were rarely any better off: they merely swelled the army of unskilled casual labourers who reckoned themselves lucky if they were able to support themselves and their families by acting as porters, by shovelling snow or working as stevedores. The impoverishment of large sections of the urban population, which had already begun in the eighteenth century, continued until it reached disastrous proportions.

The growing mass destitution was known as 'pauperism', and no one seemed able to cope with it: a leading encyclopedia, 'Brockhaus', offered a definition in 1840:

Pauperism is present wherever a numerous class of the population is able to earn no more than the most frugal living by arduous labour, and are not even certain of that minimum subsistence. Being victims of this condition and suffering it throughout their lives, and having no prospect of improvement, they sink ever deeper into apathy and brutishness, providing an ever growing number of recruits for the army of alcoholics and vices of every sort, as well as filling the poorhouses, workhouses and prisons as the ailment spreads and increases with breathtaking rapidity.

The process bid fair to end in disaster. The Scottish clergyman, Thomas Robert Malthus, had long since forecast that a constant increase in population, accompanied by a much smaller increase in resources, must inevitably lead to a breakdown of human society. The fact that Europe did not collapse in a catastrophic famine like that which was to afflict the Third World a century and a half later was due to the simultaneous development in economic progress that we usually call the Industrial Revolution.

The idea is doubtless somewhat misleading. That a fundamental change had taken place was obvious enough: hitherto every kind of work had been performed by the power of human or animal muscle, or else by natural forces – water and wind. Latterly it had been machines that had increasingly borne the burden – with incomparably greater efficiency, in fact. The exploitation of mineral resources, for instance, was placed on a totally new footing. Coal and iron, and later mineral oil, were extracted in massive quantities, processed and consumed, serving as the hallmark of the new age. The scientific spirit of enquiry was wedded to industrial enterprise: the new products were not produced simply by the expertise of skilled craftsmen, but emerged as the result of abstruse calculations in offices and laboratories. The organization of work changed in ways that entailed major social adjustments. The craftsman's workshop was replaced by the factory, the economically self-sufficient smallholding gave way to the large agrarian estate, the principle of the division of labour triumphed. The wage-earner selling his labour on the free market took the place of the craftsman or peasant who had often been bound by social or even legal convention, but who had at least enjoyed a measure of economic security.

The industrialization of Europe has now lasted some two hundred years as a coherent and unceasing process of change. It took some time, however, to affect the whole continent and it is essentially a twentieth-century phenomenon. Until the eve of the First World War, industrialized Europe was located, roughly speaking, in an ellipse extending through Lancashire, Stockholm, Warsaw and Genoa. Large tracts of countryside remained nevertheless virtually unaffected by technological and economic change – from the Netherlands, still one of the wealthiest countries in Europe, down to Spain and Russia, the poorest nations. The same was true of Austria-Hungary and Poland. Certainly, there were industrial islands everywhere in which industry flourished. Bohemia had a highly developed textile industry, Catalonia produced more cotton goods than Belgium, the textile industry in Northern Italy, especially its silk mills, had been mechanized, and foundries and machine workshops had sprung up round Moscow and St Petersburg. But the economies of these countries long remained for the most part non-industrial – with the exception of the Netherlands. Factories and railways owed their existence mainly to British, and later also to French, Belgian and German engineers and investors. Apart from geographical problems, which handicapped the larger eastern countries in particular, it was the persistence of outmoded feudal attitudes and traditional attitudes to work and property as well as an old-fashioned protectionist approach to fiscal and customs policy that obstructed the development of the inventive spirits and held back investment and the growth of demand. Europe was split into two worlds: a thriving, industrialized north-west and a largely agrarian east and south which exported foodstuffs and raw materials to the industrial centres and tended to import industrial equipment and techniques. It was a situation not unlike that which currently exists between the countries of the first and third worlds. And the political consequences were similar to those manifested in the totalitarian, mostly fascist dictatorships with their policies for development in the industrially backward countries of Europe after the First World War.

There was another feature that distinguished industrial from agrarian Europe: the economic boom had taken place mainly in areas where there had been a large increase in population and where in consequence there was a plentiful supply of cheap labour. The mines and factories sucked up workers: the pool of labour seemed inexhaustible, for the underprivileged and poverty-stricken masses were only too glad of any kind of regular employment with a guaranteed wage. In spite of all the contemporary and subsequent criticism of the wretched living conditions of the first generation of factory workers, we should bear in mind that, in comparison with the mass poverty of the pre-industrial period, the average working man or woman was now better off. Unemployment, underemployment, child labour and female labour, undercutting of wages through cottage industry, pressure on wage-rates from cut-price production in more favourable locations: all these factors tended to have less and less effect. Although there were still occasional poor harvests, as well as industrial slumps that quite frequently drove up food prices, there were no riots caused by starvation in the period following the 1848–9 revolution. Pauperism, which had seemed to be an inevitable evil in the first half of the nineteenth century, was no longer a problem in the second half of the century.

The expansion of population and production was accompanied by another revolutionary change in everyday life. The tyranny of space, the handicap of distance, which had hitherto handicapped economic expansion and the extension of centralized political authority, was overcome in the course of the nineteenth century. The transport of goods and passengers, and also the transmission of news acquired a totally new dimension. For as long as anyone could remember the duration of a journey between two given points had remained more or less constant, limited by the performance of horses on land or sailing vessels at sea, but also by vagaries of the weather or the rigours of the terrain. Over favourable country a rider might cover up to 200 kilometres a day, but how many people had a horse of that quality? Stage-coaches, which provided an overland service between large towns, managed barely 50 kilometres a day in France about 1780; the express post could cover 80 to 90 kilometres per day. But the French network of highways was indisputably the best in Europe, for the state accepted responsibility for the building of highways and arterial roads with a paved surface. In England, too, there were the turnpikes built by private contractors, and a traveller could make good progress on these, but in the rest of Europe the pace of travel was considerably slower. In Prussia, a kingdom with a great many frontiers, Frederick the Great deliberately allowed roads to fall into disrepair so as to make invasion by his enemies more difficult. It was only following the Napoleonic era, when it was a question of linking the newly acquired provinces to the Prussian heartland, that the building of modern carriageways got under way. Nevertheless, as late as 1830 the stage-coach still took forty hours to cover the distance between Berlin and Breslau. Further to the East, in Austria-Hungary – not to mention Russia – travel facilities were even more wretched. In winter and in wet weather the endless sandy tracks were virtually impassable, while in the brief summer months a sturdy pedestrian often made better time than horse-drawn vehicles.

This situation changed dramatically in the course of the nineteenth century. The network of highways became denser, and the traveller's dependence on the weather and the season of the year lessened. Express messengers with frequent and well co-ordinated changes of horses increased the speed of travel significantly: the 650 kilometres between Paris and Bordeaux could now be covered in a day and a half, whereas before the Revolution the journey had taken five days. The expense of travel declined correspondingly – with increasing rapidity, once the railway had begun to replace the stage-coach. About 1850 European railways registered 800 million passenger-kilometres: road transport by horse-drawn vehicles achieved exactly half that figure. At the same time great clipper ships were celebrating fresh triumphs in rapidity of passage and

cargo capacity: on their long voyages between Liverpool and
Melbourne, or China and San Francisco they were capable
of logging 500 kilometres per day. The career of steamships
with stern screws had also begun about this time; they catered
mainly for passenger transport, for they were not dependent
on favourable winds and could thus operate to a timetable.
The opposite shores of the Atlantic came closer together: the
millions of European emigrants now crossed the Atlantic in two
or three weeks, twice as fast as their predecessors a hundred
years earlier.

The age of mass transport had begun: huge quantities of
goods and passengers were carried in a much shorter time, over
greater distances and at lower unit cost. Agricultural produce
could be shipped across seas and continents to the great new
conurbations without deteriorating, and raw materials could
be delivered to distant destinations for processing. It was only
now that it became feasible to supply large wholesale markets,
a vital precondition for the expansion and integration of the
European economy.

Within a single generation the scale of the world in a
precisely literal sense had been changed. Hitherto the largest
economic region known to Europeans had been the Mediterranean basin. To traverse the Mediterranean from East to West
had, ever since antiquity, taken eighty days, while the passage
across the continent from Madrid to St Petersburg had taken
a similar time. It was the railway that broke open the prison
of space and distance. In 1839 the English magazine, *The
Quarterly Review*, gave an account of newly opened railway
lines and connections and ended with a prophecy concerning
'the gradual and ultimately total annihilation of space and
distance, which have hitherto been thought of as dividing
the various nations of the world in perpetuity'.[2] In 1873
Jules Verne made this vision the theme of his novel *Round
the World in Eighty Days*. Sixteen years later an American
reporter set out to make his utopia come true. Elizabeth
Cochrane of the New York daily newspaper, *The World*,
sailed from Hoboken to London, crossed the Channel to
France, called on Jules Verne in Paris and travelled on by
train to Brindisi. There she boarded a ship that took her across

the Mediterranean and through the Suez Canal to Singapore. From there she continued her journey via Hong Kong and Yokohama to San Francisco. A special train chartered by her paper carried her, together with the monkey she had bought in Singapore, as far as Chicago, leaving her ample time to reach New York. Apart from the special train, she had used only scheduled services, and the time taken for the journey was less than that envisaged in Jules Verne's story – seventy-two days, six hours and eleven minutes from New York back to New York. By the close of the nineteenth century, then, man's conceivable living space had expanded to embrace the entire globe.

But in order to be aware of this, a man did not actually have to travel: news travelled even faster and reflected more and more accurately the reality of the world. Hitherto, news had been an expensive commodity at the disposal of wealthy merchants and the ruling classes, and it still travelled relatively slowly. The fall of the Bastille was not known in London until three days after it had happened, and the news took no less than eight days to reach Vienna. There had indeed been regular postal services in Western and Central Europe ever since the sixteenth century and they had delivered letters from ordinary citizens as well as more important messages; nevertheless, despatches from foreign observers in revolutionary Paris reached Berlin, for example, at the earliest two weeks after the events they reported.

In 1794 a French engineer called Claude Chappe invented the semaphore, a mechanical telegraph employing movable vanes which were mounted on hills, on church steeples or on special masts, transmitting messages from one station to another by means of an alphabetical code. Trials demonstrated what was for those days the incredibly rapid transmission of messages: given good visibility, a message flashed from Paris to Toulon in no more than twenty minutes. Until the middle of the nineteenth century it was this semaphore that dictated the rapidity with which news might be transmitted throughout Europe, until it was finally replaced by the electric telegraph. At the same time, the railways speeded up postal deliveries to an unprecedented standard, there was naturally a vast increase in the actual number of postal deliveries, so that post offices were able to rationalize their services and reduce their charges: in 1856 a letter posted in Paris could be delivered two days later in Berlin. The telegraph, and later the telephone, reduced the time taken to deliver messages to practically nothing, and a flourishing press also played its part in disseminating news to the masses.

For there was now a large public seeking access to news. Even in the late eighteenth century news had been limited essentially to the relatively small class of individuals who could read and write. By the middle of the nineteenth century the reading public had grown significantly: in the central areas of north-western Europe including Scotland, Germany, Scandinavia, the Netherlands and Switzerland, more than three-quarters of the population could read and write; in Austria, England, France and Belgium more than half the population were literate. The population on the agrarian fringe of Europe – Russia, the Balkans, Central and Southern Italy, the Iberian peninsula – was still more than three-quarters illiterate. A reading public that had expanded at this rate stimulated an unprecedented boom in the output of newspapers and magazines, which was facilitated by new printing methods using lead type and linotype machines. Wherever state censorship did not try to suppress the free transmission of information the increasing market in books and newspapers offered not only news but also opinions and debate, leaving the choice of party to the reader's judgement. Soon a critical public emerged, eager for discussion and imposing on governments and cabinets specific aims and policies which had been formulated more rapidly and effectively than ever before with the help of the mass media.

The population explosion, the industrial revolution, the conquest of time and space, the increased availability of knowledge and information: all these factors were clearly linked and they interacted. Europe's political system was bound to adapt to such unprecedented fundamental changes. Basic assumptions about government changed: the absolutist state which had dominated the eighteenth century in Europe in a great variety of hybrid forms could no longer fulfil its function – to put it in abstract terms – on three essential levels: as regards power-sharing, as regards its efficiency as a mode of government, and as regards its legitimacy.

In political terms the decline of absolutism was most clearly manifested in its response to the demand on the part of wide sections of the population for a share in the exercise of the state's power. Alongside the old aristocratic power elite, new elites were arising everywhere in Europe. Leading functions in the state and in the army were being increasingly taken over by members of the middle class who kept the apparatus in working order, but who were excluded from the political privileges that guaranteed the status of their aristocratic superiors. They were the junior officers in the army, civil servants and secretaries in the embassies, the secretaries to regional tax inspectors, minor officials in the law courts. The anomaly was all the more glaring in so far as their aristocratic superiors were much more often at court or on their estates than in their offices. Industrialization, too, gave birth to a new echelon of leaders, the middle-class industrialists themselves, their managers, the leading employees who, as a body, wielded considerable economic power and who were eager to make their presence felt in politics as well as in business circles. The explosion in literacy and education led to the formation of an informed class of authors and their readers who refused to see why their political debates should have no practical outcome whatsoever. And, last but not least, the question of who consented to the levying of taxes or conscription into the armed forces became increasingly important on the threshold of the age of the masses. The slogan of the American revolution, 'No taxation without representation', swept through Europe, demanding new forms of representation that took account of the ineptitude of the so-called 'estates', as well as the ideologies of the new age.

As far as the efficient functioning of the political system went, the claims of the European crowns to exercise absolute authority had never been made good. Hitherto a lasting compromise with the nobility had set limits to the absolute power of the state in the person of the monarch. The vast increase in population, the development of new modes of communication, the need to rationalize the state and improve the efficiency of government prompted by industrialization: all this clearly called for a new kind of state with a centralized mechanism of government and administration, a state that could exercise its authority, its monopoly of power in the most remote areas of the country and the most subtle ramifications of society, but in conformity with recognized legal standards. Only in this way could the state avail itself of the total natural and human resources of the nation, reaching every class and group of the population in order to ensure, as compensation for the enormous social problems of industrialization, the most equable distribution of goods and opportunities in life.

The radical changes in Europe were sensed most acutely by contemporaries as a crisis in the political legitimacy of the state. The ancient myths and their interpretation on the continent no longer held water, the 'grace of god' and 'the good old order' were outworn concepts. The prince was, after all, only a man like other men, he had lost his nimbus. His elevation was no longer sanctioned by god, but by the consent of his subjects, and if this was not forthcoming, then his head was liable to fall under the guillotine. In 1830 Louis Philippe, the 'citizen king', did not swear his coronation oath on holy scripture, but on the constitution. The title of king he did not receive from god, via the Archbishop of Paris, but from parliament. And as for the 'Holy Alliance' concluded between the monarchs of Austria, Russia and Prussia on the basis of the Christian religion, it was not taken seriously by the public: 'a monument to human and princely eccentricity', remarked Friedrich von Gentz drily.

It should be noted that a crisis in moral values in Europe had set in long before the population explosion and industrialization had shattered the social order that had been based on 'estates': as Hegel stated, 'if once the realm of ideas is revolutionized, then reality will not hold out for long'.[3] The de-Christianization of large parts of the continent, the reduction of Christianity from a daily to a Sunday faith, was already under way by the end of the seventeenth century – not just in the elitist philosophy of the Enlightenment, but also as a change in collective attitudes and the practices of ordinary people. This was evident, for example, in a different manner of discussing death, or in an increasing knowledge and practice of birth control methods that had been banned by the church.

People's perception of the real world had undergone a profound change, and their attitude to the ordering of society and the state had changed correspondingly. Hitherto, the present had scarcely been distinguished from the past and the future. Embedded as they were in the firm matrix of family, village or small town, and caught up in the repetitive annual cycle of the countryside, people were barely aware of historical development: the future they expected would be no different from the past, the future order of things inevitably 'the good old order'. Of the new age, Heinrich Heine observed, 'What changes there are bound to be in our outlook and ideas! Even the elementary ideas of time and space have become uncertain: space has been annihilated by the railway and we have been left with nothing but time.'[4] Even time was felt to be unstable, racing past at a dizzy pace. Time, wrote Ernst Moritz Arndt, buries its own offspring, so that what existed yesterday has already been forgotten today.[5] Men were stunned by a jostling host of new and unheard-of ideas, all of them in stark contrast to the tranquillity prevailing in the customary 'old order' that could be scanned and intuited at a glance. The great migrations, the massive displacements of population were felt to be catastrophic, or else, with much the same social and psychological effects, as exhilarating and as evidence of something excitingly new. In 1871 the Basel historian, Jakob Burckhardt, summed up the new sense of the present age:

> Whereas our forefathers had little to suffer other than periodic wars, the last three generations have lived through a great variety of innovations – for example, the proclamation of new principles of existence, any number of newly founded states, sudden changes in whole systems of morals, culture and literature. In their startling effects on men's lives, the age of the Reformation and the era of colonization are nothing compared with our own time.[6]

The daily lives of great masses of people were radically changed, and time-honoured ties, myths and loyalties faded away. The once robust social body of the agrarian communities with their clearly identifiable social classes rooted in religion and fixed in men's minds, broke apart and set free myriads of individuals searching for new meanings in life – in so far as the struggle for a bare existence left them leisure for such speculation.

Responses to the call for a new and more meaningful community came from many different quarters. The right of the individual to liberty and the pursuit of happiness, as promised in the American – and initially in the French – Revolution became the slogan of European liberalism. It was not easy to make out exactly what liberalism was: a Spanish officer rebelling against the absolute rule of Ferdinand VII certainly had aims that differed from those of an English Whig trying to alter the constitution of the House of Commons; a member of a German student fraternity calling for German unification on a constitutional basis was very different from a Russian nobleman trying to abolish serfdom. But what they all had in common was the demand for liberty, generally understood as personal freedom, freedom of assembly and of speech, freedom of the press, freedom from arbitrary action by the state and, in general, a curb on state intervention in the social, economic and private sphere. The aim of a liberal society according to the English economist Jeremy Bentham was 'the greatest happiness of the greatest number'. The path to such a society led through liberal political institutions, above all through constitutions guaranteeing human rights and, in the spirit of Montesquieu, limiting the powers of a government as well as those of parliaments and lawcourts.

During the second half of the nineteenth century an even more radical proposition had been brought into the limelight by the opposition. As far as its organization was concerned, socialism had evolved mainly from more radical versions of liberalism, the representatives of which did not share the inclination of their more conventional colleagues to seek a compromise with the current ruling class over power-sharing, and who were prepared to go the whole hog, using revolutionary violence to bring about popular sovereignty in the spirit of the Jacobins. Their war-cry was 'Equality for all!' rather than 'Freedom for the Individual!' With the advance of industrialization and the emergence of a 'fourth estate' the myth of 'class' was invoked, the solidarity of the working class in opposition to the self-interest of the ruling class and the proprietors. All this may be seen as evidence of a dawning awareness on the part of those lower classes whose labour in the factories had made possible the growing prosperity of society as a whole.

The old world mobilized its defensive forces, devising ideologies likely to appeal to the masses. Conservatism consisted originally of a defence of organic diversity in the state and society, in defiance of the abstract principles of the Enlightenment, although Conservatism considered that it, too, was part of that intellectual movement. In the words of the Osnabrück civil servant and historian, Justus Möser, 'We have tended in fact to depart from Nature's true plan, which shows her riches in diversity, and we are opening up a path to a despotism that is determined to make everything conform to a few rules, thus eliminating Nature's diversity.'[7] The Conservative's adversary in this respect was not a particular philosophy, but any absolute authority that translated the maxims of the Enlightenment into a mode of government calculated to level out the organically evolved system of 'estates' based on social class. In the eyes of the great English Conservative, Edmund Burke, the French revolutionaries were distinguished only by the fact that they employed the levelling method with greater consistency.

This brand of enlightened Conservatism that was mainly concerned to protect freedom against the despotism of rulers as well as against the despotism of the masses changed, following the French Revolution and the Napoleonic era, and became more of a theoretical edifice defending the social and economic supremacy of the old pre-industrial elites – the crown, the nobility and the clergy – against the claims of the new elite and their political criteria. The conservative war-cry was now 'Legitimacy!' The more acute the sense of permanent crisis and incessant radical change became, the more unyielding the conservative defensive attitude grew. In the second half of the nineteenth century conservatism began to make common cause with nationalistic, populist, and ultimately with anti-Semitic movements, so that it, too, ended up as a mass movement. Political Catholicism, on the other hand, was in the last analysis the response of a minority population in islands of tradition that had been less drastically affected by changes in social standards: its representatives were simply seeking to defend themselves against the claim to supremacy of a predominantly Protestant aggressive liberalism.

In Europe during the nineteenth century, then, all manner of ideas concerning the social and political order and legitimacy took shape, evolved in a variety of ways, assumed different forms and also interacted. All these 'isms' were born from one and the same European universe of discourse and even their most extreme formulations in the twentieth century – communism and fascism – represented kindred versions of European thinking. Such trends coagulated, however, into parties and 'movements' which laid claim to absolute validity, claiming not just to stand for particular vested interests, but to embody universal and absolute truths. In this way the masses might be inflamed and incited to man the barricades, without, however, ever being able to overcome totally the rival ideologies and their followers.

The religious and civil wars of the sixteenth and seventeenth centuries once more threatened Europe in the nineteenth and twentieth century. Here again it was the power of the state that put an end to civil strife. The customary mechanism of the bureaucratic, authoritarian state was becoming less and less effective, because governments were now obliged to adopt modern political ideologies in order to justify themselves in the eyes of their own people. In the age of industrial mass civilization, the state needed a mandate that subsumed other political ideologies likely to have a mass appeal, amalgamating them and ensuring the state of the support and consent of its citizens. The key to this kind of legitimacy was the idea of the nation, an idea, it is true, that had now undergone considerable modification.

In its political sense the term 'nation' had hitherto denoted the sum total of those, who, directly or indirectly, took some part in political actions, in that they had some link with the crown, or else were represented through the estates. This meaning applied until the late eighteenth century, except that the set of politically active individuals changed following the French Revolution. In his epoch-making pamphlet published in January 1789 under the title, 'What is the Third Estate?' Abbé Sieyès defined the new, revolutionary idea of the nation as follows: Of the three estates, the nobility, the clergy and the 'third estate', – the community of the unprivileged 'common' people – it was only the third estate that sustained society, through its labour. The first and second estates were not really part of the nation, because they contributed nothing to its welfare: in fact, the nation consisted solely of the third estate, the 'people'. 'What, then, is the third estate? Everything!'[8] Montesquieu had explicitly described the nobility and the clergy as the two great pillars of the nation, but through the inversion of concepts suggested by Sieyès the 'people' and the 'nation' were identified as one and the same. The 'people' were no longer the despised, stupid masses, the 'plebs', but the 'good people', simple, innocent working folk who were now seeking from their rulers, the noble and clerical parasites, their rights as useful members of society. It was the people who constituted the nation, and only the people's nation could grant a mandate to the state and its government. This new nation, argued Sieyés, 'has been there from the very beginning, it is the origin of everything else. Its will is always legitimate for it is a law unto itself . . . '[9] It is the nation that confers its constitution on the state, and conversely it is from the nation that the state derives its powers, the nation in the shape of the free people is sovereign, as was stated in Article 3 of the Declaration of Human and Civil Rights adopted on 28 August 1789: 'The nation constitutes the principal source of all sovereignty. No assembly or individual may exercise a power that does not derive expressly from the nation.'[10] The 'nation' of the French Revolution was the body of all politically conscious citizens based on the equality of all and the sovereignty of the people. Anyone who did not pledge allegiance to the revolutionary Third Estate was automatically excluded from the nation. A native of Württemberg, Karl Friedrich Reinhard (1761–1837), tutor to a merchant's family in Bordeaux, on hearing of Louis XVI's attempted flight, decided 'that he wished to live and die as a Frenchman'. By virtue of that decision he did in fact become French and was later a leading figure in the French diplomatic service, and at one time even Foreign Minister of France. Membership of a nation, as understood in France at that time was simply a matter of a personal decision – in Ernest Renan's words, '*un plébiscite de tous les jours*'.

This novel, revolutionary idea of the nation as a whole people engaged in joint political action turned out to be more than just theoretical. It was a powerful weapon, uniting France internally to the point where enemies of the Revolution were expelled and outlawed, for the nation was 'one and indivisible'. In the war against the crowned heads of Europe it was the nation, the mass of the people, that made possible a mobilization on an unprecedented scale and the victory of the mass armies of French citizen-soldiers over the mercenaries of the absolutist states. Along with the revolutionary armies, the idea of the sovereign nation of the people began a triumphant advance across Europe. In Germany it encountered another idea and combined with it – the idea of the nation as a collective body sharing a common language and culture.

In France, with its compact territory and the institutions that had grown up there, it had seemed natural to define the nation as a political community on which the sovereignty once possessed by the crown had devolved. Such an identification of nation and state was at that point unthinkable in Germany: the basic perception her citizens had of their nation related to a community of enlightened minds sharing a common language and taking no account of territorial boundaries. As early as 1776 Adelung's dictionary had defined 'nation' as 'the indigenous inhabitants of a country, in so far as they have a common origin, speak a common language and are, in a more specific sense, distinguished from other peoples by a characteristic mode of thought or action, or by their national spirit, whether they constitute a state of their own or are dispersed throughout a number of states.'[11] What constituted a nation, then, was not a political bond, but a common language and an awareness of a common identity. The idea of a nation was defined even more precisely by the Weimar Consistorial Counsellor, Johann Gottfried Herder. He, too, linked 'nation' and 'people', but he was not thinking, like Sieyès, of politics, but of language and literature: that was where, he declared, the foundations of a nation and a people were to be found. It was in their stories and songs that a nation bared its soul. It was language and culture that constituted the soul of a people, and a people was more than just the sum total of its members: nations were spiritual entities, collective individuals, 'God's ideas'. Herder imagined the world as a vast garden in which nations had grown like plants, each in keeping with its own specific, mysterious, divine laws; no nation was superior to the others, but each was different. Every human being was fated to be a member of his nation and bound to it throughout his life through his mother-tongue. Herder's view, that states and constitutions mattered less than culture and language, reflected the continuing disparity between states and peoples that obtained in Central and Eastern Europe. Herder was subsequently regarded by the Slavs as the prophet of their national identity.

Herder's ideas became popular because they coincided with the Romantic tendencies of his age. The belief that their poets, hearkening to folksongs and writing in the language of the people, were drawing on profound sources of intuitive knowledge and were much closer to the people than their rulers or civil servants, was one of the comforting ideas by which the nations of Central and Eastern Europe compensated for their backwardness compared with the nation states of the West, and by which they affirmed their cultural identity. This was true of Germany, and it also applied to other nations in Central and Eastern Europe. They differed from the nations of Western Europe in that they lacked political institutions and even an ideological context in which a nation might define itself in terms of the current age. The nation was merely a vision of the future that could be glimpsed only in a common language and culture: a utopia adumbrated in historical sources, dim, and appealing more to the emotions than to the reason. 'What is the German's fatherland?' asked Ernst Moritz Arndt in his 'Song of the Fatherland' in 1813, the earliest German anthem. It took him a couple of verses to come up with the answer: the German's fatherland is there, wherever the German language is spoken. The objective element constituting the German nation issued, in Herder's terms, from the individuality of the people, which in turn was rooted in the language they shared. In this sense the existence of the nation did not depend on men's will: whoever had German as his mother-tongue was, ineluctably and for the whole of his life, a German.

These two views of the nation – the subjective, political view of the French Revolution, and the objective, cultural view of German Romanticism – fertilized each other, intermingled and interacted, forming the tonic keynote for the thousand voices of modern Europe. In an age when people had been uprooted, losing their bearings and any sense of their past, but were still inspired by hope for the future, the idea of the nation was attractive in three respects: it offered a sense of direction, a sense of community and a suggestion of transcendence. Identification of the individual with the nation simplified complex social and international relationships and clarified the issue of loyalty – especially in many Central European countries, where governments had frequently changed between the first partition of Poland in 1772 and the Congress of Vienna in 1815, and where today's ruler might turn out to be tomorrow's adversary. In such circumstances the idea of the nation offered a landmark and a criterion of judgement. National communities tended to emerge wherever older traditional political structures were on the point of disintegrating. In the *levée en masse* of 1793, in the wars of liberation in 1813, in the risings and campaigns fought for their emancipation by the peoples of south-eastern Europe, the new sense of a collective national identity was not just confirmed: it was actively experienced as a palpable and real phenomenon. Public festivities and celebrations, from the *fêtes révolutionnaires* of the French Revolution to German festivals celebrating the Battle of the Nations at Leipzig, confirmed a sense of nationhood over and over again, creating an authentic sense of community and reinforcing the individual's impression that he did indeed belong to a greater whole. The idea of the nation had quasi-religious undertones: since a nation has no visible physical presence, it has to be believed in. Nationalism is the secular faith of the industrial age. The new state was not sanctioned by god, but by the nation.

8

The Invention of the
'People's Nation'

The revolutionary French nation had declared itself *'une et indivisible'*, but not all its citizens saw it like that. In 1790 peasants in the south-west of France rose in rebellion because they had misunderstood the decree of emancipation proclaimed by the National Assembly and thought they had been exempted from any kind of levy or tax. Abbé Grégoire, a member of the National Assembly, looked into the causes of this misunderstanding and came to the conclusion that the language of the decree, issued in Paris, was foreign to most Frenchmen. French was spoken in no more than 15 of the 83 *départements*: in the others, *patois*, various dialects, were spoken – the Abbé counted more than thirty of them. These mostly deviated so markedly from French that the latter had to be regarded as a foreign language, known only to the urban middle classes. South of the Garonne a totally different language prevailed, the *langue d'oc*; Racine once remarked that in the *midi* he was as much in need of an interpreter as a Muscovite in Paris. It was a great shock to discover that, apart from the region round Paris, the language of Voltaire and of the Declaration of the Rights of Man was scarcely better understood in France than in the rest of Western and Central Europe. The Education Act of 21 October 1792 consequently stipulated that every child was to be taught to read and write French, and Deputy Barère declared on behalf of the Education Committee that henceforth the language must be 'as much one as the Republic'.[1] But the way was long and tortuous, and the unification of the French nation and the French language was not achieved until some time in the twentieth century.

And this in a land where, as scarcely anywhere else in Europe, the nation had been politically and culturally integrated at an early stage. The state had brought powerful pressure to bear in order to standardize the language. Had not the *Académie française* been founded in 1635 precisely because the unification of the state entailed the unification of its means of expression? The situation was little different in other Western European states – in Great Britain, say, or Spain. In those countries dialects had survived the pressures of standardization, and there were also whole sections of the population who spoke totally different languages: Welsh and Gaelic in Great Britain; Catalan, Basque and Galician in Spain. Even where state institutions designed to consolidate the nation had long existed it took a considerable time to form the unifying bond of a common language. Education systems had to be centralized, instruction had to be given in officially recognized languages. Military conscription helped, in that every recruit was obliged to understand the orders given by his superiors. The spread of literacy promoted standardization of the language, and so did the improvement in travel and communications and the growth of trade and industry.

The language issue was even more vital in those European nations which did not coincide with the territory of the states they inhabited. This problem became more acute once it was taken for granted, under Herder's influence, that a nation could not exist without its national language. Protestant nations had an initial advantage, for there the word of god had been preached in the local tongue ever since the Reformation. Translations of the Bible exercised a powerful influence on the standardization of languages. This was certainly the case with the Saxon-Meissen dialect of Luther, which was adopted as a base by later grammarians to create a uniform written Germany language, and which enjoyed the greatest prestige among the educated classes in German-speaking areas. The same was true of Bohemia where the Hussite Bible, printed in Prague in 1549 in the local dialect, had considerable influence on the standardization of the Czech language. In Hungary proponents of the old and new faiths vied with each other in attempts to influence the language through Bible translations: the Protestant Bible, brought out in 1590 by Gáspár Károly, was answered by the Catholic Church with a Counter-Reformation Bible for the nation.

But what if the rivalry of the churches did not provide a stimulus for the standardization of the vernacular? A remarkable example is Italy, where in fact a standard language had emerged during the Renaissance in the shape of the Tuscan dialect of Dante, Boccaccio and Petrarch. In the course of the succeeding centuries, however, this standard lost ground increasingly to regional dialects. The Milanese poet, Carlo Porta (1775–1821), for example, had to write his popular verse – which Stendhal praised as 'masterpieces of national literature' – in the dialect of his native city. For his appeal to his fellow countrymen on behalf of a united, democratic Italy the Jacobin patriot, Luigi Angeloni (1759–1842), was unable to find any more effective medium than a stilted idiom modelled on the classical writers of the fourteenth century. When the first Italian national assembly met in Turin in 1860, the delegates spoke French. The linguistic problem was solved virtually single-handed by Alessandro Manzoni (1785–1873): he wrote his great historical novel, *I Promesi Sposi*, from the viewpoint of the ordinary people – initially in a Lombard dialect. In the interests of national unity he later revised it, translating it into the Tuscan standard language as the latter had evolved since Dante's time. Through this 'laundering in the Arno' Manzoni turned the conversational idiom of the educated Florentine middle class into the Italian national language, thus overcoming the parochial regionalism of Italian culture. But the fact remained: in the era of Italy's unification not even all those who could read had a command of Italian. According to a realistic estimate, that amounted, in 1861, to something like 600,000 men and women, i.e. no more than 2.5 per cent of the Italian population were fully literate.

National cultures were not in fact, as Herder's disciples believed, collective entities that had surged up spontaneously from the primeval depths of the popular soul: they were largely the work of a handful of 'revivalists' – intellectuals, poets, philosophers, historians and philologists – who acted as godfathers to their nations, frequently in distant exile, in Paris, London or Vienna. Friedrich Schleiermacher hailed them, along with the founders of the world religions, as 'great men', heroes of historic stature. The revivalists were creators of language, like Adamantios Korais (1748–1833), a Greek physician living in Paris, who added elements of Classical Greek to the demotic idiom of his day to produce the modern Greek national language, *Katharevusa*. 'It is the learned members of a nation', he declared, 'who are the natural law-givers of the language spoken by the people.'[2] Law-givers of a similar kind were Barbu Mumuleanu (1794–1836), who turned Rumanian from a peasant dialect into a literary language, and the Norwegian, Ivar Aasen (1813–96), who replaced Danish in his country by a standard language *Landsmål* – concocted from various local dialects. The Serbian national movement would be unthinkable without the inspired poet, Vuk Stefanović Karadžić (1787–1864), who not only compiled a collection of folk songs, but also wrote a Serbian grammar and dictionary. And would we now have a Slovakian state without the *Grammatica slavica* of the Catholic priest, Anton Bernolàk, which appeared in 1790?

The list might be extended *ad libitum*: the majority of national languages that are now so firmly rooted in the cultural soil of Europe, were not standardized until the nineteenth century, dredged from the obscure recesses of colloquial speech, cast in the mould of a grammatically standardized literary language, and, in some cases, largely invented. And what philologists could not do, the poets did for them, for it was the poets who thought they could detect the spirit of the nations in their epics, fairy stories and folksongs. What they in fact produced was an artificial kind of literature adapted in theme and style to the taste of a middle-class readership. The brothers Grimm tried to give back to the nation 'the primeval Germanic myths long thought to have been lost' and ostensibly recorded these from peasant sources on the Upper Rhine: in fact their stories were largely drawn from earlier collections and owed their fascinatingly folksy atmosphere largely to the editors. James Macpherson's *Ossian*, a collection of Gaelic poems which appeared in English in 1762 and made a profound impression on the Romantic public throughout Europe, turned out to be fraudulent. The spirit of the people that had been invoked to justify the idea of the nation was in fact the spirit of a small group of enthusiasts.

Along with language, it was history that constituted the 'people's nation'; history was the record of a common destiny that united a people from their earliest traditions down to the present day, binding the nation together with an indissoluble bond. A nation's history was the guarantee of its existence: revolution, war, violence against all those who chose not to be part of the nation or who opposed the struggle for unification – all that seemed justified, as long as the nation could appeal to some ancient hallowed law. This was all the more the case with nations that could boast of no established institutions: 'For our present will not lack links with our past', declared the Serbian nationalist, Ilija Garašanin, in his programmatic memorandum *Načertanije* (1844),

> but past and present will form a coherent, integrated and interlocking whole, and that is why the Serbian nation and its existence as a state stand under the aegis of a hallowed historical law. Our aspirations cannot be denigrated as something novel and lacking foundation, it cannot be said that they are tantamount to revolution and upheaval; it must be admitted that they are a political necessity, grounded in ancient times, with their roots in the national life of the Serbs as a state . . . [3]

The idea was not in itself all that novel. Even in earlier times, national consciousness had been bred and nourished by mythically embroidered history: the heroic virtues of the Franks were allegedly derived from Trojan and Roman ancestors, rulers both east and west of the Rhine had traced their descent back to Charlemagne, and the legend of King Arthur was at the heart of the historical image by which the Tudors supported their claim to the English throne. But with the dawning of the modern age about 1800, with the birth and growth of people's nations, with the dizzy acceleration of people's experience of the passing moment, and expectations aroused by the age of industrialization, people's need and craving for history grew ever more acute. Every aspect of life was overgrown with a Romantic yearning for the past: the present, it seemed, had to be justified solely by its roots in history. Behind the Romantic spirit of the age there lurked a sense of bewilderment at the progressive destruction of time-honoured structures and modes of life, along with a longing for a new collective meaning to life, a longing that also had its roots in the distant past.

The new idea of the one, indivisible and immutable nation, born from the ancient spirit of its people, called for confirmation by a coherent and seamless past that had been purged of doubts and ambiguities, a past from which might be deduced the fateful continuity that justified the nation for all time. Every nation, explained the German historian, Leopold von Ranke, had been endowed by god with its own special character, and the course of history was marked by 'each nation's independent development of its own specific character in the manner ordained by god.'[4] Everywhere in Europe the nineteenth century witnessed the triumphant advance of historical study or, to be more precise, of national historiography, which constantly refined its intellectual equipment in order to tailor attractive historical costumes for the nations.

It was in Germany especially that historical studies flourished; it seemed as if history had set herself up as queen of the sciences. It had taken the shock of the French Revolution, the revolutionary wars, the collapse of the Holy Roman Empire in 1806, the defeat of that idol with feet of clay – Prussia – at Jena and Auerstädt to impart a sense of their common Germany identity to the inhabitants of Bavaria, Saxony and Württemberg, not to mention Lippe-Schaumburg, Saxony-Anhalt-Coburg and Reuss. But the newly discovered German nation had no firm frontiers -- and it was not actually a 'state', for the 'German Union' (*Deutscher Bund*), to which the European statesmen had acted as godparents in 1815 was conceived in an international spirit: it embraced, amongst others, the sovereigns of Great Britain, Denmark and the Netherlands. The constitution of Central Europe remained the principal concern of all the continental powers, while the idea of the nation was reckoned to be a 'revolutionary' and potentially destructive principle.

Since prevailing circumstances promised little support in government circles for the idea of a political nation, the German 'nation' was historically founded as a utopian projection. There were a great many historical episodes that might vouch for Germany's future. There were the Greeks, to begin with, discovered in the middle of the eighteenth century by Winckelmann and since then regarded as having a special affinity with the Germans. Had not Greeks and Romans been in classical times what the Germans and the French now were? Had not then, as now, an overbearing and powerful state dominated the West – rational, efficiently governed and organized, civilized, but lacking true culture and spirituality? In the East there had been a powerless conglomeration of states, in which, however, intellectual power and humane values had flourished? 'Dost thou know Minerva's folk?' asked Hölderlin, and replied:

> It liveth still. The Athenian soul still reigns
> Divine and serene among men.

The reference is to the Germans, and in 1807, in his *History of the Decline and Fall of the Greek Free States*, Wilhelm von Humboldt enlarged on the affinities linking Greek and Germany. For Friedrich Ludwig Jahn, who urged German youth to take up gymnastics to fit themselves for battle against the French, the Germans were a 'sacred nation'[5] on account of their similarity to the Greeks. It was no mere chance that the first major German national monument, the 'Valhalla' near Regensburg, was constructed, in spite of its nebulous Nordic name, in the shape of the Athenian Parthenon.

One of the most popular successes of the nineteenth century in Germany was Gustav Droysen's biography of Alexander the Great, published in 1833, which described the rise of a kingdom in Northern Greece – half barbarian still but able, by draconian measures, to impose order on the muddle of small

states in the south of the country. This Greek kingdom, united
by force of arms, formed the base for Alexander's visionary
advance to the East and for the transformation of Asia under
the auspices of a nobler Greek humanitarian ideal. Droysen's
book found a place on almost every middle-class bookshelf, for
it was generally taken for granted that Macedonia was Prussia,
Greece was Germany and Asia was Europe. The middle class
was meant to regard Bismarck as their Alexander, a leader
whose triumphant rise had been predicted by the historical
sciences of the nineteenth century.

The superiority of humanistic German culture, which was
to culminate in the creation of a national state, was one of the
grandiose historical ideologies of the day; another was the myth
of the German people, which seemed, ever since Herder's time,
to have been suffused with a Romantic, well-nigh sacred radi-
ance. To these ideologies was added a more rational and more
directly political idea of the people stemming from the French
Revolution: the idea of the people, in the form of the Third
Estate, exercising legitimate collective sovereignty over itself.
These two approaches, the Romantic and the more explicitly
political, both passionately committed to the 'people', met and
merged in Germany. In the winter of 1807–8 Johann Gottlob
Fichte delivered his *Addresses to the German Nation* in Berlin,
which was occupied at that time by a French army. In these
patriotic tirades the German people feature as an innocent
and uncorrupted nation fighting for its liberty against military
repression – and fighting even more vigorously against cultural
subjugation. In so doing the nation was fulfilling some higher
historical mission.[6]

The German people that had thus been discovered – over
a thousand years after the *gens anglorum* of the Anglo-Saxon
chronicler Bede – was initially enlisted to support a vision of the
future first propounded by the liberal opposition. In Heinrich
Luden's twelve-volume *History of the German People*, which
began to appear in 1825, the people were installed as the
supreme tribunal, at the bar of which every state institution
was obliged to justify its existence. Luden's vision of the future
was in keeping with the 'People's Empire' which the liberals of
the 1848 revolution had sought, a democratic state headed

by a monarch.[7] But what Luden had to say of the German nation was just as equivocal as what Fichte had said earlier: the Germans were the most deserving of nations, and their culture was superior to all others.

In principle the idea was not new: in the age of the Renaissance writers like Ulrich von Hutten and Johannes Wimpfelin had, with the indispensable allusion to Tacitus's *Germania*, set the virtues of the Germans and their descendents against the decadence and corruption of the Romans. This view was revived in the early nineteenth century: the German nation was represented as directly descended from the Germanic tribes, and all the admirable qualities Tacitus claimed to have discerned in the people of the North were now attributed to contemporary Germans – loyalty, morality, valour and simplicity – all these in contrast to their French neighbours. The fact that the Germans had Slavonic and Celtic forebears does not seem to have bothered anyone, any more than the fact, as Johannes Haller once remarked, that the most successful of Germanic nations was not the German, but the English people.

The Germanocentric limitation of the idea of the people already contained a latent virus, which, even in Heinrich Luden, was activated by the suggestion that what bound together a nation was not so much its language as its blood. This contention was launched at a level of argument remote from any historical evidence or proof, ranging via the racial theories of Count Gobineau and Houston Stewart Chamberlain to the lunacies of Adolf Hitler.

To begin with, in fact, there had been another historical perspective that seemed more promising. Even although the forces of the opposition in Germany were hopelessly divided into liberals, republicans, democrats, socialists, Catholics and Protestants, there was nevertheless a vision of the future which, precisely because it was vague and ambiguous, offered common ground to the proponents of many different ideas, uniting the forces of change, reform and revolution for more than two generations: this was the utopia of a national state embracing all Germans.

The desirability of this solution was by no means self-evident. Although the political fragmentation of the country had been deplored ever since the age of the humanists, the remedy had not been seen as consolidation into a single national state, like France or England, but as a more effective common front on the part of the princes, and more wholehearted support of the emperor. It was not territorial fragmentation that was considered the greatest evil, but the conflicting interests of the country's rulers. The multiplicity of regimes, capital cities and constitutions within the Reich was considered a positive advantage, since this was what seemed to guarantee a defence against megalomaniac despotism. As Christopher Martin Wieland summed up the situation, it was the diversity of manners and customs, as well as of theatres and universities, that fostered culture and civilized behaviour. Prosperity, too, argued Wieland, was more evenly and fairly distributed where the entire resources of a nation were not concentrated in one place.[8]

In the eighteenth century it was considered axiomatic that the Germans, as inveterate individualists, were not suited to life in a single nation state. It was in this feature that Wilhelm von Humboldt saw the essential cultural superiority of the Germans over the French. There was also another reason why a centralized political authority seemed to him a disadvantage: 'No one could then prevent Germany from becoming a nation intent on conquest, which no true German can wish, since it is a matter of common knowledge what singular advances the German nation has achieved in terms of intellect and scholarship, simply because she had not been in a position to direct her political energies abroad – and it is still not clear to what end these energies might be directed.'[9] When Humboldt, as a Prussian Minister of State not long after the Wars of Liberation wrote this, he was already bracing himself to defy the spirit of the age: any progressive impulse, any resistance to Metternich's system, any liberal protest against political stagnation or the German Union's pathological fear of demagogues was henceforth liable to be suppressed in the interests of a national state – united at home, formidably powerful abroad.

In the search for a historical model that would substantiate and justify the vision of a future state uniting all Germans, it seemed only natural to cast a glance back into the recent past. And there was Prussia – a state based on strict discipline and organized on the most modern lines, which had demonstrated by its rise from a third-rate territorial state to the status of a major European power in the course of the eighteenth century that the rigid system of European states and their balance of power might be breached. Prussia had convincingly proved her claim to lead Germany by the prominent part she had played in the War of Liberation in 1813. There was, above all, that myth of the great king, the 'Sage of Sanssouci', who had stood his ground against a host of foes and who had, by his victories over the French and the Russians, created the model German hero.

A whole generation of politically committed historians now occupied chairs in German universities: Dahlmann in Bonn, Häusser in Freiberg, Duncker and Treitschke in Berlin, Droysen in Jena, Sybel in Munich – all of them liberals and all of them convinced of Prussia's historic mission and the pernicious influence of South German, 'anti-national' Catholicism. They were by no means of the same mind as Leopold von Ranke, who had denied that history could teach the present age any lesson whatsoever. They waged political campaigns as members of parliament, as contributors to leading newspapers, as university teachers – as 'professorial prophets', as Max Weber was later to say of Treitschke – but above all as historians who shaped the German's image of history. They differed from liberals in Western Europe in that they saw the state not just as the product of natural forces, but also as the embodiment of ethical values, without which culture and social morality would not be possible. And those values seemed to be nowhere as clearly manifested as in Prussia, as Droysen declared in the *History of Prussian Policy* he began to publish in 1855. Ever since the fifteenth century, he claimed, Prussian rulers, fully aware of Prussia's German mission, had pursued an utterly consistent political line. From that, more than dubious historical thesis, Droysen drew the conclusion that the realization of the German national state through the agency of Prussia was part of 'the divine cosmic order'.[10]

Even more impact was made, however, by the popularized versions of such historical scenarios that flooded the country in hundreds and thousands of editions and reprints. Pride of place was taken by Franz Kugler's *History of Frederick the Great* (1841), which had illustrations by Adolph von Menzel, depicting, for example a 'Flute Concerto in Sanssouci' and 'Old Fritz out Riding'. These were archetypal images engraved in the hearts of Protestant Germans of every class from the nobility to the humblest labourer. They were images that may have influenced the outcome on the battlefields of Königgrätz and Sedan just as much as the military skills of the Prussian General Staff.

The historical image of Prussia had one flaw, however: generally, it applied to the Protestant parts of Germany only, omitting the mainly Catholic south of the country, Bavaria, for example, and Austria. The path from Potsdam led back into the luminous mists of an age that was more pure fantasy than truly medieval. But that was where generations of German historians believed they had found what they wanted for the future a German Reich resplendent in all its power and glory, its crown taking precedence over all other European monarchs. This was what Freiherr vom Stein had called for in a memorandum of 18 September 1812: 'In the tenth, eleventh, twelfth and thirteenth centuries Germany was a mighty Empire . . . Instead of restoring the constitution dictated by the Peace of Westphalia, it would be infinitely more fitting and in the interests of Europe generally and of Germany in particular, to restore our ancient monarchy.'[11] The idea was undoubtedly popular, and its popularity was further enhanced by the exemplary shock of violent revolution that set its seal on the middle class throughout the entire nineteenth century, fostering the nostalgic desire for what seemed to be the socially and intellectually safe and sound world of the middle ages. Max vom Schenkendorf, a poet of the War of Liberation against Napoleon, had written:

> O German Kaiser, be our King!
> Avenge the people, freedom bring!
> Break the chains that bind us fast
> And claim the victor's wreath at last!

Germany's future, then, was to be found in her past, in the middle ages. Of course, Schenkendorf's German Kaiser was not the Habsburg in Vienna, but Kaiser Barbarossa, the legendary Hohenstaufen, enthroned in his cavern on the Kyffhäuser mountain, who would return in the hour of Germany's greatest need and restore her erstwhile greatness.

The history of the German middle ages became something like a national obsession. Freiherr vom Stein founded the *Monumenta Germanica Historica*, the collection of German medieval sources that has still not been completed. The *Lay of the Nibelungs*, the 'German Iliad', began its triumphant career as one of the earliest monuments of Germany's national literature. Johannes Voigt's *History of the Teutonic Order*, Friedrich von Raumer's *History of the Hohenstaufens and their Age*, Heinrich Stenzel's work on the Frankish emperors, all of which were published in the 1820s, went through innumerable reprints; the educated classes read them as they had once devoured novels of love and romance. This image of the middle ages was provided in all its perfection in the six volumes of Wilhelm Giesebrecht's *History of the German Imperial Age*, which appeared in 1855. The age of the medieval emperors, Giesebrecht wrote in his preface, was 'the period during which our nation, strong in its unity, enjoyed its greatest power and influence, not only governing its own destiny, but also holding sway over other nations: it was an age when the German counted for most in the world, and an age when the German name had the sternest ring to it.'[12]

It would be difficult to overestimate the influence emanating from this vision of the middle ages: there was scarcely an area of culture – either highbrow or popular – that was not infiltrated by it. Lyric poets and popular novelists vied with each other in their efforts to paint a romantic and heroic picture of medieval times as an age in which the radiant splendour of the emperor and an atmosphere of Christian piety had embraced every class of society, prevailing over conflict and contradiction. Where evil existed, it invariably came from outside the charmed circle, in the shape of Roman intrigue or French duplicity. The radiant image was eagerly pounced upon by poets, dramatists and operatic composers. The novels of the day, Achim von Arnim's *Crown Guardians*, Tieck's *Heinrich von Morungen*, Hauff's *Liechtenstein*, de la

Motte Fouqué's *Magic Ring* transported the hopes and wishful visions of the nation back into the age of the Hohenstaufens. Operas like Carl Maria von Weber's *Freischütz* or Richard Wagner's *Mesitersinger* were every bit as popular in their time as Broadway musicals in our own day. The host of national monuments that sprang up in Germany at this time – the finally completed Cathedral in Cologne, the banqueting hall in the Marienburg of West Prussia, Schinkel's Kreuzberg Monument in Berlin – were mostly erected in the Gothic style, which was presumed to have been the authentic German idiom, to which architects must now return. It was many years before anyone noticed that the model for Cologne Cathedral had been the cathedral in Amiens.

And so it came about that the German state, so long and eagerly awaited and finally founded in 1871, was designed largely in the image of the middle ages. The hereditary presidency of the German Union was dignified by the title of 'Kaiser', although the position had not the slightest organic connection with the last of the Roman Emperors, the Habsburg Francis II, who had renounced the title in 1806. The newly resurrected German Union called itself an empire (*Deutsches Reich*), although it had nothing in common with the international and confessional constitution of the Holy Roman Empire. The propagandists of the latter-day empire liked to refer to the elderly Prussian king with his white beard as 'Barbablanca' to suggest that he was a reincarnation of Frederick Barbarossa. William I, in fact, would never have taken it into his head to found a German Empire, and he thought that his coronation in Versailles had been the 'most vexatious day of my life'. On that day, he remarked dolefully, the old Prussian state had been borne to its grave. His son, Frederick III, who reigned for a mere hundred days, thought in more topical terms: he wished to be styled Frederick IV, because he preferred to be numbered among the ancient Roman German rulers. His successor, William II, ill-starred in every respect, modelled himself on the Saxon Emperor, Otto the Great (912–73), embraced the latter's policy, and regarded the claims of his medieval predecessor to universal authority as the justification of German imperialism at the start of the twentieth century. In 1871 the German Empire was well on the way to becoming the leading industrial power in Europe and was scarcely matched anywhere in the modernity of its economic and scientific achievements – but the image that it cherished of itself was in fact resurrected from the dead.

These developments, so striking in the case of Germany, were paralleled elsewhere in Europe. Even those nation states of Western Europe that were ostensibly founded on strictly rational principles were no exception. The popular romantic novels of Sir Walter Scott, the elegantly elegiac essays of François René de Chateaubriand directed the public's gaze to a medieval world transfigured by a Christian faith from which allegedly both France and England derived their historical origins. Historians like Michelet and Carlyle sketched historical portraits in graphic language of great potency, aiming to make nations aware of their historical destiny. At the same time historic scenes and personalities were standardized, simplified and streamlined to ease their transition from the past into the present. Accounts given by English Whig historians deployed a simplified version of British constitutional history, representing it as a universal yardstick, a one-way street obviously leading mankind to liberty and progress. In France a scheme was laid down outlining the people's view of their own history – in defiance of the grand critical assaults on it by modern French historians. The thread tracing the identity of the French nation runs directly from the Capets down to the present day: Charlemagne and St Joan, the Sun King and Danton were all regarded as part of the living present. The *gesta dei per francos* of Guibert de Nogent from the eleventh century represented a prototype of the French national identity that has endured down to the present day; the memory of the storming of the Bastille in 1789 still has the power to unite the nation from the communists on the left to parties on the extreme Right. Even the great villains, Robespierre and Napoleon, have been rehabilitated and made to serve the greater glory of the *grande nation*.

The histories of the European nations have been constructed *ab initio* rather than reconstructed, and the more questionable the continuity of a national identity is, the more this is liable to be the case. How real was the link between the Hellenic race of ancient Greece and those Greeks who, to the delight of the European public, cast off the Turkish yoke in 1822, celebrating their *anagenisis*, the rebirth of classical Hellas? The Illyrian movement fought against the efforts of the Hungarian crown to reduce Croatia to a Hungarian province: the Croats were allegedly descendents of the ancient Illyrians, hence autochthonous and, like the inhabitants of the Balkans and of Venice in far-off times, the ruling nation among the Slavs. This view collided naturally with the historical claims of the Serbs, who traced their origins back to the medieval Serbian kingdom of Tsar Dušan, who, for his part, had already begun to challenge the supremacy of the Byzantine emperors in south-eastern Europe. Was it not, then, the mission of the Serbian nation to gather all the Balkan peoples together under its rule?

This kind of historical arrogance was not only meant to reinforce internal solidarity and the integration of a nation; it was also meant to provide evidence for more ambitious claims. Had it lacked any semblance of historical justification, the German annexation of Alsace and Lorraine in 1871 might have seemed like the arbitrary act of a conqueror. As it was, however, it might be argued that Alsace had once been German-speaking and part of the Reich, until Louis XIV exploited the weakness of the emperor and occupied Strasbourg. That was the reason why the palace of Versailles was chosen as the setting in which the Prussian King William I was proclaimed German Emperor. Through this symbolic act the 200-year-old shame of France's seizure of Alsace was to be formally expunged. Right down to the present day, given the bewildering mixture of nationalities in most parts of Europe, history is still being invoked in order to substantiate claims of a political or territorial kind, whether in the case of Greece which harks back to the empire of Alexander the Great and refuses to recognize a sovereign state under the name of Macedonia, or whether in the case of the Serbian defeat in 1389 on Kosovo Polje, the Field of Blackbirds, which is used to justify the repression of the Albanians who now inhabit the province of Kosovo. The historical memory of the nations is liable to teach them murderous lessons.

9

The 'People's Nations'
in Reality

We have described how the nations which Europeans of the twentieth century now take for granted came into being in the closing decades of the eighteenth century and the course of the nineteenth century: national mentalities bred by a distinctly limited number of scholars, journalists and men of letters – 'people's nations' potentially and in theory, but falling short still of any substantial existence. It is not easy to say, quoting Karl Marx, how the idea of the nation gripped the masses and became a material force, finding its way from the studies of the thinkers, the creators of languages and literatures, and the historians. When and for what specific reasons might a subject of the Habsburg monarchy take it into his head that he should feel above all that he was a Czech, a Hungarian, a Serb or an Italian? What prompted a citizen of Prussia, Brunswick, Sachsen-Gotha or Lippe-Schaumburg to consider himself a German, and to reckon that his membership of the German race counted for more than his loyalty to the house of his traditional ruler?

Obviously, war, enemy occupation, despoliation by an alien power and a sense of collective humiliation acted as catalysts in the emergence of a sense of national identity. It was in fact the powerful patriotic sentiments aroused by the march of Napoleon's armies across Europe that paved the way for the emergence of many European nations. The methods which had made possible Napoleon's political and military triumphs had to be turned against him: France had to be defeated by the weapons she herself had forged.

Another impulse that aroused many European peoples to a sense of their own identity in the years 1808–9 originated on the outskirts of the continent. Following the Thirty Years War and the abatement of her hegemonial ambitions Spain seemed to have turned her back on Europe, but her Bourbon monarchy survived for a time thanks to an accommodation arrived at with revolutionary France. The indirect rule that Napoleon exercised in this way did not satisfy him once he had become Emperor: he feared a British invasion of the Iberian peninsula, and he had also cast a greedy eye on the economic resources of Spanish America. A palace revolution hastened the pace of events: Napoleon then intervened and, under the pressure of a powerful French military presence, King Charles IV (1748–1819) renounced his crown, which Napoleon handed over on 4 June 1808 to his own brother Joseph (1768–1844), hitherto King of Naples. The whole of Spain rose in rebellion against the rule of a Napoleon, the insurrection being led by the clergy, who in any case detested the revolutionary ideas emanating from France. Everywhere committees, so-called *juntas*, were formed, which recognized only Ferdinand VII (1751–1833), the son of Charles IV, as King of Spain. The insurgent Spanish forces drove the French army of occupation back beyond the Ebro, while at the same time an English expeditionary force landed in Portugal and forced the French army there under the command of Marshal Junot to capitulate.

For the first time Napoleon had come up against an adversary who owed his fighting spirit to the same kind of revolutionary fervour that had inspired France for twenty years. He was no longer facing the standing army of some absolute ruler, but a loosely organized, albeit poorly trained band of fanatical *guerilleros*, who attacked in small groups and then withdrew, acknowledging no rules of warfare: they were elusive and apparently tireless. The motives of the Spanish rebels of 1808 were certainly very different from those of the French revolutionaries of 1789: the Spaniards were fighting for the traditional order, for their absolute rulers, for the Catholic faith – but above all for independence from the hated rule of the French. Napoleon failed to understand the enemy he was dealing with: as far as he was concerned, he was fighting against barbaric gangs of cattle-thieves and smugglers who were only interested in loot, and he believed he could bring the situation under control by a series of police actions. It was his false assessment of the power of a national passion to mobilize a people that brought about his downfall: '*Cette malheureuse guerre m'a perdu*,' he confessed ruefully in St Helena.[1]

French propaganda went to great lengths to play down events in Spain and to disguise French setbacks. But even French observers could not fail to notice that French army communiqués and reports in the press were not taken seriously by other subjugated European countries. A report needed only to be stamped as French for the opposite to be accepted as the truth, and even accurate accounts of events published in the *Moniteur* or in the official media of the Union of Rhenish States were scarcely credited.[2] And the field of public opinion was not the exclusive preserve of the French, even in Napoleon's day: there were any number of more or less independent newspapers and journals brought out by private publishers, who broadcast their views more or less cautiously from a national angle. There was, too, Spanish propaganda financed by England which appealed to the nations of Europe and made sure that the European press was kept well supplied with news items. Spanish proclamations, manifestos, broadsheets and pamphlets flooded Spain and the rest of Europe. Particularly common were publications modelled on proclamations by the Roman Catholic Church, such as were familiar to Catholics all over Europe. The Spanish 'Citizen's Catechism' which first appeared in Cartagena in May 1808, was distributed in hundreds of thousands of copies and translated into almost every European language. The full title was '*Catecismo civil, y breve compendio de las obligaciones del español, conomiciento practico de su libertad.*'

Tell me, child, who art thou?
A Spaniard.
What does that mean? A Spaniard?
An honest man.
How many duties hath such a man?
Three: he must be a Catholic Christian, he must defend
    his religion, his fatherland and its laws
    and die, rather than allow himself
    to be oppressed.
Who is our King?
Ferdinand the Seventh.
By what manner of love shall we be bound to him?
By the love that his virtue and his misfortune deserve.
Who is the enemy of our happiness?
The Emperor of the French.
Who, then, is he?
A new, infinitely bloodthirsty and rapacious monarch,
    the beginning of all evil, the end of all good:
    The essence of all vice and malice.
How many natures hath he?
Two: a satanic and a human nature [. . .]
Who are the French?
Former Christians and present heretics.
What hath led them into their new servitude?
False philosophy and the licence
    of their corrupted morals [. . .]
Shall this unrighteous regime soon pass away?
The opinion of those sages who understand politics
    is that its fall is close at hand . . . [3]

This text, to which many others might be added, has the hallmark of effective nationalistic propaganda, e.g. the definition
of national identity by reference to the enemy. The nation is
lauded as the hallowed victim of a foe who has strayed from the
path of righteousness, he is an incarnation of Satan and hence
outlawed from the community of men. In the fight against
him any means are justified. We must see Francisco Goya's
engravings *Desastres de la guerra* in the context of this
diatribe in order to gauge the fury and the unbridled

ferocity with which the Spanish revolt against French occupation was conducted in the cause of nationalism – a precedent for the barbaric nationalistic wars that have flouted every international convention and that are still afflicting Europe to the present day.

From the point of view of Paris, the Spanish rising had created a dangerous precedent: in December 1808 a despatch from the French embassy in Berlin reported that, 'in spite of the trifling successes of the Spaniards whom they so much admire, a remarkable number of people here have recently begun to repeat in German the rabble-rousing speeches that have of late inflamed the minds of the Spanish populace. It is high time that we answered these people – and not just through articles in the newspapers.'[4] In fact, the Prussian poet and dramatist Heinrich von Kleist (1777–1811), who was secretly in the pay of the Austrian propaganda service, was already working on a translation of the *Catecismo Civil*; it appeared in 1813 under the title of '*The Germans' Catechism*' and was circulated in numerous reprints.

Only the vaguest idea of what was happening in Spain penetrated as far as eastern Europe. What seemed most important was the fact that, in his confrontation with Spanish nationalist sentiment, Napoleon had for the first time met his match: the great Corsican was neither infallible nor invincible.

> It is a long time, it seems to me, since our anxious and gloomy forebodings turned so quickly into the most cheerful and animated expectation. Only a week ago we were thinking – and from what we then knew, quite rightly thinking – that we were on the brink of an abyss; now the only question that remains is whether we have the spirit and determination to take advantage of the highly auspicious turn of events that divine grace has once again vouchsafed us . . . It is obvious that Fortune has turned her back on Bonaparte and that his abominable career has come to a halt, that Europe may be saved, beginning with Spain . . .

This was how Friedrich von Gentz saw the situation in September 1808.[5] A British agent wrote from Königsberg:

You may imagine with what anxious anticipation everyone here is watching events in Spain, and that is understandable, for the fate of all of us depends on what
happens there, and no doubt Bonaparte has only tem-
porarily turned his gaze away from this country – if he
is victorious in Spain (which God forbid), he will always
find some pretext to coerce Prussia once again, or even to
wipe her off the map.[6]

Indeed, the possible fate of Spain posed a threat for the
whole continent: if Napoleon had ventured to sweep his Bourbon allies from their throne, who would then protect the
other crowns of Europe? This was the argument used by
the Austrian ambassador in Paris, Count Metternich, to con-
vince his chief, the Foreign Minister, Count Stadion, who
put it to the Emperor and to the Commander-in-Chief of
the army, Archduke Charles, on 13 April 1808. Napoleon
was clearly planning 'to see only kings of his own making
and of his own family and their dependents ruling throughout Europe'. Spain would inevitably be followed by Austria.[7]

This called, it seemed, for a drastic change in Austrian
policy. From this point on Austria was preparing for war
with France, and for the first time in Europe a traditional
regime was calling on the nation to form a united front
against a common foe. The lesson to be learned from Spain
was simply how to win battles, but this meant involving the
entire nation in the war effort and an enormous increase in
the resources of the state. There were, of course, familiar
ways of mobilizing a people: one of them was linked to the
name of Archduke John (1782–1859), who had learned from
Johann von Müller's *History of the Swiss Confederation* that
a people might defend itself against any attempt to subjugate
it only if it was inspired by a love of liberty, a sense of
community and a common will to resist the oppressor. In a
lengthy memorandum dated 17 May 1808 he proposed that
the entire population should be called to arms by means of a
territorial levy (*Landwehr*):

Here it is the masses that are called upon to fight, the

nation, all for one and one for all; it will not be difficult to move them to action . . . if the nation stands its ground, then Austria is invincible . . . a state in distress taking recourse to the customary measures under attack by a rapacious aggressor. This is the spur that will enable us to call up all our resources, induce us to put forth all our strength and will furnish us with yet more resources by making the cause of the state the common concern of the whole people.[8]

The suggestion was put into practice with an alacrity that was not regarded as typically Austrian: all discharged regular soldiers and all males between the ages of 18 and 45 who had hitherto been exempted from military service were enlisted in the territorial forces and first called to the colours on 27 June 1808. By the middle of August the first battalions of the reserve had already begun training.

Austria thus became, after France, the second European state to introduce universal military conscription, and she did so for much the same reasons. Apart from mobilizing the nation's resources in the interests of a decisive campaign, the intention was to do away with the old distinction between civilians and soldiers, so that the unity of the fatherland might be epitomized in its common defence.

It was realized, of course, that incorporating civilians into a military organization would not in itself necessarily turn them into zealous defenders of the state. Their enthusiasm would have to be engendered to begin with. The Austrian ambassador in Paris, Count Clemens Metternich (1763–1859), witnessed the daily application of the French system and wrote to Stadion:

Public opinion is the thing that matters most, it is something which, like religion, penetrates to the lowest level, where administrative measures have no effect. It is just as dangerous to despise public opinion as to spurn moral principles. Whereas, however, the latter may rise anew where an attempt has been made to eradicate them, this is not the case with public opinion, which calls for special consideration, assiduous and unremitting cultivation . . .[9]

The Austrian government overlooked no single channel of propaganda in its efforts to arouse public opinion. New newspapers, like the *Patriotic Bulletin (Vaterländische Blätter)* were launched with the express purpose of stirring patriotic sentiments in the hearts of the country's citizens, and a deluge of broadsheets, mostly translated from Spanish or English, descended on the populace, thousands of patriotic odes, romances and dramas were written, itinerant orators travelled up and down the country, so that the glorious gospel of the united Austrian nation might be brought to the notice of every illiterate peasant. And similar means were employed to prepare the soil of neighbouring countries for the coming conflict. In Bavaria, Württemberg and other states of the Rhenish Union, Austrian propaganda fell on fertile soil, for it coincided with the conscription of recruits to the auxiliary corps provided by the German states for the French campaign in Spain. Even in the Bavarian army, which had been numbered among Napoleon's staunchest allies, considerable misgivings were voiced concerning the Spanish venture. Austrian propaganda thus made its impact at an auspicious moment. In the conservative provinces of Bavaria, skilfully edited reports from Spain of desecrated churches and devastated farmland made a deep impression. In more recently acquired provinces of Bavaria such appeals had an effect on the traditional loyalties of the Franconian and Swabian inhabitants of the imperial cities, and on the subjects of former ecclesiastical principalities.

On 10 April 1809 Austrian troops crossed the Inn, Munich and Nürnberg were occupied, French and Bavarian contingents in the Tyrol were forced to surrender, and Archduke Charles (1771–1847), the Austrian Commander-in-Chief, pushed on in the direction of Regensburg with the intention of attacking the French corps that was stationed there. At that time it was the custom for generals marching into alien territory to issue proclamations justifying their intentions and reassuring the population who were thus to be exposed to the rigours of warfare. The Archduke Charles's proclamation, drafted by Frederick Count Stadion, brother to the Foreign Minister, and the writer Friedrich Schlegel, struck a novel note: it was not addressed to the subjects of the King of Bavaria, but to 'the German nation', and it declared 'Our cause is Germany's cause. With Austria, Germany will be a free and happy land: she can become both free and happy only with the aid of Austria. Germans! Take stock of your situation! Accept the help we offer you! Play a part in your own salvation!'[10] What the difference was between the Austrian and the German nation was not entirely clear but, on the other hand, it did not seem to present a problem. Even more explicit was a further appeal, 'To the nations of Germany!' that was issued four days later: 'Copy the fine example set by Spain. Do not shrink from the bloody battle to come, for it is certain to end in our victory.'[11]

Only a few months later the war had already been lost. The Austrian statesmen had gravely miscalculated when they opted for war. Napoleon had turned up in the Central European theatre of operations with the main body of his troops much more rapidly than anyone could have expected. Prussia was neutral, England held back. But, above all, the novel expedient in which such high hopes had been placed, simply did not work: the attempt to arouse the patriotic feelings of the people to the point where they would rebel against Napoleonic rule failed. It was only in the Tyrol and Vorarlberg that the spark ignited a conflagration. In Germany, Austrian propaganda had to circumvent the more or less stringent censorship of the Rhenish Union. It also had to contend with French counter-propaganda, which had in the past been particularly effective in Bavaria.

Not that Austrian propaganda had not reached the people to whom it was addressed: reports from the police and agents in Berlin, Kassel and Munich reveal that, even long before the outbreak of hostilities, expectations and even hopes of an Austrian success were running high amongst the population, even in the lower classes of society. But no more than a handful of Prussian and Westphalian troops were actually mustered. In open defiance of the king's instructions they went into action and were duly defeated. Their action was not sufficient to act as a primer for a general rising. The inertia of the country's citizens and peasantry, their reluctance to run risks, were simply too great to be overcome. One major reason was that they were not sure where their loyalties lay. As long as their local rulers, and above all the King of Prussia, were not prepared to desert from the French camp, and regarded resistance to Napoleon as rebellion against their own authority, then any summons to rebellion was bound to smack of Jacobinism. Where risings did take place, in Hesse and in southern Germany, for example, this happened in areas where regimes had changed several times during the preceding years. The demands of the insurgent peasantry of Marburg, Mergentheim or Stockach were invariably vague and boiled down to the restoration of the old, pre-revolutionary order. The farm labourers who joined Colonel Dörnberg in his abortive expedition to Kassel to depose Napoleon's brother, King Jerome of Westphalia, carried a red velvet banner with the old imperial eagle,[12] and in the insurgent areas of south-west Germany officials confirmed that 'the spirit of rebellion was spurred on by the hope of a return to Austrian rule.'[13] Otherwise, these risings conformed to a familiar pattern: there had always been peasant risings in those areas, whenever the old order of things was changed – in this case it was conscription into the army on the French model that triggered off the rising, or, alternatively, dissatisfaction with the burden of taxation. In 1809 there was, then, no nationwide mobilization of the people with the aim of shaking off the French yoke and founding a single nation state. But ever since the Spanish insurrection and the Austrian war of 1808 the rebellion of the European nations against Napoleon had been at the back of men's minds. With Russian, Swedish and British assistance this rebellion was finally to break out in the so-called Liberation Wars of 1813.

It is not all that easy to find out what 'mobilization of the nation' actually implied in practice, and contemporary sources are prone to exaggerate and idealize. Sources offering statistical data in the manner of present-day public opinion polls are exceptional. However, Linda Colley has carried out research into the growth of popular patriotic sentiment in England at the turn of the eighteenth century, scrutinizing the applications of volunteers to join the militia which was raised to meet the threat of a French invasion.[14] Her findings may be summed up as follows: the government's appeal for volunteers to join the colours in 1803 achieved on average a response from about 50 per cent of the male population between the ages of 17 and 55, with the Scots and Welsh being distinctly under-represented. It is noticeable that the rate of response was in step with the degree of industrialization and urbanization in any given county. Apart from artisans in the towns, it was mainly members of the upper and educated professional classes who responded to the appeal.

It is remarkable how closely these findings correspond to the impression we have of the volunteers involved in the Wars of Liberation in 1813. On 3 February of that year King Frederick William III summoned Prussia's youth to volunteer for service in light infantry units. 'The King sent out his call, and they all came,' ran the patriotic Prussian legend – but in fact the Prussian people responded to their king's patriotic appeal in a variety of ways. The 'educated classes', graduates, civil servants, students and sixth-formers were over-represented by something like a factor of five; that is also the case with urban craftsmen, who were recorded in the Prussian register of trades and occupations as constituting some 7 per cent of the population. In fact they provided no less than 40 per cent of the volunteers. The rural population accounted for about 75 per cent of Prussia's inhabitants, but no more than 18 per cent of the volunteers came from that class.

A comparison between the English and the Prussian data reveals similar trends: urban sections of the population were willing to be mobilized for the defence of their country, those groups in fact who were normally inclined to oppose the traditional political and social order and to support the spread of industrialization in its early stages – the educated class, property-owners and craftsmen. The rural population, on the other hand, who were generally credited with a particularly high degree of loyalty and regarded as especially docile, showed little sign of patriotic zeal. The comparison seems to show in general that it was not traditional loyalty to an established dynasty that played the major part in the social and intellectual mobilization of Europe against Napoleon, but rather some sense of a common cause in the spirit of the *levée en masse* of the French Revolution. Indeed, the mobilization of the masses throughout the nation was praised by the Prussian General von Gneisenau (1760–1831) as a weapon that had been 'purloined from the arsenal of the Revolution', while to subjects of the British crown, the appeal to patriotic sentiment was justified by a British officer as 'recourse to the same expedient for the defence of our independence as France has used so effectively during the last ten years'.[15]

Mass mobilization was possible only because, in the course of the world war that had raged uninterruptedly since the summer of 1792 and that was to last until it ended on the battlefield of Waterloo in 1815, the techniques of mass indoctrination and propaganda had been raised to a fine art. If we look closely, for example, at the barrage of propaganda to which the people of Prussia were subjected, and which was financed by British, Austrian and Russian subsidies as well as by Prussian money, then we can clearly identify the ideas on which national patriotic enthusiasm were built.

The main motive of volunteers during the war, a motive that overshadowed all others, was clearly of a negative nature: hatred of Napoleon and of France. Ample evidence of this may be found in the literary diatribes of Kleist, Arndt, Körner and Friedrich Schlegel. Even the mild-mannered Clemens Bretano, for example, was capable of this doggerel:

> Bayonets amain,
> Seek not in vain
> To cast off the chain:
> As far as the Seine
> Let not one foe remain!

There was an endless succession of blood-curdling ditties in this vein, which, judging by – admittedly incomplete – figures for print-runs, were circulated on a vast scale. Evidence of hatred of the enemy may also be culled from most contemporary personal accounts of the campaign that are available to us – memoirs, diaries and letters. It was hatred that provided the yeast for the ferment of those years and that constituted their emotional common denominator. This is indicated, incidentally, by the spirit in which Prussian volunteer units waged their campaigns, avoiding the taking of prisoners wherever they could. 'No quarter to be given,' was the order regularly given before an attack. Contemporary accounts of actions in which volunteer battalions were engaged remind us of the atrocities we have grown all too familiar with in the ideological mass warfare of the twentieth century.

The second major theme in appeals for the active commitment of the nation in the war of liberation was 'freedom', and there can be little doubt, in spite of subsequent assertions to the contrary, that what was meant was not a set of concrete demands for incorporation in a liberal constitution, but simply freedom from French tyranny. Certainly, various slogans, like the title of Max von Schenkendorf's popular song, 'The freedom that I mean', might be understood in more senses than one, but there is not one statement in all this war propaganda, nor in the testimony of those involved in the fighting, that put the call for 'freedom' into the context of any programme of political reform.

In the end the war was glorified as a battle for the people and their fatherland, and any amount of lip-service was indeed paid to the German people and the German fatherland. In most cases, however, these tributes were based on distinctions drawn in nebulous poetic terms between the Germans and their French enemies. Germany does figure as a cultural and linguistic entity, but there is never any suggestion that Prussian particularism might be eliminated and Prussia absorbed into a German nation state. Any suggestion of a nation in the sense implied by subsequent slogans in favour of national unification is simply lacking. The German fatherland of the War of Liberation had not yet assumed any definite shape. It was simply a poetic, historical and utopian idea that wore, in its earthly incarnation, the black and white colours of Prussia. The appeal of the Prussian King to his subjects to be 'both Prussians and Germans' which, ironically, gained him the reputation of a Jacobin with his royal colleagues of the Rhenish League, merely defined at that juncture a kind of interim coalescence of Prussia and Germany – at least from the Prussian point of view.

All these ideas and emotions were assimilated into feverish activity: the commonest syntactical feature of the versified propaganda of those years was the imperative mood, a point-blank summons lacking any specific aim, a simple 'Arise!' 'Up and away!' 'So, arise now, arise to peril and to death!' Theodor

Körner, for instance, wrote: 'Arise, my people, the beacon's flame flares up!' The laconic motto of the Lützow Volunteers was 'Through!' This lust for action at any price, in defiance of every prudent military maxim, found apt expression in Blücher's nickname, 'Marshal Forwards'. The sense of national solidarity felt by the masses – and the same might be said of all Central and Western Europe in the early nineteenth century – was thus still diffuse, not related to any positive political programme, governed merely by the image of a common foe. This alone was what seemed to establish a national identity. With the coming of peace and a return to civilian life, the sense of belonging to a great national community faded into the background for the moment. One or two generations had to elapse before a lasting awareness of national identity could be implanted in the mass of the population.

In those nation states of Western Europe that were already politically stabilized, however, there were schools and armed forces from which the idea of the nation could infiltrate into the population at large. In Central and Eastern Europe this function had to be performed by a network of books and newspapers, political parties and associations, coffee-house clubs and social gatherings. In this environment slogans and policies promoting the idea of the nation occupied the minds of the members and their friends and were thus disseminated throughout society at large.

It was mainly the existence of societies and clubs that transmitted the concept of the nation to the generality of the population. This did not happen by mere chance, for the free association of individuals, defining their own aims and free to join or leave an association as they wished, was calculated to undermine or disrupt the class-ridden system of middle-class society. 'Societies and associations', wrote Thomas Nipperdey, 'are one of the main means by which a new middle class combining the older bourgeoisie and new recruits from a variety of professions, from educated circles, commerce and industry, from the civil service and the liberal professions, gradually came to constitute the concrete reality of a specific lifestyle, and not just an idea.'[16] The nineteenth century was a century of societies constituting a network of associations with the most diverse aims and objects, and there was hardly an individual who was not a member of at least one such society. Given the prominent part played by music and song in disseminating slogans and ideas calculated to inspire the public with patriotic sentiment, the importance of choral societies can hardly be overestimated. That choral singing was regarded at an early stage as a useful channel for inspiring patriotic feeling is evident, for instance, from the statutes of the 'German Society' of Ickstein dated 24 August 1814. This was a nationalistic secret society, under police surveillance and ultimately disbanded because of its 'revolutionary plotting'. In the statutes we read:

> Since our nation is so sadly lacking in songs that befit our times, and since men, especially the untutored classes, are wont to express their feelings solemnly in song, the Society endeavours to the best of its ability to meet this need. It resolves, therefore, that every member should endeavour in his own circle of society to popularize truly German songs, such as those of Theodor Körner, and, on the other hand, to eradicate those vulgar ditties that are presently current among our people.

This suggestion seems to have been regarded by the police as particularly subversive, for in the official copy of the statutes it has been underlined and singled out by an exclamation mark.[17]

Side by side with the choral societies we find the gymnastic associations, which propagated a distinctly militant brand of the nationalistic ideology in many countries. The pattern was set by the Berlin Gymnastic Association founded in 1811 by 'Turnvater' Jahn to train German youth for eventual battle against the French. It operated with a mixture of physical culture, character training and patriotic propaganda. By 1818 there were in Germany no fewer than 12,000 gymnasts, who considered themselves pioneers in the promotion of the national idea. In 1820 the gymnastic clubs were banned under the terms of the Carlsbad Decrees, although most of them carried on with their activities underground. Following their reconstitution in 1842 the number of clubs and members grew rapidly: by 1862 there were 135,000 German gymnasts, who aspired to be the nations' preceptors through their public displays and their image as a rallying point for nationalist feeling. Similar organizations sprang up in the Habsburg dominions, promoting German patriotic sentiment in Austria, but in sharp opposition to Habsburg rule in Hungary and even more so, in Bohemia, where the founding in 1862 of the Sokol (Falcon) movement for sport and physical culture gave a powerful boost to national awareness among the Czech lower middle class. In Austria and the Catholic areas of Germany, Marksmen's Clubs (*Schützenvereine*) had long been a feature of community life, and these societies also tended to be inspired by patriotic motives. Student fraternities should also be borne in mind in this context. The universities as the focus of middle-class pride in the educational system were regarded as hotbeds of nationalistic ideas, so that they became a principal target of the Carlsbad Decrees by which the rulers of the Holy Alliance attempted in 1819 to damp down a seething eruption of nationalist feeling.

As distinct from such popular societies, the other main proponent of European nationalist movements, the liberal press operated on a rather higher social level. It was, of course, as committed as ever to the educational ideals of the middle class and addressed itself to a relatively small readership, generally in rationally argued terms. The liberal press had a dual function in the context of the 'national movement': firstly, it served as a vehicle for protests against the existing political system in a much more directly polemical sense than the societies. Indignant responses were aroused in the liberal educated classes by bans on newspapers and by political censorship. The clamour for political freedom that had been raised in these enlightened circles ever since the eighteenth century had been – in Germany at least – essentially a call for tolerance and freedom of speech. In this respect Germany differed from the bourgeoisie in Western Europe and in England: what the middle class in England understood by freedom was epitomized in free trade, while in France, Spain and Italy what was sought was active participation in the political process. In Germany the trenches dug during the religious wars had scarcely been filled in, and the measure of a citizen's freedom was his monarch's personal degree of tolerance. This is why penalized newspaper editors and censored authors played such a prominent part in the first stirrings of revolution around 1830. In the second place, it was the liberal press that encouraged the forming of political parties: 'parties', 'factions' and 'associations' crystallized round those newspapers which had first generated a public for debates in the parliamentary arena. Suggestions that were thrown up by societies and associations reflecting a public mood or an image in the public mind assumed more specific form in the press and ultimately emerged as political slogans and platforms.

In Germany and throughout Northern and Western Europe the middle class promoted the founding of societies, associations and pressure groups, rallying an increasingly large section of society behind national slogans, in spite of bans and obstructions imposed by the authorities. In Eastern and Southern Europe, however, the same function often had to be performed by secret societies, which often adopted the organizational methods of older secret societies from the eighteenth century, like the Freemasons and the Illuminati. This applied mainly to countries under foreign domination, where the secret society seemed to be the best form of organization for the clandestine preparation of insurrection. A prototype of such societies and a model widely adopted in Europe was the *Carboneria*, which had come into existence about 1806 in southern Italy and which had initially led the fight against French rule. After the fall of Napoleon and the ending of his family's rule in the Kingdom of Naples, the *Carboneria* had opposed any government which did not support the unification of Italy under a liberal constitution. The *Carbonari* took their name from the charcoal burners, presumably on account of the latter's obscure, backwoods existence. They set themselves up, not just as nationalists and democrats, but also as rigorous moralists. Their deliberately ambiguous sign of identification was I.N.R.I., which, apart from its well-known scriptural sense, was alleged to signify *Iustum Necare Reges Italiae* – 'it is right to kill Italy's kings'. Although the *Carboneria* at one time undoubtedly had a large membership – although the figure of 300,000 sometimes quoted is not supported by evidence and seems unreasonably high – it was nowhere notably successful in inciting and carrying out insurrections. The risings in Naples and Piedmont in 1820 – and in the Vatican state in 1831 – were quickly put down by Austrian troops. The leaders fled to France and Switzerland, and the *Carboneria* was revived in those countries, this time under radical republican rather than expressly nationalistic auspices, and now directing its attention to Spain, Poland and Germany. In time a virtual symbiosis came about, involving French, Italian and Polish politicians of a democratic persuasion, who founded the *Charbonnerie Démocratique Universelle* in Paris in 1831. It is almost impossible to reconstruct this organization, since it consisted of a great many clandestine leagues, lodges and semi-secret political clubs. Unrest was fomented in Lyons and Paris, partisans were despatched to Poland and support organized for an assault on the main guard-house in Frankfurt, when a handful of democrats attempted to launch a *putsch* against the *Bundestag*. But all these enterprises foundered and the *Carboneria*, a bogey of European politics since 1815, languished and dwindled, to be succeeded by a new and more energetic secret movement, more youthfully high-spirited than seriously political – the 'Young Europe' of the Italian revolutionary leader, Giuseppe Mazzini (1805–72). Mazzini had belonged to the *Carboneria*, but had been disillusioned by the sectarian nature of that organization. His own secret organization, founded in Marseilles in 1831 under the name of 'Young Italy', was soon matched by a 'Young Germany' and a 'Young Poland', which together constituted 'Young Europe'. The organization was intended to consist of small, hand-picked cells, active but strictly disciplined and inspired by a profound faith in god. These groups would lead the struggle for liberation and the establishment of national republics in the whole of Europe, inspiring the populace by their example. Mazzini's *putsch* in Piedmont in 1834 joined the long list of bungled attempts at revolution in Italy during the nineteenth century, and 'Young Europe', like other secret societies failed to make any enduring political impact. Nevertheless, the example it set constituted an unremitting emotional appeal to malcontents everywhere to rally under the banner of the nationalists, and this alone was enough to unsettle the powers that be.

It was in the Rhine crisis of 1840 that the nationalism of the masses was manifested for the first time as a distinctive factor in politics, indeed, as an issue of the utmost significance. The Rhine crisis was precipitated by the French government under the leadership of Adolphe Thiers. France had just suffered a humiliating setback in its Far Eastern policy, and the government was seeking to compensate for a loss of public confidence by adopting an aggressive posture towards France's continental neighbours, demanding, for instance, the restoration of the country's 'natural frontier on the Rhine.' Thiers was not so much manipulating public opinion as taking his lead from it. In Germany a counter-campaign was mounted to stir up public opinion there. It began in the Rhineland, but ultimately involved the whole country, reaching almost every sector of the population and clearly demonstrating the power of the national idea to unite the whole of Germany. Nikolaus Becker's 'Song of the Rhineland': 'They shall not have it, our freeborn German Rhine', became a kind of unofficial national anthem almost overnight. Max Schneckenburger's 'Watch on the Rhine' and Hoffmann von Fallersleben's *'Deutschland-Lied'* were also composed in this vortex of patriotic fervour. For the first time ministerial cabinets in Germany sensed an impulse from the grassroots that was imposing a policy on them. Metternich detected a whiff of Jacobinism in the German air: he consequently resisted pressure from Prussia and other moderately large states for changes in the military clauses of the constitution of the Rhineland states and for the taking of military precautions. At the same time the two leading German powers agreed in November 1840 on a common operational plan in case of war, referring explicitly to the 'mood of the nation'. The following year the *Bundestag* consented to the construction of federal fortifications in Rastatt and Ulm. The Rhine crisis petered out after Thier's ministry had been dismissed by the king at the end of October 1840 and replaced by a government under Guizot, who reverted to a policy based on a European balance of power. But the potential force of mass nationalism had made itself felt for the first time, and since then it has governed the policies of European states to an increasing degree as an independent political factor against which, in the long run, no claim of a government to represent its people could hope to prevail. The Rhine crisis of 1840 marked a historical dividing line: as long as the evolution of the states in Central and Eastern Europe had offered a range of viable alternatives, there had been a chance of enlisting support from the existing states among the parties and groups engaged in the political debate but it had now become obvious that there was no viable alternative to the nation state.

Part III

Nation States

10

The Revolutionary Nation
State 1815–1871

The nation state was the secular organization of the nation's power, declared Max Weber. In the nation state the nation is not content to be merely the sum total of all its members: the people are identical with the nation, which sees itself not just as a cultural, but also as a political entity. The nation as constituted by the people finds and evolves its identity within the state; it is in the context of the nation state that a people is free to govern itself, free from alien rule.

At the beginning of the nineteenth century it was far from self-evident that a state might be constituted as a nation state. The statesmen who set about shaping a new political order for Europe at the Congress of Vienna still had very divergent notions of the future community of states. For Prince Metternich (1773–1859), who was to be, along with the Russian Tsar Alexander (1777–1825) and the British Foreign Minister, Lord Castlereagh (1769–1822), the architect of the new Europe, Italy was no more than a 'geographical concept', its unification as one state unthinkable. His most intimate adviser, Friedrich von Gentz (1766–1832), declared that the existence of Germany as a single state was a perilous illusion: 'The unification of all the German tribes in a single, undivided state' was no more than a dream that had been refuted by a thousand years of experience and ultimately cast aside. 'It is incapable of realization by any operation of human ingenuity, nor can it be enforced by the bloodiest of revolutions; it is an aim pursued only by madmen.' Showing a fair degree of prophetic insight, Gentz concluded his speculation with a warning that if the idea of national unity gained the upper hand in Europe, 'then a wasteland of bloody ruins will be the only legacy that awaits our descendants.'[1]

That was the fear that haunted the statesmen of Europe as they set about refashioning the continent after the fall of Napoleon. They had looked into the abyss and escaped with no more than a fright, and they were agreed on one thing, and one thing only: there must never again be a revolution in Europe – and the very idea of a state deriving its authority from an entire nation was a revolutionary principle *par excellence*. The diplomatic correspondence of the day is full of sombre warnings of the perils of this national idea, *'une maladie grave de l'état social en Europe'*, as the French emissary to the Frankfurt *Bundestag* put it.[2] Everywhere there was an urge to return to the old, pre-revolutionary system of sovereign states ruled by ancient dynasties that had kept the peace by means of checks and balances on the model of the Peace of Westphalia in 1648. Spain and Portugal were restored under their former ruling families, Holland was enlarged by the former Austrian Netherlands, later to become Belgium, Switzerland was reconstituted, Sweden stayed united with Norway, and since the Pentarchy, the club of five major European powers, was unthinkable without France, the latter was left intact within its 1792 frontiers, playing a major part in the Viennese peace negotiations, as if there had never been a war lasting for decades between France and the rest of Europe. It was the last time in the history of Europe that statesmen were in a position to pursue a rational policy that balanced the interests of all the parties and kept the peace without taking account of the emotions of the masses and the hatred of one people for another.

Certainly, even in the deliberations at the committee meetings of the Viennese commission, the spirit of the new age was present, a dread of brute force unsanctioned by any higher idea or principle. It was the wish of the Russian Tsar Alexander I that Europe's rulers should enter into a 'Holy Alliance', a pact founded on the Christian religion and the legitimate, i.e. monarchical and dynastic order of the European states. The 'Holy Alliance' was meant to be the response to the revolutionary demand for the establishment of nation states. In his visionary enthusiasm for the idea Alexander I was convinced that he could forge a bond between the nations and the monarchs. Metternich, on the other hand, the strategist of the new order, confided in his notes, 'Abstract ideas count for very little. We take things as they are, and look for those factors that may save us from becoming prisoners of illusions about the real world.'[3]

There were others, it appeared, who were indeed prisoners of illusion: the Polish general and national hero, Tadeusz Kosciusko (1748–1817), for instance, who turned up in Vienna to demand the unification and independence of Poland, which was nevertheless once more partitioned at the behest of the major powers – this time into no fewer than five parts. Or the champion of German youth, 'Turnvater' Friedrich Ludwig Jahn (1778–1852), who made his appearance one day on the banks of the Danube, gazed at in astonishment by elegant Viennese society on account of his quaint, old-fashioned 'German costume', his luxuriant beard and his blunt, blustering manner. He was regarded as a buffoon, because he had dared to remind the German princes of the promise of German unification they had given at the time of the War of Liberation. 'Jacobins in bearskins' such enthusiasts for a German nation state were dubbed: if their demands were to be met, would it not indeed be tantamount to a European revolution?

The entire carefully balanced European system depended on Central Europe remaining fragmented, diffuse and powerless. It was on this system that the Treaty of Westphalia had depended, and the Congress of Vienna still relied on it. The statesmen assembled in Vienna were profoundly concerned because the 'Germanophiles' were bent on unifying Germany and turning her into a nation state. 'They are attempting to overturn an order that offends their pride and to replace all the governments of the country by a single authority,' the

French Foreign Minister Talleyrand wrote to Louis XVIII from Vienna.

> Allied with them are people from the universities, young-
> sters who have been primed with their theories, and
> all those who ascribe to German particularism all the
> sufferings that have been inflicted on the country in the
> course of the wars that have been fought there. The
> unity of the German fatherland is their slogan, their
> faith and their religion, they are ardent to the point of
> fanaticism . . . Who can calculate the consequences, if the
> masses in Germany were to combine into a single whole
> and turn aggressive? Who can say where a movement of
> that kind might stop?[4]

Thus, the principle of nationality was acknowledged only where it was linked to the legitimate rule of a monarch: in Great Britain, France, Spain, Portugal, the Netherlands and Sweden, i.e. in Northern and Western Europe. There were obvious reasons why, in the period of restoration following the violent upheavals of the French Revolution and the Napoleonic Wars, countries should take their place in history which already had the features of nation states. In all these cases there had long been stable states, consolidated in cultural as well as political and administrative terms, with ruling classes who had for centuries regarded themselves as 'nations'. Ever since the internal upheavals of the Glorious Revolution of 1688 in England and the great Revolution of 1789 in France, the proportion of the population participating in the process of government, either directly by election, or else by some form of plebiscite, had been steadily enlarged: in other words, what had once been 'aristocratic nations' had been turned into 'people's nations', or they were at least in process of being thus transformed. In the case of these countries it had already become perfectly clear what would apply by and large to the rest of Europe. The idea of the nation was the logically consistent answer to Europe's choice of its path into the modern age: as more and more individuals became politically aware and acquired the chance of participating in the political process, the idea of the nation gained increasing prominence. The nation and democracy became two sides of the same coin, the nation state turned out to be the appropriate contemporary setting and the guarantor of democracy and parliamentary rule. Rousseau and the politicians who had framed the constitution after the French Revolution had as good a claim to be the intellectual progenitors of this development as John Locke might have had in the aftermath of the Glorious Revolution of 1688: the nation they had visualized as a commonwealth of its citizens had now come of age.

A case in point was France. Certainly, the restoration of the Bourbons in 1814 had an effect on the country, but the attempts of the ultra-royalists and Charles I (1757–1836), successor to the prudently cautious Louis XVIII (1755–1824), to turn the state into a mere tool in the hands of the land-owning aristocracy did not succeed. Even though the third estate, hardly changed, incidentally, since the revolutionary constitution of 1791, was hamstrung by a restrictive electoral law based on a property qualification – until 1830 there were never more than 100,000 Frenchmen with the vote – the Bourbon constitution of 1814, the *charte*, nevertheless recognized the people's right to sovereignty and to political representation, while the civic principles of liberty, equality and property, albeit in strictly circumscribed terms, were endorsed in the constitution. An attempt by the King to curb the increasingly aggressive opposition through censorship and a drastic restriction of the franchise led to the revolution of July 1830 and to the proclamation of national sovereignty, i.e. to the supremacy of the chamber of deputies over the monarch's prerogative. King Louis Philippe (1773–1850) did not swear his oath of allegiance on holy scripture, but on the constitution, and the coronation ceremony did not take place in the traditional setting of a cathedral like Reims or Notre Dame in Paris, but in the presence of the Chamber of Deputies. True, the representative assembly of the people remained to a large extent the preserve of the propertied middle class, because the property qualification embodied in the electoral law was merely modified and not repealed. But unremitting pressure from a left wing extending from liberal intellectuals and industrialists eager for reform to a radical republican opposition, ensured that the regime of the *juste milieu* would be no more than a transitional phase. It was succeeded in 1848 by a radical democratic republic, which, like the republic of the first great French revolution, was, in its turn, abolished by a dictator who at once proceeded to have himself proclaimed emperor. But the regime of Napoleon III (1808–73), like that of Napoleon I, collapsed as the result of a military defeat, and was followed by the Third Republic. In spite of these numerous changes of regime undergone by France during the nineteenth century, the general trend was clear enough: it was towards a democratic form of state with elements of the plebiscite that derived its mandate, at home and abroad, from the sovereignty of the people.

The case of England was not significantly different in principle. It is true that here it was not the one and indivisible nation that had seized power. The idea of popular sovereignty and a written constitution as in France was, in terms of English constitutional tradition, what Edmund Burke called 'the rape of reality by reason'. Ever since the days of the Glorious Revolution there had emerged in England a balance of power between the crown, the higher nobility and the landowning squirearchy. A further factor was represented by the commercial middle class of the self-governing City of London. The English parliamentary system at the beginning of the nineteenth century had in fact many of the features of an *ancien régime* without an absolute ruler. The Parliament at Westminster did indeed claim to represent the nation as a whole, but not as direct representation of the people (real representation): it represented the vital interests of the country (virtual representation). But by the end of the eighteenth century at the latest, it was obvious to everyone that the English Parliament no longer satisfied even these traditional standards. It was electoral corruption and bribery of the members that acted in fact as the lubricant of the parliamentary process, and a fair proportion of the constituencies were in the hands or pockets of the crown or of noble families. Besides, the population explosion and incipient industrialization had led to considerable changes in the distribution of the population. New economic centres with their rapidly expanding populations, cities like Manchester, Birmingham and Sheffield were not represented in Parliament at all, whereas tiny constituencies like the notorious Old Sarum, which virtually existed only on paper, sent members to Westminster.

The surprising thing about the great electoral reform of 1832, which was regarded by contemporaries as downright revolutionary, was that it entailed only relatively minor changes. These changes were sufficient, however, to transform and modernize the parliamentary system to an unprecedented degree. Nothing had been further from the minds of the Whig high aristocracy who actually proposed the reform, than the democratization of the English parliamentary system. They had been trying to take advantage for their own ends of the increasingly radical criticism that had been expressed up and down the country ever since the days of the French Revolution and that primarily reflected the ideas of the American Revolution. The intention had been to carry out cautious corrections and eliminate anomalies in the electoral process, thus restoring the effectiveness of Parliament, which had been undermined by corruption. The boundaries of the constituencies were redrawn and the number of those entitled to vote was very modestly increased from some 500,000 to 813,000. But in the long run these relatively minor adjustments altered the entire political system of Great Britain. The old methods of manipulating election results and influencing members of parliament became increasingly difficult to operate: the outcome of elections became uncertain, and the response of MPs less predictable.

The power to command parliamentary majorities was seen to slip away from the crown and its supporting aristocratic elite. The autonomy of the lower house increased, and it soon became apparent that the crown could no longer exercise its most cherished privilege, the power to appoint or dismiss an administration without the consent of Parliament. In this way, the pressure of liberal – occasionally even radically democratic – public opinion, together with fundamental economic changes and consequent social changes, as well as the readiness of the upper classes to accept a gradual process of evolution, led more or less automatically to an opening up of the English political establishment, and hence to an increasingly broad mandate for government. Certainly, the process took a comparatively long time: the English electoral law was only gradually made more democratic, female suffrage was not introduced until after the First World War and, strictly speaking, the evolution of parliamentary democracy in England was not completed until 1948, when separate parliamentary representation of British universities was abolished. The process of turning England into a nation state differed from that in France, but the end result was the same.

The ways in which France and England approached national statehood influenced to varying degrees the emergence of almost all the countries of Western Europe as nation states. The revolutionary example of France, with a national constitution leading to the establishment of a nation state, was followed in 1820 by Spain (where the constitutional era lasted no more than three years and was followed by an absolutist reactionary regime), and in 1831 by Belgium. On the other hand, it was more the evolutionary English example that influenced the Scandinavian countries and the Netherlands. In these countries, where the monarchy forfeited its direct political authority and influence, it tended to become both a symbol and the representative of the nation state and its historic roots. It is no mere chance that this is where the monarchy has survived wars, revolutions and workers' governments down to the present day.

In Central Europe, that is, in Germany and Italy, the situation was totally different. The political fragmentation of this region and the direct influence exercised by the peripheral powers on the constitution and the political organization of Central Europe had not come about by accident but were the logical outcome of the overall European order. It was only the amorphous nature of Central Europe that had kept the balance of the continent over the centuries, and a glance at the map will show the reason: it was Central Europe, from the Baltic to the Tyrrhenian Sea that kept the great powers apart, kept them at a distance and prevented head-on collisions. This region was a diplomatic glacis in peacetime, the major European theatre of operations in the event of clashes. What mattered was to prevent any undue concentration of power in the centre of

Europe, for whoever controlled that territory – whether an existing major power, or some new power emerging in Central Europe itself – might, in alliance with some other European power, become mistress of the entire continent. That was why any concentration of power in Germany or Northern Italy seemed to challenge the stability of Europe. The inevitable consequence was the formation of hostile coalitions, which were all the more effective in that any Central European power aspiring to hegemony in Europe would have to assert itself on a number of fronts, without itself having defensible natural frontiers. For this reason the independence of small – indeed minuscule – Italian and German states seemed in the eyes of their neighbours to guarantee European freedom, the equilibrium of the European states, and ultimately their very existence. That is why, in the Treaty of Westphalia of 1648 the European powers combined to guarantee the existence of more than 300 miniature German principalities and imperial free cities. This was how the situation was seen by the statesmen of England, France, Russia, Prussia and Austria who were rearranging the continent of Europe at the Congress of Vienna.

On this occasion at least 'national' federations of states were planned for Germany and Italy, but it was only in Germany that a German Union (*Deutscher Bund*), more or less a secularized successor to the Holy Roman Empire, actually came into existence. It comprised no more than a loose association of thirty-nine sovereign states and municipalities with a standing conference of delegates, the *Bundestag*, as its sole common constitutional organ. It was presided over by the Austrian Emperor, but voting rights were so allocated that it was not possible for Austria or Prussia to outvote the other members. These two major powers belonged to the German Union only by virtue of their territories which had formerly belonged to the empire. The Kings of Denmark, England and the Netherlands were also members of the German Union in their capacity as sovereign rulers in Schleswig, Hanover and Luxemburg – a blatant denial of the principle of nationality. This may be seen as the final attempt to establish Germany as a field for the balancing of European interests, rather than as a compact central power.

Something similar happened in Italy; whereas, however, the German Union was by and large an alliance of German monarchs, Italy had for centuries largely been under alien rule. Austria not only regained Lombardy, but was able to round off her possessions in Northern Italy by annexing the territory of the former Venetian republic. The area under Austrian domination was also enlarged by a number of states ruled by Habsburg monarchs: Tuscany, Modena and Parma. The Papal State was restored, but Austria was granted the right to garrison the fortresses of Ferrara and Comacchio with the aim of facilitating intervention in Central and Southern Italy, if it should be necessary. Southern Italy, i.e. Sicily and Naples, were ruled by the Bourbons, as they had been before the revolutionary war, so that it was only in the north-west of the country that an indigenous dynasty was established. The Kingdom of Piedmont – Sardinia, enlarged by Liguria and Genoa, rose to the rank of a European power – on the one hand, as a link in a defensive ring against France, but also as a check to the ambitions of Austria. Thus the European powers were, if possible, even more determined than in the case of Germany to frustrate the unification of the country, especially as Metternich's attempt to create a loose Italian federation, a *Liga Italica*, foundered on account of the reservations of Piedmont and the Papal State regarding their sovereignty.

In Eastern Europe the idea of the nation state was entirely at odds with the existing political order. The mainly Slavonic East of the continent had neither states with the accent on a single nationality and adherence to constitutional principles as in Western Europe, nor the motley collection of small states such as existed in Central Europe. Eastern Europe was the preserve of great imperial systems which embraced a host of ethnic groups and did their best to thrust them into historical obscurity. The Polish-Lithuanian and Swedish Empires had indeed passed away, but the Ottoman, the Russian and the Habsburg Empire had weathered the storms of the era just past and still cast their shadow over the new age of emerging nation states. These empires were bureaucratically governed from the centre, despotically in the case of Turkey and Russia, in a legalistically bureaucratic spirit in the case of Austria.

There were times when the Prussian monarchy, with its high proportion of Polish subjects, might have been added to the list of empires. As far as the empires were concerned, the so-called 'prisons of the nations', the idea of the nation was a two-fold threat: for one thing, the idea of the sovereignty of the people was diametrically opposed to power structures that culminated and were concentrated in the person of the ruler; for another, the demand on the part of subject peoples for nation states of their own did not imply, as it did in Western or Central Europe, intrinsic or extrinsic adjustments to the state, but rebellion *against* the state, its replacement or the secession of its components. In this way, a whole belt of east European states, from Finland, through the Baltic states, Poland, Czechoslovakia, Rumania, Bulgaria, Greece, Albania and Serbia came into existence by secession from the great empires in the hundred years following the emancipation of Greece in 1829. There were, indeed, similar cases in Western Europe – we need only think of Belgium, which seceded from the United Kingdom of the Netherlands in 1831, Norway, which dissolved its personal union with Sweden in 1905, Ireland, which seceded from the United Kingdom of Great Britain in 1922, and Iceland, which dissolved its union with Denmark in 1944.

How right the founders of the Holy Alliance were to fear the explosive revolutionary force of national and liberation wars was shown even before the diplomats and statesmen had taken their leave of Vienna in 1820. In Spain, Portugal, Naples and Sicily and in Piedmont revolutions in support of national and liberal aims had broken out. As to how these problems might best be coped with, a profound difference of opinion arose between the Western powers, especially England and France, and the Eastern countries, Prussia, Russia and Austria. At the conferences of Troppau, Laibach and Verona, the eastern powers, in the spirit of the Holy Alliance and the counter-revolutionary bias of the Viennese settlement, reaffirmed their determination to 'bring back into the bosom of the grand alliance, by armed force if necessary, those states which had suffered a change of government through insurrection'. This policy was opposed by England and France. The English Foreign Minister, Lord Castlereagh, warned against 'a league of governments against their peoples', and pointed out that, in the end, the governments of England and France were responsible to 'the great tribunals of their popular assemblies'.[5]

This attitude on the part of France and England, however, was not inspired solely by virtuous liberal sentiment: both governments were eager to profit, if they could, from the explosive force of nationalism and to gain strategic advantages in the field of foreign policy. This became evident after a Greek national committee in Epidauros had declared the independence of the Hellenic people from the Ottoman Empire on 1 January 1832 and passed a constitutional law on the basis of popular sovereignty. Turkey had not been present at the conference table in Vienna, since she was still not reckoned to be a European power, but the English Foreign Minister, George Canning (1770–1827), was obviously thinking of Russian and Austrian aspirations in south-east Europe when he declared, on the occasion of the Greek insurrection, that Great Britain was the champion of small nations. French foreign policy, for its part, was notably successful in promoting revolutionary movements of a nationalistic complexion in various parts of Europe, particularly in Italy and Poland. In Italy it had not been forgotten that the movement for Italian reunification, the *risorgimento*, had had its origins during the years of French occupation between 1796 and 1815, the years of the Jacobin republics of the *triennio* between 1796 and 1799, the satellite states founded by Napoleon, as well as the Kingdom of Italy, which also owed its existence to the great Corsican. An urban intellectual class had grown up here, for whom a united Italy had seemed virtually within their grasp, and whose constitutional preferences and ideas of national unity were inspired by French models. The *Carboneria* had operated from a base in Paris following the defeat of insurgents in Naples and Piedmont by Austrian troops. A host of Polish émigré organizations also sought refuge in France, so that Paris came to be regarded almost as the second capital of Poland. Napoleon III went a stage further in seeking a foreign policy confrontation with Austria by positively encouraging the movement for the unification of Italy. His aim was to win over liberal public opinion in France and to overturn the Viennese peace settlement of 1815, thus restoring French hegemony in Europe. And so the system of European states that had been so laboriously put together in Vienna began to fall apart into two opposing blocs: in the East the great continental powers of Austria and Russia – and, to a lesser degree, Prussia – who backed the *status quo* and had reasons to fear aspirations to independence among their ethnically mixed populations, and, in the West, the long established nation states of France and England, which, as great colonial powers, had interests extending far beyond Europe, but which had spread the influence of their constitutions and political institutions throughout the continent. In the Crimean War of 1853–56 it then became perfectly clear that the old European concert had fallen silent to all intents and purposes. The direct military confrontation of the Western powers and Russia was followed by a further estrangement between the powers flanking Europe.

Growing estrangement and hostility between the powers of East and West left room in the centre of Europe for the kind of political manoeuvering that the statesmen in Vienna had been at pains to eliminate. The crisis of the European system consequent on the Crimean War opened a window – a historical opportunity for the unification of Central Europe such as had never previously existed, and was rarely to exist subsequently. The situation at the time was not dissimilar to the situation in which Europe has found itself since 1989 following the collapse of the Soviet system.

Even after the revolutions of 1848–49, it had seemed as if the desire of German and Italian patriots for a nation state of their own such as the French and the English had, was fated to remain an illusion. The 585 delegates of the German people who assembled on 18 May 1848 in St Paul's Church in Frankfurt to debate the unification of Germany on the basis of a liberal, democratic constitution were hopelessly divided as to what actually was to constitute Germany. As was the case with all professorial debates, the discussion went on endlessly. Heinrich von Gagern (1799–1880), President of this National Assembly, proposed a motion to the effect that 'Austria should not be considered as included in the German federal state'. What he was proposing was the so-called 'Little

Germany' solution of the problem, a federation of German states, excluding Austria, such as had already existed in the form of a 'German Customs Union'. Heinrich von Gagern voted for the King of Prussia as the Emperor of Germany: after all, it was all there – the fixed frontiers, the clear contours, the rational solutions – and was not Austria's power in any case undermined by internal turmoil in that state of many different nationalities, and had not the Prussian King Frederick William IV pledged his allegiance to the ideals of Germany unity and liberty? But it was only reason, and not the heart that spoke in favour of a 'little Germany' under Prussian hegemony: Germany as no more than a Greater Prussia. Opposition was fierce and it came from every section of the Assembly. The 'grand barrier of the Carpathians' was invoked, the 'invincible bulwark of the Tyrol', Bohemia, 'the head and the brow of Germany', along with the civilizing mission of the Germans in the East and in the Balkans. The fact that other nations there were fighting for their independence just as the Germans were, played virtually no part in the debates of the German National Assembly. Greater Germany, the old empire resurrected under Habsburg emperors, but anointed with a few drops of liberal oil – that was the alternative dreamed of by a majority of the assembled dignitaries.

But all their debates were in the end nothing but a waste of breath: real power did not lie with the people's delegates in Frankfurt. A German nationalist rising in Kiel against Danish rule had given birth to a provisional government, this government had been forced to seek assistance from the National Assembly. Having no forces of its own, the Assembly was obliged to borrow troops from Prussia. The Prussian force then advanced into Jutland, but this brought the European powers on to the scene. They had in any case taken a sceptical view of attempts to unite Germany, and now that the German national movement was apparently spreading to the German-speaking territories of the Danish crown, they saw their doubts confirmed. The British Ambassador, Sir Stratford Canning read the riot act to the Prussian government, pointing out that they must 'pursue a policy in line with the system of international law, the best guarantee of peace, which the enthusiasts for German unification are so successfully intent on overthrowing and consigning to contempt and oblivion.'[6] In Sir Stratford's view the agitators were the liberal pioneers of a German national state, disorder meant, for him, the unification of Germany. To the cabinets in London and St Petersburg, the proceedings of the delegates in St Paul's Church looked like a revolt against the hallowed principles of the European balance of power. French emissaries demanded guarantees of the continued existence of the sovereign territorial states of Germany, British warships demonstrated in the North Sea, Russian troops were deployed along the Prussian frontier, and under such massive pressure from the European powers Prussia withdrew her troops from Schleswig-Holstein, in spite of vociferous protests by the professorial parliament in Frankfurt.

That was the turning point: in any revolution, victory goes to the party that settles the question of power in its own favour, and the assembly in St Paul's Church was totally devoid of power. The threat of a triple intervention by the European powers was not the least of the reasons why the German revolution of 1848–49 failed in its bid to establish a German nation state in the form of a Greater Germany, with a liberal constitution and guaranteed popular sovereignty and safeguards for human rights. The fear throughout the continent of a national and democratic revolution in the centre of Europe was too powerful. The Prussian Ambassador, Karl von Bunsen (1791–1860), summed up the prevailing opinion of English politicians as follows:

That Germany should become a mighty Empire is highly improbable. Now that the old Empire has collapsed, there is much more likely to be dissolution and fragmentation under the domination, or at least the influence, of France in the West and Russia in the East. On the other hand, it is not desirable that Germany should become a unified state. Ultra-democratic elements would then have a foothold in the very heart of Europe, and English trade and industry might then be at risk.[7]

It was not until after the revolution of 1848 that a legitimate alternative to the nation was eliminated from public opinion.

During the revolution there had still been voices denying that
state and nation need necessarily be one and the same. For
example, the Slavonic congress convened in Prague in June
1848 under the chairmanship of the Czech historian, František
Palacký (1798–1876) approved an address to the Austrian
Emperor which explicitly renounced any claim to separate
Slav nationhood. The delegates merely wished that an end
should be put to the domination of the Habsburg Empire
by the Germans, and that a federative state based on equal
rights for all the nations involved should be constituted. 'We,
the sons of the great Slav race, whose various branches now
enjoy under the paternal rule of Your Imperial Majesty all
the liberties they have long sought, wish, with their tried and
proven powers and loyalty, to play a full part in the rebirth of
the Austrian state.'[8] But the troops of Prince Windischgraetz
duly stifled the 'long sought liberties' of the Bohemians and
restored the late absolutist and centralized rule of the Habsburg
domains, and the other subject peoples of Austria fared no
better. Following the suppression of the revolution, Pasquale
Mancini (1817–88), expert on international law and subsequently Italian Foreign Minister, was quite sure in 1851 that
any state in which a number of nationalities were forced into a
union was not a political organism, but a monster doomed to
extinction.[9] What, in fact, was a nation without a state? The
philosopher Hegel (1770–1831) had long since declared, the
life of a nation without a state was merely 'pre-history'. The
liberal Swiss constitutional lawyer and Heidelberg professor
Johann Caspar Bluntschli (1808–81) drew from this statement
the conclusion that, 'Every nation has the duty, and hence the
right, to found a state . . . As the human race is divided into a
certain number of nations, so the world ought to be divided
into a corresponding number of states. Every nation is a state.
Every state is a national entity.'[10]

In Italy, unlike Germany, the 1848 revolution had not even
produced a national institution like the Frankfurt National
Assembly. The various revolutionary centres, Naples, Rome,
Milan, Venice, Florence and Turin did in fact take advantage
of the weakness of the monarchical authorities in the same
way as Germany had in the spring of 1848, but then the

various factions quarrelled amongst themselves, each claiming leadership of a national movement for the unification of the country, so that in the end they were defeated one by one by Austrian, Bourbon, Spanish and French forces. But, as distinct from Germany, the revolutionary enthusiasm of 1848 was preserved until a national state was actually founded. The liberal, democratic and radical leaders of the movement for Italian unification, who had propagated their cause even before the revolution and then led the rebellion against Austria in 1848–9 – Mazzini, Gioberti, Garibaldi – went on stoking the revolutionary fires in public, whereas in Germany during the fifties a general mood of dejection and disillusion with the ideals of the revolution had set in. The Italian middle class still clung to their vision of a united Italy, inspired by the grand operas of Giuseppe Verdi, whose *Trovatore* and *Sicilian Vespers* represented thinly veiled appeals to rebel against alien rule and were regarded by the Italian public as evidence of a renewed Italian culture.

The founding of the Italian nation state may be seen as the story of liberal, aristocratic and middle-class political and cultural elites which had emerged from the *moderati*, a social class of moderate intellectuals, civil servants and members of the commercial and landowning middle class, that had grown up in the course of the nineteenth century in all the urban centres of Italy, generally under the influence of certain journals standing for liberal policies. The initial aims of *moderatismo* did not actually include the unification of Italy as a single state: they were concerned more with reform of the constitutions, education and the economy in the existing states. It was the development of constitutions in Western Europe, especially the liberal constitutional monarchy in France after 1830, that provided their models. The pioneers of Italian unification were different in their origins: they were democrats like those who had played a prominent part in Mazzini's movement, who combined their vision of a nation state with unitarian, democratic, and occasionally even socialist, ideas. The revolutionary fervour of the democrats alarmed the *moderati*, who disliked radical change and hence sought to be associated with an enlightened monarch who favoured constitutional rule: they found him in the person of Carlo Alberto (1798–1849), King of Sardinia and Piedmont.

It is fascinating to trace the process by which, following the disastrous outcome of the 1848 revolution in Piedmont, the country was infiltrated by the liberal ideas that expressed the spirit of the age. In the period of reaction following the revolution, it was Piedmont that offered a rallying point for a kind of *moderatismo* that allied itself with sections of the democratic movement to form a new version of Italian liberalism that was destined to transform the Piedmontese state. Towards the end of the 1850s Piedmont was a parliamentary state supported by a broad liberal consensus and vigorously pursuing the modernization of society, of the economy, the civil service and the whole apparatus of the state according to French and English models. Since 1852 the leader of Piedmontese policy had been Count Camille Cavour (1810–61), an enthusiastic advocate of the British parliamentary system who, during the revolution in Turin, had edited the journal *Risorgimento*, from which the movement for the unification of Italy had taken its name. As prime minister of Piedmont, he achieved a number of remarkable feats more or less at the same time: by intervening in the Crimean War on the side of England and France, he secured the support of the two powers on the Western flank of the European system. In consequence, Piedmont appeared at the Paris Peace Conference in 1856 as a member of that system. Whereas Napoleon III believed that he had found in Piedmont a weapon to be used against Austria, Cavour in fact induced him to support the unification of Italy – initially of Northern Italy only. Cavour had to pay a high price for this support: at a meeting with Napoleon III in the health resort of Plombières in the Vosges, he had to agree to cede Nice and Savoy to France. However, France, in return, was committed to the defence of Piedmont. The Emperor of the French had declared to the Prime Minister of Piedmont that he would support Sardinia(–Piedmont) to the best of his ability in a war against Austria, 'provided that it was embarked on in a non-revolutionary cause, so that it might appear . . . to be justified in the view of European diplomacy, and especially in European public opinion.'[11]

This was a recipe for unification as it applied to the states of Central Europe: changes in the map of Europe were permissible in the eyes of European diplomacy, provided they took place in a 'non-revolutionary cause'. This was tantamount to a half-hearted obeisance to the spirit of the Viennese peace settlement of 1815, but at the same time an obvious attempt to thrust it aside. The victories of the allied Piedmontese and French armies at Magenta and Solferino led on 11 July 1859 to the preliminary peace of Villafranca, by which Austria ceded Lombardy to the French, who promptly handed it over to Piedmont. Napoleon III would have been content with this shattering blow to the Habsburg Empire, but as far as Cavour was concerned, this was the critical point when his years of dedicated collaboration with the various wings of the Italian national movement were to bring returns. The pattern of a *connubio*, an alliance of Cavour's *moderati* with the moderate Left and the Democrats to form a modern liberal elite began in Turin and then spread throughout Italy. The *Società Nazionale* represented the extension of Piedmontese national liberalism to the whole of Italy. The Society was a powerful organization in towns and cities, comprising aristocratic and middle-class liberals who offered themselves as allies to Cavour and rapidly became instruments of his policy. Hardly had the war with Austria come to an end when insurrectionary movements in Central Italy swept away the rulers of the upper Italian duchies, as well as the Papal administration in Emilia-Romagna and the Marches. Provisional governments led by politicians belonging to the *Società Nazionale* called for union with Piedmont, and plebiscites in these areas resulted in overwhelming public support.

But Cavour was playing a dangerous game. Napoleon III was annoyed that the ball he had set rolling had continued on its path without any further action on his part, and the surrender of Nice and Savoy – necessary to forestall intervention by France – had entailed a grave loss of face for Cavour at a time when a wave of nationalism was sweeping through Italy. Besides, Cavour had stooped to a questionable policy of double-dealing: he had allowed the radical and democratic volunteer forces of Garibaldi and Mazzini a free hand to

incite the population of lower Italy and parts of the Papal State
to revolution, and had then intervened to restore order with
the Piedmontese army. The revolution which Cavour and his
liberal associates dreaded, and which would probably have led
to intervention by the great powers, seemed to be just round
the corner. A kind of commando operation in Sicily led by
Giuseppe Garibaldi (1807–82) in May 1860, the 'March of the
Thousand', turned out to be a brilliant triumph. Garibaldi rose
to become the popular hero of the *risorgimento* and appears in
that role to this day in the shape of majestic equestrian statues
in almost every Italian town. He attempted to capitalize on
this favourable turn of events, elevating himself to a kind of
dictator in Sicily, promising democratic reforms and dismissing
the emissary of the Piedmontese crown.

The unification of Italy thus became the prize in a race
between Garibaldi's forces and the Piedmontese army. As
Garibaldi was making his way up from the South towards
Naples, driving the remnants of the Bourbon forces before
him and then turning towards Rome, Piedmontese troops
were marching into the Papal states from the North; they
crossed the frontier into the Kingdom of Naples and joined
up with Garibaldi, who, whether he liked it or not, was
obliged to watch his national revolutionary movement being
turned by Piedmontese generals into a national victory gained
by the royal army. As a further move designed to outflank
his rival, Cavour organized plebiscites in the areas occupied
by his troops; the results were often falsified and involved
only a minority of the population, but they gave a semblance of democratic justification for the Piedmontese policy of Italian unification under a liberal constitutional monarchy. Garibaldi gave up the struggle and retired, bitterly
disappointed, into private life, while on 18 February 1861
a newly elected popular assembly representing almost the
whole of Italy met for its first session in Turin. In the presence of this parliament, Victor Emanuel assumed the title of
'King of Italy, by the grace of God and by the will of the
People'.

Venice, Rome, the Trentino, South Tyrol, Trieste and
Dalmatia were still missing and needed to make the dream

of the unity of the Italian state and the Italian people come true. Three European wars, in each of which Italy played only a minor part, made the territorial completion of the national state possible. In 1866 Venice fell to Italy as a result of the Austrian defeat by Prussia at Königgrätz; in 1871 Italian troops marched into Rome, because the French contingent which had hitherto guarded the Pope was urgently needed for the defence of Paris against the Germans; and the Adige region was ceded to Italy in 1918 after the defeat of the central powers in the First World War. It was this kind of rounding-off in the case of Italy that made clear how far territorial changes were dependent on the power constellation in Europe as a whole.

The formation of the German nation state also began with a war fought outside Germany. After a lull lasting for a decade, the issue of German unification was revived and once more thrust into the centre of political action by the Italian crisis of 1859. Austria's Italian territories were threatened by the alliance between Piedmont and France, and national passions in Germany were once more running high. Even the more sober liberals regarded Northern Italy as one of the pillars of the Reich – the modern idea of the nation state was automatically linked with the memory of the glories of the Hohenstaufen Empire which were interpreted solely as evidence of German supremacy in southern and south-east Europe. In the parliaments of the German Union, in party meetings, at academic conferences and in national rallies of choral societies, marksmen and gymnasts, through a sudden flood of periodicals and pamphlets, the impression arose that the solution of the German problem was at hand. The ancient theme of a hereditary hostility between Germany and France was gleefully resurrected, and the incorporation of Alsace and Lorraine in a new Reich was even demanded. The tidal wave of nationalism reached its peak in celebrations marking the hundredth anniversary of Friedrich Schiller's birth that were held everywhere in the German-speaking countries. The anniversary of the poet's birth, 10 November 1859, was, as it happened, also the day on which a defeated Austria surrendered Lombardy at the Peace of Zürich.

The Italian crisis of 1859 had exposed to the full light of day the inherent instability of the German Union: both the major German powers had revealed weaknesses in the eyes of the public: Austria, because she had been defeated in the war, and Prussia, because she had temporized and manoeuvred in order to stay out of the war. Nevertheless, following the defeat of the Danube monarchy, the idea of a German federal state under Prussian leadership as an alternative to an impotent German Union of dubious standing, began increasingly to gain ground. In the middle of September 1859 the German National Association (*Deutscher Nationalverein*) was founded by liberals and moderate democrats from all the German states, apart from Austria: the affinity with the *Società Nazionale* was obvious. An orchestrated campaign in the press made the preference for Prussian supremacy in Germany perfectly clear – but Prussia was not Piedmont, and King William I was not to be compared with Victor Emanuel. Whereas in Italy the liberal national movement was backed by the Piedmontese government, in Prussia there had developed ever since 1861 a deeply rooted hostility between the liberal majority in parliament and the crown. The initial dispute concerned the expansion of the armed forces and changes in their constitutional position. The intention was to achieve these aims without the consent of parliament, for the army was determined not to be beholden in any way to parliament and to remain the sole instrument by which the crown enforced its rule. For this reason a quarrel over the Prussian army turned into a dispute about the constitution, with the liberal party using its right to reject the budget – a move which Prussia's monarch and government regarded as tantamount to a declaration of war. Suddenly, the spectre of revolution was back on the scene: liberal opinion in Germany turned away from Prussia, all the more decisively, since the new prime minister, Otto von Bismarck (1815–89), appointed on 24 September 1862, was regarded as a counter-revolutionary *sans phrase*, a tool of the army and the conservatives. It appeared that he had been commissioned by the king to put an end to the constitutional dispute by every possible means and to force parliamentary liberalism to its knees. The German National Association now repudiated Prussia's mission, which it had once triumphantly proclaimed and suggested that a general German parliament, as in 1848–9, should decide Germany's future. In January 1864 the German National Association opened in Coburg its headquarters, a 'Central Office for a Volunteer Defence Corps', which not only recruited volunteers for the war in Schleswig-Holstein, but actually planned a revolution to overthrow the Prussian government under Bismarck, for which purpose rifles were purchased in London. On the eve of the war between Prussia and Austria in 1866, the prevailing mood of the German national movement was one of profound resignation. The neutrality of all the medium-sized and smaller German states, declared the weekly newspaper of the German National Association on 14 June 1866, 'was the only appropriate course of action for a German national policy', since 'the nation's banner' flew neither in the Prussian nor the Austrian camp. Bismarck was misjudged on all sides, as regards the assumptions that were made about his policy. For him, the post of Prussian prime minister was not the ultimate goal, but merely the means to a higher end. His primary concern was the extension of Prussian power and her consolidation in a revolutionary Europe, a policy which, in his view, could be pursued only through the establishment of Prussian hegemony in Germany – at Austria's expense, but in keeping with the interests of the other European powers. The means were revolutionary, but the end was conservative. Neither this 'white revolutionary' (Ludwig Bamberger) nor the principle of 'creative counter-revolution' could find a place in the political vocabulary of the nineteenth century.

'The great issues of our time will not be settled by speeches and majority decisions – that was the great mistake of 1848 and 1849 – but by iron and blood.'[12] Bismarck's conclusion, which horrified liberals of every shade, was only logical and drawn from experience of previous failures. The iron-and-blood metaphor had not in fact sprung from the mind of some war-mongering Junker: it was a quotation from a song written by one of the volunteers of 1813 who had founded the movement for unification and liberty, Max von Schenkendorf (1783–1817):

> For only iron can save us,
> Naught but blood can set us free,
> So deep in shameful bondage
> And lost in sin were we.

That had been a revolutionary pledge, and the fact that Bismarck adopted the phrase, while Schenkendorf's liberal descendants shrank from the *ultima ratio* of policy, recourse to armed force, indicated that the forces of change were not to be found 'down below' among the people. Revolution in Germany – as elsewhere in Europe – was for the most part not fomented from below, but from above.

With the benefit of hindsight, we may find the attitudes to Bismarck among liberals in the national movement between 1862 and 1866 remarkable: they range from condescending contempt (Bluntschli to Sybel: 'in a purely subordinate, indeed subservient position, he might prove useful; in a position of authority he is absurd and insufferable'[13]) to outright detestation (Baumgarten to Sybel, 'Men who spurn the constitution, reason and the law like naughty boys must be made to shake in their shoes. They must be made to feel an acute apprehension that they might one day be beaten to death like rabid dogs.'[14]) There was good reason for contempt and detestation, for Bismarck had entered the fray to put an end once and for all to attacks by the liberal opposition who were attempting to transform the authoritarian state into a parliamentary democracy such as had long existed in Piedmont. Since, in the policy of the German national movement, as in that of its Italian opposite number, national unity and freedom in domestic policy were indissolubly linked, the Prussian prime minister was reckoned to be, in the words of the *National Association Weekly* (*Wochenschrift des Nationalvereins*), 'The last shot in the locker of the reaction by the grace of God'. If the profound gulf between Bismarck and the German national movement is compared with the smooth collaboration between Cavour and the Italian national lobby in the campaign for Italian unification, then we might well conclude that the founding of a German nation state had been rendered difficult beyond any hope of realization.

In fact, the opposite was the case. Nothing would have handicapped Bismarck's plans more than an alliance with the national movement, whose intention of shattering the existing system was perfectly obvious and was looked upon with the greatest suspicion by the governments in London, Paris and St Petersburg. Bismarck actually needed the hostility of liberal and national forces in Germany in order to conceal his strength and his true aims behind the screen of his quarrel with the liberals, so that he was able to act ultimately with astonishing speed. In 1863, when a rising in Russian Poland prompted a wave of liberal sympathy throughout Europe for the oppressed Polish nation, it was only Bismarck who sided with the tsar, with an eye to Russian benevolent neutrality in the war he was seeking with Austria. Public opinion in Germany seethed with indignation. The National Association spoke of 'the man at the head of the Prussian state, condemned by his own nation, who is intent on undermining the authority and standing of that state,' and threatened revolution.[15] And the hostility of the national movement grew even fiercer when Bismarck turned his attention to the Schleswig-Holstein issue.

Ever since the 1848 revolution, the irredentist issue in Schleswig-Holstein had been a favourite theme with the national movement, and public indignation came to the boil when the Danish parliament resolved in 1863 that the whole of the duchy of Schleswig, hitherto linked only by a personal union with Denmark, should be fully integrated into the Danish state. The liberal German press hastened to declare that the first priority of national policy must be the independence of Schleswig-Holstein under a German prince, the Duke of Sonderburg-Augustenburg. Schleswig-Holstein Societies were founded in every German town, and in Frankfurt 500 deputies from all the German parliaments called for the liberation from Danish rule of the Elbe duchies, Schleswig, Holstein and Lauenburg. And, as in 1848, Prussia was once again prepared for military intervention – not, indeed on behalf of the Elbe duchies and Augustenburg's rights: the latter did have a hereditary right on his side, but not the international agreement that guaranteed the integrity of the Danish crown territories.

Unmoved by the furious outbursts of the national faction, Bismarck accordingly acknowledged the rights of the ruling Danish sovereign from the house of Sonderburg-Glücksburg. He nevertheless planned an invasion of the duchies, allegedly because Schleswig-Holstein's special rights had been infringed, and even contrived to gain the support of Austria. The distinction between the aims of the German national movement and those of the two major German powers – who now took the stage arm-in-arm, to everyone's amazement – was at first sight merely a point of law, but any formal recognition of the rights of the Danish crown was anathema to German patriots and hence an intolerable threat to the peaceful order of Europe. As Prussian and Austrian troops began to invade Holstein in January 1864, occupying the whole of Jutland by the middle of the year, the fury of the liberal public knew no bounds – not without reason, as appeared following the conclusion of a peace treaty on 30 October 1864, when it transpired that the liberated Elbe duchies were not to enter the German Union as independent states, but were to constitute a condominium administered jointly by the two victorious powers, Prussia and Austria.

Now it turned out, however, that Bismarck's contempt for the 'windbags and swindlers of the movement party', as he termed the patriotic liberals, was not entirely unjustified. In the face of Bismarck's success, the united front offered by the camp of Bismarck's opponents began to crumble visibly as eminent historians like Heinrich von Treitschke (1834–96) and Theodor Mommsen (1817–1903) now pledged themselves to Bismarck's manifestly unscrupulous, but none the less successful policy, and even a democrat like Franz Waldeck (1802–70), on the extreme left wing in the Prussian chamber of deputies, declared bluntly that he could see no alternative to Bismarck's design.

Faced with the *fait accompli* of the Danish war, which was later to be seen as the first war of German unification, the national movement had shown itself to be vociferous but impotent, and when the quarrel between Prussia and Austria became critical, with each side holding back only in the hope of laying the blame for the outbreak of war on its opponent, when the Prussian advance-guard ultimately crossed the Bohemian frontier on 21 June 1866, then the liberal public was shocked, but paralysed and incapable of action. And when the outcome of the war was settled by the Battle of Königgrätz on 3 July 1866 with Prussia emerging as victor and Austria retiring from the battle for supremacy in Germany, then the national movement collapsed overnight as an independent political force in Germany. The liberal lawyer, Rudolf von Ihering (1818–92), who had pilloried Bismarck on account of his 'desecration of all the principles of legality and ethics' just before war broke out, wrote after Königgrätz:

> I bow before the genius of a Bismarck who has achieved a masterpiece of political tactics and initiative. I have forgiven him everything he has done so far, indeed, what is more, I have convinced myself that it was all necessary, that everything that seemed to us who were not in the know to be criminal arrogance, turned out in the end to be the indispensable means to a single end . . . For a man of action of this stamp . . . I would give a hundred men of liberal convictions, of impotent integrity.[16]

Following Austria's exit from the German Union in 1866, a North German Confederation was formed, a coalition of all the German states north of the River Main, under Prussian leadership, a little German, greater Prussian nation state which had even at this stage, all the features of the German Reich that succeeded it: an alliance of sovereign monarchs, of whom one, it is true, was more sovereign than the others. 'All the armed forces of the alliance,' it was stated in the treaty dated 18 August 1866, 'are under the supreme command of His Majesty, the King of Prussia.' Following a war declared by a single cabinet, there was now to be an alliance of cabinets. This would have been scarcely more than a loose federation of states, had not the treaty specified as its central justifying feature a federal constitution to be agreed 'in collaboration with a parliament convoked jointly by the contracting states (Art. 2)'. In this way the alliance of monarchs was to be

complemented by a popular assembly elected in free, equal
and secret ballots by all male citizens over the age of 25. The
South German states – Bavaria, Württemberg, Baden and parts
of Hesse – were linked with the North German Confederation
only by individual treaties, but their full membership was only
a matter of time and fresh opportunity. The opportunity arose
with the Franco-Prussian War of 1870–1, which, through the
implementation of treaties of alliance with the South German
states, turned into a Franco-German War.

The political unification of the German belligerents kept
pace with events in the war, which ended with the defeat of
France. The mood of exhilaration among the German population as expressed by public opinion put such pressure on
the cabinets of the South German states that they had no
alternative but to continue along the road to union with the
North German Confederation. The path from the outbreak of
war to the proclamation of William I (1797–1888) as German
Emperor in the Hall of Mirrors in Versailles was short, but
strewn with obstacles – Bavaria's consent to the title of emperor
for the Prussian king even had to be purchased by an annual
contribution to the private purse of Ludwig II. The German
Empire that came into existence on 1 January 1871 with
the ratification of a new imperial constitution by the South
German parliaments and the Reichstag of the North German
Confederation, differed from the North German Confederation
only by its extension to South Germany and the introduction
of the titles of 'Emperor' and 'Empire', which meant nothing
in constitutional terms, but added symbolic force to the legitimacy of the new German nation state.

As the North German Confederation had previously done,
the new empire defined itself in its constitution as a 'perpetual
union for the defence of the federal territory and the laws
obtaining within it, as well as for the welfare of the German
people', as the preamble put it. The supreme head of this
federation continued to be the King of Prussia, who accepted
the office of President of the Federation, and in this capacity
'bore the title of German Emperor (Art. 11)'. In fact there
was not the least constitutional connection between William I
and the last of the Roman Emperors, the Habsburg, Francis

II (1768–1835), just as the Greater Prussian, Small German Empire had no connection with the erstwhile Holy Roman Empire. But the minds of those groups who propagated the idea of a German national state, for the most part the liberal middle class, had for generations past been conditioned by images and myths of a regressive Romantic utopian resurrection of the alleged medieval glories of the Empire – and this myth was so potent that no German nation state could be endorsed without reference to it. The title of Emperor, moreover, as Bismarck was clearly aware, had a variety of implications. It was in keeping with the particularistic ideas of the South German princes in so far as it emphasized the federative aspect of the ancient Reich. Conservatives of the old school, who found it hard in any case to stomach a new constitution, were comforted by the idea of a Christian, Romantic, divinely ordained imperial dignity as a defence against any secular leaning towards liberalization. Liberals and democrats saw the imperial title in the light of the 'people's emperor', as already adumbrated in St Paul's Church. At the same time the link between the late war and the proclamation of the emperor in Versailles offered the nation a suggestive glimpse of a military leader in the style of Caesar or Bonaparte. The ambivalence of his new title was not the least of the reasons why William I was taken aback: he complained of the 'illusory office of Emperor', and believed that, with the proclamation of the new empire, the old Prussia had been borne to its grave.

The German and Italian approaches to a national state were clearly linked, as the dates of their beginning and culmination show: 1848, 1859 and 1871 were the stages in each case which led to a unified and regularly constituted state. In this respect the formation of national states in Central Europe represents a single process. We find, in Germany as in Italy, a social vanguard, an elite of property-owning and educated aristocrats and members of the middle class who tended to cut themselves off from the lower classes – the *Società Nazionale* was characterized, in the words of one of its historians, by 'repudiation of the higher aristocracy, embarrassment as regards the artisan class and outright fear of the peasantry'.[17] The corresponding German organization, the National Association, deliberately pitched its subscription at such a level that only the affluent could afford to join: it was only in Saxony or on the Upper Rhine that any significant number of tradesmen or farmers belonged to gymnastic or choral societies or marksmen's associations. Middle-class liberalism kept an uneasy balance between aristocratic conservatism and the constant dread of social revolution from below. The middle-class proponents of the national idea – middle-class in the sense that they gave priority to middle-class and liberal values, ideas and aims – comprised for the most part respectable citizens, pillars of society, for whom the nation state was not intended to be, as has often been claimed, primarily a national economic community. The idea of a rising, class-conscious, capitalist bourgeois creating, along with the nation state, the concept of the market and the instrument of the class struggle, may now be regarded as outmoded. In fact, the urbanization and industrialization of Italy, apart from a few economic islands (Piedmont, Lombardy, Liguria) were far too under-developed to offer a positive basis for a politically viable capitalist bourgeoisie while, north of the Alps, the German Customs Union under Prussian auspices had been established ever since 1834, and an integrated market in commodities and capital had come into existence, even in the absence of a national state.

In Germany, as well as in Italy, there were a number of political reasons which prompted a motley collection of minor aristocrats, professors, teachers, writers, journalists, Protestant parsons, civil servants, and, as one group among many, men of private means – collectively known as the bourgeoisie – to demand the founding of a nation state. The main reason was the absence of any overriding legitimate authority. It was not only the fact that the ancient, feudal, class-ridden order of society had collapsed, or that the church, the nobility and local authorities had forfeited their exclusive claims to unquestioning obedience on the part of their subjects: Central Europe, both north and south of the Alps, had long been a theatre of war for the European powers, with the result that, in the turbulent years between the French Revolution and the Congress of Vienna, men had lived through a whole series of rapidly changing regimes – today's ruler might well turn out to be tomorrow's foe. And with the rapid alternation of political authorities, new political arrangements had constantly cropped up: republicanism to the point of Jacobinism, Bonapartism, *ancien régime*, with more or less explicit versions of Enlightenment reforms, cautious restoration with echoes of the Napoleonic legacy, or simply pure reaction. The nation state offered a way out of this wilderness that lacked any kind of political norms or directives. What was needed, it seemed, was a strong state with institutions so firmly and durably established that they could defend the achievements of liberalism in the long term and advance them still further. Such a state must have a mandate from the entire nation based on its history and culture. The nation state offered a new community, a common bond; in general, but emotionally potent, terms it made 'sense'. This was sufficient reason for educated, politically zealous Central Europeans to aspire to something which their neighbours in the West manifestly already possessed.

Such affinities between Germany and Italy might be pursued further: in each case there was a dominant authoritarian state in the north of the country, which had originally belonged only in part to the nation: the house of Savoy had been directly subject to the old empire, with traditions that were more French than Italian, while a considerable area of Prussia had lain outside the German Union (and, before that, outside the Reich) – indeed its claim to be a kingdom originated outside the context of the Reich, and it included a fair number of Poles among its subjects. In both cases a statesman in the Bonaparte mould had not hesitated to appeal to the emotions of the masses in order to achieve his aim of national unification and, finally, in each case an alliance between these statesmen on the one hand and a liberal national movement on the other, had followed the founding of the state – the *Destra storica* in Italy, born of an alliance of moderate democrats and liberals, and the National Liberal party in Germany, which the National Association had formed in 1866, and which would henceforth orchestrate in parliament Bismarck's plans for German unification.

Certainly the differences between the two states were also considerable. The more or less highly industrialized 'little' German Reich differed from an Italy that still had a mainly agrarian economy. South of the Alps, a man of property still meant an agrarian landowner, which is why, by and large, there was no agrarian reform in Italy – the broad mass of the Italian peasantry and rural proletariat remained indifferent to the issue of a national state, with consequences for Italy's political culture that can still be observed today. On the other hand, the liberal elite of the country, who created the Italian nation state, were uncompromisingly committed to French and English constitutional models. The West and its political culture, Enlightenment, the idea of human rights and popular sovereignty: all this was not felt to be somehow alien and hostile, but a pattern that ought to be adopted. How very different was the case of Germany, where the identity of the new nation, issuing as it did from a war against France and born of the memory of the war of liberation against Napoleon in 1813, was defined in defiance of the West and its traditional values. The proclamation of the emperor was deliberately staged in the Palace of Versailles as a posthumous humiliation of Louis XIV, whose 'campaigns of plunder' at the end of the seventeenth century had devastated the Palatinate and led to the separation of Alsace from the Reich. The fact that France was to be Germany's 'arch-enemy' but Italy's 'traditional friend' made a vital difference to political culture on both sides of the Alps.

As far as Europe was concerned, the rise of German and Italian nation states was tantamount to a revolution in the double sense the statesmen of 1815 had had in mind when they specified peace terms for the continent in Vienna. For one thing, the revolution affected the European system of states and the principle of checks and balances that was based on the fragmentation of Central Europe. The dismay in the cabinets of the major and lesser European states was very great at the prospect of an unprecedented concentration of power at the very heart of the continent. It was put into words by the leader of the opposition in Great Britain, Benjamin Disraeli (1804–81), who declared in the House of Commons on 9 February 1871 that the founding of the German Empire was nothing less than 'the German Revolution, a more momentous political event than the French Revolution of the previous century . . . There is not a single diplomatic tradition,' Disraeli went on, 'which has not been swept away. We have a new world, new influences are at work, new and unknown factors and dangers with which we must come to terms, and which, at a time when everything is new, are still hard to estimate . . . '[18]

But it was not only the system of European states that was revolutionized: in the new nation states themselves there had been revolutionary changes. Whereas in Western Europe it had been the state that had created the nation, in Central Europe it had been the nation that gave birth to the state. The founding of the nation state has been described as 'a revolution from above', as a reversal of policy at home and abroad effected by the leading statesmen, Bismarck and Cavour. It was Bismarck himself who coined the concept.[19] In the case of Italy, however, it became evident – and this is what worried the European powers – that there had in fact been close collaboration between the prime minister of Piedmont and the forces of 'revolution from below', involving not just the *moderati*, to which group Cavour himself belonged, but also the democratic revolutionary partisans of Garibaldi and Mazzini.

In the case of Germany, too, the path to the founding of the new Reich may be described as marked by the collaboration of Bismarck with the national movement – a collaboration, it is true, *malgré lui*. The gulf separating Bismarck from the liberal publicists was doubtless deeper than that which lay between Cavour and the liberal press. But public opinion in Germany was already such a powerful force that not only Bismarck but every German government since the 1848 revolution had to try to win over this potential factor and adjust its policies accordingly. That is demonstrated, for example, by the fact that none of the medium-sized German states dared form an alliance with a power outside Germany, although the Viennese protocol regulating their union specifically reserved the right of all the German states to form alliances with foreign powers. A policy of a 'third Germany', a confederation of German states with French backing on the lines of the Rhenish Union of 1806 would have entailed incalculable risks in domestic policy two generations later.

Thus, the pattern of a 'revolution from above' must be seen

in relative terms, even in the case of Germany. It is true that the German Empire was not united by speeches and majority decisions but by blood and iron. Nevertheless, there was no single factor in its successful outcome that was in the long run opposed to mass nationalism. Bismarck himself made the point in his memoirs: 'Even if motions in regional parliaments and in newspapers and at marksmen's jamborees were incapable of bringing about German unification, liberalism nevertheless exerted a pressure on the monarchs that made them more inclined to make concessions to the advantage of the Reich.'[20]

Bismarck's policy did indeed shatter the outward cohesion of the national movement, but it was that movement which dictated, if not the means, then the aim of his policy. Without the influence, however diffuse, of the movement for national unification which gave the cause an aura of legitimacy, what would have emerged ultimately would not have been a German Empire, but simply a Greater Prussia. The same is true, *mutatis mutandis*, of Piedmont. That Bismarck was playing a risky game when he put mass nationalism on a leash, may have been more obvious to him after his fall from office in 1890 than it had been previously. At any rate, his successors proved themselves to be incapable of taming this particular tiger.

11

The Imperialist Nation State 1871–1914

The year 1871 marked a historical hiatus that was even deeper than contemporaries realized at the time. Instead of the jumbled territorial patchwork that had marked the map of Central Europe for centuries, there had come into being two massive powers, namely Germany and Italy, which represented an alien element in the European system of checks and balances. The powers on the periphery of Europe, Russia in the East, England and France in the West, each responded in characteristic fashion and so emphatically that, by the beginning of the twentieth century, the great European powers had changed their policies, and the intellectual climate had also undergone a radical change.

It was France that underwent the most profound change following the *année terrible* of 1870–1. The traumatic experience of the humiliating surrender of French regimental colours at Sedan, the siege of Paris, total defeat by the combined German armies, the loss of Alsace and Lorraine, the Commune in Paris and other domestic upheavals were quite deliberately countered by an appeal to national solidarity and by an educational programme in a nationalistic spirit. Even today, any educated Frenchman is familiar with a quotation from Ernest Lavisse (1842–1922), the historian who headed the campaign to cultivate a republican brand of nationalism:

> Since that ghastly year I have never for a moment given way to despair, but have sought tirelessly to impart to millions of our children the hope and confidence I bore within myself. I have time and time again stressed what we owe to our lost provinces. The single tower of Strasbourg Cathedral is never out of my sight. I constantly see it soaring alone into the heavens: I am Strasbourg, I am Alsace, I send you greetings and I am waiting.[1]

Patriotic regeneration and republican education were to be two sides of the same coin. The entire educational system, non-clerical and republican in its basic policy, was placed in the service of the nationalist cause: the teaching of history and citizenship was to be the starting point of the country's regeneration. It was above all the elementary schools, reformed by the left-wing republican Minister of Education, Jules Ferry (1832–93) which served as the instrument for the re-education of France in a nationalistic spirit. Every Frenchman became familiar at school with G. Bruno's *Le Tour de la France par deux enfants: devoir et patrie*, the thrilling story of fourteen-year-old André Valden and his seven-year-old brother, Julien. Shortly after the Franco-German war the two homeless orphans are forced to leave their native town, Phalsburg, which has been annexed by Germany, and set off on a journey which leads them through the whole of France. The refugee children with the German-sounding surname ultimately find a new home in their fatherland, the unique merits of which they have now come to know. The book first appeared in 1877, and in the course of the next thirty years went through twenty reprints, each of which was adapted to reflect current events and political priorities. The *Manual général* prescribed for the training of elementary school teachers and published in 1881 by Ferdinand Buisson, a close colleague of Jules Ferry, required a map showing Alsace and Lorraine to be displayed in every classroom, flanked by a banner draped in mourning crêpe. At the prize giving on the last day of the school year teachers were instructed to write on the blackboard, 'Child, thou art to be a warrior!' In pursuit of this policy, *bataillions scolaires* were formed in the elementary schools to provide the children with pre-military training. The generation that grew up in the aftermath of the Franco-German war was inoculated with republican, nationalistic and military ideas and values – entirely in keeping with the spirit of the Jacobins and the latter's sense of mission, to which the teachers and historians of the Third Republic specifically alluded. It was no mere coincidence that the *Marseillaise* was adopted as the French national anthem in 1879, while the 14 July, the anniversary of the storming of the Bastille, was declared a national holiday the following year.

The generation of republicans that came to power in the 1870s also forged a bond with the nationalism of the Great Revolution, insisting that their fatherland, in spite of all the defeats it had suffered in the interim, was still the leader of mankind, in that it defended the virtues of Enlightenment and republicanism against the forces of reaction and militarism embodied in Prussia. The nation's unshakeable sense of mission had been expressed in the middle of the nineteenth century by the historian, Jules Michelet (1798–1874), when he spoke of the 'pontificate of modern civilization' represented by France as the pioneer of the modern socially progressive and enlightened state: the French idea of civilization had thus become the very core of a national religion.

In the mid-eighties, however, the climate changed. Hitherto it had been the anti-clerical, republican left-wingers in French politics who had set the tone, adopting the cause of the nation and its link with 1789. Now the centre of gravity had shifted, the defence of the nation's values became increasingly the concern of the anti-republican, anti-democratic, Catholic right. Whereas left-wing intellectuals had been prone to attack the officer corps and the call to avenge the defeat of 1871 – Rémy de Gourmont's shocking article on the army, 'our beloved plaything', had appeared in the *Mercure de France* in 1891 – the officer corps itself began to change in its composition. Aristocrats and the sons of the wealthy bourgeoisie became more and more dominant. They had often been educated in Roman Catholic schools which were fiercely hostile to the lay state schools, and they inspired the cadet schools and officers' messes with anti-republican sentiment. The glorification of the army, which had been promoted even by pillars of the republican establishment, was now turned against the republic, the monarchical and clerical Right claimed the army as its own preserve, along with the cult of the lost provinces and the prospect of revenge.

To this was added profound dissatisfaction with the 'opportunist Republic', which was publicly reproached with losing sight of major national priorities, despite all its efforts to educate the nation. The colonial policy of Jules Ferry's cabinet, encouraged by Bismarck, had led at the beginning of the eighties to the conquest of Tunis and northern Indo-China, but it was seen, even in republican circles as a diversionary manoeuvre drawing attention away from the 'blue line of the Vosges', an underhand and clandestine collaboration with Germany. Was this not France's evil genius at work once again, the spirit that was to blame for the defeat of 1871, the cowardice of the regime and its lack of patriotic fervour? The League of Patriots (*ligue des patriotes*) founded by men who had once been impeccable republicans, like Paul Déroulède (1846–1914) and Ferdinand Buisson, tried to promote the national issue in the minds of their fellow countrymen by organizing national festivals, encouraging the cult of national symbols and figures such the Maid of Orleans, and the idea of revenge. The statue in the Place de la Concorde representing Strasbourg was draped in mourning as a constant reminder of France's first priority, the recovery of Alsace. The League of Patriots inclined more and more towards anti-parliamentary, populist and revanchist attitudes and moved ever closer to the movement led by General Georges Boulanger (1837–91), Minister of War in Freycinet's 1886 cabinet, who was extremely popular as a spokesman for the 'little man' and who was directly elected in a number of constituencies in the 1888 elections.

Under Boulanger, '*Général Revanche*', who demanded an anti-republican revision of the constitution and who liked to see himself as the saviour of his country – as both Napoleons had done before him – the conservative and monarchist Right fell in behind the banner of nationalism and began for the first time to mobilize the masses in support of a *doctrine nationaliste*; hitherto such appeals to popular support had been the weapon of the Left. In fact Boulanger came to grief on the eve of the *coup d'état* that had been planned and was forced to flee into exile in 1889, but the nationalistic Right had in the meantime formed itself into a *parti nationaliste*, which constituted a rallying point for all those who were unwilling to accept a democratic, anti-clerical republic, and who saw in an open society and the interplay of parliamentary and social forces a threat to the national consensus that had to be revived, if France was to recover her place in Europe and in the world.

But, first of all, France herself had to be restored. Apart from the republican government's seemingly lethargic pursuit of military revenge in a confrontation with Germany, there were the financial scandals that swamped France in the eighties, as if to underline the corruption and depravity of the republican authorities. 'There are political problems at home that govern problems of foreign policy', wrote Déroulède:

> We cannot hope to achieve anything abroad before we have cured our domestic ills. Our country is sick, debili-tated, and needs a general course of treatment . . . Before we can win back Alsace and Lorraine, we must rediscover France . . . That is why, on the League's banner, above the slogan, 'Revision of the Frankfurt Treaty', we have written the words, 'Reform of the parliamentary regime'.[2]

To the Right, it seemed absolutely certain that the nation was threatened from within as well as from abroad. The accusations which politically active intellectuals like Edouard Drumont (1844–1917), Maurice Barrès (1862–1923) or Charles Maurras (1868–1952) flung at the republic, were echoed in many quarters. Cosmopolitanism, internationalism and freemasonry were allegedly undermining the unity of the French nation, and the Jews in particular were France's internal enemy number one. A work in two volumes by Edouard Drumont, *La France juive*, appeared in 1886 and proved to be an instant bestseller. In fact it was an inelegant and clumsy piece of work, a concoction of Jewish life and customs, Parisian gossip and *chronique scandaleuse* lacking any logical sequence of ideas. The author simply lashed out in all directions – masonic lodges, which had been cited during the French Revolution as subversive organizations, were allegedly again at work planning revolution. Girls' grammar schools, those 'appalling dens of vice', were luring women away from their true domestic vocation. Those who were pulling the strings behind the scenes and who were to blame for France's decline, were the Jews, who featured in this fanatical piece of propaganda as destructive parasites who were responsible for Europe's decadence and who therefore ought to be combatted by every nation.

This was merely the prelude to a wave of anti-Semitism which was to reach its climax in the Dreyfus affair of the following decade. A Jewish captain of artillery on the General Staff, Alfred Dreyfus (1859–1935), was accused of acting as a spy for the German General Staff, tried by court martial in an atmosphere of intense public emotion, and sentenced to imprisonment and dishonourable discharge from the service – unjustly, as it subsequently transpired. The battle for the rehabilitation of this Jewish officer with the German-sounding name was in fact a battle for the soul of France. Various organizations took up the cause of Dreyfus, sensational rhetorical duels were fought in parliament, cabinets fell and several ministers of war were forced to resign, and the popular press took a fervent interest in the case. When at last the prolonged and ferocious opposition of the Ministry of War and the General Staff had been overcome and Dreyfus half-heartedly rehabilitated, the nation had been split into two camps. On one side stood the leading representatives of the Third Republic, who began to found parties and trade union organizations: the *Parti radical* in 1901, the *Parti socialiste* (SFIO), in 1905, the umbrella organization of the trades unions (CGT), along with a host of human rights committees, anti-clerical leagues and people's universities. On the other side stood the *Bloc national*, those who had been on the losing side in the Dreyfus affair and who in their resentment closed their ranks against the anti-militarists, the 'godless', the Jews, the intellectuals who had espoused the case of Dreyfus, the workers' parties and the unions. Members of the middle class who resented the rise of the working-class movement were drawn into the wake of the reactionary bloc by the spokesmen of the Right.

French nationalism assumed its ultimate form around the turn of the century. In his trilogy, *Le roman de l'énergie nationale* (1897–1903) and in his essays, *Scènes et doctrines du nationalisme* (1902), Maurice Barrès fought against individualism, the cult of the ego, which he believed to be the main cause of the corruption of French civilization. The nation ranked above the ego and had therefore to be regarded as the supreme priority in a man's life. The individual had no choice but to submit to the function assigned to him by the nation, 'the sacred law of his lineage', and to 'hearken to the voices of the soil and the dead'. The nation's heritage had to be defended against the corrupting effects of egoism within, and the infiltration of Alsace by German culture.

Less mystical and more directly political were the demands of Charles Maurras. He, too, takes as his starting point the danger threatening the nation, invasion by 'anti-French' forces of individualism and cosmopolitanism, of democracy and socialism, in short, by the 'stupid nineteenth century'. (Léon Daudet). What was needed was a revival of royal, Catholic, pre-Revolutionary France, the expulsion of the poison that had been injected into the nation by the Revolution. The nation was the supreme political reality, its renewal and restoration a rational demand, so it was only rational for a patriot to be a monarchist. The somewhat dubious logic of this conclusion led Maurras to the view that the battle against the 'fateful errors of democracy' must be waged by violent means, as a revolution against the republican institutions of the Revolution.

The *Action française* represented the ultimate step from literature to political action. Founded by Maurras in 1898, it was originally no more than a small coterie of writers, but in 1908, with the appearance of a periodical under the same name, it came to the notice of the public and had a considerable impact. The paper was sold in the streets by a corps of volunteers, the *Camelots du roi*, i.e. the Royal Partisans, the first organized paramilitary street rowdies and agitators, later to be clothed in uniform shirts and boots. In the provinces the leadership of the *Action française* was often in the hands of members of aristocratic families, who were embittered because they had been ousted from the public life of the Third Republic – although

this rarely applied to the higher aristocracy. The frequent claim
that the membership was drawn from the petty bourgeoisie is
hard to sustain. It is true that a considerable percentage of the
members came from the lower middle class – tradesmen, commercial travellers, small shopkeepers – but about half of the
members were university graduates, often lawyers. The student
element attracted particular attention by the spectacular brawls
it provoked, for instance, in the academic year 1908–9, when
a certain Professor Amadée Thalamas announced a lecture
on the seemingly harmless subject of 'Teaching Methods'.
A few years previously, however, Thalamas had made some
derogatory remarks about Joan of Arc, who had been chosen
as a kind of patron saint by *Action française*. The result was a
violent riot and street battles between gangs of students. The
whole thing was not much more than a storm in a teacup,
but the impassioned speeches for and against Thalamas in
the Chamber of Deputies and on public platforms showed
how deeply French society was split into two blocs, each of
which claimed to represent the nation. In the case of France,
a paradoxical situation arose, in which the appeal for national
unity did not unite the country, but divided it. It took the *union
sacrée*, the common front formed by the parties in response to
the German declaration of war on 3 August 1914 to bridge the
gulf between the two camps.

However topical many features of French nationalism in
the Third Republic may seem, especially in the light of its
continuation after the First World War, it must be realized
that as a movement it was basically defensive, negative and
backward-looking. 'We are the victims of defeat, even before
we come into the world', declared the philosopher, Charles
Péguy (1873–1914). 'We were born as a defeated nation.
We were born shortly after invasion and defeat, as a nation
conquered on the battlefield.'[3] To fear of the modern age,
which had destroyed hierarchies and threatened beauty, which
was dominated by money rather than by ideas of honour,
there was joined an awareness of defeat, of humiliation and
weakness in comparison with the Protestant powers – not
only Germany, but England as well. It is notable, however,
that French nationalism was mainly aimed at the continent of

Europe and took little interest in the colonies. Colonial enterprises were to some extent suspected of being merely a device for distracting attention from the problem of Alsace–Lorraine and the rehabilitation of the country.

England, too, reacted to the revolution in the European order that took place in 1871. Changes on the continent had given this leading colonial power reason to reflect on the major asset of its overseas empire. Moreover, changes in the franchise in 1867 and 1884 had introduced a broader cross-section of the public to politics, and both the major parties, the Conservatives and the Liberals, were faced with the task of integrating the new voters into their programmes. In a celebrated speech at the Crystal Palace on 24 June 1872, the British Prime Minister, Benjamin Disraeli, had declared that a pivotal feature of Conservative policy was the fact

> that the English people, and especially the working classes of England, are proud to belong to a great nation and wish to maintain that greatness – that they are proud to belong to an Empire, and that they are determined, if they can, to maintain that Empire – that they believe in general that the greatness and the Empire of England are to be attributed to the country's time-honoured institutions.[4]

After a sharp attack on the Liberals, who had neglected the Empire in their eagerness for reform in domestic policies, Disraeli arrived at the conclusion:

> It is a matter of whether you wish to be a comfortable England organized on continental lines that will fall victim to an inevitable fate in the foreseeable future, or whether you wish to be a great country, a country in which your sons, if they rise in the world, can achieve eminent positions, and gain not just the esteem of their fellow countrymen, but the respect of the whole world.[5]

Disraeli belonged to that generation of English Conservative statesmen who saw the England of their day caught up in a breathtaking economic boom, as the mistress of world trade, but who also detected the basic problem of their age in the deep division of the nation into distinct groups and individuals who cared only for their own interests. In his youth Disraeli had written a socially critical novel in which he had deplored the division of England into two nations, that of the 'haves' and that of the 'have-nots'. It was clear to him that a return to traditional, tried and trusted social relationships, to the union of the two nations in one, could be achieved only if everyone, including the members of the working class, was prepared to take an interest in the fate of the nation as a whole. There seemed to be two ways in which this could be done: the solution, step by step, of the country's social problems, and, secondly, the creation of a British Empire spanning the globe and sustained by national pride.

The idea was not new: years previously, the historian, J. A. Froude had pointed out in *Frazer's Magazine* the boundless scope that England had for expansion overseas, given the changes in the European balance of power. In his epic poem, *Idylls of the King*, Alfred, Lord Tennyson, had raised England from the status of a second-rate island to an 'Ocean-Empire with her boundless homes'. *Greater Britain*, published by Charles Dilke in 1868, proved to be a huge success. The art historian and social critic, John Ruskin, invested the idea with fateful significance: England seemed for him to be the 'regal island, a source of light to the entire world, a centre of peace', for which reason she must 'found colonies as far afield and as rapidly as she can'[6] for the benefit of all mankind. Disraeli, then, was simply picking up ideas that had long been in the air and had already achieved a degree of popularity. What he did, however, was to turn these ideas into essential planks in the platform of a political party and the state which it governed.

Following the rule of the Liberals and their Manchester school notions of *laissez-faire*, which had lasted for a whole generation, in the Conservative era of Disraeli and his successor, Salisbury (1830–1903), the state set out to ensure the domestic equilibrium of Great Britain and to maintain her power abroad. While the social consequences of industrialization were tackled by a whole series of measures in social policy under the slogan of 'Tory democracy', the government proceeded to consolidate England's overseas possessions, which had hitherto been acquired in an almost absent-minded fashion: they were extended in competition with rival continental powers and ultimately turned into a judicially and constitutionally coherent global empire. In this process British settlers in the colonies of Canada, Australia and New Zealand played a relatively minor part. The true source of imperial power was to be found in India and the adjoining territories, and comparisons with the Roman Empire were frequently quoted. When, in 1876, he persuaded Queen Victoria (1819–1901) to assume the title of Empress of India, Disraeli achieved a masterstroke in the consolidation of the nation. Growing enthusiasm for the crown – which had been distinctly lukewarm under the Georges from the House of Hanover – was now combined with the vision of a resplendent, wealthy, exotic continent under English rule, and the dream of an imperial monarchy acquired a further degree of actuality. Was not England repeating the legendary exploits of Alexander the Great, was not the English crown heir to the great Macedonian who had conquered the entire known world and united East and West? The popular novels of Rudyard Kipling (1865–1936) toyed over and over again with this theme: the short story, *The Man who Wanted to be King*, is manifestly a parable – the tale of an English adventurer who stumbles on Buddhas with classical Greek profiles in a remote Himalayan valley, and a people who greet him as a reincarnation of Alexander . . . The strategic links with India were looked upon as the empire's arteries; on the one hand, the sea passage around Africa, hence the 'Cape–Cairo axis' and, on the other, the passage through the Mediterranean via Gibraltar to the Near East and thence by the overland route via Mesopotamia, Persia, Afghanistan and Baluchistan. Great Britain was prepared to enter into open and fair competition for supremacy in the world, but when the lines of communication with India seemed threatened by Russian troops in the Hindukush, by French expeditions in Syria or on the White Nile, or German railway engineers in Mesopotamia, then the British popular press seethed and Whitehall thought of military intervention.

The colonial expansion of the British Empire at the height of the imperial phase between the 1880s and the First World

War was, in percentage terms much less than that of England's rivals – after all, it was not a matter of building a new colonial empire, but of rounding out possessions that had been acquired long since. But the very extent of these colonial dependencies makes it obvious that we are dealing with a unique phenomenon (see table: areas in thousands of square kilometres).

	Great Britain	France	Germany	Spain	Italy
1881	22,395	526	0	432	0
1895	29,021	3,577	2,641	1,974	247
1912	30,087	7,906	2,907	213	1,590

Source: Wolfgang J. Mommsen (ed.): *Imperialismus*, Hamburg 1977, p. 371

As distinct from the situation of France or Germany, the island kingdom of Great Britain could afford to take a view of the world in which great European wars featured as mere sideshows in a global battle for oceans and continents – a battle from which Britain had invariably emerged victorious, whether against Spain or France. But who was to say that this would always be so? The great historian of imperialism, John Robert Seeley (1834–95), whose work, *The Expansion of England* (1883), sold 80,000 copies within two years, warned of the fate which had befallen great powers like Sweden, Holland or Spain in the past, so that they had declined into second-rate status. He suggested two expedients to forestall the decline of the British Empire: on the one hand, continued expansion, and, on the other, an integrated system of government, so that England might keep her place in future alongside the new world powers, the USA and Russia. With the declining expansion of the empire in the 1890s and later, it was the second suggestion that took priority. 'Constructive imperialism' was the latest watchword and it implied the realization of the most grandiose ideal that statesmen of any age or any country had ever envisaged:

'the creation of an empire such as the world had never seen', in the words of the colonial secretary, Joseph Chamberlain (1836–1914), who was the principal spokesman for the 'constructive imperialism' movement. He went on, 'We must work towards the unification of the states bordering the oceans; we must consolidate the British race'.[7] A first step towards this aim was to be the formation of an economic union, to be followed by military and political alliances. At the same time, however, thought was given to more effective integration of the motherland, with Chamberlain and his colleagues planning to reduce the part played in government by the parties and by Parliament; they were inclined to place vested interests before the interests of the nation and proposed introducing elements of the plebiscite into the British constitution under the slogan of 'more democracy'. In their view, imperialism, national interests and democracy seemed to be only different aspects of the same overall endeavour: to save the nation from the decline that was threatened by class antagonisms and socialism at home, and growing competition from Germany, France and Russia abroad. 'Democracy has been achieved, a democratic national policy has replaced utilitarianism, and imperialism has become the very latest and the highest embodiment of our democratic nationalism. It is a conscious expression of our race.' This was how the Duke of Westminster defined the connection between democracy and imperialism.[8]

These were not just the ideas of a small Conservative elite and a handful of Liberals, as many historians believe, but a pervasive public opinion shared by all social groups and classes. Towards the end of the nineteenth century there had been established in England a national consensus, binding the nation together in a social and cultural sense, which helped the country to overcome its social conflicts, the painful problem of Irish Home Rule, and the loss of England's hitherto unchallenged economic and political supremacy as a world power. Imperialism and nationalism were merely two sides of the same coin. The major issue affecting the internal unity of the kingdom – its relations with the Irish minority seeking their independence – was invariably represented in public as inseparable from Great Britain's imperial mission. The proponents of 'constructive imperialism' were at the same time opponents of Home Rule, i.e. Irish self-government, because the latter was a threat to the unity of the empire. Teaching in the schools encouraged the national consensus, as did popular literature and the reading matter offered to the young. In the traditional theatre and on the stages of the music-halls imperialism became a central idea, the visual arts, including architecture, paid homage to it, and the popular press across the spectrum from the *Daily Telegraph* to the *Daily Mail* and the *Daily Express* preached imperialism. In its first issue in 1896 the *Express* announced that it was 'neither the mouthpiece of a political party nor the instrument of any social clique . . . Our policy is patriotic, our policy is the British Empire'.[9]

The national consensus rested on certain clearly defined assumptions. To begin with, there were the unique features of the British character, which explained and justified the worldwide expansion of Great Britain. The British national character was endowed with a special talent for government – for self-government, as well as the government of subject peoples: the British were 'the greatest governing race the world has ever seen', to quote Joseph Chamberlain.[10] This implied not only the superiority of the British over all other white races, and *a fortiori* over non-white races, but also a moral justification of the empire: Great Britain's imperial mission was in the interests of civilization and of mankind in general. Somewhere in the background there was the idea of service as well as rule. 'The white man's burden', as Kipling called the duty of civilizing the world and converting it to Christianity, lay squarely on the shoulders of England. Opposed to all this was the unseemly envy of upstart rivals for world leadership, against whom England might prevail only if she went on extending her power. In 1911 they were singing in the music-halls of Drury Lane:

> There are enemies around us who are jealous of our fame,
> We've built a mighty empire and they want to do the same,
> And they think that they can do it, if we drop off for a nap
> While they fight our friends and neighbours and wipe them
>   off the map.[11]

Unlike the France of the Third Republic, which was deeply

divided on issues that called for a national consensus, in England an extraordinary measure of agreement prevailed on ideas of the state, the nation, the empire and Britishness. In the case of Germany, in a sense, the features of France and England were combined.

In Germany, too, the 'internal consolidation of the Reich', the striking of a balance throughout the nation between conflicting social groups and interests was the primary issue in domestic politics. A great multitude of intersecting and mutually hostile social and economic interests coagulated into parties, mass organizations, pressure groups and lobbies. The situation was rendered even more complex by the existence of outsiders: the emergence of the new German nation state had engendered problems with minorities: there were sizeable French, Polish and Danish ethnic groups in the population of the Reich – and the place and function of Jews in Germany was a hotly disputed issue. Bismarck's mode of government tried to solve such problems by segregating such of the larger groups as could not be assimilated into a monarchical, authoritarian state, and branding them as 'enemies of the Reich'. These included, first and foremost, the Catholics of the Centre Party. Ever since the middle of the nineteenth century they had been offering dogged resistance to attempts by the Protestant state to achieve political and cultural centralization. The so-called 'cultural battle' (*Kulturkampf*) was ostensibly waged over state supervision of schools and the appointment of parish priests, but it was in fact an attempt by the Protestant state to make German Catholic politicians conform to Prussian national policy, in spite of their international affiliations. Incidentally, this was not simply a German problem: a 'cultural battle' was being simultaneously waged – albeit with other assumptions and in other forms – in France, Spain and Italy. And since the end of the seventies in Germany there had also been a battle against social democracy. August Bebel (1840–1913) inspired mortal terror in government circles and amongst the affluent when he declared in the Reichstag on 25 May 1871 that the Paris Commune was nothing but a minor preliminary skirmish compared with what his contemporaries might expect in the way of social revolution. Bismarck's legislation of 1878, aimed

against socialism, was the state's response to the challenge of
the 'party of revolution', although it seems innocuous enough
in the light of the methods of political persecution customary
in the twentieth century: after all, the Social Democratic Party
continued to exist and grew stronger from one election to the
next. At the same time, the imperial government introduced,
step by step, a system of state insurance that became a model
for the whole of Europe as a mode of turning destitute socialists
into Conservative citizens of modest means. As far as that went,
however, the social policy conceived in a spirit of East Elbian
patriarchalism proved to be a failure, for, following the repeal
of the anti-socialist legislation in 1890, the rush to join the
Social Democratic ranks became more marked than ever.

The most effective instrument of the national integration
of Germany as a 'retarded nation state' (Helmut Plessner)
was certainly the army. The army regarded itself as the sole
guardian of the state and the monarchy – not just against
foreign aggressors, but also against the enemy within, the
Social Democrats, Catholics and Liberals. In the course of
time the image of the Prussian officer increasingly ousted that
of the middle-class liberal in public esteem. The civic virtues of
the educated and affluent middle class had played a vital part
in German history during the nineteenth century; now it was
no longer these virtues that set social standards, but the image
of the Prussian officer. Certainly, in the German provinces,
especially in the regional capitals of the 'Third Germany',
as well as in South Germany, the simpler assessment by the
middle class of its own political function, inherited from the
first half of the nineteenth century, still persisted. But it was
the growing political weight of the Prussian trinity – Imperial
court, rural estate and barrack square – that made the deepest
impression on the German mentality. There was, too, the
high esteem which the army had enjoyed ever since the Wars
of Liberation: it might well be said that the army was the
pride of the nation. Respect for the army devolved on every
single one of its members, gaining him enhanced status in
his social milieu. This is why universal conscription was not
felt to be an imposition but an honour and an opportunity
for social advancement; weapons and uniform were invested

with a Romantic and glamorous aura, which was sedulously fostered, with the exception of a few liberal papers, by the press and in literature. Even in civilian life it was important for a man to have 'served'. Civil servants and teachers derived their self-respect from their status as officers of the reserve and in their offices and schools they applied the criteria they were familiar with from their army service. This militaristic mentality was bound to have an influence on political judgements – initially affecting the country's subjects, and ultimately its rulers.

The main reason for this lay in the 'inner consolidation of the Reich', which had not proceeded according to plan. Germany remained inwardly fragmented, ancient territorial and denominational differences could not be overcome in such a brief period, nor could the profound social gulfs be bridged which had opened in the wake of industrialization between industry and agriculture, the nobility and the middle class, capital and labour. The political parties, which ought really to have absorbed and smoothed out these divisions, proved unequal to the task, not least because, under German constitutional arrangements, they were not obliged to accept political responsibility or forced to compromise. As a result they were more concerned with philosophical issues and ideological programmes than practical politics: they served their adherents more as secular churches than as effective pressure groups. The German party system was a mass of irreconcilable antagonisms, a tangle of trenches and redoubts.

And the whole political system was intersected and overlaid with organized interests. Between the various pressure groups, as between the various parties, there was no common language and consequently a deeply rooted inability to arrive at social and political compromises. Where common sense, or dedication to some ulterior common criteria should have prevailed, what dominated the social system was an ideological battle of all against all, the sole common denominator being an imperial German nationalism that reached deep into the working-class movement, in spite of protestations to the contrary on international platforms. But this nationalism was bloodless and shallow: with the founding of the Reich the

utopia that had furnished two generations of German patriots
with the meaning and measure of their political action and a
sense of their own identity had vanished and been replaced by
the economy. What was missing was a middle-class culture
of common sense, common practices such as were taken for
granted as governing the political culture of Germany's western
neighbours. Lacking, too, was a unifying idea that would have
pointed the way beyond the present into the future.

There was only one court of appeal, then, competent to
resolve this comparatively dramatic social situation, alone
assuming the burden of all the efforts being made to resolve the
various clashes and conflicts, including the problem of national
identity and the ultimate meaning of things: this court of appeal
was in fact the state itself, the authoritarian Prussian–German
state which was responsible for administration, education and
the distribution of wealth and privilege, a state which felt
itself competent to deal with everything from social services
to bye-laws governing the lay-out of cemeteries, with a civil
service and armed forces subscribing to an ideology in which
they existed above and beyond the conflicting interests of
society, caring only for the welfare of the entire body politic
– in essence an anti-democratic, totally authoritarian ideal.
Its authoritarian character was emphasized all the more in
that the proper representative of the people, the Reichstag
was widely regarded as a forum for meaningless gossip and
petty squabbles and was little respected. As one Conservative
member remarked, the emperor could shut the Reichstag down
at any moment with the help of a lieutenant and a squad of
ten men. The image of 'Father State' standing above a feckless
people and all their quarrels was deeply rooted, and this was
illustrated by the fact that German Social Democracy, the great
counterpart to the state, itself duplicated the state apparatus
down to the last detail of its spirit and structure. 'But the
foe that we must beat/ Is the blindness of the masses in
factory and street.' That was not the motto that hung in
every Prussian office, but a couple of lines from the Social
Democratic 'workers' Marseillaise'.

The army and the official state as factors holding the nation
together were augmented in the nineties by a feeble impersona-

tion of an English model – the vision of Germany's world-wide mission, the imperial temptation. The small continent of Europe seemed too cramped for the enormous economic and political potential that was being generated in Germany. Confinement within the scope of modest domestic develop-ments and saturated markets was felt by the German middle class as degrading and discriminatory in comparison with their European neighbours. National politics had hitherto implied the unification of Germany and the subsequent consolidation of the Reich; since the nineties, however, German politics had meant world politics, as expressed by Max Weber (1864–1920) on the occasion of his inaugural lecture in 1895:

> Once . . . the unity of the nation had been achieved and its political appetite had been satisfied, an oddly 'unhistorical' and unpolitical spirit took possession of the German middle class, intoxicated with success, but longing only for peace and quiet. German history seemed to have come to a halt, the present moment was, it seemed, the total fulfilment of the millennia that had preceded it . . . As far as *our* development is concerned, what matters most is whether a major political issue is liable to confront us once more with the great questions of political power. We ought to realize that the unification of Germany was a youthful prank perpetrated by a nation in its old age, from which it should have refrained on account of the cost, in case it turned out to be the end, rather than the starting point of a policy for Germany as a world power.[12]

Aspirations to world power, then as the mission of the German people, as its apotheosis: that was a distinct departure from Bismarck's policy, which had been strictly confined to Central Europe. It was not the old Prussian upper class, uncivi-lized and yet awe-inspiring in the view of foreign observers, concerned only to maintain its social status at home and devoid of ambitions in foreign policy, that had prompted an excursion into imperialistic adventure. Those who had promoted it were rather the liberal, educated and affluent middle class, the heirs of the German national movement, who, as their economic potential grew, were intent on expansion and global status.

It is hard to distinguish here between carefully calculated economic policy on the one hand, and, on the other, the desire to compensate for national frustration at the sight of imperialistic expansion by neighbouring countries – France, England and Russia. Unlike these states, however, in Germany the sense of mission was limited to 'global politics', without any ulterior intellectual principle to recommend it. Shortly before the outbreak of the First World War the pan-German writer, Friedrich von Bernhardi, confessed ruefully, 'We lack any clearly defined political and national aim that might capture the imagination, move the nation's heart and prompt it to take concerted action.'[13] Behind the makeshift slogan, 'global politics' there lurked for the most part the example of British imperialism, which Germany tried to oppose and to emulate at one and the same time. 'The world must not at some point become either English or Russian', wrote the influential historian and publicist, Hans Delbrück, 'but if the world outside Europe were divided absolutely into two languages, then it would be impossible for European states thus excluded to hold out for long against such superpowers. That is why Germany is obliged to pursue a colonial policy on a grand scale . . .'[14]

Bismarck had responded to the demand for German colonies and spheres of influence reluctantly and in a dilatory fashion. This was the era of colonial adventurers like Carl Peters (1856–1914) and Gustav Nachtigall (1834–85), who hoisted the German ensign over East Africa and Cameroons. With the aid of a vociferous press, mass organizations and business associations, they more or less forced the Reich to annex these territories as a protectorate. The situation changed under Bismarck's successor: under pressure from mass organizations like the 'German Colonial Society', founded in 1887, and, above all, the 'Pan-German Union', founded in 1894, the establishment of German colonies in Africa and the Pacific Ocean became a feature of German foreign policy. South-west Africa (now Namibia), East Africa (now Tanzania), Togo and Cameroons became German protectorates, as did Tsingtau in China, a part of New Guinea and several archipelagos in the South Seas. It was still possible to arrive at gentleman's agreements with European neighbours over the partition of the world, as was shown by the Congo Act, agreed at an international conference in Berlin in 1885, the German–British Zanzibar Settlement of 1891, and finally by the Treaty of Algeciras in 1906, which settled the Moroccan question.

Two further initiatives in Germany's global policy, however, turned out to be more perilous. One was the extension of the axis of German influence beyond Vienna and south-east Europe into the territory of the Ottoman Empire as far as Mesopotamia. International tension reached a critical point with a pompous state visit to the Middle East by Emperor William II (1859–1941) in 1897, which was seen as a provocation by both Russia and England, and with the start of the construction of a railway to Baghdad in 1899. This seemed like an attack on Russia's aspirations in the Balkans and on the Bosphorus, as well as a threat to Britain's position in the Middle East. Any conflict in this area was bound to have repercussions on the peace of Central Europe.

Secondly, there was German policy for the High Seas Fleet. Ever since 1897, when Bernhard von Bülow (1849–1929) assumed responsibility for German foreign policy and, almost simultaneously, Admiral Alfred von Tirpitz (1849–1930) was appointed head of the admiralty, the two men had vigorously encouraged the building of a German Navy that would be capable of holding its own against the most powerful of the maritime nations – at that stage, still England. This move was not just a matter of cleverly calculated power politics; it was backed by an upsurge of national enthusiasm and a desire for self-assertion as compensation for feelings of inferiority vis-à-vis the manifest superiority in many respects of the 'English cousin'. It was backed, too, by a veritable mass movement led by the 'German Fleet Association', the most powerful of German pressure groups with over one million members. The awareness that England's interests would be threatened in their most sensitive area, and that consequently England would feel obliged to line up with the European flanking powers, Russia and France, played no part whatsoever in the public debate of the time. As had previously been the case with the unification of the Reich, an atmosphere of vague mass emotion was created in opposition to the rationale of the European balance of power. This time, however, the popular mood had its spokesmen in the nation's political leadership, above all, in the person of the Emperor himself, who never missed an opportunity, by his martial bearing and speeches, to alarm and provoke those responsible for British foreign policy.

The change in European ideas of the nation that took place in the nineteenth century may best be observed in the example of Italy. The idealistic nationalists of the *Risorgimento* had dreamed in the spirit of Mazzini of the brotherhood of the European nations and had assigned to the nation state an educational responsibility that would issue in civil liberties and power-sharing. These ideas underwent a radical change in the era of the prime minister Francesco Crispi (1819–1901), who ruled in an autocratic fashion between 1887 and 1896. It was an age of vigorous industrial progress which brought benefits to very few individuals, while social tensions grew ever more acute. Not only industrial workers, but also agricultural workers, especially in central and southern Italy, organized themselves: strikes and administrative repression raised the temperature on both sides, and Crispi took advantage of a virulent nationalistic mood to distract attention from such internal conflicts and also to increase the prestige of his nation. He rejected irredentism, the demand for the unification of all the Italian linguistic areas with the motherland, having noted how fragile the European alliances were. Instead he encouraged colonial expansion, sending troops to Eritrea, Somaliland and Ethiopia. He owed his electoral landslide victory of 1895 to the effervescent enthusiasm of the middle class for his colonial policy: a year later the Battle of Adowa took place, in which the Italian Army suffered a crushing defeat by Abyssinian troops.

This defeat was the cause of renewed trauma. The younger generation who made their appearance and put their stamp on Italian public life around the turn of the century were utterly convinced of the hollow pretensions and hypocrisy of their liberal fathers and the state which the latter had founded, the *raison d'être* of which seemed to go no further than *trasformismo*, a permanent time-serving compromise between the parties of the Left and those of the Right. Artists and writers took their lead from French models like Charles Maurras and Maurice Barrès. Gabriele d'Annunzio, Giovanni Papini or Filippo Tommaso Marinetti praised their nation as a 'chosen people', proposed action outside parliament in the name of the patriotic collective that had to be protected against the individualism of the modern age, and called for conflict, danger, technical advance and war. In the light of this irrational and Romantic nationalism, the imperial expansion of Italy beyond the Mediterranean seemed to be a prime condition for the rebirth of the Italian nation. Enrico Corradini celebrated the conquest of Libya in 1912:

> In truth, we thought it impossible that we should be of one mind on any single issue: all of a sudden we found ourselves at one, when confronted with this greatest of all human exploits, this war story in real life which goes beyond the limits of our imagination, the real life drama, in which we forty million Italians scattered across five continents are the pioneers, the advance guard of the hundreds of thousands of our sons who are fighting in Africa against a foe on the verge of defeat, with the whole of modern mankind and the history of ages still to come as onlookers.[15]

On the one hand, then, the disintegration of modern society, on the other the unifying experience of war viewed in aesthetic terms, from which a new nation must arise like a phoenix from the ashes: this was the quintessential experience that inspired the generation of 1914 – in France no less than in Germany and Italy.

However differently the European nation states may have coped at the end of the nineteenth and the beginning of the twentieth century with their internal tensions or with threats from abroad, real or imagined, the characteristic mark of the age may be detected behind whatever differences of approach there might be: 'integral nationalism', to quote Charles Maurras's term for his comprehensive and uncompromising theory. Whereas the *Risorgimento* nationalism of the nineteenth century had in principle manifested

certain liberal features, and was preached by a small elite
of highly respected individuals on the assumption that all
the social classes of a nation were equal, mass 'integral
nationalism' proceeded from the assumption that the nation
was supreme and absolute: *'Du bist nichts, Dein Volk ist
alles'* ('Thou art nought, thy people is all'); *'La France
d'abord'*; 'My country, right or wrong', these or similar slogans were the commandments to which 'integral
nationalism' committed its loyal adherents, and by which
it sanctioned the use of physical force against those of any
other faith.

This was in principle nothing new; even the radical Jacobin brand of nationalism during the French Revolution had
displayed totalitarian tendencies: the nation was *'une et indivisible'*, egalitarian and homogeneous, and anyone who did
not emphatically declare his faith in the nation would have
to reckon with physical annihilation. As a widespread political
phenomenon, it is true, integral or totalitarian nationalism is
distinctly more modern. It needed the established nation state
as the context in which it might be fully deployed: state and
nation tended to interact and influence each other more and
more, and state interests and policies tended increasingly to
coincide with expressions of national egoism, an unhappy
combination that began to make its appearance in all the
European states and to dictate European politics more and
more comprehensively towards the close of the nineteenth
century. The European concert, in which the self-interest of
individual states was moderated by the overall balance of
power, gradually fell silent, was heard only at abortive conferences that were convened less and less frequently and ultimately
gave way to the discordant antagonisms of the great powers
and their rival alliances.

With the dissolution of the European system of states, a
morbid fear of impending danger and decline grew up in
individual states: the disintegration of society, above all the
spectacle of striking and demonstrating workers, alarmed the
upper classes of the nation states, no less than the threat of
international rivalry that seemed to offer no choice other
than expansion overseas or else decline and fall – either in

a process of gradual decay, as with the former major powers, Sweden, Holland or Spain, which had ended up becalmed in the lee of history, or abruptly through war. Such nightmare visions of impending perils and panic first began to appear in the seventies and eighties, became more and more alarming by the turn of the century, and had reached their deafening and shattering crescendo by the outbreak of the First World War, which affected the whole of Europe. Across the whole political spectrum, from the radical Left to the extreme Right, France was hypnotized by the 'blue line of the Vosges on the horizon', by the German peril and the shame of 1871. England was all too acutely aware that she had lost a supremacy that had long been taken for granted, the superiority of the nation at sea had no longer been guaranteed after 1900. Germany was not just competing with England in world markets, she was setting out to build a fleet that reawakened in England the old fear of invasion. Saki's novel, *When William came*, described the conquest of Britain by the Germans, and instantly became a bestseller. Studies of industrial efficiency comparing England, Germany and the USA showed in England's case, 'signs of American enterprise and German organization . . . but the spirit of enterprise has evaporated, and the organization has been bungled'.[16] In Germany there was a growing fear of 'encirclement', a lethal alliance of the powers on the periphery of Europe against the central powers. This fear was associated with widespread feelings of inferiority and a tendency to think that Germany had been cheated in the partition of the colonial world. In Italy colonial fever, rendered even more acute by the defeat in Ethiopia, was endemic and associated with irredentism, the demand for the Brenner Pass as Italy's natural frontier.

The often irrational obsession with a country's inferiority or impending hazards in the social area, which underlay, not only the mood of the public, but also the action taken by governments, was matched by what seemed like an equally irrational sense of superiority and almost missionary zeal. A memorandum by Cecil Rhodes (1853–1903) from the year 1877 certainly represents an extreme case, but statements in the same tenor might be heard in similar contexts from publicists of the other European powers:

> I claim that we are the leading race in the world, and the more of the world we populate, the better it will be for mankind . . . Since [God] has obviously made the English-speaking race the chosen instrument by which He means to produce a state of society based on justice, freedom and peace, then it is bound to be in keeping with His will if I do everything in my power to provide that race with as much scope and power as possible. I think that, if there is a God, then He would like to see me do one thing, that is, to colour as much of the map of Africa British red as possible.[17]

Cecil Rhodes made his contribution to this end by occupying and annexing Bechuanaland and what was later to become Rhodesia.

This sense of mission, which now seems to us overwrought, if not actually grotesque, was common to all the states of Europe at the beginning of the twentieth century and did a great deal to inflame antagonism between nation states. That applied even to Russia, whose thrust in the direction of Asia, the Pacific and the Indian Ocean had taken second place since the end of the nineteenth century to a vision of an empire of all the Slav nations under Russian leadership which would serve primarily as a barrier to Germany and Austria and a feared 'Germanization' of Eastern Europe. The military chauvinist, General Fadejew (1824–84), declared, 'The Slavonic masses are a kind of cosmic nebula which, given a centre of gravity, might solidify to form a world. That is why each of these fraternal nations must be liberated, and the independence of each secured by a firm alliance with Russia.'[18] The electrifying effect of these words was probably greater abroad than with the Russian public, but the course of Russian policy in the Balkans up to the July crisis of 1914 is evidence of the extent to which the tsar was committed to his image of the 'Tsar as Liberator', not only at home, but also outside Russia, for instance, *vis-à-vis* Bulgaria or Serbia.

For every European nation state the former system of international relations seemed to be giving way to a world of mutual hostilities, and at the same time enemies had begun to rear their heads at home. This applied above all to the threat of socialism, which had made its appearance as the ideological rival to nationalism, in that it substituted class solidarity for national solidarity. As early as 1848 Karl Marx and Friedrich Engels had declared in their *Communist Manifesto* that workers had no fatherland, and in a Social Democratic *Manifesto addressed to the Working People of Austria* it had been stated in May 1868 – in German, Czech, Polish, Italian, Rumanian and Hungarian – that 'the age of division into nationalities is past, the principle of nationality survives only on the agenda of reactionaries. . . The labour market knows no national frontiers, world trade crosses all language barriers. Capital, which rules everywhere, and the expression and measure of which is money, cares nothing for alleged racial descent.'[19] In the course of time the attitudes of socialist leaders to the nation state diversified and ranged from emphasis on the nations' right to self-determination, via theorists like Lenin (1870–1924) and the Austrian Marxist, Otto Bauer (1882–1938), to Rosa Luxemburg's (1870–1919) uncompromising repudiation of the very idea of the nation. But from the point of view of the establishment in every European state, any appeal to class solidarity and internationalism was simply an unprecedented provocation and was met with ferocious hostility to such 'footloose riff-raff'. Both ideologies, nationalism and socialism, were essentially revolutionary, but nationalism had a long head-start over socialism, for the nation and the state were closely linked, while socialism rejected the existing state in principle and could not avail itself of the state's ideological reserves, such as the idea of national integration and solidarity.

The antithesis, 'national–international', in domestic politics was broadened in the context of the cultural conflict which broke out in a number of states, and in the course of which 'ultramontane' Catholicism was increasingly ranked side by side with socialism. Bismarck stated his conviction 'that the state is threatened in its very foundations and imperilled by two parties which have in common their opposition to the nation and the consolidation of the nation state. In my judgement all those who are in favour of reinforcing the state element, the capacity of the state to defend itself, must stand together against those who threaten and attack it.'[20] The more a nation state felt threatened, the more the unifying consensus was called in question, the larger loomed the spectre of its internal foes. To Catholics and socialists were added ethnic minorities – Poles, Danes, Alsatians in Germany, the people of the Celtic fringe in Great Britain (a problem that bulked so large that, at one time, Scotland was officially referred to as 'North Britain') or the inhabitants of Southern Italy. These were all minorities that may not have been attacked in the strict sense, but which were often discriminated against, handicapped in their cultural development, and excluded from any chance of improving their social status in the countries where they lived.

It was above all the Jews who represented an obvious anti-image to the ideal of national unity. 'Integral' nationalism at the turn of the nineteenth and twentieth century already had markedly anti-Semitic tendencies, which were manifested in ways that differed from one country to another. As compared with their co-religionists in Eastern Europe, Jews in Central and Western Europe regarded themselves as culturally assimilated, but often attracted feelings of social envy, because they lived in better economic circumstances than their non-Jewish compatriots. Popular anti-Semitism, nourished by economic factors, was combined with acute cultural anti-Semitism as Jewish emigrants from the east, driven out by social ostracism and pogroms in Russia, made their way into Western Europe. Their seemingly alien culture, their uncompromising orthodoxy were felt to be outlandish, incomprehensible and dangerous. Popular hostility to the Jews was thus provided with an additional basis. Heinrich von Treitschke's anti-Semitism was confined to the argument of national integration: 'All that we ask of our Israelite fellow-citizens is simple: they should become Germans and feel themselves simply to be Germans – without detriment to their faith and time-honoured, sacred memories which we all of us respect.'[21] But the works of Houston Stewart Chamberlain (1855–1927) and Count Gobineau (1816–82) had already begun to appear. They proclaimed that the Jewish 'race' was different in principle from others, and inferior to them. About the year 1886 Edouard Drumont gave free rein to his imagination:

> The only one to gain from the Revolution was the Jew: everything stems from the Jew, and everything finds its way back to the Jew. Here, what we are dealing with is the conquest of an entire nation, its subjugation as serfs to a tiny but tenaciously united minority . . . What we have is the exploitation of a subservient race by a master race.[22]

In the figure of the repulsive Jewish merchant, Ehrenthal, in Gustav Freytag's immensely successful novel *Soll und Haben* (*Debit and Credit*), and the greasy banker Schwartz in Paul Féval's *Habits noirs* and the profoundly evil fence, Fagin, in Charles Dickens's *Oliver Twist*, popular novelists created clichés that could readily be seized upon and adapted by nationalistic rabble-rousers. The German Social Reform Party, founded in 1875 by the Prussian Court Preacher, Adolf Stoecker (1835–1909) featured anti-Semitic demands in their party programme and in 1892 sixteen of their members were elected to the Reichstag. In 1898 there were anti-Jewish riots in a number of French towns in connection with the Dreyfus affair. They were incited by anti-Semitic propaganda in Edouard Drumont's paper, *La Libre Parole*, and even in liberal England, where the assimilation of Jewish residents had made most progress, there were brawls in the slums of London's East End in protest against Jewish immigrants from Eastern Europe. None of this agitation was notably successful, however, and it soon died down, except in the case of the Austrian Christian–Social Party, which took power in the City Hall of Vienna in 1895 under the popular Lord Mayor, Karl Lueger (1844–1910), whose crude anti-Semitism made a deep impression on the youthful Adolf Hitler (1889–1945). The image of the 'Jew' as the enemy had been identified and might be invoked at any time when there was a need to discredit liberal or socialist policies or to explain away social inequalities or setbacks to national unity.

And so the 'traditional enemy' abroad was joined by an

enemy at home, who was regarded as a threat to the nation's very existence. In the conduct of political campaigns at home there was often a tendency to exaggerate friction with other states as a way of encouraging loyalty at home. Internal and external conflicts tended to influence each other, each rendering the other more acute. The idea of the nation which, in the transition from the eighteenth to the nineteenth century, had been a utopia encompassing all parties in a union of people, culture and state, became, in the succeeding age of nation states and industrial mass civilization, a polemical factor in domestic policy: it no longer stood above the parties uniting society, but itself turned into a party and divided society. By setting itself up as an absolute 'integral nationalism', it refused to recognize the rights of its opponents in domestic and foreign policy, and became a party advocating civil war on a national and European scale. For one of its essential features was that the ideas and categories of *Risorgimento* nationalism, of a Herder or Mazzini, concerning the existence side by side of liberal, constitutional nations, and the equality of all nations, no longer obtained.

These ideas were soon superseded by the grim doctrine of Charles Darwin (1809–82) concerning natural selection and the survival of the fittest, the pseudo-scientific version of which, 'social Darwinism', was extremely popular as the product of middle-class late Enlightenment. The law of nature, on which this idea was allegedly based, was a battle of all against all, peace was an illusion of the weaker party, at best a breathing space in an eternal struggle for existence; only he who was superior in moral and physical resources would survive. That the human species was not adapted to peaceful co-existence was taken as axiomatic by every social and political group, whether it subscribed to the Marxist idea of the class struggle, the populist notion of the perpetual antagonism between nations, or the recently propounded ideology of the battle between rival races. It was an epoch in which ideas of humanity and natural justice lost ground to the seductive appeal of anti-democratic and anti-individualistic ideologies which were ostensibly founded on physical laws of nature, and in which the nation counted for infinitely more than the individual. Heinrich von Treitschke was able to launch to great effect the proposition that the individual should be ready to sacrifice himself 'for a higher collective, of which he is a member; he counts for something only in so far as he is part of his nation'. Moreover, the regenerating function of war was discovered and most eloquently put into words by Friedrich Nietzsche (1844–1900). Nietzsche was himself a scathing critic of William II's Reich and of its citizens, but his catch-phrases – 'the will to power', the master race and the superman, the 'blonde beast', and the triumph of the strong nations over the weak – were liable to all kinds of abuse. In vulgarized form, his concept of an elite race had the same effect as the irrational and elitist theories of Vilfredo Paredo (1848–1923) in Italy, or Georges Sorel (1847–1923) in France. The latter diagnosed bourgeois society as mindless and decadent in peacetime and suggested that there were only two remedies: 'A great foreign war that might invigorate us once again and at least bring to power men with the will to govern; or else a mighty expansion of the power of the working-class which would reveal the true nature of revolution to the bourgeoisie and force them to turn away in disgust from all their humanitarian platitudes . . . '[23] And in Oswald Spengler, the prophet of a 'decline of the West', his readers might find the blunt statement, 'Man is a beast of prey.'

Politics meant war, and war was needed to incinerate the evils of the new age, which ranged from individualism to socialism, so that a nation might arise rejuvenated from the ashes. This was not the view of a handful of extremists: it was the view that might be found in popular as well as serious periodicals and newspapers in the period between 1880 and 1914. For the present-day observer such literature is a veritable treasure-trove of evidence revealing the nucleus of 'social Darwinism' that sustained popular nationalism in those days – in the Anglo-Saxon parts of the world as well as in France, Germany or Italy. When the British Field-Marshal Roberts constantly referred during the Boer War to the inexorable struggle between nations as a biological necessity, praising it as an effective remedy that had made a man of many a weakling and fitted many a nation to govern

a worldwide empire, then he was merely echoing many other
authors of the day who were vigorously beating the same
drum: like the German General Friedrich von Bernhardi, for
instance, whose 'Germany and the next War', first published
in 1912, was reprinted nine times in the next two years and
exhorted politicians to look on war as a 'moral necessity',
which would purge the nation and lead it on to its higher
destiny.

This growing readiness on the part of the masses to go to
war as a cure for the nation's ills was to be found everywhere
in Europe in the years just before the First World War, and it
began to change the very nature of society. National integration
was increasingly pursued through military organization. In
1910 the 16,500 Prussian Servicemen's Associations numbered
1.5 million members; the 'German Warriors' League' also had
1.7 million members in 1910, and the 'Kyffhäuser League'
could muster as many as 2.5 million members. These figures no
doubt included a good many multiple memberships, but there
were also a large number of paramilitary youth organizations,
like 'Young Germany' or the 'Youth Defence Force', and if we
count the supporters of the 'Fleet Association' and the 'Defence
Association', who drummed up support for the Conservatives
at elections, then the total of Germans mobilized in this way
came to something like 5 million, i.e. a sixth of all the nation's
men or juveniles, and more than double the number of trade
unionists at that time. It is numbers of this order that must
be borne in mind when we visualize the 'integration of the
nation'.

It is clear, all the same, that what was happening in Germany, where the craving for a national consensus bordered
on the neurotic, was simply a particularly striking instance
of a European phenomenon. We must also bear in mind that
the nationalistic organizations that rallied support for parties
reckoned to be ultra-Conservative or nationalistic were prone
to exert pressure on governments to adopt aggressive foreign
policies and otherwise put their stamp on public opinion in general. The 'Pan-German Union', founded in 1894 had 18,000
members by 1901, including 5,400 university teachers, 5,000
small businessmen, 3,700 civil servants, artists and teachers,

as well as 2,700 independent tradesmen. Similar mass organizations, although possibly not as influential, were the *Action Française* in France, the *Associazione Nazionalista Italiana* or *Italia Irredenta* in Italy, and the British 'Primrose League' and 'Greater Britain' – all of them more or less anti-democratic, illiberal and aggressively nationalistic – and, in the case of Germany and France, anti-Semitic as well. This amounted to a deafening chorus of 'integral nationalism' that did more to drive the peoples of Europe into the First World War than all the mistakes of their leaders, diplomats and generals put together.

The ideal nation state had still not made its appearance: the apparatus of the state, which was governed by rational and clear-cut administrative criteria and which was ready to compromise in foreign policy was still at odds with a one-sided nationalism that was much given to aggressive posturing. At this stage nationalism was still a social phenomenon rather than a feature of the state. It provided the consensus that middle-class society needed to come to terms with the disintegration of the old agrarian world and its reorganization into distinct social classes, as well as with the disorder and ugliness of the dawning industrial age. But leading politicians at the end of the nineteenth and the beginning of the twentieth century had been unable to resist the temptation to harness public enthusiasm for national aspirations in order to advance their policies at home and abroad – whether to serve the unification and inner cohesion of the new states of Europe, or, in the case of France to overcome the shock of the defeat of 1870–1, or else to secure popular support for imperialist expansion, as in the case of England and Russia. The Bonapartist ventures of Bismarck, Cavour, Ferry and Disraeli all backfired, but the populist spirit of the nationalist movements, once conjured up, remained, captivated the public imagination and imposed its political aims on the rulers. 'But very often, gentlemen,' the German Chancellor, Theobald von Bethmann Hollweg (1856–1921), declared before the Reichstag on the eve of the outbreak of the First World War, 'wars are not planned or brought about by governments. Nations have often been driven into wars by vociferous and fanatical minorities. This danger still exists and is possibly even more acute today, since the public, the nation's mood and agitation have gained in scale and significance.'[24] Barely two years later the critical point had been reached.

12

The Total Nation State 1914–1945

If the hackneyed metaphor of the 'turning point in world history' ever made sense, then it applied to the outbreak of the First World War. Looked at in the cold light of day, it was by no means the first world war in a series – the conflict between England and France for the acquisition of an overseas empire between 1740 and 1763, in which the war between Prussia and Austria over Poland was no more than a sideshow, has a better claim to that distinction. If we compare the number of casualties in the First World War in relation to the scale of the armies involved, then the losses were not greater than in the Napoleonic wars, and yet the 'Great War', as contemporaries quite rightly began to call it, was a totally unprecedented experience for Europe. The self-destruction of Europe, which has not come to a halt even today, began in the July days of 1914.

'The Great War through which we have just passed differed from all previous wars in the vast military resources employed and in their fearful power of destruction, and from all other modern wars in the ruthlessness with which it was fought,' said Winston Churchill (1878–1965), who was anything but a pacifist.

> The horrors of all were combined, and it was not just armies, but entire populations that were involved . . . Neither armistices nor negotiations mitigated the struggle of

the armies. The wounded died wretchedly between the hostile forces, the dead fertilized the fields, merchant ships, neutral vessels and hospital ships were sunk and all on board abandoned to their fate, or else killed as they swam to safety. Every effort was made to force whole nations into submission by starvation, without regard to sex or age. Cities and cultural monuments were wrecked by artillery fire, bombs were dropped at random. Poison gases of all kinds stifled or burned the soldiers, liquid fire destroyed their bodies. Men fell from the heavens in flames or suffocated slowly in air pockets in sinking ships. The size of the armies was limited only by the population of their countries. Europe and large parts of Asia and Africa were turned into a single desolate battlefield, on which after years of struggle not just armies but whole nations perished. When it had all passed, torture and cannibalism were the only expedients which the civilized, scientifically educated Christian states had denied themselves – and that, only because they would have been of doubtful utility.[1]

That was the point: war was no longer waged only on the battlefield, but also in the hinterland, and everyone, whether soldier or civilian, man or woman, was somehow involved, either at the battle-front or, as it was significantly called, on the 'home front'. The whole of society was at war, and the hour of the state had come.

People did not realize that at first: indeed, in August 1914 the tide of national enthusiasm ran high in all the belligerent states, for it was still believed that the soldiers would be home for Christmas. Instead, the war went on, lasting longer and longer, and in spite of the warning example of the American Civil War, none of the states involved was prepared for a war of attrition lasting for years. On the other hand, the war had so stimulated and reinforced the popular national consensus that, for the first time in the history of industrial societies, a far-reaching concentration of power in the hands of the state commanded universal support. With the *union sacrée* invoked by President Poincaré in the face of German aggression, the deep division of opinion which had just previously split the middle-class government majority from the socialists over the issue of a three-year term of military service, was overcome. In Great Britain the campaign of the Suffragettes and the dispute over Irish Home Rule were forgotten. English society, no less than the continental states, succumbed to the patriotic fever, which ran riot in panic fear of 'krauts' landing by night on England's beaches, or in the suspicion of German spies in every walk of life. The anxious question of a child overhearing a conversation about her German governess – 'Oh, mummy, must we really kill poor Fräulein?' – has its place in the stock repertoire of anecdotes recounted by British historians.

In the capitals of the belligerent powers people danced in the streets and garlanded the departing troops with flowers as if they were sacrificial victims. In Germany especially public enthusiasm for the war was unbounded, and the 'spirit of 1914' was henceforth to be invoked for two generations, when it seemed vital to place absolute national unity above self-interest and the criticism of individuals. How deeply the 'spirit of 1914' had permeated the population involved in the war – not only in Germany – is evident, for instance, in the widespread craze for altering names. The Berlin Chief of Police von Jagow, ordered the removal of all French and English words in public places, so that the 'Hotel Bristol' and the 'London Bar' perforce vanished from the map, while the 'Hotel Westminster' was renamed 'Hotel Lindenhof' and the 'Café Piccadilly' turned into the 'Café Vaterland'. The military commander in Breslau banned a confectionery factory from using the term 'bon-bon' in its advertisements. In Great Britain, many residents, even some who had lived in the country for generations, changed their German-sounding names, taking their lead from the Royal Family, who no longer wished to be called Hanover, but Windsor. The Rue d'Allemagne in Paris was henceforth called Rue Jean Jaurès. Bizarre details of this kind may seem trivial, but they indicate a degree of national fervour such as had never been known in previous wars. It was all part of the same pattern when the socialist parties in almost all the belligerent states joined the common front of their own state, fully supporting the war effort, in spite of ardent appeals by the Socialist International in Brussels. Only the Russian and the Serbian socialists refused to toe the national line. The famous statement by the Kaiser, that he no longer recognized parties, but only Germans, applied *mutatis mutandis* to all the warring states. When there were no parties but only nations, there was virtually no limit to the authority of the state.

Montesquieu's doctrine to the effect that parliamentary powers should never devolve on the executive had never had many supporters in Great Britain, so the Westminster Parliament had little hesitation in passing, on 8 August 1914, a Defence of the Realm Act, commonly known as DORA, which was followed by additional emergency legislation. In – totally justified – confidence in the constitutional loyalty of the British crown, Parliament gradually encouraged the executive to encroach on the preserve of the legislature. The British Cabinet was in any case in a position to claim that it was acting as a kind of executive committee of Parliament, since a coalition government including all the parliamentary parties had been formed in 1915 ; since December 1916 the Cabinet had had, in the person of David Lloyd George (1868–1945), an exceptionally capable and determined leader. His war cabinet of no more than six members exercised a kind of dictatorship, and the parliamentary system was largely suspended for the duration of the war.

The parliament in Paris, on the other hand, steadfastly refused throughout the war to accede to government requests for an enabling law. At the beginning of the war the Chamber did indeed pass a number of measures that represented a virtual dictatorship – restrictions on basic civil rights, extensions to the powers of courts martial, the so-called 'Carnet B', which made it easier to prosecute suspects – but there was never any doubt that the civilian leadership was firmly in control, and that the government was still controlled by the Chamber of Deputies in the time-honoured Jacobin tradition. On the other hand, in Italy, which entered the war on the side of the Entente in 1915, parliament to all intents and purposes surrendered its powers to the government, hardly ever met and handed the country's finances over to the executive, which for its part underwent a process of profound change. New ministries sprang up, together with an almost endless list of commissions and offices, and, above all, a kind of shadow government in the shape of a *Comitato per la mobilitazione industriale* under the chairmanship of a general. The new Italian leadership consisted of bureaucrats, military men and industrialists, who had one thing in common: a fondness for authoritarian solutions to political problems. The liberal parliamentary structures of the Italian body politic, which were barely fifty years old, wilted under the pressures of the world war.

The voluntary self-emasculation of parliament was nowhere effected as thoroughly as in Germany. Hitherto there had been no emergency legislation; on 4 August 1914 the government of the Reich submitted a batch of war measures to parliament, and it was the party chairmen who, on their own initiative, deplored the fact that the government might find itself in the position of having to act quickly and without debate in parliament, so that it would be advisable to have an enabling law. The representative of the Reich government, State Secretary von Delbrück, replied that the government had already thought of that but had not ventured to put the question to parliament; he personally would not advise any such voluntary surrender of parliamentary powers. It was of no avail: in their access of patriotic zeal the members insisted on giving the government power to enact legislation without the approval of parliament. Nevertheless, they seem to have had second thoughts, for their renunciation of power was stowed away in an obscure paragraph of a bill stipulating the extension of the validity of cheques and bills of exchange. Henceforth, the Imperial Council (*Bundesrat*), i.e. the representative assembly of the rulers of the Reich, was invested for the duration of the war with the power to enact any legislative measures 'to deal with deficiencies in the economy'. Since the war was increasingly turning out to be an economic undertaking, in which raw materials had to be procured, handled and administered, living accommodation allocated and the labour force organized, the scope of these powers went far beyond strictly economic issues and furnished the government of the Reich with well-nigh dictatorial authority. Some 80 per cent of all the laws and mandatory orders promulgated in Germany during the war were enacted on this basis. Moreover, the Imperial Council delegated plenary secondary powers, so that the governmental bureaucracy – and in wartime that meant by and large the military authorities – effectively became part of the legislature.

In fact, total war called for forms of decision-making, control and organization that had been unknown in any more or less liberal constitutional state before the war. It was not only in the belligerent countries, but also in most of the neutral countries that the state assumed control of the rationing of raw materials and food, as well as control of production deemed essential for the war effort. This control included not only the armaments industries and all its sub-contractors, but also transport and communications: the first economic measures relating to the war that were introduced in England and France provided for the nationalization of the railways. In the course of the war most countries also introduced legislation to regulate labour relations, at least in areas vital to the war effort; such legislation, for instance, limited the free choice of employment and compelled employers to accept trade union organizations as partners in negotiation, in order to avoid disputes and increase production in armaments factories. And there were the actual operations of the war itself, the recruitment of millions of men and their replacement in civilian jobs, generally by women – a development that paved the way for fresh measures relating to family life. The placing of huge government contracts with industry, the requisitioning of foodstuffs, horses and vehicles had a profound effect on the economy and entailed a vast increase in government expenditure, which could no longer be met by long-term loans, so that the money supply increased dramatically; since, at the same time, most goods and services had become scarcer, the result was price increases, which then had to be checked by state regulation of prices and incomes.

Similar problems arose in all the countries of Europe: the state gained ground everywhere, because it had no rival. The attendant growth of bureaucracy in every area of life was indeed severely criticized: the proliferation of offices, departments and committees led to an intensification of the paper war but rarely to any perceptible gain in efficiency. But seen in the light of a war economy, the nineteenth century state with its free trade principles and its confinement to a few regulative functions seemed to be truly a thing of the past; the future obviously belonged to the economically efficient regulatory state: in comparison with its unlimited authority, the mercantilism of the absolutist state paled into insignificance. Socialism, which seemed to have succumbed to the 'spirit of 1914', triumphed in the form of a militaristic socialism run by generals and bureaucrats. Walther Rathenau (1867–1922), managing director of the mighty German AEG electrical company and the highly efficient organizer of the country's raw material supplies for the conduct of the war, outlined in 1915 in a lecture delivered to university professors in Berlin, the future prospects for a national economic policy:

> I would like to give you an account of our economic warfare policy, which is without historical precedent, which will have great influence on the course and successful outcome of the war, and which will, as far as we can see, affect us all for a long time to come. It is an episode in our economic history which approximates very closely to the methods of Socialism and Communism.[2]

That the world of the future would be governed by 'state socialism' was a generally accepted view; the visionary Rathenau was not the only one who anticipated this. In France, as well as in Italy and England, a lively debate on the nationalization of industry began: during July and August 1916 the London *Times*, scarcely to be suspected of socialist sympathies, published a series of articles under the title, 'The Elements of Reconstruction', the authors of which made the case for a 'national plan', drawing a contrast between 'the old chaotic world of independent economic enterprise which benefited only uncontrolled private profit' and 'the new system of a coordinated economy, in which the public interest is a controlling partner.'[3] The British government itself had expressed the same thought in different words: it reported in 1918, that 'the war has brought about a transformation of the social structure and of government, many aspects of which will be with us for a long time.'[4]

From total war to the total state? The idea did not seem to be all that eccentric. There was, for instance the figure of General Erich Ludendorff (1868–1937), the closest colleague of Field-Marshal von Hindenburg (1874–1934) and the real head of the German Army's Third Supreme Command, who had effectively been the commander-in-chief of the German armed forces since 29 August 1916 and who since then had been busy mobilizing men and materials for the conduct of the war, and exercising a decisive influence on the war economy and German domestic policy as a whole. Ludendorff's handling of the wartime economy was assumed to be highly efficient, an assumption that was not entirely borne out by the facts, but was claimed in official propaganda. At any rate, both Lenin and Hitler were unstinted in their admiration of Ludendorff's organizational achievements.

Ludendorff presumably knew what he was talking about, then, when he summed up his experience in his book, *The Conduct of War and Politics*, which appeared in 1922. Like every other member of the German General Staff, he had been brought up on the classical theory of General von Clausewitz (1780–1831) and was familiar with the latter's famous dictum to the effect that war was merely the continuation of politics by other means. Clausewitz had wished to impress on his brothers in arms that a state engaged in a war should keep its ultimate political goal in view: war should never be an end in itself.

Ludendorff, however, took a different view of Clausewitz: certainly, even war was not just a military problem, political issues were not eliminated by war, they persisted. But had Clausewitz, asked Ludendorff, not been wrongly interpreted in the past? Was it really in order to draw a sharp distinction between the conduct of war, on the one hand, and politics on the other, and to assign to the former the role of servant, and to the latter the role of master? Ludendorff was thinking entirely in the middle-class spirit of the time, in the spirit of the late Enlightenment, the power philosophy of Nietzsche and the theory of social Darwinism, when he declared that this was the point where Clausewitz had been misunderstood. In fact, war and politics were one and the same, there was no such thing as peacetime, relations between the nations were a perpetual conflict – which was not always pursued with weapons of war – and within every country there were always forces seeking to subvert the state and the nation, and to undermine their morale.

War and politics, then, coincided and could only come to their joint conclusion when the enemies of the state had been defeated and destroyed in their ethnic substance. Consequently war must end either in victory or in annihilation, and not, as spineless civilians like to think, in peace by negotiation or concession. Such solutions were nothing but wishy-washy compromises which gave the enemy time to recover his strength. It further followed that the military and civilian leadership must be one and the same. But it was only logical that the supreme command should be in the hands of a soldier, for only a soldier was capable of so organizing the nation that it could wage total war: such organization must be on purely military lines. Politics, then, culminated in total war, and that implied total mobilization of the nation and its resources. The responsibility for carrying out such a plan fell on an individual somewhat vaguely identified in Ludendorff's writings as 'the great generalissimo', by which Ludendorff presumably meant none other than himself.

With the ideas of 'total war' and 'total mobilization' an element hitherto foreign to the military mind had made its appearance on the military and political scene. The concentration of all available forces under a single command for the sole purpose of annihilating another nation was an idea that had fleetingly come to the surface during the nationalistic phase of the War of Liberation in 1813, but it had been rejected by the military and political leadership of the European states. Conservative reaction had implied not only the rejection of democracy, the republican constitution and liberal legislation, but also a return to the rational political principles of the absolutist era. These principles, however, had included, amongst other things, the right of every state to exist. What General Ludendorff proceeded to put into practice after the end of 1916 were repressed ideas from the murkier areas of the middle-class mind: the unleashing of war without conventional political constraints, implying that the nation had first claim on the individual, in the spirit of the maxim 'Thou art nought, thy nation is everything': this was the assumption underlying the total mobilization of the political, economic and military resources of the nation, an assumption that opened up the way directly to totalitarian dictatorship. And the general was not alone in his views: using very similar arguments, Charles Maurras had called for a warrior king who would prepare France for war, since war was the ultimate authentic truth for mankind; and for the former socialist, Benito Mussolini (1883–1945), who had turned into an ardent nationalist on the outbreak of war, war was the most splendid chapter in all Italian history, and democracy was seeking to deprive the Italian people of the fruits of victory. Democracy meant decay, and only the state that craved war and expansion was fit to survive.

Whether, had the central powers won the war, Ludendorff would have had the chance to implement his vision of the total state, is questionable. Even during the war he had been unable to outwit the Reichstag, which passed a motion in 1917 calling for a peace 'without annexations or indemnities' and opposing the wide-ranging proposals for territorial conquests that had been put on record by the supreme command of the German forces. There was a further factor to be taken into account: the war had also encouraged certain countervailing trends. Trade unions had been recognized by the state and by the employers as representing the workers' interests. In almost all the combatant countries, socialist politicians had been appointed sooner or later to government posts, and the extensive employment of female labour in the economy had led to the franchise being extended to include women in almost all the democratic states of Europe immediately after the war.

But the old liberal, *laissez-faire* state of pre-war days was never resurrected. It had in any case existed only as an approximation to an ideal: since the end of the nineteenth century all the European states had begun to intervene officially in the economy and in social issues. The Prussian–German state had acted as a pioneer in this respect, passing bills for insurance against accident and sickness, introducing retirement pensions and regulating domestic industry by means of protective tariffs, as well as curbing the most blatant excesses of companies and corporations through legislation on cartels and subsidies. It even tried to influence market prices directly by itself engaging in industry, e.g. in the coal-mining industry and in the generation of electric power. If staunch liberals were wont to point to England as the model of a liberal, *laissez-faire* state, then they were under a very common misapprehension – even this model of liberalism and free enterprise had had to face the accusation brought against it by the liberal periodical, *The Economist* in 1894 that in the course of time the state had assumed the function of universal provider. In 1911 the socialist, Sidney Webb (1859–1947), had noted with satisfaction that the English state 'at least registered, inspected and controlled all those industrial activities in which it was not itself engaged'.[5]

It was the war which had made irreversible the movement towards a state committed to intervention in social and economic issues. Even demobilization, the discharge and economic reintegration of millions of soldiers could only be managed by the state. The trade unions had no intention of being thrust back into their pre-war role, but demanded the eight-hour day, more effective participation in the management of factories and a more active social policy. Unemployment insurance, introduced before the war only in Great Britain, was now added in many other countries, including Germany, to older social security measures. In those areas devastated by the war, private enterprise alone was unable to cope with reconstruction; the state once again intervened as organizer and investor. Living accommodation was scarce everywhere and often had to be rationed, and it was the state which exercised control here, too, fixing rents and subsidizing the building of homes. The communications and transport networks were also restored and further developed, especially through the provision of suburban travel facilities. In a number of states in eastern Central Europe land reforms were introduced, and here, too, little was done without state intervention.

All this through the power of democracy? So it might seem, but the reality was different. The extension of state activity, increasing intervention in the economy and the provision of social services were a response to a problem that arose after the First World War in most European states: the breath-taking rapidity with which democracy forfeited its credentials and its credibility as a viable form of government, unable, it seemed, to correct the massive distortions in society and the economy wrought by the war. The case of Germany speaks for itself: with the victory of the entente in the autumn of 1918, it had looked for a moment as if democracy had won the day in Europe. Even Ludendorff reckoned that Germany might be given the benefit of a tolerable peace only if she turned into a parliamentary democracy. It was Ludendorff and the German High Command who virtually ordered the majority parties in the Reichstag – the Social Democrats, the Catholic Centre Party and the Liberals – to assume power. The last government of the old empire, the cabinet of Prince Max of Baden, was answerable to the Reichstag and functioned under an effective parliamentary and democratic constitution. It was as the plenipotentiary of this government that State Secretary Matthias Erzberger signed an armistice in the Forest of Compiègne on 11 November 1918.

This turned out to be a fateful move. For one thing, the first German democracy did not come into being as a result of its own efforts or through a parliamentary initiative, but as the last resort of a desperate General Staff. And, of course, Weimar democracy was born at the worst possible moment, a moment of defeat, with which its birth and its *raison d'être* would for ever be associated. And, finally, the circumstances were to prove fateful, in so far as it was civilian politicians, and not those truly responsible for the hopeless military situation, the officers of the Supreme Army Command, who were called upon to conduct the armistice negotiations. By combining his request for an armistice with the wish for reversion to a strictly parliamentary regime Ludendorff had saddled a convenient scapegoat with the responsibility for defeat and surrender. The legend of 'the stab in the back', which was to poison public life in the Weimar Republic, had its origin in this move.

Besides, there was no suggestion of lenient peace terms. Instead, there was the Treaty of Versailles, reparations, years of insulting discrimination and setbacks in foreign policy, an infinite sense of humiliation. All this might be borne only if the profoundly shaken self-esteem of the whole German people could unload on to some scapegoat or other the insults they had suffered. And the scapegoat they found was democracy and those who supported it. The rabble-rousing formula to the effect that 'republic' and 'democracy' were no more than synonyms for cowardice and betrayal became a stock feature of the nationalistic agitation that was believed by millions of individuals. From 1920 onwards the democratic parties were never able to command a stable majority in the Reichstag.

As a democracy the Weimar Republic was thus a feeble state without any inherent sanction or support: it sought to avoid civil war and to purchase the favour of the electorate by subsidies and the redistribution of assets. Demands were made on the state by vested interests from every quarter on a scale far beyond anything that had obtained before the war, and they were duly met. The amounts of money involved are evident from the sharp increase in public spending, particularly in the social services sector. In 1929 the burden of taxation was twice what it had been in 1913, i.e. 18 per cent instead of 9 per cent. On the eve of the First World War, social expenditure by the central government, the provinces and local government had totalled 337 million marks; by 1929, however, it amounted to 4 billion 751 million marks per annum, i.e. an increase by a factor of no less than 13. In this way the unloved state of the Weimar Republic tried to buy the loyalty of various vested interests through promises of subsidies and support – promises which had to be redeemed in the event of crisis.

And when the crisis arose as the national economies of the

industrial states plunged into the most severe slump in modern economic history following 'Black Friday', 25 October 1929, as banks collapsed, the industrial production of Europe fell by a half within three years, and a third of the working population of Germany were unemployed, then all the guarantees offered by the government had to be honoured at one and the same time, and the German state proved unequal to the task. In England, where the slump was scarcely less dramatic than in Germany, responsibility for dealing with the consequences was borne on many different social and administrative shoulders: the constitution weathered the storm unscathed. In Germany, on the other hand, the Weimar state was brought to its knees by the combined pressure generated by the expectations of many different social groups. And since the loyalty of the German people to their constitution depended on the success of that constitution and its political institutions in resolving the conflicting claims of the social partners, the very basis of the constitution was at risk, if the government policy of redistributing assets were to fail. In its attempt to act like a powerful state, parliamentary democracy in Germany cut the ground from under its own feet and itself dealt the trump cards to the National Socialists, who at once set about building the totalitarian state, of which General Ludendorff had only dreamed.

Other democracies survived the worldwide slump, although they suffered severe damage. The states which survived the crisis were for the most part those in which democratic and parliamentary institutions were so solidly grounded in tradition and custom that they were beyond the range of debate: France, where the tradition of a revolutionary, democratic national state had had a sufficiently firm footing ever since 1789, and a string of peripheral states in the west and north-west of the continent, in which constitutional monarchy and the corresponding parliamentary institutions provided a robust political framework: Great Britain, the Netherlands, Belgium, Luxemburg, Norway, Denmark and Sweden. But such states were by no means the rule in Europe.

Most of the post-war democracies were sandwiched between extremes of the Left and Right at a time when social and economic problems continued to escalate. In any case, the democrats no longer had confidence in their mandate to rule and were reluctant to risk civil war by fighting revolution with revolutionary means. It was not only that the democracies seemed feeble and lacking in self-confidence; they were unprepossessing, for their appeal was addressed to reason rather than to the emotions: they were simply grey and boring. The generation that had emerged from the trenches at the end of the war had been born and grown up in the *fin de siècle*, they had experienced the *belle époque* as the high noon of philistine satiety, of mindless snobbery, of middle-class vulgarity, and were deeply convinced of the hollowness, duplicity and sterility of the liberal pre-war era. During the war their detestation of the respectable establishment was confirmed, the bourgeois world of the post-war period seemed to them to be radically false and doomed to destruction. The political affiliations of their elders found little support in this younger generation: the parents liberal or conservative, their sons and daughters socialists or National Socialists: that was the normal situation throughout Europe at the time.

Liberal democracy had lost from the start, not because it was liberal, but because it was dull, and an obstacle to those thrilling experiences for which the spirit of the time yearned. In this respect the extremes of Left and Right were at one, for Right and Left were not differentiated by their attitude to the present. What mattered to both extreme movements was the shaping of the future – and even here they resembled each other, in that they both envisaged a strong state that would rule with a mailed fist. Democracy could not be accommodated' in such visions in any circumstances: by its very nature it is based on the pluralism of political parties and interests, and it can work only if there is a readiness on the part of all parties concerned to compromise and strike a balance – not just between kindred interests, but also between conflicting interests.

That was part and parcel of the traditional European system of states, which functioned in a rational fashion, as long as individual states kept the stability of the whole in view, along with their own interests. They had thus aligned their policy, as it were on a diagonal meridian bisecting an angle between their own and the general interest. This equilibrium in the relations between the states of Europe had been destroyed by the World War. Instead, an allegedly high-minded principle had been introduced into European politics with the peace treaties of 1919. It was a principle that soon proved to be divisive and destructive: the principle of national self-determination. Henceforth it was the wish of the American President Woodrow Wilson (1856–1924) and of the victorious Entente that every people should have the right to form a nation state on its own: Europe was to be a continent of sovereign national states.

It was not clear to Western politicians sitting round their green baize tables in Versailles, St Germain and the Trianon, that it was this very principle that would plunge Europe into war and civil discord. The unity of state and nation in Western Europe was reckoned to be a precondition of progressive, democratic politics, while the problems of the statesmen's own minorities, e.g. the Indians in the USA, the Scots, the Welsh and the Irish in Great Britain, the Bretons and Alsatians in France seemed to have been made less acute by providing for their participation in legislative bodies. In Central and Eastern Europe, where homogeneous ethnic communities on a large scale hardly existed, where linguistic, denominational and cultural affiliations overlapped, and where an ethnic mixture within relatively small areas was the rule, the demand that nation, language and state should coincide was ludicrous. The nations which rose in 1918 and 1919 from the ruins of the great empires of Eastern Europe – the Ottoman Empire, Russia and, above all, Austro-Hungary – were merely the agencies of national majorities ruling over sizeable minorities, who in most cases were the victims of unremitting persecution. 'There is not a single people or province of the Habsburg Empire to which the achievement of independence has not brought those torments which ancient poets and theologians predicted for the damned souls in Hell,' was Winston Churchill's view.[6] Official figures relating to the size of these minorities are pitched as a rule well below the estimates of scholars, minority spokesmen and committees of the League of Nations.

Country	Date	Percentage of total population
Albania	1930	22.3
Bulgaria	1930	10.3
Czechoslovakia	1921	52*
Estonia	1931	11.8
Hungary	1920	10.4
Latvia	1930	26.6
Lithuania	1923	26.6
Poland	1921	30
Romania	1930	29
Yugoslavia	1931	57

* unofficial estimate
Source: Paul Lendvai: 'Sprengstoff im gemeinsamen Haus. Nationalitätenkonflikte in Osteuropa', in: *Europäische Rundschau* 2/91, p. 17.

Whereas it was the threat of socialist revolution that darkened the horizon in West and Central Europe, in Eastern Europe it was the unresolved problem of nationalities that was most likely to bring about a state of emergency and subsequent dictatorial measures. Of the newly created states that had emerged from the ruins of the multi-ethnic empires of Eastern Europe only one was able to preserve its democratic mode of government – Czechoslovakia, but it was in fact that country's ill-starred minorities policy that offered the pretext for the Sudeten crisis of 1938 and the annexation of Czech territory by Germany.

The famous prophecy of the British Foreign Minister, Sir Edward Grey (1862–1933) on the outbreak of the First World War had been fulfilled in a more profound sense than its author had ever imagined: 'The lamps are going out all over Europe: we shall not see them lit again in our lifetime.' Europe had passed through the bloodbath of a world war, and instead of its old cohesive balanced system of nation states, a multitude of states had emerged, only to fall apart in hostile alliances, pacts and understandings. In the eyes of the losers in the war, especially in the view of those two outcasts from the international community, Germany and Russia, the League of Nations in Geneva was nothing but a tool of the victorious powers. There was scarcely a European frontier that was not disputed, and the idea of revenge, a revision of the Paris peace treaties of 1919, was prevalent, not only among the losers but also with many of the victors who felt that they had not received their fair share of the spoils of war.

The political fragmentation of the continent was matched by its economic fragmentation. The world's economic system had been only partly salvaged following the war, and it collapsed once again under the pressure of a worldwide slump in 1929. New frontiers, of which there were many, meant more and more barriers to trade, restrictions on imports, and exchange control regulations: the states of Europe found themselves on the way back to the model of the hermetically sealed commercial state. Domestic antagonisms were no less vicious than the hostility between individual states: extremist parties – nationalists and communists – gained ground at the expense of the democratic centre. It was the extremists who set the tone of the public debate, while the ethnic minorities of Eastern Europe clamoured for the right to form their own nation states that had been granted to other, more fortunate ethnic communities. Such ethnic pressure groups threatened the internal law and order of the newly created states that had issued from the Habsburg, Russian and Ottoman empires. In other words, Europe was once again on the brink of war, either between rival nation states, or else within newly created states themselves.

The latent danger of civil war between the two world wars invited the same response that had put an end to the civil and religious wars of the sixteenth and seventeenth centuries – the development of a strong, centralized state authority: at that time absolutism, now its contemporary equivalent, the authoritarian, or even outright totalitarian state, as it had been visualized by the advocates of 'integral nationalism' of the *fin de siècle*, and as it had shaped the pattern of society through the imperialistic and nationalistic mass organizations of the immediate pre-war era. This pattern of social and political organization had been endorsed in the large-scale battles of the war, and it was now on offer as a remedy for a post-liberal Europe that was ailing and lacking the balance it had formerly had. The era of the total state had dawned.

When the President of the Reich, Paul von Hindenburg, appointed Adolf Hitler Chancellor of Germany on 30 January 1933, this seemed in no way sensational in the European context. The illusion of Hitler's Conservative supporters that they could accommodate him into their scheme of things and then 'push him into a corner' was by no means shared by everyone, but it had to be admitted that dictatorships were becoming the order of the day in Europe. Where dictatorship was not the order of the day, as in the France of the *République des camarades*, the kind of domestic stability that prevailed was hardly an advertisement for democracy. There was a widespread impression that the democracies had come to grief during the great economic crisis and that the transformation of the liberal state into a welfare state had been no more than a transitional phase which was bound to be succeeded by the advent of a totally authoritarian state. Now the day of the strong men and of national concentration had arrived – all eyes were turned on Mussolini, a dictator who was openly admired by liberals throughout Europe during the early years of his regime.

If we do not count Lenin's regime in the Soviet Union, Benito Mussolini (1883–1945) was the first of the European dictators, but he was not the only one. His seizure of power in Rome in 1922 was followed by an uninterrupted series of authoritarian revolutions – in 1923 in Bulgaria, Spain and Turkey, in 1925 in Albania, in 1926 in Poland, Portugal and Lithuania, in 1929 in Yugoslavia, in 1930 in Romania. Hitler's seizure of power in 1933 was followed in the same year by the establishment of the Dollfuss regime in Austria. In 1934 Estonia and Latvia became dictatorships, as did Spain and Greece in 1936. By 1939 only eleven European states out of twenty-eight had democratic governments.

The number of dictatorships includes the Soviet Union,

which had declared a national policy of 'socialism in one country' once the worldwide revolution had obviously failed to materialize. Later on, during the Second World War, Stalin declared that the battle against Hitler was the 'Great Patriotic War', so that, in the case of the Soviet Union also, we are dealing with a dictatorial regime appealing to national solidarity on patriotic grounds. It is true that the Soviet Union and its hostile counterparts, the authoritarian and Fascist dictatorships, were based up to a point on conflicting ideologies, but they were alike as far as their constitutional pattern was concerned. They shared an official totalitarian view claiming absolute validity, a centralized mass movement organized as a monolithic political party, total control of the means of coercion and media of communication and, last but not least, total bureaucratic control of the economy through political directives, socialization and nationalization. Certainly, these features were not present to the same degree or at the same stage of development everywhere but, by and large, all the European dictatorships in the period between the two world wars had the hallmarks of totalitarianism, or at least aspired to them.

It was not only the losers in the First World War – Germany, Russia, Austria, Turkey – but also many of the victors who joined the camp of the dictators. The outcome of the war rarely matched the exaggerated expectations which had been aroused by groups bent on the annexation of territory, or even by governments themselves, while the war was still in progress. Disappointment was particularly acute in Italy. The country's territorial gains had in fact been considerable – Trieste, the Trentino and South Tyrol became Italian, but a great deal more had been expected. The Allies had refused to consent to the annexation of Dalmatia and Fiume (Rijeka), a protectorate of Albania and an Italian sphere of influence in Asia Minor, so that the Italian negotiators had left the conference dissatisfied and humiliated. The catch-phrase *'vittoria mutilata'*, the crippled victory, went the rounds in Italy, and the situation was aggravated by the fact that the burden of the war had made Italy's social problems more acute. The budget deficit had to be met by massive increases in taxation, the promises of a fair land reform that had been made to the demobilized soldiers were never fulfilled, while spectacular commercial bankruptcies brought about by speculative trading on the stock market helped to make the crisis even more acute. There was an endless series of factory occupations and long-term strikes, and the government in Rome changed every few months. During the elections of 1919 the democratic state gave every sign that it was in its death-throes: the poll was scarcely more than 50 per cent of the electorate. It was a classical situation of potential civil war which was rendered even more critical by the total collapse of Italian liberalism. The liberal government of Giovanni Giolitti (1920–1) refused to intervene in the grave unrest affecting industry and agriculture, and this gave the Fascist, Benito Mussolini, the chance to put himself forward as the sole force opposing communism. Neither the prefects nor the police took steps to deal with violent action by the Fascist *squadri*, and even great liberal newspapers like the *Corriere della Sera* remained silent in the face of violent terrorism by various local Fascist gangs. When the socialists ultimately called a general strike in August 1922, Mussolini's chance to declare open war on socialism had come. His 'march on Rome' on 28 October 1922, carefully coordinated with royalist and Catholic groups, was launched into a virtual power vacuum: King Victor Emanuel III refused to give his prime minister, Luigi Facta, authority to declare martial law and appointed Mussolini as Facta's successor.

Mussolini's rise to power in a sense set the pattern for many of the greater or lesser 'Leaders'. The preconditions were similar in many cases. There was almost always a middle class of property-owning or educated individuals, historically the advocates of the national idea, who felt themselves ill done by or suffering under a sense of national discrimination as a result of defeat or 'lost victories', loss of national territory or the denial of territorial ambitions. This was the case in a material as well as a psychological sense, for this was the class that had forfeited its prosperity in the inflation that gripped Europe in the aftermath of the war, so that its members felt threatened with decline into a faceless proletariat.

These people suffered under an archetypal dread of masses

of insurgent workers forcing their way from the discordant din of their grimy factories into their sitting-rooms and threatening the hallowed inheritance of their bourgeois culture. The cry, 'peace to the cottages, war on the palaces!' which had taught the aspiring middle class to fear socialism in the previous century had gained a fresh topical reality, not only in the bloody turmoil of the Russian revolution, but also in the civil wars and social unrest of the post-war era in Central and Western Europe. The current social situation was felt to have deteriorated drastically: the Spanish philosopher, Ortega y Gasset (1883–1955) expressed this feeling as follows: ' The masses are simply lacking in morality, for morality is essentially a sense of subordination, a concept of service and duty.'[7] There were still those who believed in traditional standards and had a vision of a world where everyone knew his place, where seniority and subordination were felt to be as divinely ordained as wealth and poverty. European society in the industrialized nations, as well as those countries which were on the threshold between an industrial and agrarian economy, was deeply uneasy: any sense of security seemed to have gone for good.

The Fascist parties held out the promise of that security in an unprecedented form, Mussolini in Italy, Hitler in Germany, as well as all the minor 'leaders' who copied these eminent models – Corneliu Codreanu (1899–1938) in Romania, José Antonio Primo de Rivera (1903–36) in Spain, Joris van Severen (1894–1940) in the Flemish provinces of Belgium, and Leon Degrelle (1906–94) in the Walloon areas – all possessed considerable personal magnetism and knew how to concoct an explosive mixture of ideas and images. The mixture combined grievances against war profiteers, currency speculators and black marketeers and generally all those who had allegedly profited from the privations of the workers and soldiers. In this connection, especially in Germany, France and Eastern Europe, it was the caricatured image of the Jew that was most effective as a racist version of the socialist stereotype of the capitalist. Other ingredients involved the application of military metaphors to political life, the psychological mobilization of the masses for civil war, and glorification of action for its own sake. It was the primacy of action over reason that constituted the basically irrational character of National Socialist and Fascist propaganda and ensured its effectiveness in the fight against the scarcely credible programmes of the Conservative, Liberal and Socialist democratic parties. The myths of the nation and of race played a prominent part in the pronouncements of the Fascist and National Socialist parties. Behind the accusation that the democracies had betrayed the nation lay an inflated, indeed absolute adulation of the 'nation', with the party and its leader as its sole champions and representatives. In most cases the burning issue was the revision of the outcome of the First World War, often entailing even more extensive territorial demands. The Germans were allegedly a 'people denied living space', obstructed in their natural development by the cramped living conditions and urbanization of Central Europe. Consequently, in some vaguely defined way or other, Germany would have to expand to the East and acquire new colonies. Greater Finland, imperialist expansion in Africa, the Mediterranean as *mare nostro* of the Italian nation, a Greater Netherlands: these ambitions were all simply extensions of ideas that had once been deployed in support of 'integral nationalism' even before the war.

In public speeches by Hitler or Mussolini policy statements and theories played only a minor part. It was primarily the personal impression made by these two great demagogues that captured and focused the desires and dreams of their listeners as in a burning glass, devising impressive and suggestive names for their wishes and reflecting them back on the mass of the people. They fascinated their followers and the electorate, dredging up from the irrational collective pre-conscious depths all manner of fears and prejudices and putting a name to them. In this respect Fascists and National Socialists proved to be far more modern than their political rivals. The traditional parties, in their ideological and programmatic orientation and through the process by which they had evolved, were the heirs of an age of rationalism, when it was believed that men had only to be familiarized with a political programme in order to be convinced of its truth. It was not clear to the leaders of such parties that men are not rational by nature, but can become so only by a great effort of will. Hitler, on the other hand, was well aware of this and counted on the emotional deficit which the established parties had ignored. 'The driving force behind all the mightiest upheavals on earth was always to be found less in some rational and objective conviction amongst the masses than in a fanatical mood that seized them,' he wrote, 'and sometimes in a kind of hysteria that drove them irresistibly on. The man who wishes to win over the broad mass of the people must know the key that will open their hearts. And that is not weakness, but will-power and strength.'[8] It was from this realization that Mussolini drew the conclusion that democracy had alienated the nation from its true 'style' – 'that is, a line of conduct, colour, power, the picturesque, the mystic; in short, everything that really counts in the minds of the masses. When we play the harp, we use all its strings: from brute force to religion, from art to politics.'[9] Anyone who reads Hitler's or Mussolini's speeches nowadays may find it hard to understand the effect they had on their listeners. These listeners were desperate, hunted men, tormented by demons, hungry for miracles and thrills, caring nothing for contradictions in political manifestos, logical errors or factual discrepancies. The 'Duce' and the 'Führer' demanded their faith and their devotion and offered in return certainty and security in a new community that would protect and care for them: that was what their followers were looking for, and that was what they found.

The success of the Fascists and the Nazis was evident from the figures: even before they came to power the Italian *Partito Nazionale Fascista* (PNF) and the National Socialist German Workers' Party (NSDAP) were mass movements, the former with 300,000, the latter with as many as one million members. They far outstripped the 'middle-class' parties of the time, which had still not contrived to shed their reputation as parties for 'respectable citizens' only. The hard core of most political parties was formed by soldiers who had returned from the war and found it hard to settle down in civilian life. They were embittered by the outcome of the peace negotiations and, unencumbered by any sort of traditional loyalty, they were intent on extending the war into the peace that had succeeded it. It was such activists who constituted the revolutionary yeast in the Fascist parties: we need only recall Gabriele d'Annunzio's legionaries who placed the Italian government in an acutely embarrassing position when they occupied Fiume on 11 November 1919, or their successors in the Fascist party, the *squadri d'azione*, specialists in bloody street battles. Or the German Free Corps, who had crushed the nascent Soviet republics and communist risings in the German civil war of 1918–19, and had ejected the Polish volunteer units which had forced their way into the eastern provinces of Prussia. The members of these Free Corps were aggrieved and felt let down because they had not been embodied in the minute *Reichswehr*, the regular army Germany was allowed under the terms of the Versailles Treaty. Many of them ended up in Adolf Hitler's private army, the SA. The same was true of the 'Archangel Michael Legion' of Corneliu Codreanu in Romania, the Estonian 'League of Freedom Fighters' under General Larka, or the members of the *Croix de Feu* in France. These party political armies were uniformed and organized on military lines and served as instruments of propaganda and civil warfare.

The military trappings, which were characteristic of all the Fascist parties and which underlined the monolithic mass nature of such movements, were not a true reflection of traditional military patterns of hierarchy and subordination. Armies are governed by principles of order and obedience: the subordinate takes orders from his superior officer, whoever the latter might be: 'officers of the General Staff have no names' (Helmuth von Moltke). In the armies of the Fascist parties, and in the parties themselves, on the other hand, the distinction between the 'Leader' and his followers, derived from pre-war notions of the ethnic community and reinforced by the 'battlefield experience' of the world war, was essential. At the head of the party stood the leader, Führer, Duce, Caudillo or Poglavnik, whose real or reputed charisma made him the actual embodiment of the party, which paid fanatical homage to him.

The Fascist parties of Europe regarded themselves as 'movements', permanently standing by and exerting the unremitting pressure on the political institutions of the democracies that would make them ripe for a 'takeover' of power. With the transition from the 'movement phase' to the 'system phase', however, a point was reached at which essential differences might be detected. In both Italy and Germany there was a mixture of *coup d'état* and a legitimate assumption of power, of threats of civil war and a formally correct appointment of the party leader as the head of government. This was followed by a transitional period, in which the institutions of democracy and other political parties still retained limited freedom of action, before a totalitarian state under the authority of the single legitimate party was established. In Italy this transitional phase lasted from 1922 to 1926, when all parties and organizations in opposition to the government were dissolved, whereas in Germany the brief lapse of time between the end of January 1933 and the death of President Hindenburg on 2 August 1934 was sufficient for the installation of the National Socialist regime.

In no other European country, however, was the establishment of a dictatorship in any way linked with the triumph of a Fascist movement. In Latvia, for instance, the leader of the Peasants' Union, Karlis Ulmanis (1877–1941), had recourse to a *coup d'état* in May 1934, and banned not only the Social Democratic Party but also the Fascist 'Thunder-Cross' movement, and proceeded to pursue a nationalistic policy under the slogan, 'Latvia for the Latvians'. The authoritarian regime of the Estonian President Konstantin Päts (1874–1956) did not hesitate to disband the radically nationalistic 'Freedom Fighters' on the grounds that they were 'a threat to public order', and under the Polish Marshall Pilsudski (1867–1935), who had risen to power in 1926 in a military *putsch*, the various Fascist groups dwindled into insignificance. In Portugal the leader of the Fascist national syndicalists, Rolâo Preto, was exiled by the dictator Salazar (1879–1968) and the movement was banned. In Romania in 1938, as previously in Yugoslavia, it was the king who launched a *coup d'état* and immediately banned Codreanu's Fascist 'Iron Guard'. In spite of the wartime alliance with National Socialist Germany, Marshall Ion Antonescu (1882–1946), who had governed Romania since 1940, disbanded the 'Iron Guard' and had its leader, who had fled to

Germany, sentenced to death. The Fascist Dollfuss dictatorship in Austria, backed by the Home Guard (*Heimatwehren*)
organization, was indeed anti-Marxist and anti-democratic and
modelled itself on Mussolini's Italy. It was content, however,
with the establishment of a strictly authoritarian regime and
had no very extensive political ambitions: the more radical
National Socialist movement was banned in Austria.

In Spain between the two world wars a military insurrection with the aim of bringing down the democratic government was twice attempted: in 1923 by the Captain General of Catalonia Miguel Primo de Rivera (1870–1930), and
in 1936 by a group of generals, among whom Francisco
Franco (1892–1975) rapidly took the lead. Neither Primo
de Rivera nor Franco were really Fascists, but simply soldiers
who wished to replace a 'decadent' and inefficient democracy
by a nationalistic and centrally organized military dictatorship,
and who were thus following a tradition that reached back
into the nineteenth century. The *Unión Patriótica*, which was
formed in 1925 with the aim of mobilizing the population
in support of a dictatorship led by Primo de Rivera, consisted mainly of old-style Conservatives who simply wanted
to encourage patriotic sentiment. It was not until 1933, when
Primo de Rivera's regime had long since collapsed and democracy had been restored, that a Fascist party made its appearance
in Spain – the '*Falange Española*' under its *Jefe* (Leader),
José Antonio Primo de Rivera (1903–36), the son of the
former dictator. Its programme was both nationalistic and
anti-democratic, but like that of the Romanian Iron Guard
or the Hungarian National Socialist Party it also entailed a
social revolution. But Franco used the *Falange* merely as an
instrument during his *putsch* and, once he had gained power,
he combined the *Falange* with the *Requetés*, the militia of
the Carlist monarchists, to form a single mass organization
under the direction of Franco himself. Such militant organizations were in any case subordinate to the general staff
of the armed forces, so that military control by the party
was permanently guaranteed. Manuel Hedilla (1898–1970),
the successor to José Antonio Primo de Rivera, was placed
under arrest, and the *Falange* became little more than a claque

for the Franco regime. In 1941 a confidential German report
stated,

> the *Falange* was meant to bring together the broad masses
> of the nationalists and the Reds and to provide a base for
> an ideology. It has not succeeded in this task. Rather,
> it has tended to become a mere tool in Franco's hand
> and has been set up as his private executive . . . In these
> circumstances it is distinctly compromising for National
> Socialism, if the German press, unaware of the true state
> of affairs, equates the *Falange* with the NSDAP and praises
> it accordingly.[10]

On closer inspection it is clear that we must distinguish
between two separate phenomena: on the one hand, the rise
of Fascist parties and movements in Europe, which affected
every country and influenced the climate of opinion on the
continent, especially during the thirties; and, on the other hand,
dictatorially governed states that were often lumped together
and condemned as 'Fascist', although a seizure of power in the
sense that the Fascists became the sole ruling party and bent
the state to their will, took place only in Italy and Germany.
The Fascist states that came into existence during the Second
World War, i.e. in Slovakia, Hungary and Croatia, owed their
brief span of life only to German bayonets. All the other
dictatorships in Europe between the wars, the states governed
by Pilsudski, Horthy, Salazar, Antonescu – and even the Franco
regime – were either purely military dictatorships, or else
authoritarian governments run by civilian politicians – but
they were not Fascist states. They were ruled by a conservative
establishment which had gained power with the aid of the
army and which was able to seal the local regime off from
revolutionary suggestions emanating from the extreme Left or
Right. The traditional state was not substantially impaired,
but its authority was extended, if necessary by force, to ensure
social stability. Such authoritarian dictatorships endeavoured
to demobilize the masses and to exclude them from any significant participation in public life. Instead, their ruler offered the
population social models that guaranteed property rights and
the kind of social integration which harked back to notions

of the community that had prevailed before the industrial revolution: ideologies based on the corporate state or on an official discrimination between different social classes were especially popular with such regimes.

The states created by Mussolini and Hitler were totally different. Their basic foundation was the single unitarian party, which claimed to be a 'movement' rather than a party like other parties of the liberal parliamentary system they so detested. They were intended to carry the spirit of revolution into the structure of the state and society at large and to ensure its perpetual advance. They did their best to keep the mass of the population in a constant state of agitation and readiness for 'action'. The entire nation was to be mobilized by means of propaganda, parades, demonstrations and through the perpetual ritualization of public life: it was to be integrated and constantly made aware of its own nature. The ultimate aim was the conversion of the nation into a socially coordinated and politically homogeneous mass that acknowledged only one single will – the will of the Leader – and only one moral value – the nation. It was only logical, then, for the law of 9 December 1928 to proclaim the Fascist Grand Council, the supreme consultative body of the *Partito Nazionale Fascista* the 'supreme organ' that was 'to co-ordinate and integrate all the activities of the regime that had emerged from the revolution of October 1922 ', and hence represent 'the unity of party and state' at the highest level. Party and state were bound ever closer together: the *fasci* became the emblem of the state, the *squadri* were turned into a state militia.

But Mussolini wished the party to function like the Bolshevik party in Russia under Lenin's leadership – acting as a kind of transmission belt by which the political will of the leadership might be passed on to the entire state. Mussolini's idea of the state was strongly influenced by Hegel's worship of it. In Mussolini's view the state stood above the nation and the party. The nation, he declared, was a huge collective personality, 'united by an idea constituted by its will to exist and to exercise that will', only so far, indeed, 'as it is a state. But it is not the nation which gives birth to the state as in the antiquated naturalistic sense which served as the basis of literature in the nineteenth century. On the contrary, it is the nation that is created by the state, which imparts its will-power and its actual existence to a people aware of its own moral integrity . . . '[11] In fact, during Mussolini's years in power the balance moved towards a nationalization of the Fascist regime: the party tended to lose its political function and degenerated into an institution dedicated to the care and comfort of its own members, offering them chances of advancement to attractive government jobs.

In National Socialist Germany the state, the party and the people were much more closely welded together than in Fascist Italy. Under a 'Law to Secure the Unity of Party and State', enacted on 1 December 1933, the NSDAP became the 'embodiment of the German idea of the state and was consequently indissolubly bound up with the state'. Adolf Hitler deliberately gave priority to his party function when he assumed the title of 'Leader and Chancellor of the Reich'. The Party extended its authority far beyond its own members to embrace the entire nation. In 1939 the 36 *Länder* and provinces of the country were duplicated at party level by 40 *Gaue* or districts with governors (*Gauleiter*) who tended increasingly to assume governmental responsibilities. Below the *Gaue* were counties (*Kreise*), then local groups (*Ortsgruppen*), cells, and at the foot of this organizational pyramid, 'blocks', each with responsibility for some 50 households. The block superintendents (*Blockwarte*) and cell leaders (*Zellenleiter*) kept the closest possible watch on the private lives of the population. They were in a position to check on the loyalty of every individual to the regime and to report deviants, so that they were both party officials and police officers. Through a whole network of affiliated organizations covering every social and professional group the party extended its control over further millions of citizens, irrespective of their attitude to National Socialism. Control was exercised through compulsory membership of professional or occupational associations run by the Nazis, from the National Socialist League of Medical Practitioners to the German Workers' Front, the former trade union organization which had simply been incorporated into the party. There was no escape, because membership dues were deducted from wages and salaries along with income tax and social security contributions.

Wherever the party seemed too unwieldy for the task of educating the population in its baleful ideology, then its elite organizations took over: the SS, the Security Service – SD (*Sicherheitsdienst*) – and the Gestapo, the secret state police, which had been developed by Heinrich Himmler (1900–45) and Reinhard Heydrich (1904–42) into an all-powerful instrument designed to purge, terrorize and 'educate' the nation. It was with such crack troops that Himmler constructed a new elite based on the racial theories of National Socialism: anyone who did not belong to the old establishment of the aristocratic, the wealthy and the educated might apply to join the new elite, provided his physique conformed to the model of 'nordic man'. The former chicken-breeder Himmler looked on his crack troops in their black uniforms as an 'Order of Germanic Clans', whose marriages were dictated by strict genealogical rules.

The transformation of the German nation into a homogeneous entity in line with the standards of the NSDAP was accelerated by the pressures of the Second World War. Those features that had marked the image of National Socialism from the outset now came into full prominence: comprehensive militarization and uniformity. Hitler was convinced – thus endorsing Ludendorff's vision during the First World War – that war was the ultimate aim of politics, a characteristic perversion of the familiar Clausewitz doctrine. This celebrated dictum took precedence over everything else as the incontrovertible principle of Hitler's view of the world. The next logical step he deployed time and time again in his writings, in innumerable speeches and conversations: politics in essence meant the securing of a nation's living space. This living space could be conquered and retained only by perpetual struggle, so that politics was merely a kind of never-ending war, and armed conflict the only logical conclusion – the 'most potent and truly classical' expression of politics, as Hitler put it, but also of life itself. Living in a world of perpetual peace, on the other hand, men were bound to degenerate and be superseded by animals, which instinctively obeyed the law of nature. 'As long as the

earth revolves around the sun', he declared in solemn tones
to the Bulgarian ambassador Draganoff in December 1940,
'as long as there is warmth and cold, fertility and infertility,
storm and sunshine, so long will the struggle last, among
men and among nations . . . If men lived in the Garden of
Eden, they would rot. Whatever men have become, they have
become through battle.'[12] There are hundreds of examples of
such statements by Hitler, for it was this obsession with the
idea of war that drove him on. One of his closest collaborators
spoke of his 'pathologically aggressive nature'. This obsession
went far beyond its starting point in social Darwinism and was
nurtured to a degree it is hard for us to fathom by Hitler's
experience at the front during the First World War. This
was what governed the feelings, the violent behaviour and
the ideology of National Socialism. As Hitler used to say over
and over again, as far as he was concerned the world war had
never come to an end.

When the essential purpose of a community is war, then
earlier distinctions cease to count. German society in the
Wilhelmian era had been a militaristic society in the sense
that there was a marked tendency to apply the standards of
the army to civilian life, and to make the Potsdam lieutenant
of the regiment of guards the prime social model. Nevertheless,
distinctions were clearly evident. The officer with all the arrogance of an elite stood quite apart from the civilian, who could
at best achieve nothing more in his bearing than a caricature of
the admired military model – Heinrich Mann's Professor Unrat
was, in point of fact, not a soldier, but a pitiably laughable
'subject'.

Now in the Third Reich, the situation was quite different.
In conformity with the Leader's will the nation was organized
on totally military lines, it was promoted, as it were willy-nilly,
from the contemptible status of the civilian to that of the
soldier. Anyone exercising a public function naturally wore a
uniform, however un-military his job might be. Lawyers were,
in the official propaganda jargon, 'officers of the law'. Academ-
ics became 'soldiers of scientific knowledge'. No area of life,
not even the professions, escaped the principle of order and
obedience in the name of leadership. Under the auspices of this

kind of assimilation to military routine, roll-calls and parades were constantly held throughout the country, in government offices, in schools and universities and in factories, so that the whole population literally toed the line. As Goebbels himself put it, 'In the new Germany we have only one commander, Adolf Hitler. Our regiment is called Germany!' Military service of one kind or another, dictated by Hitler's express will, was to become the mode of life of every German. In this militaristic state subject to its Leader, the old military legacy of Prussia merged with the Romantic German national consciousness to generate the monstrous image of a totalitarian regime founded on terror and compulsion. The identification of 'inner veracity' with terrorism and concentration camps, and an 'outer veracity' with a determination to wage aggressive war: this was what now went to form a grotesque mask combining the features of a militaristic Prussia and a nationalistic Germany, with its gaze fixed upon the person of the Führer, the supreme militarist.

A distinction might well be drawn here between Fascist Italy and Nazi Germany. Mussolini's Italy never entirely lost certain features of a middle-class state under the rule of law; daily life was not obviously affected by a process of political assimilation, the totalitarian aspirations of the Fascist party were no more than an imposing façade behind which Italian society hardly changed – like the *Vittoriano*, the Italian national monument at the end of the Corso in Rome, Fascism was a vast marble stage devoid of depth. Attempts by the regime during the Second World War to stimulate a sense of national solidarity by substituting the more intimate *voi* for the form of address, *Lei*, and by replacing the handshake by the Fascist salute, were generally regarded as silly and presumptuous and not taken seriously.

In Adolf Hitler's Germany, however, a truly totalitarian dictatorship held sway. Government by terrorist methods and political and social assimilation were the order of the day, and the registration and administrative regimentation of the so-called *Volksgenossen* had gone to extreme lengths. The monstrously distended National Socialist Party went on steadily expanding and smothered the state and its bureaucracy with countless political initiatives, like some malicious cancer, robbing the

state of its most important responsibilities and undermining
the integrity of its servants. Broadly speaking, it might be said
that the National Socialist Party, which claimed to embody the
will of the German people, had done everything in its power to
dismantle and dismember the German state.

What was true internally applied abroad as well. Mussolini
waged war quite differently from Hitler. Mussolini was totally
under the spell of Enrico Corradini's heroic imperialism from
the period before the war: he carried it to its logical conclusion,
but never advanced beyond it. 'The Fascist state is the will to
wield power and to rule,' he declared.

> The Roman tradition is its driving force. In the doctrine
> of Fascism 'impero' is not simply a territorial, military
> or commercial idea, but an intellectual or moral con-
> cept . . . For Fascism the ambition to 'impero', i.e. to the
> expansion of the nation, is an expression of its vitality.
> Its opposite, the wish to stay put at home is a symptom
> of decline. Nations which rise or which are revived, are
> imperialistic, only peoples in decline can afford to hold
> back . . . [13]

In the wars of Fascist Italy against Ethiopia, in its participation
in the Spanish civil war, and in alliance with Germany in the
Second World War, the central issue for Mussolini was the
pursuit of a more or less classical colonial policy of expansion
and spheres of influence on the pre-war pattern. The aims
were never clearly defined, but largely determined by the
current political or military constellation. They were indeed
proclaimed and justified in bombastic terms, with Mussolini
representing himself as a direct descendant of the Roman
Caesars. Racist undertones played only a minor part in the
Italian campaigns: in Italy, it is true, there was racist legislation
modelled on the Nürnberg laws, but it was never consistently
applied: it failed partly because of bureaucratic inefficiency,
and partly on account of the humane instincts of the Italian
people.

Hitler's war, on the other hand, was of a totally different
kind. It was often believed that Hitler's bid for global power,
as Hermann Rauschning and, later on, Alan Bullock, Hitler's

eminent biographer, tried to explain in their works, was nihilistic, irrational, unprincipled and governed by sheer lust for power. Seen in this light, the Second World War and the events leading up to it were simply an attempt by a reckless opportunist to achieve conquests more or less without risk. This 'revolution of nihilism', as Hermann Rauschning called National Socialism, was, then, unique, something that fell more or less outside the context of German history: there was no rational explanation for the outbreak of the Second World War.

In the meantime, however, historical research has revealed factors that, even in the era of the Wilhelmian Reich and the First World War, had some affinity with the aims of the National Socialists. We know that Hitler's anti-Semitism had precedents in thinkers of the nineteenth century and that the massacre of entire populations had already been practised in colonial wars: we need only think, confining ourselves to a German example, of the suppression of the Herero rising in south-west Africa in the years 1904–7. And the theory of the Germans as a 'people without living space' was prefabricated: at the end of the nineteenth century the geopolitician Friedrich Ratzel, for example, had already advanced the view that history was only the record of a permanent struggle for living space. This argument had been taken up during the First World War by powerful interests in support of demands for annexations that ranged from the Channel coast of the continent to the Ukraine.

In unleashing the Second World War was Hitler acting within a tradition of German thought and German policy? Are National Socialism and its consequences the ultimate truth concerning the history of Germany? That, too, has often been claimed, but it is just as false as the opposite proposition. Neither anti-Semitism, nor the 'living space' theory, nor the propensity for genocide are confined to Germany. The truly murderous excesses, the totally destructive effects came about only when these elements were combined in Hitler's mind and thus acquired a totally novel character. From the very first day of Hitler's appointment as Chancellor of the Reich, i.e. from 30 January 1933, the policy of the Reich adhered, although with a certain amount of tactical flexibility, to the basic principles of Hitler's thinking and his vision of history as a perpetual, ruthless battle between nations for 'living space'. This a nation needed for its demographic growth, which must be governed by the principle of racial purity. As early as 1930 in an address to students in Erlangen Hitler declared, 'Every creature strives to expand and every nation strives for global mastery. Only those who keep this goal in view are on the right road.'

Up to this point Hitler's thinking had run more or less on the lines of classical nationalism in its inflatory imperialistic phase. Cecil Rhodes and Enrico Corradini had preached the doctrine in much the same terms. But then came the critical step which hurled the idea of the nation into a murderous racial ideology, drawing from the concept of the one and indivisible nation a consequence from which even the most rabid nationalists of the nineteenth century had recoiled. In Hitler's view only racially superior and homogeneous nations were fit to rule in the long run: throughout the course of history they had been prevented from doing so by opponents of the Aryan race, by Judaism, which was subversive by its very nature. The Weimar Republic and the Western democracies had already succumbed to this 'subversion', the Soviet Union was in fact the first state to be totally infiltrated by Jews and was thus a source of infection for the rest of the world. Hitler's pathological reasoning led him to the conclusion that the German body politic must be rid of Jews and the country must seek the living space to which it was entitled in the wide open spaces of Eastern Europe, where the Germans would assume the role of the master race, while the allegedly inferior Slavs were to act the part of slave nations. According to this demented logic the world war had to be fought simply in order to exterminate the Jews.

The German leadership in the Second World War, then, was not primarily concerned to revise the outcome of the first war, as many of Hitler's Conservative backers believed, and as a good many people still believe: the issue was not just mastery in the classical sense of European foreign policy, nor the acquisition of export markets, nor the release of inner tensions through military activity – all that might be said of Mussolini, but not of Hitler. None of the reasons for going to war hitherto familiar from the history of Europe applies to Germany's actions in the Second World War. In Hitler's own words the issue was 'the launching of the final campaign against the Jewish–Bolshevik arch-enemy' in a vast theatre of war dominated by National Socialism.

Everything that had happened prior to the assault on the Soviet Union, then, was merely tactical preparation. The attack on Poland was designed simply to seize territory for the deployment of German forces against the East. The war against France was meant to secure Germany's rear, as was the attempt to come to an understanding with Great Britain on the basis of a division of the world between the two powers. Following the defeat of Poland, millions of Jews had been rounded up and herded together in the ghettos of Polish cities, while Jews in Germany were identified and singled out for 'treatment'. All this was simply a prelude to what was to happen following 'Operation Barbarossa' – war against the Soviet Union and the deliberate, utterly ruthless extermination of the Jews as the precondition for German mastery of the whole world. Stalingrad and Auschwitz were linked and mutually dependent.

How important this aim was for Hitler is evident from the vigour with which he pursued the policy of eradicating European Jewry, even when the strategic situation was already hopeless. Even during the summer campaign against Stalingrad in 1942 the German armies had been handicapped by shortage of transport, because at the same time trains were being re-routed throughout the whole of Central and Western Europe to carry consignments of Jews on their way to extermination camps. Hitler was only being consistent when, facing imminent defeat, he wished to see the entire German nation destroyed, since it had proved to be too feeble to establish the global rule of the Aryan race on the bones of the Jews.

The most horrifying feature of the Second World War was not just the mass killing, the scale of which it is hard to grasp, but also the tyranny of a homicidal idea. Hitler's war blew apart all the recognized standards of reason and policy. We now know into what an abyss of infamy men may be led, when totalitarian ideology is linked with total power. In Hitler's 'Third Reich' we may observe just what a totalitarian state is capable of, if it is conceived and designed with the utmost consistency. What happened in the Third Reich was a totally logical development, for it was all implicit from the outset in an idea which defined, confirmed and justified the nation by reference to its enemies – the image the nation has of itself and the image of its enemy are but two sides of the same coin. As the idea of the nation became totalitarian, as it came to be conceived as absolute and sacred in the ideologies of 'integral nationalism' and Fascism, and ultimately in its most consistently extreme manifestation in National Socialism, then the enemy was also magnified and seen in absolute terms – and so the war came, a war which burst asunder all the bonds that European civilization had hitherto imposed on it.

Part IV

Nations, States and Europe

13

Nations, States and Europe

Do we really know now what the outcome was to be when, on 1 September 1939, German troops began their attack on Poland? The Second World War and its consequences: it meant hecatombs of dead – historians speak of 55 million, but no one knows exactly how many there were – it meant a flood of refugees on an apocalyptic scale, it meant industrialized, technically efficient mass murder, it meant the advance of the Soviet Union into the heart of the Old World, and it meant the beginning of the end of the German nation state. It is true that Europe seems to have entered a new historical era since Eastern Europe underwent a sudden change in 1989–90, since the Soviet Union retreated to its original stronghold, with its empire falling apart and Russia shrinking back to the frontiers it had had in the eighteenth century.

But we still cannot be sure that we have come to the end of an era that began with shells bursting on the Westerplatte in Danzig and the howling of dive-bombers over Cracow and Warsaw. It is possible that future generations will see in this era the final great explosion in which Europe perished, as a star in a supernova which flares up and dies, to continue its existence merely as a cold, black, shrunken cinder in the heavens. Those of us who survived the cataclysm would then be living in a continent where the erstwhile forms of life merely glowed dimly here and there under the ashes, while barbaric civil wars and internecine feuds tore to shreds the once stable system, while in fact Europe's heirs – America, Japan, China, and perhaps Russia – would have long since gained hegemony throughout the world, while the hungry states of the Third World were merely awaiting their chance to fall upon the remaining wealth of their moribund former masters.

That would be the worst case, which may not necessarily come to pass, even although Europe has already taken steps in that direction. One thing at any rate is certain: the appearance of the continent in 1945 was totally different from what it had been following the First World War, which had ended with the triumph of the principle of nationality. There was indeed no lack of voices proclaiming once again that Europe – now liberated and democratic – may become a family of nation states, as declared in Article 2 of the Atlantic Charter. In fact, all the pre-war European states were restored in 1945, with the exception of the Baltic states annexed by the Soviet Union. It was even initially the wish of the Allies that Germany should exist as a single state, although, immediately following her capitulation, sovereignty was invested in the commanders-in-chief of the four major victorious powers.

However, attempts to reconstruct the traditional order of states in Europe failed, because the preconditions were lacking. The history of Europe may be seen as a series of attempts to restore the former unity of the continent by elevating one of its major powers to a position of hegemony, beginning in the sixteenth and seventeenth century with Spain, which exploited the wealth of its overseas empire, and was inspired by its mission to restore the Catholic unity of Europe. Spain was succeeded by France which twice aspired to hegemony in Europe: the first time under Louis XIV, and again, borne up by the sense of mission inspired by the French Revolution, under Napoleon Bonaparte. England took advantage of successive defeats suffered by France to establish, at the beginning of the eighteenth and again during the nineteenth century, a kind of indirect hegemony in Europe, although the country's main interest lay in the overseas empire. Ever since the Congress of Vienna, Russia had been advancing her interests in the direction of Central and South-East Europe. All these attempts had come to grief, however, because of the resistance of the other European states, which formed coalitions in opposition to the ascendant power in each case, so that sooner or later the overall balance of power on the continent was restored.

The attempt of the German Reich, twice in the course of the twentieth century, to achieve supremacy in Europe also forms part of this pattern of alternating attempts at hegemony and restoration of a balance of power. Adolf Hitler's world war released such unique destructive forces, however, that Europe itself did not have the resources to restore the balance, and salvation had to come from outside the continent – from the steppes of Asia and from across the Atlantic. Europe paid for its rescue by its division and by its partial absorption into the spheres of interest of the two superpowers, the United States of America and the Soviet Union.

This was obvious even before the war came to an end. The wartime conferences of the Allies dealt with Europe from the outset more or less from outside, in the context of a global policy. Europe itself had very little say in what its future was to be. Of the European powers it was Great Britain, under its determined and purposeful wartime leader, Winston Churchill, that made every effort to extend its worldwide power and influence into the post-war period. British policy was aimed primarily at retaining the Commonwealth countries that were scattered all round the world. Under General de Gaulle (1890–1970) France, as a defeated nation, made every effort to resume its place in the company of the great powers, but was initially excluded from major policy decisions. No small part in military operations as well as in the shaping of European policies after the war, was played by the resistance movements in those parts of Europe that had been occupied by the Germans, and a number of these movements had put forward suggestions for a European union after the war, although these proposals had had little in the way of practical consequences. During the war, it is true, the latent antagonism between the liberal Western powers and the Soviet Union had been played down in the interests of the anti-Hitler front, but it had by no means been eliminated. Stalin's expansionist intentions rapidly became apparent and roused the suspicions of his

Western allies, as well as strengthening their determination to curb over-ambitious Soviet policies in Europe.

What that entailed was the establishment of spheres of influence. As early as 9 October Churchill suggested to Stalin in so many words that the degree of influence, of the Western powers and the Soviet Union respectively, in the Balkans should be defined in percentages. Thus, in Romania Soviet influence should amount to 90 per cent, that of the Western powers to 10 per cent; in Greece, Western influence should be 90 per cent, the Soviet share 10 per cent, while in Yugoslavia each of the blocs should have 50 per cent influence. The same would apply to Hungary, but in Bulgaria the Soviet Union would have a share of 75 per cent, and the Western powers only 25 per cent. In hindsight the idea seems like an absurd juggling with illusory figures, but Churchill took it much more seriously than he subsequently admitted in his memoirs, and even Stalin was much attracted by the idea. To that extent the great powers had already moved away from the idea of the nations' right to self-determination, and subsequent decisions taken by the 'Mighty Trio', Stalin, Roosevelt and Churchill at the Yalta Conference of 4 – 11 February 1945 confirmed their policy. True, there was no mention of 'spheres of influence', because President Roosevelt did not care for the term, but in fact all the decisions taken at Yalta were concerned with the influence of the West in competition with Soviet influence, whether in the Balkans, in Poland or in Central Europe generally.

The partition of Europe had therefore already been on the cards at the end of the war, and it was then made even more radical by the Cold War. Given the fierce rivalry between the opposing sides, nation states had very little chance of asserting exclusive rights: following the explosion of the atomic bomb over Hiroshima on 6 August 1945 and the first Soviet atomic bomb in August 1949, a situation arose in which the sovereignty of individual states had to be redefined: henceforth, in any grave crisis only the nuclear powers had total freedom of action, while the sovereignty of the other European states depended at best on whichever major power had deployed its nuclear shield over its sphere of influence, dictating the domestic, political, ideological and economic factors that were to prevail under that shield. The traditional right of nation states to self-determination had been superseded by a bipolar policy that governed them militarily, ideologically and economically.

This applied above all to those parts of Europe which included those countries that had formed a *cordon sanitaire* confining the Soviet Union after the First World War, with the addition of the Soviet occupation zone in Germany and, until the state treaty of 1955, Austria. Already in the spring of 1945 Stalin had made it clear in discussion with Yugoslav communists that: 'This war was not like wars in the past. Whoever occupies a given territory will impose his own social system on that territory. Everyone will impose his own system as far as his armies can advance. It is bound to be like that.'[1] In the years following the war the Soviet Union was careful to take account of national differences between the countries under its control: they were allowed to choose their own 'path to Socialism', provided that the supremacy of the Soviet Union in domestic and foreign policy was acknowledged. This was a period when the communist regimentation of Eastern Europe was proceeding apace, when communists were represented in the French government, when communists in alliance with the Nenni Socialists were on the threshold of power in Italy and a civil war involving the communists had once again flared up in Greece. In this situation, to Stalin's surprise, the United States government under Harry S. Truman (1884–1972) resolved to resist the further expansion of Soviet power in Europe. The Truman doctrine of 12 March 1947 offering American support to nations that were not yet under Soviet domination, together with the Marshall Plan of the same year, designed to boost the European economy, were evidence of a will to resist on the part of the West that was regarded by Stalin as a positive threat. Soviet interference in the internal affairs of Eastern European states became more blatant, rival political parties vanished to make way for undisputed rule by a Communist Party subservient to Soviet policy, but with the ostensibly 'democratic' support of 'block parties'.

Within the Soviet sphere of influence there was no longer room for nation states to pursue their own line of development. The 'national communist' policy of Wladislaw Gomulka, who had sought a compromise with the Polish peasantry and some kind of understanding with the Catholic Church, was abruptly halted in 1948. The Polish Army, which had allegedly been infiltrated by right-wing deviationists, was taken firmly in hand through the appointment of a Soviet citizen, Marshall Konstantin Rokossovsky, as Polish Minister of Defence. Soviet policy-makers had greater problems with Yugoslavia, because there were no Soviet troops stationed there, who could, if necessary, impose Stalin's will on the country. Consequently, when the Communist Party of Yugoslavia, under the leadership of Marshall Tito (1892 – 1982), broke away from Moscow and declared a policy of independence, the Soviet response was no more drastic than a torrent of vulgar abuse of the 'Tito clique' and an attempt to isolate Yugoslavia. In fact it was only later that Yugoslavia's 'path to Socialism' was justified as 'national communism', like the claim of the Romanian leadership to an independent foreign policy in the seventies and eighties. In fact, Tito had broken away from Moscow primarily because Soviet foreign policy seemed to him too nationalistic, too much gov-erned by tactical considerations and excessively dictated by the interests of the Soviet Union. It was the 'nationalist' Tito who, with the support of communist liberation movements, was determined to promote the international aims of communism to the point of world revolution.

From that point on, until the collapse of the Soviet empire at the end of the eighties, 'nationalism' was regarded by the Sovi-ets as a dangerous 'right-wing' deviation. Following Stalin's death in 1953, it did seem for several years as if the Soviet leadership was once again prepared to tolerate independent policies on the part of nations within the Soviet sphere of influence, but in November 1956 the member of the Politburo responsible for ideological questions, Suslov, declared that, for countries on their way towards socialism, certain principles must be observed – such as the 'leading part played by the Marxist–Leninist Party', the 'defence of socialist achievements against attacks by internal and external enemies' and pro-letarian internationalism. What the last of these principles meant in practice had been shown by the Soviet intervention in Hungary in October 1956. The Soviet Union was not prepared to tolerate a 'national communism' that called in question the monolithic union of the states allied in the Warsaw Pact and the undisputed leadership of the Soviet Union. The Brezhnev doctrine, which was proclaimed when troops of the Warsaw Pact marched into Czechoslovakia in 1968, was no more than a more precise formulation of the 'principle of socialist internationalism'. Socialist states consequently had no more than 'limited sovereignty' and a 'limited right of self-determination'. Wherever there was a risk of autonomous developments in a single state, then there arose the possibility of 'fraternal assistance' by the allied socialist states and, above all, by the Soviet Union – even if such assistance required the use of tanks. The *pax sovietica* smothered the aspirations of peoples and states and the ethnic minorities of Eastern Europe, keeping them in check by the constant threat of police action or full-scale military intervention. It seemed as if the political elites of these states were so firmly tied to the Communist Party of the Soviet Union that the national interests of individual states were to be totally subordinated to the common interests of Comecon and the Warsaw Pact. The ideological justification might be summed up in these terms: nationalism was a product of consciousness, but consciousness depended on the form taken by actual social existence, so that, in the age of socialism, 'middle-class nationalism' was superseded by 'socialist patriotism' and 'proletarian internationalism'.

This did not mean that the Soviet Union was unable to appeal to the national interests of states in Western Europe, in circumstances where the victors and the vanquished might be played off against each other. The German–Soviet Rapallo pact of 1922, an alliance between the two outcasts of the international community after the First World War, had set the example. In principle Stalin was harking back to this old Rapallo policy when, in notes to the Western powers and the Federal Republic of Germany in 1952, he offered German reunification in return for Germany's neutrality and a limitation of German sovereignty. This appeal to the interests of a German national state was undoubtedly meant to torpedo proposals for the incorporation of the Federal Republic of Germany into a Western military alliance. No responsible

West German politician was so unrealistic as to pick up the nationalist card dealt by Stalin. In Europe, as planned in Yalta, it was scarcely disputed that Western Germany's true national interest lay precisely in the renunciation of its national interest in the time-honoured classical sense.

As far as Western Europe was concerned, it was also an indisputable fact that its leading power, i.e. the United States, had set the acceptable pattern. Almost everywhere outside the Eastern bloc liberal parliamentary democracy was adopted as the model, the attractions of which went beyond the member states of the Atlantic Alliance and influenced the neutral states of the West, from Finland and Sweden to Austria and Switzerland. It was only on the fringes of Europe, in Spain, Portugal and Greece, that authoritarian regimes were able to survive for a time.

As distinct from the course of events after 1918, the Western type of parliamentary democracy, derived ultimately from French and British constitutional traditions, was established in an unexpectedly firm fashion. Judging by experience between the wars, democracy had been feeble, vulnerable, inefficient and lacking in credibility, but the situation was now quite different, because certain essential circumstances had changed. There was now, for one thing, an awareness of the dangers that threatened democracy and that were now taken into account in the constitutional provisions for the defence of democratic institutions. This applied with particular force to the Federal Republic of Germany: the Basic Law of 1949 may be read in large measure as a draft explicitly intended to correct the failings of the Weimar Constitution. It applies also, however, to the constitution of the French Fifth Republic, which put democracy in the French political parties on a sound footing. There was also the fact that the mass migration of peoples and other social upheavals in the aftermath of the Second World War had disrupted the social structures of Europe, bringing benefits in the shape of a more pragmatic attitude and the elimination of ideology from politics, and reinforcing the readiness of different groups in the population to compromise on disputed issues. The democracies of Western Europe also benefited from a worldwide economic boom that lasted for the best part of twenty years, and in which the European economies had a major share. The annual increase in the gross national product of all the economies of Western Europe was sufficiently great to allow for a redistribution of income, to guarantee social peace and harmony, and to accustom men to the advantages of parliamentary democracy without the unremitting struggle for their daily bread. For the first time the nations of Western Europe were united in the realization that to be a democrat was to be on the winning side.

The decision by the United States not to withdraw, as it had done after the First World War, but to guarantee the security of Western Europe, guarding it through the Marshall Plan and the NATO Alliance against any advance by the Soviet Union, did what was needed to encourage the formation of unions and alliances within Europe itself. Even during the war, resistance movements against Nazi oppression had been aware that they had a common cause in the spirit of Europe's humanist and Christian tradition. Carl Goerdeler (1884 – 1944) declared in a peace plan dating from the autumn of 1943, 'And so the combination of the European nations in a Confederation of European States seems to us an imperative necessity. Its aim must be to secure Europe absolutely against the occurrence of a European war . . . '[2] And in July 1944 a 'Declaration on European Cooperation' drafted by resistance groups from a number of European countries, called for the institution, after the war, of a European government, a European Court of Justice and a common European Army.[3] Europe's resistance to Hitler's dictatorship was thus one of the roots of the European movement following the Second World War; another was the Cold War. Without the two great despots, Hitler and Stalin, a unification of Europe, capable for the first time in history, of setting up enduring international institutions, would scarcely have been possible. If we look at the development of a European 'Us-awareness' in the period extending from the Battle of Salamis to the present day, we find an explanation that is as simple as it is depressing: Europe has always united only in opposition to something, never in favour of something. Europe becomes aware of its identity primarily when it is a question of warding off a common, real or imagined enemy, but it tends to lose its sense of identity once the threat has passed. When the Arabs invaded Gaul and were defeated at Tours and Poitiers, when the Mongols attacked Hungary and Silesia, when the Turks were encamped before Vienna, then the unity of Europe was invoked. It was even invoked on the occasion of the Boxer rising in 1900, when the nightmare of a Chinese 'Yellow Peril' seemed to have become reality. The rising was put down by a united European expeditionary force – and this was only fourteen years before the outbreak of the First World War seemed to have totally eliminated any prospect of united European action.

The risk of a new world war, an attack by troops of the Warsaw Pact on Western Europe, had indeed been reduced by the nuclear stalemate between East and West, but it was revived following the outbreak of the Korean War in 1950. The readiness of Western Europe to enter into military alliances increased, as did the realization that the economic, military and political integration of the continent entailed the abandonment of isolated national policies. When Winston Churchill, in a speech in Zürich on 16 December 1946, called for the creation of a 'United States of Europe' – still an alarming idea at that point in time – based on a partnership between France and Germany, he left out Great Britain. The exclusion of Churchill's own country was in keeping with the classic British policy of a balance of power in Europe which, through a system of pacts, would pacify an unruly continent on England's threshold, so that Britain might be free to devote herself to the overseas possessions of His Britannic Majesty. But the collapse of the British and French colonial empires made it obvious in the course of the fifties that the era of European hegemony had finally come to an end, that Europe had been thrown back on its own resources and could only maintain its position in alliance with the United States, if it could combine and concentrate what was left of these resources. The foundation of a 'Common Market for Coal and Steel', also known as the 'Montanunion', through which production of coal and steel in France, Germany, the Netherlands, Belgium and Luxemburg was governed by a common authority, was a first step towards the economic integration of Europe – a first step on a path which has currently reached a conclusion in the present-day 'European Union' with its vast superstructure of commissions, councils, general directorates and civil servants. From the point of view of the modern observer the world of the late nineteenth and early twentieth century, the so-called '*Gründerzeit*' of economic expansion and international commercial rivalry, has long since vanished: the hopeful rhetoric which ushered in European unification now strikes us as hardly less astonishing than the unquestioning willingness of the parties concerned to renounce something of their autonomy in pursuit of this aim.

In these circumstances had not the nation state become obsolete? In the forties, and even more so in the fifties, there were powerful forces in Europe openly working towards that end. It was the decade of the Christian Democratic parties, a novelty in European politics – major mass parties, in spite of their religious affiliations. These parties were appealing everywhere for the formation of coalitions and for a truce in the battle between labour and capital. Their great founders, Alcide de Gasperi (1881–1954) in Italy, Robert Schuman (1886–1963) in France, Konrad Adenauer (1876–1967) in Germany, Paul Henri Spaak (1890–1972) in Belgium, were all committed to the unification of Europe as a bulwark of the Christian West against Bolshevism. This was not just an example of political and economic opportunism, but an idea held in common which was manifestly relevant to a great common tradition in European history and thought. Seen in this light, the history of the European nation state had indeed come to an end.

Illusions had run riot, especially on the German side. The dream of a German nation state during the nineteenth century had seemingly held out great promise for the future of the German people, but the reality had been overshadowed by defeat, collapse and criminality. The national hope of a Reich embracing the whole German race had been realized only in the nightmare of Hitler's 'Great German Reich'. The path to unification had ended in oppression, persecution and the murder of dissidents and minorities: the monstrous and unprecedented deeds committed in the name of the German people were epitomized in the atrocities of Auschwitz and

Treblinka, and their outcome was the destruction of the German nation state.

The Swiss historian, Jakob Burckhardt, had once remarked ironically on the 'triumphant veneer' of German historical writing: when the veneer peeled off, the German identity disintegrated. The approach to Europe, then, was for many Germans an attempt to escape from the nation's past. Invoking the 'end of the nation state' may perhaps remind us of the story of the fox and the sour grapes. Pride in one's own nationality, the driving force behind mass nationalism in former times, has been deflated in the second half of the present century, not just in Germany, but in the whole of Western Europe – although the degree of decline in national pride seems to vary from country to country. In 1981 an opinion research institute carried out a survey of adults over the age of eighteen in the countries of the European Community and the USA, asking their informants whether they were proud of their nation. The percentage of those who claimed to be 'very proud' was scored as follows:

	Percentage of 'very proud'
The Netherlands	19
Federal Republic of Germany	21
Belgium	27
Denmark	30
France	33
European Community overall	38
Italy	41
Spain	49
Great Britain	55
Ireland	66
USA	79

Source: Institut für Demoskopie Allensbach. Internationale Wertestudie 1981–2.

We may be struck straight away by the low figure for the Federal Republic of Germany, but it does not differ very significantly from the data for the other countries of north-western Europe. Otherwise, the figure for the European Community is remarkably low in comparison with the figure for the USA. Certainly, the figures are no more than a kind of snapshot, but there is plenty of evidence that European integration has not been just a process on a high political and bureaucratic level: the populations of the individual states have also been involved. Beyond the national cultures and the special features that have marked the course followed by each state, the societies of Western and Central Europe have become more and more alike during the first half of the twentieth century. As the industrialization of the continent has spread to reach its periphery, the pattern of employment in most European countries has tended to become more and more homogeneous. This was always true of industry proper, but it applies now to the service sector as well. The former educational gradient between North and South, and also in some respects between rich and poor, has been gradually levelled out. The urbanization of Western and Central Europe has given birth to a common urban culture in which similarities outweigh differences. Among the major factors involved has been the evolution of the welfare state, in one form or another, throughout Europe, so that the living conditions of Europeans in the various countries of the continent are much more similar than when they are compared with the United States of America, say, or Japan. The instant mass distribution of news and cultural events, as well as mass tourism, have naturally played their part in eliminating the alienation of European nations from each other.

Any academic who takes part in international conferences and has experienced the problems that may arise from the clash of different cultures and academic traditions – not to mention the problem of different languages – is well aware that marked national characteristics still exist. Even a community sharing the same communications networks has still to be established in Europe, as was demonstrated by the example of the European Business Channel, an English-language television station which was set up in Geneva in 1990 to transmit via satellite a news programme for the commercial elite of the continent, and which had to close down within a year. It turned out that the expectations of European businessmen in terms of news output were still governed by national interests. In each European country a different blend of regional, national and international news items was looked for, and only the existing national programmes were in a position to meet that demand. It is obvious all the same that the societies of the European countries – for the moment, mainly the Western European countries – are becoming more and more like each other in certain vital areas, although the social and economic integration of Europe is often not clearly acknowledged. In particular, cultural differences have proved to be stubbornly persistent, and the linguistic disunity of Europe still plays a major part, in spite of the triumphant advance of English as an international medium of communication.

By and large, Western Europeans have settled down comfortably in their half of the continent. Their economic integration has become, step by step, increasingly firm: the European Economic Community, originally an alliance of six states – France, Italy, the Federal Republic of Germany, Belgium and Luxemburg – was widened to include Great Britain, Ireland, Denmark, Spain, Portugal and Greece, while on the more distant horizon there are already signs of a somewhat vague political entity – the 'United States of Europe', a defensive idea born of fear of communism and adherence to the hegemonial power of the West. It was not often observed that the unification of Western Europe would be based on quite different premises from those which produced the United States of America two hundred years ago: de Gaulle's 'Europe of the Fatherlands' found few supporters outside France precisely because of its realistic point of departure.

The unification of the free area of the continent seemed to be within reach. One of the major disappointments of the post-war period was that the principle of the nation state appeared to have retained its unassailable rights, in spite of a fair degree of success in economic and political integration. There are even clearer grounds for disappointment, in that we are currently faced with a revival of much that had seemed doomed to vanish along with the old Europe. We would have to look a long way back into history to find a moment when the situation of Europe looked so precarious and its future so uncertain. Almost overnight we find ourselves in a dramatically changed world, from which all the familiar landmarks of the past decades have vanished. The Iron Curtain, which had marked the bottom line of European policy for almost half a century, has fallen, the spirit of Yalta has evaporated from Europe, and what is left is a host of national, regional, economic and social factors which have emerged reluctantly from the secure ideological retreats they occupied during the Cold War: they now have to come to terms with a new situation and arrive at new and rational understandings.

The pressure of the Soviet Army had scarcely been removed before White Russia began to make territorial claims on Lithuania, the little Moldavian Republic fell apart into opposing nationalistic camps, there were bloody clashes between Romanians and Hungarians in Siebenbürgen, and the multi-national state of Yugoslavia fell apart in a war involving Serbs, Croats, Bosnians, Slovenes and Albanians. As early as 1990, Vaclav Havel predicted that 'the Yugoslav tragedy may well be repeated everywhere in post-communist Europe'. Following years of fatal underestimation of the nation and national consciousness, the breath-taking rapidity with which nationalistic and particularistic movements have spread has had the impact of a major culture shock on Western observers. Even one of the commonest Western assumptions seems to have been refuted: in particular, the belief that the urgent need of Western capital and Western investment would put sufficient pressure on the East European states to damp down nationalistic fervour and encourage peaceful assimilation to Western democratic models. The West European disciples of material prosperity have had to concede that national sentiment may prove to be more powerful than economic interests. This is apparent in the case of German industrial investment in the Czech Republic or in Poland, where the investors have not always been wholeheartedly welcomed. In fact, the relatively prominent German presence in the economies of these states has given added force to nationalistic arguments that have had a negative effect of the creation of a market economy, and even on the introduction of liberal political reforms. There are strong – and in the light of historical experience, understandable – fears in Poland and in the Czech Republic that Germany might exploit its economic strength to the future detriment of the interests of these states. This argument is employed above all by the successors of the old communist parties as a weapon against democratic and liberal changes – as may be seen in every election campaign.

Francis Fukuyama's prophecy concerning the 'end of history' and the triumph of Western democracy over a 'toothless and trifling European nationalism', as he puts it, is, to say the least, premature. Even in Western Europe national and regional aspirations have been aroused which are liable to slow down the process of European integration – as might have been observed recently in the Danish, French and British responses to the Maastricht Treaty. And how might the European Community formulate a common policy towards Eastern Europe, when the traditionally centralized states of Western Europe are also faced with demands by their national minorities for independence, or at least autonomy? A common European response to the Yugoslav crisis has been lacking to some extent because of domestic political problems that have arisen in the case of Great Britain, France, Spain and Italy with regard to Ireland, Corsica, Catalonia and the South Tyrol respectively.

At the same time, the close bonds between Western European states that guaranteed their collective security have been loosened. Given the re-unification of Germany and the security interests of particular states which became evident, for instance, against the background of the Gulf War, possible conjunctions and alliances which might have been regarded as long-since historically defunct, have been retrieved, as it were, from the bowels of history. In Paris the Polish Prime Minister evidently felt it appropriate to invoke the ancient friendship between Poland and France, in tactical exercises practised in the Foreign Office in London the Anglo-French *entente cordiale* has reappeared in phantom form, and the bogey of a renewed German–Russian alliance has alarmed readers of the Sunday supplements. The public response to the Maastricht Conference of 1991, in particular, public concern at the absence of any democratic component, has shown that it is not only the specific interests of the Western European states, but also the traditions rooted in the societies of those states that will turn out to be an obstacle delaying the process of European integration. One need only recall the outcry that was raised in Germany when the rumour spread that the future European common currency would not be a German 'mark', but a French-sounding 'écu'. No other European decision has had such a profound influence on the German attitude to European integration as this proposal. Following the Maastricht Conference the consent of the German population to a possible unification of Europe declined from 72 per cent to 42 per cent, and the picture was little different in the other member states of the European Community.

A generation which never knew either National Socialist or communist dictatorship and which, moreover, does not feel militarily threatened, is inclined to see Europe in its current state as a bugbear: a welter of bureaucratic institutions acting in ways that are often hard to understand, as a continent of butter mountains and milk lakes, the scene of savage quarrels between Dutch and French pig-breeders – a continent without any coherent common mentality and lacking any real necessity or popular sanction. The prospect of separate nation states in place of all this seems once more to have eclipsed what Europeans have in common. Even in issues of fundamental common interest, like peace-keeping or protection of the environment, the attitude and behaviour, not just of governments, but also of the nations themselves, differ from each other.

There can be no doubt that the poison of mass nationalism to which Europe almost succumbed once before, has lost none of its virulence. But it would be a mistake to look on the current turbulence purely from a negative and potentially destructive angle. Without the unifying and mobilizing force of nationalism in the countries of Eastern Europe their liberation from communism would scarcely have been feasible. National self-determination and the change from a Leninist class-war ideology to a fundamental national consensus offered the sole common bond that united the many different groups and interests in these countries. In an age in which traditional forms of religious faith have lost some of their force, it is the idea of the nation that inspires men engaged in a struggle against alien

and despotic rule with a new faith and new objectives that seem
to them satisfying, credible and meaningful.

It is not so much division into nations that threatens Europe
as the determination to found a nation state for every ethnic
group, however small, in which the impractical and illusory
unity of nation, language and territory may be achieved. The
impracticability of such a design is rendered even more prob-
lematic by the legacy of the Romantic idea of the nation as
propounded by a Herder or a Fichte: these thinkers did not
talk in terms of institutions and constitutions, of popular sovereignty and human rights, but of history, language, culture and
the kindred blood flowing from time immemorial through a
people's veins and guaranteeing its integrity over the millennia.
It is this concept of the nation that was, and still is, more potent
in Central and Eastern Europe than the unifying force of liberal
and democratic ideas, and this is what makes nationalism such
a dire danger for Europe. The course of German history in the
nineteenth and the first half of the twentieth century, built on
the mystical concept of a people bound by ties of blood that
demanded the unification of all Germans into a single state,
was doomed to fail in 1945 with the diabolical disaster of the
first German nation state. How right Ernest Renan was when
he wrote to a German colleague following the annexation by
the Reich of Alsace–Lorraine:

> Instead of the criteria of a liberal policy, you have estab-
> lished in our world such ethnographic and archaeological
> policies as will ultimately seal your own fate . . . What
> will be your answer, if one day the Slavs come and lay
> claim to Prussia, Pomerania, Silesia and Berlin, simply on
> the grounds that these place-names are Slavonic, if they
> behave on the banks of the Oder as you are now behaving
> on the banks of the Moselle, if, on the basis of some map
> or other, they point to villages that were once inhabited by
> Slavs? . . . Germany has mounted a mettlesome steed that
> will bear her to places where she has no wish to go.[4]

Renan's prophecy has been fulfilled with uncanny accuracy,
but it seems that Europe has learned nothing from the lesson
of 1945. Wars and conflicts are still being waged for historical

and ethnic reasons, whether in Kosovo, where the fateful Battle of the Field of Blackbirds in 1389 allegedly established perpetual Serbian rights, or in the blockade of Macedonia by Greece, because Greece claims to be the sole heir to the Macedonian empire of Philip II and Alexander the Great – although any cultural continuity between ancient Hellas and the modern Greek state is extremely dubious. The fact that the baleful principle of ethnocracy, the primacy of a nation united by bonds of blood, is still capable of threatening democracy and plunging Europe into fresh and exacting trials of strength has been amply demonstrated by the ghastly mass murder now being committed in what was once Yugoslavia. It is not the idea of the nation as such that must be overcome in Europe, but the fiction of an objective and ineluctable identity of people, nation, history, language and state that was ordained by fate. Even faced with the impossibility of ever realizing any such idea in the narrow confines of Europe without war, permanent oppression, 'ethnic cleansing' and mass murder, this fiction has led, time and time again, to the mass neurosis of 'integral nationalism', to the conviction that the nation inevitably embodies the supreme values of a community, and that this community is manifested in the ethnically pure state.

A glance at the actual situation, at least in Western Europe, makes it obvious that the nation state is obsolete on a number of levels. In questions ranging from the need for more extensive markets, through issues of defence and the fight against crime, the organization of transport and communications, to problems of the environment, individual state institutions have proved to be too limited in resources and competence. The nation state, which was indispensable in the last century as the setting for the emerging industrial society and for the solving of its problems and conflicts, and which, moreover, provided the necessary context for democratic constitutions and institutions, is no longer on its own able to meet the needs of men: more comprehensive arrangements are needed.

What purpose do national frontiers serve within Europe, if constitutional arrangements and economic systems are continually becoming more similar? What is the sense of a German–Polish frontier, if Germans and Poles on both sides of the frontier are able to work and live under identical conditions? What has long applied to the Alemannic race in Switzerland, Alsace and Baden, what applied to the Danish and German inhabitants of Schleswig, might now become a fact of life for German and Polish Silesians, the Austrian and Slovenian inhabitants of Carinthia, the Greeks and Yugoslavs of Macedonia, the French and Spanish Basques. The nation state has indeed become less important, but it is not yet superfluous, for many of its political and judicial functions and administrative structures cannot be dispensed with for the time being. Only the matrix of the nation state is at the moment capable of serving as a shield for free and democratic institutions.

The nations themselves are no more obsolete than the idea of the nation state. The conviction held by many dedicated Europeans in the forties and fifties that 'nations' were no more than a consequence of an inflated ideology and could be got rid of at any time, foundered on the realities of the existing political structures – and even more drastically on the mental attitude of the majority of Europeans. The European nations, still utopian figments at the beginning of the nineteenth century, turned out to be, in the present age, living cultural and intellectual entities – more indeed: an expression of that pluralism, without which Europe would inevitably lose its essential character. Robert Schuman, a native of Lorraine and the prime mover in the establishment of the Montanunion as well as a pioneer of European integration, observed in the fifties much more clearly than many others of his generation that Europe could not simply take leave of its history.

> Political frontiers were the result of a time-honoured historical and ethnic process of evolution, of a long struggle for national unity; no one would dream of abolishing them. In past ages they were often adjusted by violent conquest or advantageous marriages. All we need to do nowadays is to reduce their significance. Our European frontiers should do less and less to impede the exchange of ideas, persons and goods. In future a sense of solidarity bringing nations together ought to take precedence over our outmoded nationalisms. Patriotic feelings once had

the advantages of endowing states with a tradition and a stable inner structure. But now a new storey has to be erected on the ancient foundations, and the edifice that will supersede the states will be erected on national foundations. Thus, the glorious past will not be denied, the efforts of the nations will be deployed jointly in the service of a community that goes beyond the individual states.[5]

If there is a lesson to be learned from the many abortive attempts to unite Europe, then it is that European integration can be achieved only with the collaboration of the nations, recognizing their legitimate individual characteristics, just as the nations for their part must learn that they are not 'one and indivisible', but that they are composed of a multitude of ethnic, linguistic and regional entities.

Lasting unification of the diverse elements in Europe cannot be brought about by a centralistic, monolithic state armed with every kind of competence and authority, such as seems to be adumbrated in the present European Commission in Brussels with its comprehensive political powers in economic matters. A European constitution can endure only if it takes full account of the nations, their long history, their languages and their states. There are also regions and provinces to be considered, most of them, too, the product of age-old traditions; they have become home, and hence dear to the hearts of those who live there. And there are the local communities, in which the familiar processes of daily life unfold, and in which decisions of immediate local relevance are taken.

All this can be welded into a single whole only if the Europe of the future is conceived in the spirit of what is now called 'subsidiarity', i.e. a relatively loose structure on a number of political levels, in which only those issues which cannot be dealt with on the lower level are passed on to a superior authority.

In certain respects we Europeans are facing a situation similar to that which arose at the beginning of the nineteenth century: once again, unprecedented economic, political and technological changes are impelling us in the direction of integration. As distinct from the era of nascent nation states in the nineteenth century, however, it is now governments that are setting the economic and administrative course and pace, while the population of the continent has so far shown little enthusiasm for the grand goal of a united Europe under the slogans of freedom and self-determination. For evidence of this lack of enthusiasm we need only compare the percentage poll in elections to the European Parliament with the corresponding figures for national parliamentary elections. It seems clear that arguments for Europe appeal only to people's heads, while arguments *against* Europe appeal to their hearts.

The critical obstacle to a powerful European sense of identity lies in the Europeans themselves. Since men acquire a sense of community by reference to their common past, they see themselves largely in terms of their history. 'A nation', writes the French sociologist, Edgar Morin, 'is held together by its collective memory and by shared standards and rules. A national community draws on a past extending over many years, a past that is rich in experience, in trials and tribulations, joys and sorrows, defeats, triumphs and glory, all of which are passed on in every generation to every individual through his home and his school and thus lodged deep within him.'[6]

In the historical memory of Europeans, then, it is still their national identity that bulks largest. Just as we sometimes cannot see the wood for the trees, we Europeans cannot see our continent for the nations that constitute it. But we will learn to think and to recognize Europe, so that it becomes a reality. In the course of a thousand years we Europeans have grown used to our ancient states and nations; they will still be with us for a long time to come, and we shall still need them. But they have constantly changed in the past, and they will go on changing in the future, they may gradually fade away and recede into the background to make way for one united Europe, the shape of which we can at present only dimly discern.

Notes

Notes to Preface

1 Francis Fukuyama: *The End of History*, New York 1992.
2 Otto Hintze: 'Wesen und Wandlung des modernen Staats' (1931), in Hintze: *Staat und Verfassung. Gesammelte Abhandlungen zur allgemeinen Verfassungsgeschichte*, ed. Gerhard Oestreich, 3rd edn Göttingen 1970, pp. 470–96.
3 Cf. G. A. Almond and J. S. Coleman (eds): *The Politics of Developing Areas*, Princeton 1960; L. W. Pye and S. Verba (eds): *Political Culture and Political Development*, Princeton 1965; Wolfgang Zapf (ed.): *Theorien des sozialen Wandels*, Cologne and Berlin 1971.

Notes to Chapter 1 The Advent of the Modern State

1 G. W. F. Hegel: *Vorlesungen über die Philosophie der Geschichte* ed. F. Brunstädt, Stuttgart 1961, p. 497.
2 Luis Diez del Corral: *Der Raub der Europa*. Eine historische Deutung unserer Zeit, Munich 1959, p. 247.
3 Leopold von Ranke: 'Das politische Gespräch' in: *Sämmtliche Werke*, Leipzig 1887, vol. 49/50, p. 329.
4 Jacob Burckhardt: *The Civilization of the Renaissance in Italy*. Trans. S. G. C. Middlemore, Phaidon Press, Vienna and London, n.d., p. 2.
5 *Monumenta Germaniae Historica* Epp. pont. I, 357 (5. 7. 1231), Trans. Horst Günther, Frankfurt, 1989, p. 13.
6 *Recueil des actes de Philippe Auguste*, I, 4/6.

7   William of Ockham: *Tract against Benedict V*; Dialogus III, trac. II, 1/4, 2/17.
8   Hans K. Schulze: *Hegemoniales Kaisertum. Ottonen und Salier*, Berlin 1991, p. 92.

Notes to Chapter 2   Christianity and Reasons of State

1   Johan Huizanga: *Herbst des Mittelalters*, ed. Kurt Köster, Stuttgart, 8th reprint 1961, p. 33.
2   Niccolò Machiavelli: *The Prince*, trans. Peter Whitehorne (1560), reprinted London 1905, chapter 25, p. 349.
3   Ibid., p. 350.
4   Niccolò Machiavelli: *Reflections on the first ten books of Titus Livius*, book I, chapter 3, p. 17.
5   Machiavelli, *The Prince*, chapter 18, p. 323.
6   Francesco Guicciardini: *Opere*, ed. Roberto Palmarocchi, Milan 1941, vol. II, p.667.
7   Francesco Guicciardini: *Dialogi e Discorsi del Reggimento di Firenze*, Bari 1932, p. 667.
8   Machiavelli, *The Prince*, chapter 9, p. 294.
9   Cf. Fernand Braudel: *Das Mittelmeer und die mediterrane Welt in der Epoche Philipps II*, Frankfurt 1990, vol. II, pp. 28, 37.
10 Cf. Hellmut Diwald: *Anspruch auf Mündigkeit* (Propyläen Geschichte Europas I), Berlin 1975, p. 272.
11 Antonio de Nebrija: *Gramática de la lengua castellana*, ed. J. González-Llubera, Madrid 1926, pp. 3–9. Cf. Horst Rabe: 'Die iberischen Staaten im 16. und 17. Jahrhundert', in Theodor Schieder (ed.): *Handbuch der europäischen Geschichte*, Stuttgart 1979, vol. III, p. 587.
12 Romans, chapter 13, verse 1.

Notes to Chapter 3   Leviathan

1   Cardinal de Retz: *Mémoires*, ed. Maurice Allem (Bibliothèque de la Pléiade 53), Paris 1956, p. 63f.
2   Ibid., p. 65.
3   Jean Bodin: *Les six Livres de la République avec L'Apologie de R. Herpin*, Facsimile edn, Paris 1583, Aalen 1962, p. 1.
4   Ibid., p. 122.
5   Paul Hazard: *The European Mind 1680–1715*, Pelican Books, London 1964, p. 307.
6   Louis XIV: *Mémoires*, 1662.
7   Pierre Goubet: *Ludwig XIV und zwanzig Millionen Franzosen*,

Berlin 1973, p. 286f.

8 Cf. Friedrich Foerster: *Friedrich Wilhelm I, König von Preussen*, Potsdam 1834, vol. I, p. 35.

9 Frederick William I's instructions for his successor, January 1722, in *Acta Borussica: Behördenorganisation* ed. G. Schmoller et al., Berlin 1893, III, no. 249, p. 450.

10 Ivo Schöffer: 'Die Republick der Vereinigten Niederlande von 1648 bis 1795' in Theodor Schieder (ed.): *Handbuch der europäischen Geschichte*, Stuttgart 1968, vol. IV, p. 654.

11 Max Weber: 'Politik als Beruf' in Weber: *Gesammelte politische Schriften*, ed. Johannes Winckelmann, 2nd augmented edn, Tübingen 1958, p. 494.

12 Michael Roberts: *The Military Revolution, 1560–1660*, Belfast 1956; G. N. Clark: *War and Society in the Seventeenth Century*, Cambridge 1958; Geoffrey Parker: *The Military Revolution*, Cambridge 1988.

13 Otto Hintze: 'Wesen und Wandlung des modernen Staats', in Hintze: *Staat und Verfassung. Gesammelte Abhandlungen zur allgemeinen Verfassungsgeschichte*, ed. Gerhard Oestreich, 3rd edn, Göttingen 1970, p. 479.

14 Cf. Friedrich Brie: *Imperialistische Strömungen in der englischen Literatur*, Halle 1928, p. 56.

Notes to Chapter 4   The Constitutional State and the Rule of Law

1 Charles Montesquieu: *De l'Esprit des Lois*, Editions Garnier Frères, Paris 1961, vol. I, book XI, chapter 3, p. 162.

2 Johann Wilhelm von Archenholtz: *England und Italien*, Leipzig 1785, vol. I, p. 16.

3 Frederick the Great: *'Regierungsformen und Herrscherpflichten (1777)'* in: *Ausgewählte Werke Friedrichs des Grossen in deutscher Uebersetzung*, ed. Gustav Berthold Volz, Berlin 1918, vol. II/2, p. 26.

4 Max Weber: *Wirtschaft und Gesellschaft. Grundriß der verstehenden Soziologie*, ed. Johannes Winckelmann, Tübingen, 5th edn 1976, chapter III.5, p. 128ff.

5 Carl Gottlieb Svarez: *Vorträge über Recht und Staat*, ed. H. Conrad and G. Kleinheyer, Cologne 1960, p. 635f.

6 Ibid., p. 586.

7 Jean-Jacques Rousseau: Introduction to *Narcisse, Oeuvres Complètes*, Bibliothèque de la Pléiade, 153, Editions Gallimard, Paris 1964, vol. II, p. 968f.

8 Cf. *Geschichte in Quellen*, gen. eds Wolfgang Lautemann and Manfred Schlenke: *Amerikanische und Französische Revolution*, ed. Wolfgang Lautemann, Munich 1981, p. 90.

9 Jean-Jacques Rousseau: *Du contrat social, Oeuvres Complètes*, Bibliothèque de la Pléiade 169, Editions Gallimard, Paris 1964, vol. III, p. 380.

10 Karl Freiherr vom Stein zum Altenstein: 'Ueber die Leitung des preussischen Staats. Denkschrift vom 11. 9. 1807', in Georg Winter: *Die Reorganisation des preussischen Staates unter Stein und Hardenberg*, Leipzig 1931, part I, vol. I, pp. 369, 462.

11 Cf. Reinhardt Koselleck: *Preussen zwischen Reform und Revolution. Allgemeines Landrecht, Verwaltung und soziale Bewegung von 1791 bis 1848*, Stuttgart 1967, p. 160.

12 Jean-Jacques Rousseau: *Du contrat social*, book I, chapter I, edn cit. p. 351.

Notes to Chapter 5　　What is the 'Nation'?

1 Hanno Kesting: *Der Befreier Arminius im Lichte der geschichtlichen Quellen und der wissenschaftlichen Forschung*, Detmold 1991, 20th edn (!), pp. 3, 128.

2 'Le 17 Septembre 1985, au Mont Beuvray François Mitterand, président de la République a proclamé site national Bibracte haut lieu de l'histoire de France. Ici s'est faite l'union des chefs Gaulois autour de Vercingetorix.'

3 Ernest Renan: *Oeuvres Complètes*, Paris n.d., vol. 1, pp. 903–4.

4 Cf. also: Emile Durckheim: *Les règles de la méthode sociologique*, Paris 1950, 11th edn; Theodor Geiger: 'Die Gruppe und die Kategorien Gemeinschaft und Gesellschaft', in *Archiv für Sozialwissenschaft und Sozialpolitik*, 58, 1927, pp. 143–73; Peter B. Hofstätter: *Gruppendynamik*, Hamburg 1957; René König: 'Gruppe', in *Soziologie*, ed. R. König, Frankfurt 1964, pp. 104–12; Kurt Lewin: *Resolving Social Conflicts*, New York 1948; H. W. Riecken and G. C. Homans: 'Psychological Aspects of Social Structure', in *Handbook of Social Psychology*, Cambridge, Mass. 1974, vol. II, pp. 156–312; M. Sherif and C. W. Sherif: *Groups in Harmony and in Tension*, New York 1953.

5 Karl Ferdinand Werner: 'Volk, Nation, Nationalismus, Masse: Mittelalter', in Otto Brunner et al. (eds): *Geschichtliche Grundbegriffe, Stuttgart 1992, vol. VII, p. 223.*

6 Bernard Geunée: 'Etat et nation en France au Moyen Age', in

Revue Historique 237 (1967), p. 27.

7   Philippe de Commynes: Memoirs, Penguin Books, London 1972, p. 144.

8   Cf. Hagen Schulze and Ina Ulrike Paul (eds): *Europäische Geschichte. Quellen und Materialien*, Munich 1994, p. 1104.

9   William Stubbs (ed.): *Select Charters and Other Illustrations of English Constitutional History from the Earliest Times to the Reign of Edward the First*, 9th edn revised by H. W. Davis, Oxford 1913, p. 480, no. II.

10 Ibid., p. 460, no. VIa.

11 Cf. J. A. Watt: *The Church and the Two Nations in Medieval Ireland*, Cambridge 1917, p. 184ff.

12 Georges Duby: *27 juillet 1214. Le dimanche de Bouvines*, Paris 1973.

Notes to Chapter 6   Nation States and National Cultures

1   Severinus de Mozambano (Samuel Freiherr von Pufendorf): *De statu imperii germanici* (1667), ed. Harry Bresslau, Berlin 1922, p. 94.

2   Goethe and Schiller: *Xenien* (1796), ed. E. Schmid and B. Supan, Weimar 1893, p. 14.

3   William Shakespeare: *Richard II* Act II, scene 1, 40–7, 50.

4   Cf. Kurt-Ulrich Jäschke: 'Imperialismus, Nationalismus und Nationenentstehung im mittelalterlichen England', in Jörg Albertz (ed.): *Was ist das mit Volk und Nation?*, Berlin 1992, p. 90f.

5   Cf. Karl J. Holzknecht (ed.): *Sixteenth-Century English Prose*, New York 1954, p. 478.

6   Cf. ibid., p. 412.

7   Speech on 22. 1. 1665: in *Oliver Cromwell: Letters and Speeches*, ed. Thomas Carlyle, vol. III, p. 168.

8   *The Globe Edition of the Works of Edmund Spenser*, ed. R. Morris, London 1929, p. 138.

9   William Blake: 'Jerusalem', in *The Poems of William Blake* ed. W. H. Stevenson, London 1971, p. 489.

10 John Milton: *Milton's Prose*, ed. M. W. Wallace, Oxford 1925, p. 333.

11 Pellisson et d'Olivet: *Histoire de l'Académie française*, ed. Ch. L. Livet, Paris 1858, vol. I, p. 33.

12 Francisco de Quevedo: 'España difendida y los tiempos de ahora' (1609) in: *Obras completas*, Madrid 1961, vol. I, p. 521.

13 Cf. Hartmut Boockmann: *Das Mittelalter*, Munich 1988, p. 191.

14 Johannes Lysura: 'Aufzeichnung zur Reichsreform (12–13. 5. 1454)', in: *Deutsche Reichstagsakten. Aeltere Reihe*, ed. Historische Kommission der Bayerischen Akademie der Wissenschaften, Göttingen 1969, vol. 19/1, p. 245.

15 The Mainz Chancellor Martin Mayr to Enea Silvio Piccolomini, 31. 8. 1457, quoted from Bruno Gebhardt: *Die gravamina der deutschen Nation gegen den römischen Hof*, Breslau, 2nd edn 1895, p. 10.

16 Erasmus von Rotterdam: *Studienausgabe*, vol. 2: *Sive laus stultitiae*, Darmstadt 1975, p. 102.

17 Jacob Grimm: *Deutsche Grammatik* (1819), ed. Wilhelm Scherer, Berlin 1870, p. XI.

18 Justus Möser: 'Der Autor am Hofe', *Sämtliche Werke*, ed. Ludwig Schirmeyer, Berlin 1943, vol. 6, Section 2, p. 12.

19 Friedrich Gottlieb Klopstocks Oden, ed. Franz Muncker, Stuttgart 1889, vol. 1, p. 222.

20 Germaine de Staël: *De l'Allemagne* (1813), Paris 1862, p. 24f.

Notes to Chapter 7 The Pivotal Period

1 Carlo Vivanti: *Le campagne del Mantovano nell'età delle riformi*, Milan 1959, p. 224f.

2 *Quarterly Review* 1839 (63), p. 22.

3 Hegel to Niethammer, 28. 10. 1808, in Johannes Hoffmeister (ed.): *Briefe von und zu Hegel*, vol. I (Georg Friedrich Hegel: *Werke*, vol. XXVII), Hamburg 1952, p. 253.

4 Heinrich Heine in 'Lutetia. Berichte über Politik, Kunst und Volksleben', part 2, LVII, 5. 5., Paris 1843, in Heinrich Heine: *Werke und Briefe*, VI, Berlin 1952, p. 478f.

5 Ernst Moritz Arndt to G. A. Reimers, 6. 1. 1826, in: *Briefe*, ed. Emil Dühr, Darmstadt 1973, II, p. 326.

6 Jacob Burckhardt: *Historische Fragmente*. Posthumous papers, collected and edited by Emil Dürr, Stuttgart 1957, p. 279.

7 Justus Möser: 'Der jetzige Hang zu allgemeinen Gesetzen und Verordnungen ist der gemeinen Freiheit gefährlich,' in Möser: *Patriotische Phantasien. Ausgewählten Schriften, ed. Wilfried Zieger, Leipzig 1986, p. 98.*

8 Emmanuel Joseph Sieyès: 'Was ist der dritte Stand?' (1789) in Sieyès: *Politische Schriften 1788–1790*, ed. E. Schmidt and R. Reichardt, Darmstadt, Neuwied 1975, p. 122ff.

9 Ibid., p. 166f.

10 Reprinted in Jacques Godechot (ed.): *Les constitutions de la France depuis 1789*, Paris 1970, p. 33f.

11 Johann Christoph Adelung: *Versuch eines vollständigen grammatisch-kritischen Wö rterbuches der hochdeutschen Mundart*, Leipzig 1776, vol. 2, p. 488f.

Notes to Chapter 8   The Invention of the 'People's Nation'

1 Cf. Suzanne Citron: *Le mythe national. L'histoire de France en question*, Paris 1987, p. 272.

2 Cf. Karin Apostolidis-Kusserow: 'Die griechische Nationalbewegung', in Norbert Reiter (ed.): *Nationalbewegungen auf dem Balkan*, Berlin 1983, p. 116.

3 Dragoslav Stranjaković: ' "Načertanije" Ilije Garašanina' in: *Glasnik istoriskog društva u Novom Sadu IV* (1931), p. 78. Cf. also: Wolf Dietrich Behschnitt: *Nationalismus bei Serben und Kroaten 1830–1914*, Munich 1980, p. 56f.

4 Leopold von Ranke: 'Zur Geschichte Deutschlands und Frankreichs im 19. Jahrhundert', in: *Sämtliche Werke*, ed. Alfred Dove, Leipzig 1887, vol. 49–50, p. 78.

5 Friedrich Ludwig Jahn: *Deutsches Volkstum*, Lübeck 1810, p. 76.

6 Johann Georg Fichte: *Reden an die deutsche Nation*, Berlin 1808.

7 Heinrich Luden: *Geschichte des Teutschen Volkes*, 12 vols, Gotha 1825–9.

8 Christoph Martin Wieland: 'Der allgemeine Mangel deutschen Gemeinsinnes', preface to Schiller's *Historischer Calender für Damen für das Jahr 1792*, Leipzig 1792, p. 118.

9 Wilhelm von Humboldt: 'Ueber die Behandlung der Angelegenheiten des deutschen Bundes durch Preussen, 30. 9. 1816', in: *Gesammelte Werke XII*, p. 53f.

10 Johann Gustav Droysen: *Geschichte der preussischen Politik*, Leipzig 1855–86, 5 parts in 14 vols.

11 Freiherr vom Stein: 'Ueber die deutsche Verfassung. Denkschrift, 18. 9. 1812', in: *Briefe und amtliche Schriften*, ed. E. Botzenhart and W. Hubatsch, Stuttgart 1961, vol. III, p. 745–51.

12 Wilhelm Giesebrecht: *Geschichte der deutschen Kaiserzeit*, Leipzig 1855, vol. 1, p. 9.

Notes to Chapter 9   The 'People's Nations' in Reality

1   E. de Las Cases: *Mémorial de Sainte-Hélène*, ed. A. Fugier, Paris 1961, I, p. 609.

2   'Contrôle de Police Militaire du Gouvernement Général de Prusse à Berlin', in: Geheimes Staatsarchiv Berlin, IV. HA B no. 226, notes dated 17. 7. 1807 and 18. 9. 1808; unsigned draft of a report for the Secrétariat d'Etat, Berlin 1. 5. 1809, in: Archives Nationales Paris, AF^{iv} 1690.

3   Synoptic reprint of the Spanish original with a number of translations, including Kleist's 'Katechismus der Deutschen' in: Rainer Wohlfeil: *Spanien und die deutsche Erhebung 1808–1814*, Wiesbaden 1965, p. 309ff.

4   Unsigned note, Berlin, December 1808, in: *Archives du Quai d'Orsay Paris*, C.P. Prusse/242.

5   Gentz to Ompteda, Teplitz, 4. 9. 1808, in: F. von Ompteda (ed.): *Politischer Nachlass des hannoverschen Staats- und Cabinets-Ministers Ludwig von Ompteda aus den Jahren 1804–1813*, vol. I, p. 397ff.

6   Heinrich Hahn (i.e. the former British Consul-General Lewis de Drusina) to the Foreign Office, no place noted (Königsberg), 13. 12. 1808, in: Public Record Office London FO 64/78.

7   Cf. Helmut Rössler: *Graf Johann Philipp Stadion*, Vienna and Munich 1966, vol. I, p. 291.

8   Cf. ibid., p. 393.

9   Cf. Heinrich Hammer: *Oesterreichs Propaganda zum Feldzug 1809*, Munich 1935, p. 25.

10   In Helmut Rössler: *Oesterreichs Kampf um Deutschlands Befreiung*, Hamburg 1940, vol. I, p. 498.

11   Copy in: Bayerisches Hauptstaatsarchiv Munich, MA 2390.

12   Ambassador Reinhard to Talleyrand, Kassel, 24. 4. 1809, in: Archives du Quai d'Orsay Paris. C.P. Westphalie/3.

13   Oberstvogteiamt Ueberlingen to Hofcommissair von Wechmar, 15. 6. 1809, in: Generallandesarchiv Karlsruhe, 48/4195; von Wechmar to the Cabinetts-Ministerium, Donaueschingen, 24. 6. 1809, in: ibid., 48/4161; von Wechmar to the Cabinetts-Ministerium, Donaueschingen, 2. 7. 1809, in: ibid.

14   Linda Colley: *Britons. Forging the Nation 1707–1837*, New Haven and London 1993, pp. 283–320.

15   Ibid., p. 318.

16   Thomas Nipperdey: *Deutsche Geschichte 1800–1866. Bürgerwelt und starker Staat*, Munich 1983, p. 268.

17 Copy in: Bayerisches Hauptstaatsarchiv Munich, MA 7737.

Notes to Chapter 10   The Revolutionary Nation State 1815–1871

1   Friedrich von Gentz: 'Französische Kritik der deutschen Bundesbeschlüsse von 1819', in: Gentz: *Schriften*, ed. Gustav Schlesier, Mannheim 1838, vol. II, p. 200f.

2   Count Reinhard to Decazes, Frankfurt, 26. 3. 1819, in: Archives du Quai d'Orsay Paris, C.P., Allemagne 758.

3   Clemens Fürst von Metternich in his 'Autobiographische Denkschrift', in: *Aus Metternichs nachgelassenen Papieren*, ed. Richard Fürst von Metternich-Winneburg, Vienna 1881, vol. I, p. 216.

4   Talleyrand to Louis XVIII, Vienna, 17. 10. 1814, in: *Talleyrands Briefwechsel mit König Ludwig während des Wiener Kongresses*, ed. G. Pallain, German ed. Paul Bailleu, Leipzig and Paris 1881, p. 47.

5   Cf. Werner Markert: 'Metternich und Alexander I', in: Walther Hubatsch (ed.): *Schicksalswege deutscher Vergangenheit*, Düsseldorf 1950, p. 164.

6   Sir Stratford Canning to Lord Palmerston, 3. 4. 1848, from M. Stürmer: 'Die Geburt eines Dilemmas', in: *Merkur 35* (1981), p. 5.

7   Bunsen to King Frederick William IV, 1. 9. 1848, quoted in H. Precht: *Englands Stellung zur deutschen Einheit 1848–1850*, Munich and Berlin 1925, p. 74.

8   Address of the Prague Slavic Congress to Emperor Ferdinand I, from: H. Schulze and I. U. Paul: *Europäische Geschichte. Quellen und Materialien*, p. 194.

9   Pasquale Stanislao Mancini: 'Della Nazionalità come fondamento del diritto delle genti', quoted from: Theodor Schieder: *Typologie uhd Erscheinungsformen des Nationalstaats*, in *Historische Zeitschrift* 202 (1966), p. 60.

10 Johann Caspar Bluntschli: 'Die nationale Staatenbildung und der moderne Staat', in: Bluntschli: *Gesammelte kleine Schriften, Aufsätze über Politik und Völkerrecht*, Nördlingen 1881, vol. II, p. 90.

11 Cavour to King Victor Emanuel II, 24. 7. 1858, in: Luigi Chiala (ed.): *Camillo Cavours gedruckte und ungedruckte Briefe*. Authorized translation by M. Bernardi, Leipzig 1887, vol. III, p. 2.

12 Otto von Bismarck: *Die gesammelten Werke*, Friedrichsruh

Edition. Berlin 1926, vol. 10, p. 139.

13 Johann Caspar Bluntschli to Heinrich von Sybel, beginning of February 1863, in: Johann Heyersdorff and Paul Wentzke (eds) *Deutscher Liberalismus im Zeitalter Bismarcks*, Bonn 1921, vol. I, p. 131.

14 Hermann Baumgarten to Heinrich von Sybel, 22. 5. 1863, in: ibid., vol. I, p. 151.

15 A. Pf.: 'Die neue Heilige Allianz', in: *Wochenschrift des Nationalvereins*, No. 156, 24. 4. 1863.

16 Rudolf von Ihering to Bernhard Windschied, 19. 8. 1866, in: Karl-Georg Faber: 'Realpolitik als Ideologie', in: *Historische Zeitschrift* 203 (1966), p. 16.

17 In: Raymond Grew: *A sterner plan for Italian Unity. The Italian National Society in the Risorgimento*, Princeton 1963, p. 233f.

18 Cf. W. F. Monypenny and G. E. Buckle: *The Life of Benjamin Disraeli, Earl of Beaconsfield*, London 1929, vol. II, p. 473.

19 Bismarck's Circular to the Prussian Missions, 27. 5. 1866, in: *Gesammelte Werk*, vol. 5, no. 359.

20 Otto Fürst von Bismarck: *Gedanken und Erinnerungen*, Stuttgart 1899, vol. I, p. 293.

Notes to Chapter 11   The Imperialist Nation State 1871–1914

1 Cf. Pierre Nora: 'Ernest Lavisse, son rôle dans la formation du sentiment national', in: *Revue Historique* 228 (1962) p. 73.

2 Cf. Raoul Girardet: *Le nationalisme français, 1871–1914*, Paris 1966, p. 129.

3 Cf. Jacques Droz: 'Der Nationalismus der Linken und der Nationalismus der Rechten in Frankreich, 1871–1914', in: *Historische Zeitschrift* 210 (1970), p. 11.

4 Disraeli. Speech at the Banquet of the National Union of Conservative and Constitutional Associations, at the Crystal Palace, on 24 June 1872.

5 Ibid.

6 Cf. Colin C. Eldridge: *England's Mission, the Imperial Idea in the Age of Gladstone and Disraeli 1868–1880*, London 1973, p. 11.

7 Speech by Joseph Chamberlain, Glasgow, 6. 10. 1903.

8 Duke of Westminster: 'Practical Imperialism', in: *Nineteenth Century* 72 (1912), p. 870.

9 Cf. John M. MacKenzie: *Propaganda and Empire*, Manchester 1984, p. 24.

10 Cf. Wolfgang Mock: 'The Function of "Race" in Imperialist Ideologies', in: Paul M. Kennedy and Anthony Nicholls (eds): *Nationalist and Racial Movements in Britain and Germany before 1914*, London 1981, p. 194.

11 Cf. Mackenzie: *Propaganda*, op. cit., p. 56.

12 Max Weber: Inaugural Lecture, Freiburg, 1895, in: Weber: *Gesammelte politische Schriften*, Tübingen 1963, p. 21.

13 Friedrich von Bernhardi: *Deutschland und der nächste Krieg*, Stuttgart and Berlin, 6th edn 1913, p. 5.

14 Hans Delbrück: 'Unser Programm', in: *Preussische Jahrbücher* 95 (1899), p. 383f.

15 Enrico Corradini: *La conquista di Tripoli*, Milan 1912.

16 Arthur Shadwell: *Industrial Efficiency*, London 1909, p. 653.

17 Cecil Rhodes: 'Draft of Ideas' (1877) in: *The Last Will and Testament of C. J. Rhodes*, ed. William T. Stead, London 1902, pp. 57, 97f.

18 R. A. Fadejew: *Gedanken über die orientalische Frage (1870)*, Cf. L. Zimmermann (ed.): *Der Imperialismus, seine geistigen, wirtschaftlichen und politischen Zielsetzungen*, Stuttgart 1955, p. 15f.

19 Cf. A. Klima: 'Die Entstehung der Arbeiterklasse und die Anfänge der Arbeiterbewegung in Böhmen', in: Wolfram Fischer (ed.): *Wirtschafts- und sozialgeschichtliche Probleme der frühen Industrialisierung*, Berlin 1968, p. 438f.

20 Otto von Bismarck: Speech in the Prussian Parliament, 24. 4. 1873, in: *Gesammelte Werke*, Friedrichsruh Edition, vol. 11, p. 298.

21 Heinrich von Treitschke: 'Unsere Aussichten' (1879), quoted from: H. Schulze and I. U. Paul: *Europäische Geschichte. Quellen und Materialien*, p. 963f.

22 Edouard Drumont: *La France Juive*, quoted ibid. p. 965.

23 Georges Sorel: *Réflexions sur la violence*, German trans. by Ludwig Oppenheimer, ed. Georg Lichtheim, Frankfurt 1969, p. 90f.

24 Bethmann Hollweg, 12. 4. 1912, in: *Shorthand records of the proceedings of the Reichstag*, Berlin 1912, vol. 284, col. 1300.

Notes to Chapter 12   The Total Nation State 1914–1945

1 Winston S. Churchill: *The World Crisis*, London 1923, vol. I, p. 10f.

2 Walther Rathenau: *Die Organisation der Rohstoffversorgung*,

lecture to the Deutsche Gesellschaft, 20. 12. 1915, in: Walter Steitz (ed.): *Quellen zur deutschen Wirtschafts- und Sozialgeschichte vom Ersten Weltkrieg bis zum Ende der Weimarer Republik*, Darmstadt 1993, p. 40.

3   Cf. Arthur Marwick: *Britain in the Century of Total War*, London and Sydney 1968, p. 76.

4   Ibid., p. 78.

5   Cf. Jan Romein: *The Watershed of two Eras. Europe in 1900*, Middletown, Conn. 1978, p. 275.

6   Winston S. Churchill: *The Second World War*, London 1961, 3rd edn, p. 6.

7   José Ortega y Gasset: *Der Aufstand der Massen*, Berlin 1930, p. 140.

8   Adolf Hitler: *Mein Kampf*, Munich 1939, p. 371.

9   Benito Mussolini: *Opera Omnia*, vol. XVIII, Florence 1955, p. 438.

10 Anon.: 'Memorandum über meinen Aufenthalt in Spanien vom 25. Februar bis 28. März 1941', in: State Archives, Prague, cf. Francis L. Carsten: *Der Aufstieg des Faschismus in Europe*, Frankfurt 1968, p. 240f.

11 Cf. Benito Mussolini: *Der Geist des Faschismus. Ein Quellenwerk*, ed. Horst Wagenfuhr, Munich 1943, 5th edn, p. 6f.

12 Cf. Joachim Fest: *Hitler*, Frankfurt, Berlin and Vienna 1973, p. 831f.

13 Benito Mussolini: ed. cit. Horst Wagenfuhr, p. 24f.

Notes to Chapter 13   Nations, States and Europe

1   Milovan Djilas: *Gespräche mit Stalin*, Stuttgart 1962, p. 156f.

2   *Europa. Dokumente zur Frage der europäischen Einigung I*, ed. on behalf of the Foreign Office of the Federal Republic of Germany, Bonn 1962, p. 101.

3   Ibid., p. 105.

4   Ernest Renan to David Friedrich Strauss, 13. 9. 1870. Cf. Hans Kohn: *Wege und Irrwege. Vom Geist deutschen Bürgertums*, Düsseldorf 1962, p. 176. Also in: David Friedrich Strauss: *Krieg und Friede, zwei Briefe an Ernest Renan nebst dessen Antwort auf den ersten*, Leipzig 1870, p. 32ff.

5   Robert Schuman: *Für Europa. Vorwort von Konrad Adenauer*, Geneva 1963, pp. 219ff.

6   Edgar Morin: *Europa denken*, Frankfurt 1988, p. 168.

Bibliography

General

Akzin, B.: *State and Nation*, London 1964.
Albertini, M. et al.: *L'idée de nation*, Paris 1969.
Albertini, M.: *Lo stato nazionale*, 2nd edn, Naples 1980.
Alter, P.: *Nationalismus*, Frankfurt 1985.
Anderson, B.: *Imagined Communities. Reflectious on the Origin and Spread of Nationalism*, London 1983.
André, P. J.: *Le réveil des nationalismes. La nouvelle évolution du monde*, Paris 1968.
Barker, E.: *National Character and the Factors in its Formation*, 4th edn, London 1948.
Bay, C. et al.: *Nationalism. A Study of Identification with People and Power*, 3 vols, Oslo 1950–3.
Bell, W. and Freeman, W. (eds): *Ethnicity and Nation Building. Comparative, International and Historical Perspectives*, Beverly Hills 1974.
Bendix, R.: *Nation Building and Citizenship. Studies of our Changing Social Order*, Berkeley 1977.
Boerner, P. (ed.): *The Concept of National Identity. An Interdisciplinary Dialogue*, Baden-Baden 1986.
Braunthal, J.: *The Paradox of Nationalism*, London 1946.
Buse, D. K.: *German Nationalism. A Bibliographic Approach*, New York and London 1985.
Chabod, F.: *L'Idea di nazione*, Bari 1961.
Clément, M.: *Enquête sur le nationalisme*, Paris 1957.
Deutsch, K. W.: *Nationalism and Social Communication, An Enquiry*

into the Foundations of Nationality, Cambridge, Mass. 1953.

Deutsch, K. W. and Merrit, R. L.: *Nationalism and National Development. An Interdisciplinary Bibliography*, Cambridge, Mass. 1970.

Deutsch, K. W.: *Nationalism and its Alternatives*, New York 1969.

Deutsch, K. W. and Foltz, W. J. (eds): *Nation-Building*, New York 1963.

Eisenstadt, S. N. and Rokkan, S. (eds): *Building States and Nations*, Beverly Hills n.d. (1947).

Fougeyrollas, P.: *Essor et déclin des sociétés modernes*, Paris 1987.

Gellner, E.: *Nations and Nationalism*, Oxford 1983.

Guiomar, J. Y.: *L'Idéologie nationale: nation, représentation, propriété*, Paris 1974.

Haarman, H.: *Die Sprachenwelt Europas. Geschichte und Zukunft der Sprachnationen zwischen Atlantik und Ural*, Frankfurt and New York 1993.

Hayes, C. J. H.: *Nationalism: A Religion*, New York 1960.

Hayes, C. J. H.: *The Historical Evolution of Modern Nationalism*, 3rd edn, 1968.

Hertz, F.: *Nationality in History and Politics. A Psychology and Sociology of National Sentiment and Nationalism*, 3rd edn, London 1951.

Hobsbawn, E. J.: *Nations and Nationalism since 1870*, Cambridge 1990.

Hotz, F. O.: *Nationality in History and Politics. A Study of the Psychology of National Sentiment and Character*, London 1945.

Jessup, P. C.: *The Birth of Nations*, New York 1947.

Kamenka, E. (ed.): *Nationalism. The Nature and Evolution of an Idea*, New York 1976.

Kemiläinen, A.: *Nationalism: Problems Concerning the Word, the Concept and Classification*, Jyväskylä 1964.

Kohn, H.: *The Idea of Nationalism. A Study in its Origins and Background*, New York 1944.

Kohn, H.: *Essai sur l'étude de l'histoire du sentiment national*, Oslo 1951.

Kohn, H.: *Nationalism: Its Meaning and History*, Princeton 1955.

Leclercq, J.-M.: *La nation et son idéologie* Paris 1979.

Lemberg, E.: *Nationalismus*, 2 vols., Reinbeck 1964.

Martelli, R.: *La nation*, Paris 1979.

Minogue, K. R.: *Nationalism*, London 1967.

Nationalism. A Report by a Study Group of Members of the Royal Institute of International Affairs, London 1939. 3rd edn, New

York 1966.

Le nationalisme: facteur belligène. Colloques de 4, 5, 6 Mai 1971, ed. Institut de Sociologie, Solvay. Centre de Sociologie de guerre, Brussels 1972.

Pinson, K. S.: *A Bibliographical Introduction to Nationalism*, New York 1935.

Ploncard d'Assac, J.: *Doctrines du nationalisme*, 2nd edn, Paris 1965.

Pomian, K.: *L'Europe et ses nations*, Paris 1990.

al-Razzazz, M.: *The Evolution of the Meaning of Nationalism*, Garden City 1963.

Renan, E.: *Qu'est ce que c'est une nation?* (Conférence faite en Sorbonne le 11 Mars 1882), Paris 1882.

Shafer, B. C.: *Nationalism: Interpreters and Interpretations*, 2nd edn, New York 1963.

Smith, A. D.: *Theories of Nationalism*, 2nd edn, London 1983.

Snyder, L. L.: *The Dynamics of Nationalism. Readings in its Meaning and Development*, Princeton 1964.

Snyder, L. L.: *Varieties of Nationalism. A Comparative Study*, Hinsdale 1970.

Symmons-Symonolewicz, K.: *Modern Nationalism. Towards a Consensus in Theory*, New York 1968.

Symmons-Symonolewicz, K.: *Nationalist Movements. A Comparative View*, Meadville 1970.

Szücs, Jenö: *Nation und Geschichte. Studien*, Budapest 1981.

Véliz, C.: *Centralismo, nacionalismo e integración*, in: *Estudios Internacionales* 3 (1960), pp. 3–22.

Vergnand, P.: *L'Idée de la nationalité et la libre disposition des peuples dans ses rapports avec l'idée de l'Etat*, Geneva 1955.

Weingärtner, A.: *Nation und Staat*, Vienna 1979.

Winkler, H. A. (ed.): *Nationalismus*, Kronberg im Taunus 1978.

Winkler, H. A. and Schnabel, T.: *Bibliographie zum Nationalismus*, Göttingen 1979.

States

Addio, M. d': *Lo Stato democratico. Origini, formazione ed evoluzione storica* (Politica e Società, Saggi e Documenti 6) Bergamo 1979.

Amado, J.: *L'Etat et les sociétés*, Paris 1987.

Anderson, J.: *The Rise of the Modern State*, Brighton 1986.

Balladore, P. G.: *Dottrina dello Stato*, 2nd edn, Padua 1964.

Bellomo, M.: *Società e istitutizioni in Italia tra Medioevo ed età moderna*, 2nd edn, Catania 1977.

Breuer, S. and Treiber, H. (eds): *Entstehung und Strukturwandel des Staates*, Opladen 1982.

Browne, R. W. (ed.): *Leviathan in Crisis. An International Symposium on the State, its Past, Present and Future by 54 Twentieth Century Writers*, New York 1946.

Brunner, O.: *Land und Herrschaft. Grundfragen der territorialen Verfassungsgeschichte Oesterreichs im Mittelalter*, 4th edn, Vienna and Wiesbaden 1959.

Burdeau, G.: *L'Etat*, Paris 1970.

Chodak, S.: *The New State. Etatization of Western Societies*, Boulder 1989.

Claessen, H. H. M. and Skalnik, P. (eds): *The Early State*, The Hague 1978.

Cohen, R. and Rogers, E. (eds): *Origins of the State*, Philadelphia 1978.

Culture et idéologie dans la genèse de l'Etat moderne. Actes de la table ronde org. par le Centre national de la recherche scientifigue et l'Ecole Française de Rome, Rome 1985.

Dehio, L.: *Gleichgewicht oder Hegemonie. Betrachtungen über ein Grundproblem der neueren Staatsgeschichte*, Krefeld 1948.

Deutsch, K. W.: *Functions and Transformation of the State: Notes toward a General Theory*, Berlin 1980.

Dyson, K. H. F.: *The State Tradition in Western Europe. A Study of an Idea and Institution*, Oxford 1980.

Evans, P., Rueschemeyer, D. and Skocpol, T. (eds): *Bringing the State Back In*, Cambridge 1985.

Hartung, F.: *Staatsbildende Kräfte der Neuzeit*, Berlin 1961.

Hättich, M. (ed.): *Zum Staatsverständnis der Gegenwart*, Munich 1987.

Held, D.: *Political Theory and the Modern State. Essays on State Power and Democracy*, Cambridge 1989.

Herzog, R.: *Staaten der Frühzeit. Ursprünge und Herrschaftsformen*, Munich 1988.

Heydte, F. A. Freiherr von: *Die Geburtsstunde des souveränen Staates*, Regensburg 1952.

Hintze, O.: *Wesen und Wandlung des modernen Staats* (1931), in: Hintze: *Staat und Verfassung. Gesammelte Abhandlungen zur allgemeinen Verfassungsgeschichte*, ed. G. Oestrich, 3rd edn Göttingen 1970, pp. 470–96.

Hofmann, H. H. (ed): *Die Entstehung des modernen souveränen*

Staates, Cologne 1967.

Huber, E. R.: *Nationalstaat und Verfassungsstaat. Studien zur Geschichte der modernen Staatsidee*, Stuttgart 1955.

Iaboni, E.: *La Concezione dello Stato nelle dottrine filosoficogiuridiche*, Padua 1976.

Laski, H. J.: *The Foundations of Sovereignty and other Essays*, London 1931.

Les grands Empires, Brussels 1973 (Recueils de la société Jean Bodin pour l'histoire comparative des institutions, vol. 31).

Loock, H.-D. and Schulze, H. (eds): *Parlamentarismus und Demokratie im Europa des 19. Jahrhunderts*, Munich 1982.

Lowie, R. H.: *The Origin of the State*, New York 1962.

Lucinge, R. de: *De la naissance, durée et chute des états*, ed. M. J. Heath, Geneva 1984.

Mager, W.: *Zur Entstehung des modernen Staatsbegriffs*. Akad. der Wiss. und Lit. in Mainz. Abh. der Geistes- und Sozialwiss. Klasse, no. 9, Mainz 1968.

Maravall, A.: *Estado moderno y mentalidad social*, 2 vols, Madrid 1972.

Mitteis, H.: *Der Staat des hohen Mittelalters*, 8th edn, Weimar 1968.

Naf, W.: *Staat und Staatsgedanke*, Berne 1935.

Oestreich, G.: *Geist und Gestalt des frühmodernen Staates*, Berlin 1969.

Passerin D'Entrèves, A.: *La Dottrina dello Stato*, 2nd edn, Turin 1967.

Poggi, G.: *The Development of the Modern State. A Sociological Introduction*, Stanford (Calif.) 1978.

Schneider R. (ed.): *Das spätmittelalterliche Königtium im europäischen Vergleich*, Sigmaringen 1987.

Skalweit, S.: *Der 'moderne Staat'. Ein historischer Begriff und seine Problematik*, Opladen 1987.

Solari, G.: *La Formazione storica e filosofica dello Stato moderno*, Naples 1974.

Strayer, J. R.: *On the Medieval Origins of the Modern State*, Princeton 1970.

Voigt, R. (ed.): *Abschied vom Staat – Rückkehr zum Staat?*, Baden-Baden 1993.

Weihnacht, P. L.: *Staat. Studien zur Bedeutungsgeschichte des Wortes von den Anfängen bis ins 19. Jahrhundert*, Berlin 1968.

Nations

Agnew, H.: *Czech National Consciousness between Enlightenment and Romanticism, 1780–1815*, Ann Arbor 1981.

Alonso, A.: *Castellano, español, idioma nacional: Historia espiritual de tres nombres*, Buenos Aires 1949.

Alter, P.: *Die irische Nationalbewegung zwischen Parlament und Revolution. Der Konstitutionelle Nationalismus in Irland*, Munich 1971.

André, P.-J.: *Le réveil des nationalismes*, Paris 1958.

Armbruster, A.: *Romanitea românilor. Istoria unei idei*, Bucharest 1972.

Armstrong, J.: *Nations before Nationalism*, Chapel Hill 1982.

Auriac, J. d': *La Nationalité française. Sa formation*, Paris 1913.

Banac, I.: *The National Question in Yugoslavia. Origins, History, Politics*, Ithaca and London 1984.

Baranyi, G.: *Stephen Szechenyi and the Awakening of Hungarian Nationalism 1791–1841*, Princeton 1956.

Baumann H. and Schröder, W. (eds): *Nationes. Historische und philologische Untersuchungen zur Entstehung der europäischen Nationen im Mittelalter*, vol. III, Sigmaringen 1980.

Beaune, C.: *Naissance de la nation France*, Paris 1985.

Behschnitt, W. D.: *Nationalismus bei Serben und Kroaten 1830 –1914. Analyse und Typologie der nationalen Ideologie.* (Südost-europäische Arbeiten 74), Munich 1980.

Beumann, W. T. (ed.): *Beiträge zur Bildung der französischen Nation im Früh- und Hochmittelalter*, Sigmaringen 1983.

Beumann, H. and Schröder, W. (eds): *Aspekte der Nationalbildung im Mittelalter*, Sigmaringen 1978.

Bluhm, W. T.: *Building an Austrian Nation*, New Haven 1973.

Boyce, D. G.: *Nationalism in Ireland*, London 1982.

Bradley, J. F. N.: *Czech Nationalism in the Nineteenth Century*, New York 1984.

Brandt, J.: *The National Movement in Scotland*, London 1978.

Brian, G.: *Scottish Nationalism and Cultural Identity in the Twentieth Century*, Westport 1984.

Brock, P.: *Nationalism and Populism in Partitioned Poland*, London 1971.

Brock, P.: *The Slovak National Awakening: An Essay in the Intellectual History of East Central Europe*, Toronto 1976.

Chaunu, P.: *La France. Histoire de la sensibilité des Français à la France*, Paris 1982.

Citron, S.: *Le mythe national. L'histoire de France en question*, Paris 1987.

Colley, L.: *Britons. Forging the Nation 1707–1837*, New Haven and London 1992.

Conze, W.: *Die deutsche Nation. Ergebnis der Geschichte*, Göttingen 1963.

Dann, O. and Dinwiddy, J. (eds): *Nationalism in the Age of the French Revolution*, London and Ronceverte 1988.

Davies, C. A.: *Welsh Nationalism in the Twentieth Century. The Ethnic Option and the Modern State*, New York 1989.

Deutsch, K. W.: *Die Schweiz als ein paradigmatischer Fall politischer Integration*, Berlin 1976.

Diaz del Corral, L.: *La monarquia hispánica en el pensiamento politico europeo*, Madrid 1976.

Djordjević, D.: *Révolutions natoinales des peuples balkaniques 1804–1914*. Belgrade 1965.

Düding, D.: *Organisierter gesellschaftlicher Nationalismus in Deutschland (1808–1847)*, Munich 1984.

Duijker, H. C. and Frijda, N. H.: *National Character and National Stereotypes*, Amsterdam 1960.

Dunlop, J. B.: *The Faces of Contemporary Russian Nationalism*, Princeton 1983.

Ehlers, J. (ed.): *Ansätze und Diskontinuitäten deutscher Nationsbildung im Mittelalter*, Nationes, vol. 8, Sigmaringen 1989.

Elviken, A.: *Die Entwicklung des norwegischen Nationalismus*, Berlin 1930.

Essen, L. v. d.: *Le sentiment national dans les Pays-Bas*, 2nd edn, Brussels 1944.

Farmer, K. C.: *Ukrainian Nationalism in the Post-Stalin Era. Myth, Symbols and Ideology in Soviet Nationalities Policy*, The Hague 1980.

Fishman, D. A.: *Language and Nationalism. Two Integrative Essays*, Rowley, Mass. 1973.

Gaeta. F.: *Nazionalismo italiano*, Naples 1965.

Garber, K. (ed.): *Nation and Literatur im Europa der Frühen Neuzeit*, Tübingen 1989.

Gewehr, W. M.: *The Rise of Nationalism in the Balkans 1800–1930*, New York 1931.

Girardet, P. (ed.): *Le nationalisme français*, Paris 1983.

Graus, F.: *Die Nationenbildung der Westslawen im Mittelalter*, Sigmaringen 1980.

Harrie, C.: *Scotland and Nationalism. Scottish Society and Politics,*

1707–1977, London 1977.

Hitchins, K.: *The Rumanian National Movement in Transylvania, 1780–1848*, Cambridge 1969.

Holtzmann, W.: *Das mittelalterliche Imperium und die werdenden Nationen*, Cologne 1953.

Hroch, M.: *Die Vorkämpfer der nationalen Bewegung bei den kleinen Völkern Europas. Eine vergleichende Analyse zur gesellschaftlichen Schichtung der patriotischen Gruppen*, Prague 1968.

Hugelmann, H. G.: *Stämme, Nation und Nationalstaat im deutschen Mittelalter*, Stuttgart 1955.

Immer, I.: *Struggle for Slovakia, 1780–1918*, Ann Arbor 1979.

James, H.: *A German Identity, 1770–1990*, London 1989.

Jeismann, M.: *Das Vaterland der Feinde. Studien zum nationalen Feindbegriff und Selbstverständnis in Deutschland und Frankreich 1792–1918*, Stuttgart 1992.

Joachimsen, P.: *Vom deutschen Volk zum deutschen Staat. Eine Geschichte des deutschen Nationalbewusstseins*, 4th edn, Göttingen 1967.

Koenigsberger, H. G.: 'National Consciousness in Early Modern Spain', in: *Politicians and Virtuosos. Essays in Early Modern History*, London 1985.

Kohn, H.: *Prelude to Nation-States: The French and German experience, 1789–1815*, Princeton 1967.

Kohn, H.: *Prophets and Peoples. Studies in 19th Century Nationalism*, New York n.d.

Koppelmann, H.: *Nation, Sprache, Nationalismus*, Leyden 1956.

Lefebvre, H.: *Le Nationalisme contre les nations*, Paris 1988.

Leoni, F.: *Origini del nazionalismo italiano*, Naples 1970.

Lestocquoy, J.: *Histoire du patriotisme en France des origines à nos jours*, Paris 1968.

Mitchinson, R. (ed.): *The Roots of Nationalism. Studies in Northern Europe*, Edinburgh 1980.

Molinelli, R.: *Per una storia del nazionalismo italiano*, Urbino 1966.

Mosse, G. L.: *Die Nationalisierung der Massen. Politische Symbolik und Massenbewegungen in Deutschland von den Napoleonischen Kriegen bis zum Dritten Reich*, Frankfurt 1976.

Newman, G.: *The Rise of English Nationalism. A Cultural History 1740–1830*, London 1987.

Niederhauser, E.: *The Rise of Nationality in Eastern Europe*, Budapest 1982.

Reiter, N. (ed.): *Nationalbewegungen auf dem Balkan (Balkanologische Veröffentlichungen 5)*, Wiesbaden 1983.

Renouvin, P.: *Le sentiment national et le nationalisme dans l'Europe occidentale*, Paris 1963.

Robek, A.: *Lidoré zdroje národniho obrozeni*, Prague 1974.

Samuel, R. (ed.): *Patriotism. The Making and Unmaking of British National Identity*, 3 vols, London 1989.

Sánchez-Albornoz, C.: España. Un enigma històrico, 2 vols, Buenos Aires 1956.

Sánchez-Albornoz, C.: El drama de la formación de España y los españoles, Barcelona 1973.

Schieder, T. and Burian, P. (eds): *Sozialstruktur und Organisation europäischer Nationalbewegungen*, Munich 1971.

Schulze, H.: *Der Weg zum Nationalstaat. Die deutsche National-bewegung vom 18. Jahrhundert bis zur Reichsgründung*, Munich 1985.

Schulze, H.: *Gibt es überhaupt eine deutsche Geschichte?*, Berlin 1989.

Sestan, E.: *Stato e nazione nell'alto medioevo. Ricerche sulle origini nazionali in Francia, Italia, Germania*, Naples 1952.

Seton-Watson, H.: *Nations and States. An Enquiry into the Origin of Nations and the Politics of Nationalism*, London 1977.

Skendo, S.: *The Albanian National Awakening 1878–1912*, Princeton 1967.

Smith, A. D.: *Nationalist Movements*, London 1976.

Tipton, C. L.: *Nationalism in the Middle Ages*, New York 1972.

Urban, Z. *Problemy slovenského národniho hnuti na konci 19. stoleti*, Prague 1972.

Venero, M. G.: *Historia del Nacionalismo Catalàn*, 2 vols, Madrid 1967.

Walicki, A.: *Philosophy and Romantic Nationalism. The Case of Poland*, Oxford 1982.

Nation States

Anderson, P. R.: *The Background of Anti-English Feeling in Germany 1890–1902*, 2nd edn, New York 1969.

August, T. G.: *The Selling of the Empire. British and French Imperialist Propaganda, 1890–1940*, Westport and London 1985.

Barclay, G. St: *Twentieth-Century Nationalism*, London 1971.

Beales, D.: *The Risorgimento and the Unification of Italy*, London 1971.

Benaerts, P. et al.: *Nationalité et nationalisme 1860–1878*, Paris 1968.

Bertelsen, I. S.: *Non-State Nations in International Politics*, London 1977.

Bertsch, G. K.: *Nation-Building in Yugoslavia: A Study of Political Integration and Attitudinal Consensus*, Beverly Hills 1971.

Bossenbrook, W. J. (ed.): *Mid-Twentieth Century Nationalism*, Detroit 1965.

Brackmann, A.: *Der mittelalterliche Ursprung der Nationalstaaten*, Berlin 1936.

Brandt, H.: *Nationalstaat und Nationalismus im 19. Jahrhundert*, Paderborn 1981.

Breuilly, J.: *Nationalism and the State*, Manchester 1982.

Büsch, O. and Sheehan, J. J. (eds): *Die Rolle der Nation in der deutschen Geschichte und Gegenwart*, Berlin 1985.

Buthman, W. C.: *The Rise of Integral Nationalism in France with Special Reference to the Ideas and Activities of Charles Maurras*, 2nd edn, New York 1970.

Campanella, M.: *Stato-Nazione e ordine sociale*, Milan 1984.

Chadwick, H. M.: *The Nationalities of Europe and the Growth of National Ideologies*, Cambridge 1945.

Cobban, A.: *The Nation State and National Self-Determination*, 2nd rev. edn, London 1969.

Droz, J.: *Le nationalisme en Europe centrale de 1871 à 1939*, Paris 1963.

Eldridge, C. C.: *The Imperial Idea in the Age of Gladstone and Disraeli, 1868–1880*, London 1973.

Esman, J. (ed.): *Ethnic Conflict in the Western World*, Ithaca 1977.

Fallers, L. A.: *The Social Anthropology of the Nation State*, Chicago.

Fehrenbach, E.: 'Ueber die Bedeutung der politischen Symbole im Nationalstaat', in: *Historische Zeitschrift* 213 (1971), 296–357.

Friedrich, J.: *Europa – Nation im Werden?*, Bonn 1972.

Geyer, P.: *Der russische Imperialismus. Studien über den Zusammenhang von innerer und auswärtiger Politik 1860–1914*, Göttingen 1977.

Gille, H.-W.: *Nation heute. Probleme des Staatsbewusstseins und Nationalitätsgefühls*, Munich 1972.

Godechot, J.: *La Grande Nation. L'expansion révolutionnaire de la France dans le monde*, vol. I, Paris 1950.

Guiomar, J.-Y.: *L'idéologie nationale. Nation, représentation, propriété*, Paris 1974.

Hättich, M.: *Nationalbewusstsein und Staatsbewusstsein in der pluralistischen Gesellschaft*, Mainz 1966.

Hanak, P. (ed.): *Die nationale Frage in der österreichisch-ungari-*

schen Monarchie 1900–1918, Budapest 1960.

Hartl, H.: *Nationalitätenprobleme im heutigen Südosteuropa*, Munich 1973.

Hartley, A.: *Gaullism. The Rise and Fall of a Political Movement*, New York 1971.

Holt, E.: *Risorgimento. The Making of Italy 1815–1870*, London 1970.

Hopkins, M.: *The Relationship between Nation States and Aspects of Multinational Association in the Modern International System*, Ann Arbor 1975.

Kann, R. A.: *Das Nationalitätenproblem der Habsburger Monarchie. Geschichte und Ideengehalt der nationalen Bestrebungen vom Vormärz bis zur Auflösung des Reiches im Jahre 1918*, 2 vols, 2nd edn, Graz and Cologne 1964.

King, R. R.: *Minorities under Communism: Nationalities as a Source of Tension among Balkan Communist States*, Cambridge, Mass. 1973.

Kluke, P.: *Selbstbestimmung. Vom Weg einer Idee durch die Geschichte*, Göttingen 1963.

Knapp, W.: *Unity and Nationalism in Europe since 1945*, Oxford 1969.

Koch, H. W.: *Der Sozialdarwinismus. Seine Genese und sein Einfluss auf das imperialistische Denken*, Munich 1973.

Kohn, H.: *Die Slawen und der Westen. Die Geschichte des Panslawismus*, Vienna 1956.

Lendvai, P.: *Eagles in Cobwebs. Nationalism and Communism in the Balkans*, Garden City 1969.

Lengyel, E.: *Nationalism The Last Stage of Communism*, New York 1969.

Lepsius, R.: *Extremer Nationalismus. Strukturbedingungen vor der nationalsozialistischen Machtergreifung*, Stuttgart 1966.

Lill, R. and Valsecchi, F. (eds): *Il nazionalismo in Italia e in. Germania fino alla Prima Guerra Mondiale*, Bologna 1983.

MacCartney, C. A.: *National States and National Minorities*, London 1934.

Mackenzie, J. M.: *Propaganda and Empire. The Manipulation of British Public Opinion 1880–1960*, Manchester 1984.

Mandić, O.: *Ende und Auflösung der Nation*, Munich 1967.

Meier, V. E.: *Neuer Nationalismus in Südosteuropa*, Opladen 1968.

Meinecke, F.: *Weltbürgertum und Nationalstaat*. New edn, (Werke vol. 5), Munich 1962.

Mommsen, W. J.: *Der moderne Imperialismus*, Stuttgart 1971.

Moody, T. W. (ed.): *Nationality and the Pursuit of National Independence*, Belfast 1978.

Nacionalismo y Regionalismo en España. El horizonte politico institucional, ecónomico, social e internacional de nuestro tiempo. Seminario celebrado en Córdoba, 23–25 de febrero 1984, Cordoba 1985.

Nationale Minderheiten in Europa. Eine Darstellung der Problematik mit Dokumenten und Materialien zur Situation der europäischen Volksgruppen und Sprachminderheiten, ed. R. Grulich and P. Pulte, Opladen 1975.

Pi-Sunyer, O.: *The Limits of Integration: Ethnicity and Nationalism in Modern Europe*, Amherst 1971.

Plessner, H.: *Die verspätete Nation. Ueber die politische Verführbarkeit bürgerlichen Geistes*, Stuttgart 1959.

Poliakov, L.: *Le mythe aryen. Essai sur les sources du racisme et des nationalismes*, Paris 1971.

Robbins, K.: *Nineteenth Century Britain. Integration and Diversity*, Oxford 1988.

Romeo, R.: *Il giudizio storico sul Risorgimento*, Catania, 2. 1967.

Salvatorelli, L.: *Spiriti e figure del Risorgimento*, Florence 1962.

Schieder T.: *Nationalismus und Nationalstaat. Studien zum nationalen Problem im modernen Europa*, ed. Otto Dann and Hans-Ulrich Wehler, Göttingen 1991.

Schmidt, G.: *Der europäische Imperialismus*, Munich 1985.

Schulze, H. (ed.): *Nation-Building in Central Europe*, Oxford /Hamburg and New York 1987.

Singh, H.: *Nationalism after World War II*, Jullunder City 1967.

Snyder, L. L.: *Macro-Nationalism. A History of the Pan-Movements*, Westport 1984.

Snyder, L. L.: *German Nationalism. The Tragedy of a People. Extremism Contra Liberalism in Modern German History*, 2nd edn, Port Washington 1969.

Stambrook, F. G.: *European Nationalism in the 19th Century*, Melbourne 1969.

Sternhell, Z.: *Maurice Barrès et le nationalisme français*, Paris 1972.

Tilly, C. (ed.): *The Formation of National States in Western Europe*, Princeton 1975.

Tinker, H.: *Race Conflict and the International Order. From Empire to the United Nations*, New York 1977.

Wilharm, I.: *Die Anfänge des griechischen National staats 1833 –1843*, Munich and Vienna 1973.

Woolf, S. J.: *The Italian Risorgimento*, London 1969.

Index

Aachen, 102, 115
Aasen, Ivar, 162
Abbasid empire, 68
Abd al-Rahman III of Cordoba,
20
absolutism, 48–68; administration,
54–6; and aristocracies, 62–3,
86–7; armed forces, 56–7,
67; bureaucracy, 54, 60, 67,
68, 87; decline, 81, 148–50;
Denmark, 61–2; enlightened,
77–81; and estates, 49, 60,
61–2, 86–7, 89; exceptions to
European adoption, 64–6, 68;
force, monopoly of legitimate,
66, 67; France, 17, 48–60, (see
also Louis XIV); generation
of idea, 49–52; international
relations, 66–71; and justice,
54–5, 66, 87; mercantilism, 57,
271; philosophical justification,
49–52; power-sharing, 149,
152; prepares way for reforms,
86–7, 88–9; and provinces,
58, 87; Prussia, 62–4, 77–81,
89; sovereignty, 50–1, 53,
55, 56, 66–7; totalitarianism

compared, 282; warfare, 61,
67; Württemberg, 60–1
Académie française, 125, 134, 160
Action française, 237–8, 263
Adelung, Johann Christoph, 156
Adenauer, Konrad, 315
Adige region, 217
administration: absolutist, 54–6;
armed forces, 63; medieval,
5, 13, 14, 16–17, 21, 22,
24, (church) 4, 10, 16;
Napoleonic, 87–8; Roman
imperial, 4, 5, 10, 16, 100
Adowa, Battle of, 252
Afghanistan, 241
Africa, 250, 256, 287, 299
Agincourt, Battle of, 36
agriculture, 28, 138, 143–4, 146,
228
Albania, 207, 281, 283, 284
Albanians in Kosovo, 174, 319
Alesia, 96
Alexander I, Tsar, 90–1, 197, 199
Alexander III, the Great, of
Macedon, 165–6, 174, 241
Algeciras, Treaty of, 251
Alsace: French annexation, 174,